Early Childhood Education

04/05

Twenty-Fifth Edition

EDITORS

Karen Menke Paciorek

Eastern Michigan University

Karen Menke Paciorek is a professor and program coordinator of early childhood education at Eastern Michigan University in Ypsilanti. Her degrees in early childhood education include a B.A. from the University of Pittsburgh, an M.A. from George Washington University, and a Ph.D. from Peabody College of Vanderbilt University. She co-edits, with Joyce Huth Monro, *Sources: Notable Selections in Early Childhood Education* and is the editor of *Taking Sides: Clashing Views on Controversial Issues in Early Childhood Education* (McGraw-Hill/Dushkin). She has served as president of the Michigan Association for the Education of Young Children and the Michigan Early Childhood Education Consortium. She presents at local, state, and national conferences on curriculum planning, guiding behavior, preparing the learning environment, and working with families. She currently serves as Secretary on the school board for the Northville Public Schools, Northville, Michigan.

Joyce Huth Munro

American Association of Colleges for Teacher Education

Joyce Huth Munro is Associate for Professional Issues and Liaison at the American Association of Colleges for Teacher Education in Washington, D.C. She has been an administrator and professor at colleges in Kentucky, South Carolina, and New Jersey. Her current writing and research focuses on discovering what makes quality teacher education programs. She is coeditor, with Karen Menke Paciorek, of *Sources: Notable Selections in Early Childhood Education* (McGraw-Hill/Dushkin). At regional and national conferences, she presents seminars on innovative methods of teacher education and curriculum design. Dr. Munro holds an M.Ed. from the University of South Carolina and a Ph.D. from Peabody College at Vanderbilt University.

McGraw-Hill/Dushkin

2460 Kerper Blvd., Dubuque, Iowa 52001

Visit us on the Internet
http://www.dushkin.com

Credits

1. **Trends and Issues**
   Unit photo—Tim Hall/Getty Images
2. **Child Development and Families**
   Unit photo—© Royalty-Free/CORBIS
3. **Care and Educational Practices**
   Unit photo—SW Productions/Getty Images
4. **Guiding and Supporting Young Children**
   Unit photo—Mel Curtis/Getty Images
5. **Curricular Issues**
   Unit photo—D. Berry/PhotoLink/Getty Images

Copyright

Cataloging in Publication Data
Main entry under title: Annual Editions: Early Childhood Education. 2004/2005.
1. Early Childhood Education—Periodicals. I. Menke Paciorek, Karen, *comp.* II. Munro, Joyce H.   Title: Early Childhood Education.
ISBN 0–07–286126–6   658'.05   ISSN 0272–4456

Twenty-Fifth Edition

Cover image © 2004 Photodisc Collection/Getty Images
Printed in the United States of America   1234567890QPDQPD54   Printed on Recycled Paper

Editors/Advisory Board

Members of the Advisory Board are instrumental in the final selection of articles for each edition of ANNUAL EDITIONS. Their review of articles for content, level, currentness, and appropriateness provides critical direction to the editor and staff. We think that you will find their careful consideration well reflected in this volume.

Staff

To the Reader

In publishing ANNUAL EDITIONS we recognize the enormous role played by the magazines, newspapers, and journals of the public press in providing current, first-rate educational information in a broad spectrum of interest areas. Many of these articles are appropriate for students, researchers, and professionals seeking accurate, current material to help bridge the gap between principles and theories and the real world. These articles, however, become more useful for study when those of lasting value are carefully collected, organized, indexed, and reproduced in a low-cost format, which provides easy and permanent access when the material is needed. That is the role played by ANNUAL EDITIONS.

Twenty five years ago Dr. Judy Spitler McKee, a Professor at Eastern Michigan University, was asked to compile the first edition of *Annual Editions: Early Childhood Education*. The profession was just beginning to take shape as schools around the country were beginning to offer a degree in the new field of early childhood education. We want to take this opportunity to thank Dr. McKee for her efforts to develop this annual reader which is used today at over 550 colleges and universities. Dr. Karen Menke Paciorek joined Dr. McKee in 1985, and when Dr. McKee retired from teaching in 1990, Dr. Joyce Huth Munro joined the team. For twenty-five years we have worked diligently to bring you the best and most significant articles in the field. We realize this is a tremendous responsibility to provide a thorough review of the current literature—a responsibility we take seriously. Our goal is to provide the reader with a snapshot of the critical issues facing professionals in early childhood education.

Early childhood education is an interdisciplinary field that includes child development, family issues, educational practices, behavior guidance, and curriculum. *Annual Editions: Early Childhood Education 04/05* brings you the latest information in the field from a wide variety of recent journals, newspapers, and magazines. In selecting articles for this our Silver Anniversary edition, we were careful to provide you with a well-balanced look at the issues and concerns facing teachers, families, society, and children. There are three themes found in readings chosen for this twenty-fifth edition of *Annual Editions: Early Childhood Education*. They are: (1) the great attention being focused on the health, especially the weight and diet, of young children in America today, (2) the importance of appropriate early childhood programs being available for children, and (3) the vast amount of research that supports the need for quality early childhood programs for all children, but especially children at risk. It is especially gratifying to see issues affecting children and families covered in magazines other than professional association journals. The general public needs to be aware of the impact of positive early learning and family experiences on the growth and development of children.

Continuing in this edition of *Annual Editions: Early Childhood Education* are selected World Wide Web sites that can be used to further explore topics addressed in the articles. These sites will be cross-referenced by number in the topic guide. We have chosen to include only a few high-quality sites. Students are encouraged to explore these sites on their own, or in collaboration with others, for extended learning opportunities.

Given the wide range of topics included, *Annual Editions: Early Childhood Education 04/05* may be used by several groups—undergraduate or graduate students, professionals, parents, or administrators—who want to develop an understanding of the critical issues in the field.

The selection of readings for this edition has been a cooperative effort between the two editors and the advisory board members. We appreciate the time the advisory board members have taken to provide suggestions for improvement and possible articles for consideration. We couldn't produce this book without the assistance of many. The production and editorial staff of McGraw-Hill/Dushkin ably support and coordinate our efforts.

To the instructor or reader interested in the history of early childhood care and education programs throughout the years, we invite you to view our other book, also published by McGraw-Hill/Dushkin. *Sources: Notable Selections in Early Childhood Education*, 2nd edition (1999) is a collection of 46 writings of enduring historical value by influential people in the field. All of the selections are primary sources that allow you to experience firsthand the thoughts and views of these important educators. Available also is the first edition of *Taking Sides: Clashing Views on Controversial Issues in Early Childhood Education*. This book is also published by McGraw-Hill/Dushkin and edited by Karen Menke Paciorek. Eighteen controversial issues facing early childhood professionals or parents have been selected. The book can be used in a seminar or issues course.

We are grateful to readers who have corresponded with us about the selection and organization of previous editions. Your comments and articles sent for consideration are welcomed and will serve to modify future volumes. Take time to fill out and return the postage-paid article rating form on the last page. You may also contact either of us at kpaciorek@emich.edu or jmunro@aacte.org

We look forward to hearing from you.

Karen Menke Paciorek
Editor

Joyce Huth Munro
Editor

Contents

UNIT 1
Trends and Issues

Ten selections consider developments in early childhood education.

Unit Overview xviii

The concepts in bold italics are developed in the article. For further expansion, please refer to the Topic Guide and the Index.

UNIT 2
Child Development and Families

Ten selections consider the effects of family life on the growing child and the importance of parent education.

The concepts in bold italics are developed in the article. For further expansion, please refer to the Topic Guide and the Index.

The concepts in bold italics are developed in the article. For further expansion, please refer to the Topic Guide and the Index.

UNIT 3
Care and Educational Practices

Nine selections examine various educational programs, assess the effectiveness of several teaching methods, and consider some of the problems faced by students with special needs.

The concepts in bold italics are developed in the article. For further expansion, please refer to the Topic Guide and the Index.

UNIT 4
Guiding and Supporting Young Children

Eight selections examine the importance of establishing self-esteem and motivation in the child and consider the effects of stressors such as dealing with grief.

The concepts in bold italics are developed in the article. For further expansion, please refer to the Topic Guide and the Index.

UNIT 5
Curricular Issues

Nine selections consider various curricular choices. The areas covered include play, developmentally appropriate learning, emergent literacy, motor development, technology, and conceptualizing curriculum.

Unit Overview **150**

The concepts in bold italics are developed in the article. For further expansion, please refer to the Topic Guide and the Index.

The concepts in bold italics are developed in the article. For further expansion, please refer to the Topic Guide and the Index.

Topic Guide

This topic guide suggests how the selections in this book relate to the subjects covered in your course. You may want to use the topics listed on these pages to search the Web more easily.

On the following pages a number of Web sites have been gathered specifically for this book. They are arranged to reflect the units of this *Annual Edition.* You can link to these sites by going to the DUSHKIN ONLINE support site at *http://www.dushkin.com/online/.*

ALL THE ARTICLES THAT RELATE TO EACH TOPIC ARE LISTED BELOW THE BOLD-FACED TERM.

Academics

Accountability

Achievement

Aggression

Allergies

Assessment

At-risk children

Autonomy

Behavior

Blocks and games and toys

Bullying

Child care

Child development

Children

Classroom management

Cognitive development

Cognitive development, child

Constructivist curriculum

Cooperation

Cost, educational

Creativity

Curriculum

Developmentally appropriate practice

World Wide Web Sites

The following World Wide Web sites have been carefully researched and selected to support the articles found in this reader. The easiest way to access these selected sites is to go to our DUSHKIN ONLINE support site at *http://www.dushkin.com/online/*.

AE: Early Childhood Education 04/05

The following sites were available at the time of publication. Visit our Web site—we update DUSHKIN ONLINE regularly to reflect any changes.

General Sources

Children's Defense Fund (CDF)
http://www.childrensdefense.org
At this site of the CDF, an organization that seeks to ensure that every child is treated fairly, there are reports and resources regarding current issues facing today's youth, along with national statistics on various subjects.

Connect for Kids
http://www.connectforkids.org
This nonprofit site provides news and information on issues affecting children and families, with over 1,500 helpful links to national and local resources.

Eric Clearing House on Elementary and Early Childhood Education
http://www.ericeece.org
This invaluable site provides links to all ERIC system sites: clearinghouses, support components, and publishers of ERIC materials. You can search the massive ERIC database and find out what is new in early childhood education.

National Association for the Education of Young Children
http://www.naeyc.org
The NAEYC Web site is a valuable tool for anyone working with young children. Also see the National Education Association site: *http://www.nea.org*.

U.S. Department of Education
http://www.ed.gov/pubs/TeachersGuide/
Government goals, projects, grants, and other educational programs are listed here as well as many links to teacher services and resources.

UNIT 1: Trends and Issues

Child Care Directory: Careguide
http://www.careguide.net
Find licensed/registered child care by state, city, region, or age of child at this site. Site contains providers' pages, parents' pages, and many links.

Early Childhood Care and Development
http://www.ecdgroup.com
This site concerns international resources in support of children to age 8 and their families. It includes research and evaluation, policy matters, programming matters, and related Web sites.

Global SchoolNet Foundation
http://www.gsn.org
Access this site for multicultural education information. The site includes news for teachers, students, and parents as well as chat rooms, links to educational resources, programs, and contests and competitions.

Goals 2000: A Progress Report
http://www.ed.gov/pubs/goals/progrpt/index.html
Open this site to survey a progress report by the U.S. Department of Education on the Goals 2000 reform initiative. It provides a sense of educators' future goals.

Mid-Continent Research for Education and Learning
http://www.mcrel.org/standards-benchmarks
This site provides a listing of standards and benchmarks that include content descriptions from 112 significant subject areas and documents from across 14 content areas.

The National Association of State Boards of Education
http://www.nasbe.org/
Included on this site is an extensive overview of the No Child Left Behind Act. There are links to specific state's plans.

UNIT 2: Child Development and Families

Administration for Children and Families
http://www.dhhs.gov
This site provides information on federally funded programs that promote the economic and social well-being of families, children, and communities.

The AARP Grandparent Information Center
http://www.aarp.org/grandparents
The center offers tips for raising grandchildren, activities, health and safety, visitations, and other resources to assist grandparents.

All About Asthma
http://pbskids.org/arthur/grownups/teacherguides/health/asthma_tips.html
This is a fact sheet/activity book used to educate children about asthma. It gives tips on how to decrease asthma triggers within your house or school. It has both English and Spanish versions of some of the materials.

Changing the Scene on Nutrition
http://www.fns.usda.gov/tn/Healthy/changing.html
This is a free toolkit for parents, school administrators, and teachers to help change the attitudes toward health and nutrition in their schools.

I Am Your Child
http://www.iamyourchild.org
Rob Reiner's I Am Your Child Foundation features excellent information on child development.

Internet Resources for Education
http://web.hamline.edu/personal/kfmeyer/cla_education.html#hamline
This site, which aims for "educational collaboration," takes you to Internet links that examine virtual classrooms, trends, policy, and infrastructure development. It leads to information about school reform, multiculturalism, technology in education, and much more.

The National Academy for Child Development
http://www.nacd.org
The NACD, an international organization, is dedicated to helping children and adults reach their full potential. Its home page presents links to various programs, research, and resources into

such topics as learning disabilities, ADD/ADHD, brain injuries, autism, accelerated and gifted, and other similar topic areas.

National Parent Information Network/ERIC
http://npin.org

This clearinghouse of elementary, early childhood, and urban education data has information for parents and for people who work with parents.

National Safe Kids Campaign
http://www.babycenter.com

This site includes an easy-to-follow milestone chart and advice on when to call the doctor.

Parent Center
http://www.parentcenter.com/general/34754.html

Parenting resources can be found at this site as well as information for assisting children who are facing stressful situations as a result of terrorism.

Zero to Three
http://www.zerotothree.org

Find here developmental information on the first 3 years of life—an excellent site for both parents and professionals.

UNIT 3: Care and Educational Practices

Canada's Schoolnet Staff Room
http://www.schoolnet.ca/home/e/

Here is a resource and link site for anyone involved in education, including special-needs educators, teachers, parents, volunteers, and administrators.

Classroom Connect
http://www.classroom.com/login/home.jhtml

A major Web site for K–12 teachers and students, this site provides links to schools, teachers, and resources online. It includes discussion of the use of technology in the classroom.

The Council for Exceptional Children
http://www.cec.sped.org/index.html

Information on identifying and teaching gifted children, attention deficit disorders, and other topics in disabilities and gifted education may be accessed at this site.

National Resource Center for Health and Safety in Child Care
http://nrc.uchsc.edu

Search through this site's extensive links to find information on health and safety in child care. Health and safety tips are provided, as are other child-care information resources.

Online Innovation Institute
http://oii.org

A collaborative project among Internet-using educators, proponents of systemic reform, content-area experts, and teachers who desire professional growth, this site provides a learning environment for integrating the Internet into educators' individual teaching styles.

UNIT 4: Guiding and Supporting Young Children

Child Welfare League of America (CWLA)
http://www.cwla.org

The CWLA is the United States' oldest and largest organization devoted entirely to the well-being of vulnerable children and their families. Its Web site provides links to information about issues related to morality and values in education.

UNIT 5: Curricular Issues

Association for Childhood Education International (ACEI)
http://www.udel.edu/bateman/acei/

This site, established by the oldest professional early childhood education organization, describes the association, its programs, and the services it offers to both teachers and families.

California Reading Initiative
http://www.sdcoe.k12.ca.us/score/promising/prreading/prreadin.html

The California Reading Initiative site provides valuable insight into topics related to emergent literacy. Many resources for teachers and staff developers are provided.

Early Childhood Education Online
http://www.ume.maine.edu/ECEOL-L/

This site gives information on developmental guidelines and issues in the field, presents tips for observation and assessment, and gives information on advocacy.

International Reading Association
http://www.reading.org

This organization for professionals who are interested in literacy contains information about the reading process and assists teachers in dealing with literacy issues.

PE Central
http://www.pecentral.org

Included in this site are developmentally appropriate physical activities for children, also containing one section dedicated to preschool physical education. It also includes resources and research in physical education.

Phi Delta Kappa
http://www.pdkintl.org

This important organization publishes articles about all facets of education. By clicking on the links in this site, for example, you can check out the journal's online archive, which has resources such as articles having to do with assessment.

Reggio Emilia
http://www.ericdigests.org/2001-3/reggio.htm

Through ERIC, link to publications related to the Reggio Emilia approach and to resources, videos, and contact information.

Teacher Quick Source
http://www.teacherquicksource.com

Originally designed to help Head Start teachers meet the child outcomes, this site can be useful to all preschool teachers. Domains can be linked to developmentally appropriate activities for classroom use.

Teachers Helping Teachers
http://www.pacificnet.net/~mandel/

Basic teaching tips, new teaching methodologies, and forums for teachers to share experiences are provided on this site. Download software and participate in chats. It features educational resources on the Web, with new ones added each week.

Tech Learning
http://www.techlearning.com

An award-winning K–12 educational technology resource, this site offers thousands of classroom and administrative tools, case studies, curricular resources, and solutions.

Awesome Library for Teachers
http://www.neat-schoolhouse.org/teacher.html

Open this page for links and access to teacher information on everything from educational assessment to general child development topics.

www.dushkin.com/online/

Future of Children
http://www.futureofchildren.org

Produced by the David and Lucille Packard Foundation, the primary purpose of this page is to disseminate timely information on major issues related to children's well-being.

National Institute on the Education of At-Risk Students
http://www.cfda.gov/public/viewprog.asp?progid=1062

The institute supports a range of research and development activities to improve the education of students at risk of educational failure due to limited English proficiency, race, geographic location, or economic disadvantage. Access links and summaries of the institute's work.

Prospects: The Congressionally Mandated Study of Educational Growth and Opportunity
http://www.ed.gov/pubs/Prospects/index.html

This report analyzes cross-sectional data on language-minority and LEP students and outlines what actions are needed to improve their educational performance. Family and economic situations are addressed plus information on related reports and sites.

We highly recommend that you review our Web site for expanded information and our other product lines. We are continually updating and adding links to our Web site in order to offer you the most usable and useful information that will support and expand the value of your Annual Editions. You can reach us at: *http://www.dushkin.com/annualeditions/*.

UNIT 1
Trends and Issues

Unit Selections

Key Points to Consider

- What were some of the key studies from over 20 years ago that provided the foundation for the importance of early childhood education?

- Should the federal government pay for preschool so all children can attend prior to entering kindergarten? If so, how will this affect private companies in the business of providing early care and education?

- What are some of the benefits to children and their families of statewide universal preK programs?

- Why does investment in preschool education return seven dollars for every one dollar invested in the preschool program?

- How can standardized tests affect young children before, during, and after taking tests?

- What are some of the similarities that exist between children's play and the engineering profession?

- If America were to "design a preschool system the way we built our Interstates highway system" how would it be structured?

- How could the current standards movement in education threaten young children and how they are taught?

 **Links: www.dushkin.com/online/**
These sites are annotated in the World Wide Web pages.

Child Care Directory: Careguide
http://www.careguide.net

Early Childhood Care and Development
http://www.ecdgroup.com

Global SchoolNet Foundation
http://www.gsn.org

Goals 2000: A Progress Report
http://www.ed.gov/pubs/goals/progrpt/index.html

Mid-Continent Research for Education and Learning
http://www.mcrel.org/standards-benchmarks

The National Association of State Boards of Education
http://www.nasbe.org/

There has been much attention and focus on the importance of early childhood education in the past year. It appears that public officials and private citizens are finally beginning to see the benefits of quality early childhood education for young children. Complete journal issues, such as *Education Leadership* in April 2003 have been dedicated to early childhood education and state governors, such as Jennifer Granholm of Michigan, have dedicated an entire education summit agenda to the topic. We are beginning to see some progress. The dilemma facing professionals in the field now is how to convince legislators, community leaders, and business people to make the monetary investment that is needed to provide quality preschool programs for all who want to attend.

This unit is called Trends and Issues, and lays out concerns as well as strategies for addressing some of the problems facing early education today. The unit begins with "Investing in Preschool" and ends with "Preschool: the Most Important Grade". In both, the authors extol the many benefits of preschool education and its effects on a lifetime of learning. Also included are articles such as, "Does Universal Preschool Pay?" When families have access to a preschool program that is conducive to stimulating the learning of their child, they are most fortunate. According to the National Day Care study, only one in seven programs provide such optimal care and education. That means the majority of children in America who attend preschool programs are not receiving the care or education that will be necessary for fully enhancing their learning abilities. The debate over offering universal preschool to all children has drawn the attention of many politicians and business leaders. Will the availability of preschool for all children ensure they enter school ready to learn and have higher achievement levels? Many people question spending money on preschool programs that appear, to the untrained eye, to be large blocks of time to just play. The fact that Alexandra Starr's article was published in *Business Week* highlights the importance of this issue to our country and its economic development. Another unusual source included in this edition is *American Scientist*. The editors find great pleasure in collecting articles on early childhood education from non-education sources. In the May-June edition of *American Scientist* is

Henry Petroski's speech at a conference sponsored by the national Aeronautics and Space Administration. In it he describes the connection between children's play and engineering. He said if one wants to observe the future engineers of the world, they need only to watch young children at play.

Two articles in this unit examine the trend of high stakes testing and pressured children. Too often children come into school with knots in their stomach in anticipation of the day ahead of tests and work, much of which is not in keeping with best practices on how children learn. Schools that are more like pressure cookers than places where children can work and learn in a supportive environment are not effective learning environments. There are those who would say school shouldn't be fun, the purpose is to work hard and get ahead. There is strong evidence that adults are more productive in the work force when they are in a supportive and collegial environment. Now we need to create the same environments for students. Enjoy reading this section, which provides a view of important issues facing early childhood education today.

Investing in Preschool

Money spent on early childhood education is money well spent

By Gerald W. Bracey

"There are problems we do not know how to solve, but this is not one of them." *Washington Post* columnist David Broder wrote in January 2002. "The evidence that high-quality education beginning at age 3 or 4 will pay lifetime dividends is overwhelming. The only question is whether we will make the needed investment."

This statement stands in rather stark contrast to one by educational psychologist Arthur Jensen in 1969: "Compensatory education has been tried, and it apparently has failed." Apparently, the operative word in Jensen's comment was "apparently."

The years between the Jensen and Broder statements have produced a great deal of evidence about the effects of early childhood education, and the evidence is indeed overwhelming. It is also less well-known than it ought to be, and it certainly has not had the policy of influence it should have. The three major, well-controlled studies of early childhood education differ in some respects but produced highly similar results. In addition, long-term positive outcomes have been found from Head Start. A careful look at these research findings will show why it pays to provide preschool education to all children.

The Perry Preschool study

The best known and longest term of these studies is referred to as the High/Scope Perry Preschool Project. From 1962 through 1965, 123 African-American children whose parents applied to a preschool program in Ypsilanti, Mich., were randomly assigned to either receive preschool or not (the program did not have room for all applicants).

Random assignment is important in research design. It does not guarantee that the groups will be the same, but it eliminates any systematic bias—only chance differences will occur. Fifty-eight children were assigned to the experimental group, 65 to the control group.

Children who entered the program in 1962 received one year of preschool at age 4. In subsequent years, children received two years of the program at ages 3 and 4. All 123 students re-

ceived the same sequence of tests and interviews over the years. Testers, interviewers, and subsequent teachers did not know whether the children had been in the experimental group or the control group.

The parents were screened for socioeconomic status, and the children were given the Stanford-Binet IQ test. The children had IQs between 60 and 90 and no evidence of physical handicap. The parents had completed 9.4 years of school, on average, and only 20 percent had completed high school—fewer than the average for all African Americans, which was 33 percent. The half-day program lasted for eight months and included weekly 90-minute home visits by project staff.

The Perry project used a curriculum developed at the High/Scope Educational Research Foundation based on the concepts of Jean Piaget and other theorists who view children as active learners. The teachers rarely assessed specific knowledge, as might happen in a classroom using direct instruction; instead, they asked questions that allowed children to generate conversations with adults.

Instruction focused on what the curriculum developers considered 10 categories of key preschool experiences: creative representation, language and literacy, social relations and personal initiative, movement, music, classification, seriation (creating series and patterns), number, space, and time. The school day included individual, small-group, and large-group activities.

The study so far has looked at the children as they moved through school and at ages 19 and 27. A study of the adults at age 40 is in progress.

What the Perry study found

By the time they were 19, the students who attended preschool had higher graduation rates and were less likely to have been in special education. They also scored higher on the Adult Performance Level Survey, a test from the American College Testing Program designed to provide simulations of real-life situations. Researchers estimated that—in constant 1981 dollars—A K-12 education cost $34,813 for preschoolers and $41,895 for those who had not attended preschool.

By the time the students turned 27, some 71 percent of the preschool group had attained a high school diploma or GED, compared to 54 percent of the control group. Forty-two percent of the preschool children reported making more than $2,000 a month, compared to only 6 percent of those in the control group. Thirty-six percent of the preschoolers, but only 13 percent of the control group, owned their own homes. The preschool group had longer and more stable marriages.

Preschool did not turn the kids into angels, but it made them more at ease in society. The control group's females had an out-of-wedlock birth rate of 85 percent, compared to 57 percent of the preschool group. Control group members suffered twice as many arrests as preschoolers, and five times as many of the control group (35 percent) had been arrested five or more times. Two females in the control group had been murdered.

At the time, researchers estimated a cost-benefit ratio of $7.16-to-$1—that is, considering the cost of the preschool vs. the cost of special education, retention in grade, and incarceration and considering other benefits of preschool, the public saved more than $7 for every $1 invested in preschool. In contrast, between 1958 and 1981, the Dow Jones Industrial Average had little more than doubled, and from 1962 to 1985 it rose by only 64 percent.

The Chicago study

A similar cost-benefit ratio emerged from a later study, the Chicago Child-Parent Center Program (CPC). In 2001, when the preschoolers were 21, researchers estimated that, factoring in the participants' reduced crime rates (17 percent vs. 25 percent for those in the control group), higher high school completion rates (61 percent vs. 52 percent), and fewer special education placements (14 percent vs. 25 percent)—plus a significant difference in retentions in grade—the program had returned $47,549 to the public.

The one-year program cost $6,788 per child in constant 1998 dollars, yielding a ratio of almost precisely 7-to-1 ($47,549-to-$6,788). An intervention program initiated after children had begun school returned a much smaller amount.

The CPC study was much larger than the High/Scope Perry Preschool Project, consisting of 989 children who received preschool education, 179 who began kindergarten with no preschool, and 374 who were enrolled in other preschool programs. However, students in the CPC were not randomly assigned.

Because the CPC program was offered in 20 centers, it was more diffuse than the Perry program. Initially, teachers had wide latitude over what materials to incorporate, although later they all incorporated a program developed through the Chicago Board of Education. This program emphasized three general areas of development: body image and gross motor skills, perceptual-motor and arithmetic skills, and language. The language skills taught ranged from the auditory discrimination of sounds to building sentences to story comprehension and verbal problem solving. Arthur Reynolds, the senior researcher in the project, classified seven of the 20 centers as teacher oriented, 10 as child oriented, and three as giving equal emphasis to teacher-initiated and child-initiated activities.

Both the Perry and CPC projects emphasized parent involvement with the children. Project staff made home visits, and parents often accompanied children on field trips.

The Abecedarian study

Researchers at the University of North Carolina, Chapel Hill, conducted the third study, called the Abecedarian Project. It differed from the first two in that it identified children at birth, and those who participated in the study received full-day day care for 50 weeks a year.

Early interventions consisted of "age-appropriate" adult-child interactions, such as talking to children, showing them toys or pictures, and offering infants a chance to react to sights or sounds in the environment. As children grew older, the content of the interactions became more conceptual and skill oriented and, for older preschoolers, more group oriented. Some students participated in the program only until school began; some until age 8. A school-only intervention was also available to another group of children once they reached kindergarten or first grade. For this group, parents were provided with activities and encouraged to use them with their children.

The children in a separate control group were not completely left to fend for themselves. Researchers supplied them with iron-rich formula, reducing the possibility that differences in nutrition could affect brain growth. Social work and crisis intervention services were also available to control-group families. If assessments indicated developmental lags, the family was referred to a relevant agency for follow-up. A number of families sent their children to other preschool programs available in the area. It seems likely that these various programs provided at least some members of the control group benefits similar to those provided by the Abecedarian program. This means that any differences between the preschool and non-preschool group are smaller than they would be if the control group had attended no program at all.

Of the 111 children in the original study, 104 took part in a follow-up at age 21 (four children had died, one had been withdrawn from the study, one had developed a severe physical condition that prevented inclusion, and one declined to take part).

Young adults who had received preschool intervention had completed more years of schooling (12.2 vs. 11.6), but this was largely due to the high number of females, who are less likely to drop out of school than males. More were still in school (42 percent vs. 20 percent), and more had enrolled in four-year colleges (35.9 percent vs. 13.7 percent). Forty-seven percent of the preschool group had skilled jobs, such as electrician, compared to 27 percent of the controls. Those in the preschool group were less likely to smoke or use marijuana but no less likely to use alcohol or indulge in binge drinking. Cocaine use was denied by virtually all participants in both groups.

Tests administered at ages 8, 12, 15, and 21 showed that the program paid off in both reading and mathematics. Specifically, for children who participated for eight years, the program had a large impact on reading, ranging from an effect size of 1.04 at age 8 to .79 at age 21. Effect sizes for math ranged from .64 at age 8 to .42 at age 21. (An "effect size" is a metric for analyzing the impact of a program or intervention. The greater the effect size, the greater the impact.)

For those receiving only a preschool intervention, the effect sizes in reading ranged from .75 at age 8 to .28 at age 21. For math, the impact grew over time, being .27 at age 8 and .73 at age 21. Smaller effect sizes were seen for those who had been in a school-only program. In reading the effect size ranged from .28 at age 8 to .11 at age 21. Math effects went from .11 to .26 over the same period.

What about Head Start?

Some have discounted the results from these three studies because they are model programs and perhaps cannot be generalized or because they consider the effects small. In their controversial book *The Bell Curve,* Richard J. Herrnstein and Charles Murray managed to dismiss the studies on both counts—and to dismiss Head Start at the same time. After concluding that Head Start programs neither raise intelligence nor display "sleeper effects" (higher graduation rates, less crime, improved employability), the authors had this to say: "Perry Preschool resembled the average Head Start program as a Ferrari resembles the family sedan.... The effects [from Perry Preschool] are small and some of them fall short of statistical significance. They hardly justify investing billions of dollars in run-of-the-mill Head Start programs."

Several rejoinders to the Herrnstein-Murray contentions are available. One can point to longer-term effects now displayed by the three programs (*The Bell Curve* was published in 1994). Or one can point to the effect sizes produced by the Abecedarian and Perry projects (effect sizes have not been published for the CPC program). Not even Herrnstein (were he alive) or Murray would call those effects small.

(Labeling an effect size small, medium, or large is a matter of judgment—there is no formula for such a calculation, no point decisively dividing middle from small or large from middle. Most would call the preschool-only treatment effects in the Perry project "moderate.")

One can also point to studies that show that "run-of-the-mill" Head Start programs, as varied as they might be, do produce long-term results. Researchers looking at such outcomes found that white students who attended Head Start were more likely to finish high-school and attend four-year college. The trend for African-American students was not significant, although they were less likely to have had run-ins with the law. For both races, there also appeared to be a spillover effect to younger siblings. The young brothers and sisters of students who attended Head Start do slightly better in school and are significantly less likely to have been arrested.

The lack of a significant achievement trend for African American students themselves could be discouraging. However, the same researchers found in another study that African

Americans who attended Head Start also attended schools that had lower test scores than did other African Americans. For whatever reason, this was not true for white students. Thus, the implication is that long-term effects are not seen for African Americans because of the quality of their schooling after Head Start—not because Head Start itself is ineffective. In connection with other findings of preschool effects, this result points to the need to provide for high-quality preschool experiences for minority children while simultaneously improving their schools.

Taken together, the focused research and the Head Start research affirm Broder's conclusion. We know how to provide these services, but we're not doing it. According to *Cellblocks or Classrooms? The Funding of Higher Education and Corrections and Its Impact on African-American Men,* a study released in August 2002 by the Washington-based Justice Policy Institute, the increase in state spending on corrections between 1985 and 2000 was twice what it was on higher education ($20 billion vs. $10.7 billion). And, the study reported, there are now more African-American men in jail than in colleges and universities.

Something as remote from adulthood as preschool affects the odds of landing in jail in favor of both the individual and society. And that's not all. About the same time as the Justice Policy Institute study was released, *The New York Times* reported a side-effect of welfare reform: the "no-parent family." Many more mothers now have jobs, but this leaves their children with no caretakers. The kids are shuttled around to relatives and friends. Obviously these children could benefit from good preschool programs. The question is, as Broder asked, do we have the will to make the investment?

Gerald W. Bracey (gbracey@erols.com) is an associate with the High-Scope Educational Research Foundation and an associate professor of education at George Mason University, Fairfax, Va.

Resources

Bernstein, Nina. Side Effect of Welfare Law: The No-Parent Family," *New York Times,* July 29, 2002.

Berrueta-Clement, John B., Lawrence J. Schweinhart, W. Steven Barnett, Ann S. Epstein, and David P. Weikart. *Changed Lives: The Effects of the Perry Preschool Program on Youths Through Age 19.* Ypsilanti, Mich.: High/Scope Educational Research Foundation, 1984.

Campbell, Frances A., Craig T. Ramey, Elizabeth Pungello, Joseph Sparling, and Shari Miller-Johnson. "Early Childhood Education: Young Adult Outcomes for the Abecedarian Project." *Applied Developmental Science,* vol. 6, 2002, pp. 42-57.

Campbell, Frances A., Elizabeth P. Pungello, Shari Miller-Johnson, Margaret Burchinal, and Craig T. Ramey. "The Development of Cognitive and Academic Abilities: Growth Curves from an Early Childhood Experiment." *Developmental Psychology,* vol. 37, 2001, pp. 231-242.

Currie, Janet, and Duncan Campbell. "School Quality and the Longer-Term Effects of Head Start," *Journal of Human Resources,* Fall 2000, pp. 755-774.

Garces, Eliana, Duncan Thomas, and Janet Currie. "Longer-Term Effects of Head Start." National Bureau of Economic Research,

Working Paper 8054, December 2000. www.nber.org/papers/w8054.

Justice Policy Institute. *Cellblocks or Classrooms? The Funding of Higher Education and Corrections and Its Impact on African American Men.* Washington, D.C.: Justice Policy Institute, August 2002. www.justicepolicy.org.

Reynolds, Arthur J., Judy A. Temple, Dylan L. Robertson, and Emily A. Mann. "Age 21 Benefit-Cost Analysis of the Chicago Child-Parent Center Program." Paper presented to the Society for Prevention Research, Madison, Wis., May 31-June 2, 2001.

Reynolds, Arthur J., Judy A. Temple, Dylan L. Robertson, and Emily A. Mann. "Long-Term Effects of an Early Childhood Intervention on Educational Achievement and Juvenile Arrest. *Journal of the American Medical Association,* May 9, 2001.

Schweinhart, Lawrence J., Helen V. Barnes, and David P. Weikart. *Significant Benefits: The High/Scope Perry Preschool Study Through Age 27.* Ypsilanti, Mich.: High/Scope Educational Research Foundation, 1993.

Chapter 2

Overview of Existing Policies and Programs for Young Children

To appreciate the deficiencies in how the United States approaches early learning, it is necessary first to understand what current arrangements look like and why they work the way they do. The nation has a patchwork of early care and education opportunities that evolved to meet different and traditionally separate objectives: fostering child development (giving young children access to education and other services that would prepare them for formal school) or meeting labor market needs (providing working families with child care). Today there is growing recognition of the significance of early learning for efforts to improve K–12 education, while changing patterns of work and welfare have created new incentives to provide early education to the growing number of young children who spend time in out-of-home care. While education and care for young children are, therefore, increasingly intertwined activities, public policies still tend to reflect their separate origins as either child development or labor market programs.

BACKDROP: CHANGING SOCIETAL PERSPECTIVES ON EDUCATION, WORK, AND WELFARE

Changing societal perspectives on education, work, and welfare make the education and care children receive before they enter school of growing importance for the general public and not just for parents. Education reformers increasingly recognize that their efforts to improve student achievement are affected by differences in children's development that are already evident when formal schooling begins. With most parents, mothers as well as fathers, now working, employers know that it is more important than ever for their employees to have access to high-quality child care arrangements to help them balance their work and family responsibilities. New welfare policies require low-income mothers of even very young children to work.

Efforts to reform elementary and secondary education have drawn attention to early education. There is growing emphasis on holding schools accountable for successfully educating *all* of their students. Reformers are increasingly aware that gaps in knowledge and skills are already evident when children enter kindergarten. Narrowing these gaps (especially those linked to children's race and family incomes) after children enter school has proven to be one of educators' most intractable challenges.

Ensuring that all students receive an adequate education may depend crucially on ensuring that they enter school ready to learn. In fact, courts in two states have recently ordered state officials to provide preschool education to children at risk of later educational problems. Plaintiffs in school finance lawsuits challenged the legality of state school funding laws on the grounds that insufficient and inequitable funding denied some students their constitutional rights to an adequate education.[a] In finding for the plaintiffs, courts in New Jersey and North Carolina included in their mandated remedies the provision of publicly-funded preschool programs for at-risk youngsters.[1] (The North Carolina court specified access for 4-year-olds, while the court in New Jersey included 3-year-olds as well.) Since school finance policies are under legal challenge in many states, it is likely that court-ordered preschool for at least some children will spread beyond New Jersey and North Carolina.

Access to preschool can also help families balance child-rearing and work. While individuals may still debate whether changing patterns of work and family are desirable, the irreversible reality is that it is now the norm in the United States for women to work. This is true of all women, including mothers of children who have not yet reached kindergarten age. Between 1950 and 2000 the civilian labor force participation rate of women 20 years of age and over increased from 33 to 60 percent. In 2000, 73 percent of women with children were in the labor force, including 72 percent of those with children 3- to 5-years-old and 61 percent of those with children under age 3.[2]

Moreover, public policy has shifted in its expectations about low-income mothers' participation in the workplace.

6

Women's Labor Force Participation Rate: 1950-2000

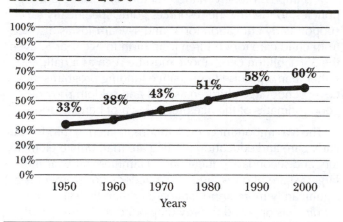

Source: U.S. Department Of Labor, *Report On The American Workforce*, (Washington, D.C.: Department of Labor, 2001), p. 126, table 5.

Labor Force Participation Rate of Women with Children: 2000

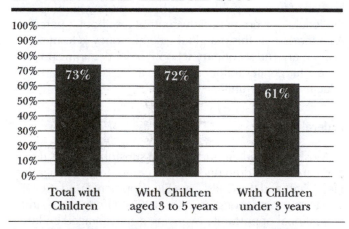

Source: U.S. Department Of Labor, *Report On The American Workforce*, (Washington, D.C.: Department of Labor, 2001), p. 127, table 6.

In the early 1990s over 90 percent of mothers receiving Aid to Families with Dependent Children ("welfare") were not in the paid labor force. Prior to 1996 states were not allowed to require public assistance recipients who were single parents caring for infants to participate in work-related activities.[3] This stipulation changed with passage of the Personal Responsibility and Work Opportunity Reconciliation Act (PRWORA). As of October 1999 most states still continued to exempt individuals with very young children from participating in work activities, but 16 states set the age limit at 3 to 6 months and 4 had no criteria for exemptions. In 23 states mothers of children over age 1 could be required to work. Only 5 states had an age limit higher than age 1.[4] Thus most single mothers became subject to PRWORA's assumption that adults, even those

with young children, should be self-supporting and that public benefits should be contingent on meeting work or work preparation requirements.

WHO CARES FOR AMERICA'S PRESCHOOLERS?

Because the United States has not approached the provision of early care and education in a systematic way, there is little routine and up-to-date information about who cares for young children. Another consequence of the nation's unsystematic approach is the lack of any universally accepted classification scheme for early care and education providers that would definitively describe the services they offer. The situation is further complicated by the fact that many young children are in multiple arrangements: for example, a child may spend part of the week in a child care center or preschool program and another part in a family day care setting (in a non-relative's home) or being cared for by relatives. Despite these difficulties, an overview of preschool arrangements can be pieced together from a variety of special (and not always strictly comparable) surveys.

In 1999, 59 percent of 3- to 5-year-olds who had not yet entered kindergarten participated in some kind of center-based program, variously called day care, nursery school, prekindergarten, preschool, and Head Start. The older the child, the more likely he or she was to be enrolled in a center-based program for at least some part of a week: 46 percent of 3-year-olds, 69 percent of 4-year-olds, and 76 percent of 5-year-olds. Just 23 percent of these children had parental care only: 31 percent for 3-year-olds, 18 percent for 4-year-olds, and 14 percent for 5-year-olds.[5] The remaining children were more likely to be cared for by relatives or in family day care settings operated by non-relatives than in center-based programs. Infants and toddlers were more likely than preschoolers to be in family-based rather than center-based care.

Center-based providers vary in the extent to which they are organized to provide educational experiences for preschool children and whether they offer services on a full- or part-day basis. There are no hard and fast rules distinguishing centers, but those labeled "day care" are more apt to be full-day programs meeting the child care needs of working parents (i.e., 9 to 10 hours a day). Nursery schools, prekindergartens, preschools, and Head Start are more apt to include instruction as an important and integral aspect of their service and, like many public kindergartens, may be part-day programs (2–4 hours) operating only during the regular school year. Even when educationally-oriented providers offer "full-day" services, full-day generally refers to the length of the typical elementary/secondary school day (6–7 hours) rather than the 9 to 10 hours offered by centers oriented to the child care needs of working parents.

The number of centers caring for children who have not yet entered kindergarten is unknown but totals well over 100,000.[b] The Children's Foundation 2001 survey of child centers found 111,506, based on reports from state child care licensing offices.[6] However, states differ in the extent to which they include or exclude educationally-oriented preschool programs from their child care licensing requirements.[c] The Foundation also reported that there were 304,958 regulated family child care homes in 2000, mostly serving six or fewer children,[7] and estimated that there were 4 unregulated family day care homes for every regulated one.[d]

Center providers operate under a variety of auspices. Some are operated by nonprofit groups, including religious organizations. Some are profit-making businesses, both single centers and large corporate chains. In some places the public school system offers prekindergarten classes, although often these are open mainly to children who are at risk of not being ready to succeed in school because of poverty, limited English, disabilities, or other factors.

States have the primary responsibility for setting standards for and regulating early care and education providers. The major exception is that the federal government requires that the states have basic child care safety and health requirements in place in order to receive funds from the Child Care Development Fund (see the next section). Even here, states set the health and safety requirements as well as procedures for ensuring the compliance of both regulated and nonregulated providers; and states vary in the extent to which their practices are consistent with recommendations of experts.[8] More generally, states differ in their rules about which providers are subject to regulatory standards and what standards must be met. As noted above, there are substantial numbers of providers (especially family-based providers but also including some centers) who are eligible for public subsidies but are exempt from any regulation except basic health and safety rules.

WHO PAYS FOR EARLY CARE AND EDUCATION?

In keeping with the traditional view that early care and education are individual consumer goods rather than an investment with important public benefits, families bear the largest responsibility for providing care and education for preschool children.

It is estimated that in 2001, public and private spending on early care and education for children from birth to age 5 will total $50–55 billion, with parents paying 50–55 percent, the federal government paying 25–30 percent, and state and local governments paying 15–20 percent. Corporate and philanthropic investments could amount to 1–5 percent but are difficult to estimate.[9] If the unpaid time of mothers and fathers engaged in child care is considered, the parental share is obviously much higher. Other costs that are not included in this total are those of relatives and others who take care of children on an unpaid basis or at a below-market rate.

It is impossible, given the structure of current funding policies, to identify the resources going specifically to support early education for 3- and 4-year-olds as distinct from child care for children from birth to age 4 or 5. Even the $50+ billion cited above must be seen as a ballpark rather than a precise figure, since funding programs may cover school-age children as well and seldom provide good estimates of the age break-down of beneficiaries.

The two important considerations to keep in mind about early care and education funding are that, unlike elementary and secondary education, (1) families still bear the largest share of costs, and (2) the federal government is a significantly more important partner than the states in *funding* (as opposed to providing or administering) early care and education. This latter fact is easily obscured by the state's lead role in administering programs and in the wide discretion states have to structure program parameters. But the American approach to financing early care and education has evolved quite differently from our approach to financing public elementary and secondary education. In the latter case, states and localities bear 93 percent of the burden of funding public schools, parents pay nothing, and the federal government only contributes about 7 percent. As important as this marginal federal money is to many elementary and secondary schools, federal funding policies have a far greater influence on the availability of early education opportunities.

Federal Funding

Most of the federal funding that subsidizes education and care for children under age 5 comes from 2 programs, Head Start and the Child Care Development Fund (CCDF). The former has its origins in the 1960s' efforts to expand educational opportunity by giving disadvantaged children a "head start" in school. CCDF is designed to support working parents by helping them with the costs of child care. Reflecting their different goals, the two programs operate in quite different ways.

Head Start. Head Start provides grants to local agencies to provide comprehensive early childhood developmental, educational, health, nutritional, social, and other services to low-income children and their families. Ninety percent of participants must be from families whose income is below the poverty line or from families who are eligible for public assistance. Most Head Start programs are half-day and part-year. While children from birth through kindergarten are eligible, only 6 percent of the 857,664 children enrolled in FY 2000 were under age 3. Fifty-six percent were age 4. (The remainder were age 3 (33 percent) or age 5 (5 percent)). Nationwide, 1,535 Head Start grantees provided services in 18,200 centers at an average cost of $5,951 per child.[e] Head Start appropriations have risen rapidly over the last decade, from $1.6 billion in 1990 to $6.2 billion in 2001.[10]

Head Start is the oldest of the federal early care and education programs, having enrolled its first children in 1965. With strong roots in the Community Action Program of the War on Poverty, Head Start has traditionally given local grantees wide flexibility in program structure. Grantees must comply with federal program standards, which Congress in 1998 modified to place more emphasis on school readiness.

CCDF. The Child Care Development Fund was formed during the 1996 welfare reform by consolidating several existing child care programs. The fund provides grants to states for subsidizing the child care costs of eligible families and for improving the overall quality and availability of child care services. Some CCDF funds are subject to matching requirements.

States give CCDF subsidies in the form of certificates or outright cash to parents to purchase child care services or through grants and contracts to providers who enroll eligible children. In FY 1999 only 11 percent of the children participating in CCDF were served through grants or contracts; 83 percent were served through certificates and 6 percent through cash to parents. In that year 29 percent of CCDF children were served in settings "legally operating without regulation," as distinguished from regulated settings.[11] Eligible settings include centers, family day care homes, and relatives if they live in a separate residence. Federal law requires that CCDF providers comply with applicable state or local health and safety requirements but otherwise leaves it up to states to set licensing standards and determine reimbursement rates.

Parents share responsibility for paying child care fees, on a sliding scale basis, although states may waive fees for families below the poverty line. States set subsidy levels and fee schedules.

Children up to age 13 who reside with a family whose income does not exceed 85 percent of the state median income are eligible to participate; however, states are free to set lower eligibility limits, and most do. Parents must be working or in education or training or the child must be in need of protective services.

Federal funding for CCDF in FY 2001 was $4.5 billion. The General Accounting Office (GAO) estimates that 1.3 million children under age 5 participated in CCDF in FY 1999 and that 70 percent of total budget authority for the program went for children in this age group.[12]

Although children benefiting from CCDF may receive care that helps them prepare for school, school readiness is not an explicit goal of the program. There are no national performance standards for services or staff other than the basic requirements noted above that states must have and enforce health and safety rules.

Other federal funding. Head Start and CCDF provide roughly three-quarters of the federal subsidies available for early care and education. Smaller but still important subsidies flow from Temporary Assistance for Needy Families (TANF), from special education programs, and from Title 1 of the Improving America's Schools Act.[13]

Under TANF, the program that replaced Aid to Families with Dependent Children in the 1996 reform of federal welfare legislation, states can use some of their welfare block grant on child care. TANF in recent years has been an important source of child care funds, reaching 350,000 children under age 5 in FY 1999 at an estimated cost of $1.3 billion.

Children with disabilities get federal aid under "special education" programs. GAO reports that 1.1 million children under age 5 participated in special education in FY 1999, but these figures cover 3 different programs and may include duplicated counts of students. Total spending on special education services for children under age 5 was $835 million.

Title 1 grants for supplemental educational and related services to educationally-disadvantaged children in low-income areas mostly are spent by local districts on elementary education, but about 300,000 children under age 5 benefited from Title 1 funds in FY 1999.

In addition to these direct expenditure programs, several tax credits and exclusions help families and employers pay for employment-related dependent-care expenses. Unlike direct federal early care and education programs, tax benefits are not targeted to lower-income families.

State And Local Funding

Prekindergarten. As of 1998–99, 42 states (including the District of Columbia) invested in state prekindergarten initiatives offering regularly-scheduled group experiences for young children to help them learn and develop before entering elementary school.[14] Beyond this fundamental similarity, the initiatives were quite diverse:

- Some programs were available only in public school settings, while others (such as Georgia's) made use of a variety of settings.
- Some states only supplement federal Head Start programs, while others have developed separate initiatives. A number of states sponsor multiple initiatives.
- Georgia offers prekindergarten to all 4-year-olds whose parents want them to participate. To qualify to participate, Georgia Pre-K providers must offer services 5 days a week, for at least 6.5 hours per day, for 36 weeks a year. Providers are reimbursed $2,219 to $3,475 annual per child. Georgia officials estimate that approximately 63,500 4-year-olds, or 58 to 60 percent, are participating, with another 12,000 4-year-olds enrolled in Head Start centers that are not Pre-K providers.
- New York and Oklahoma have launched school-district-based initiatives to open prekindergarten to all 4-year-olds, regardless of income, but not all districts

GEORGIA'S PREKINDERGARTEN PROGRAM PROVIDERS

In 1993 Georgia established a prekindergarten program for 4-year-olds with funds from the state lottery. Originally targeting at-risk children, in 1995 the program was opened to all children whose parents want them to participate. Eligible providers include:

Public Schools	Private Schools
Department of Family Services	Head Start Agencies
For-Profit Child Care Agencies	Nonprofit Child Care Agencies
Hospitals	Vocational/Technical Schools
Universities	Churches
Atlanta Job Corp	Military Bases
YMCAs and YWCAs	

SOURCE: Karen Schulman, Helen Blank, and Danielle Ewen, *Seeds of Success: State Prekindergarten Initiatives—1998–1999* (Washington, D.C.: Children's Defense Fund, 1999), p. 186.

in these states participate. New York, which restricts district participation because of limited funding, appears to be currently serving roughly a quarter of its 4-year-olds and Oklahoma around half.

- Enrollment rates in states that restrict access to prekindergarten reach or exceed 20–30 percent in a few cases, but generally are much lower.[f] These states have adopted varying approaches to setting priorities about whom to serve. Most state programs are limited to low-income families and children with other risk factors. (Even then, most states do not serve all eligible children.) Some states focus on serving all children in selected communities, generally chosen because they are home to significant populations of disadvantaged families.

- Some states limit a child's eligibility for prekindergarten to one year. Others define eligible children to include both 3- and 4-year-olds or even all children from birth to age 5.

- Many state pre-K initiatives offer only part-day (2 to 4 hours a day), part-year services, although there are exceptions such as Connecticut, Massachusetts, and Hawaii.

- Some initiatives (particularly those that follow a public school model and focus on public school settings) focus comparatively narrowly on education goals, while others provide a more comprehensive array of services including health care and various family supports.

- States may distribute pre-K funds directly to providers or may distribute them to communities or school districts, which in turn distribute funds to individual providers. Hawaii and Arizona distribute some or all funds directly to parents.

- Many but not all state pre-K initiatives require providers to meet quality standards that are higher than the state's child care licensing standards. For example, New York State has no pre-service requirements for teachers in child care centers, while prekindergarten teachers are required to be certified in elementary education.[15]

In 1998–99 states spent approximately $1.7 billion on their pre-K initiatives and served 750,000 children.[16] Total state spending was quite uneven: the 10 highest spending states accounted for over three-quarters of state spending on pre-K initiatives, although they accounted for just over one-half the pre-K age population. The 5 top spending states (California, Georgia, Illinois, New York, and Texas) accounted for about half of all state pre-K spending.[17] State spending per enrolled pupil varied widely as well, from $7,000 in Connecticut (for children enrolled in full-day programs) to less than $2,000 in 14 state initiatives. While the various initiatives are not directly comparable, in that they cover different services, a sense of the meaning of these average expenditure levels can be gained by comparing them with the $5,147 average annual cost in the federal Head Start program in FY 1998.[18] Some states require localities to provide matching funds or permit them to supplement state money. These additional local dollars may come from school districts or from community programs and organizations.

Child care. Most state spending on child care is actually federal money, from federal appropriations for CCDF or from state decisions to transfer money from the TANF block grant to CCDF or to spend TANF funds directly for child care. In addition to meeting their required state match for these funds, however, states do expend some of their own

FULL-DAY, FULL-YEAR PREKINDERGARTEN INITIATIVES

Several states provide the necessary funding for full-day and/or full-year prekindergarten for eligible children and also require that it be offered by at least some percentage of programs.

Connecticut reimbursed providers $7,000 per child in 1998–99 for children participating for the full day and full year. The state also required that at least 60 percent of available prekindergarten slots be for full-day/full-year participation, to meet the needs of full-time working families. Based on local planning processes that were required to assess the need for these programs, several communities decided to go beyond minimum requirements and have all their prekindergarten programs operate on a full-day, full-year basis. Connecticut's program is open to all 3- and 4-year-olds where offered, but is limited to school districts with high concentrations of poverty. About 6,300 children were served in school year 2001–02, roughly 7 percent of the state's population of 3- and 4-year-olds.

Massachusetts requires that at least one-third of the children participating in its prekindergarten initiative be provided with full-day classes. This requirement reflects the initiative's orientation toward meeting the needs of working families. The state also promotes full-day/full-year programming by encouraging local councils under its Community Partnerships for Children to consider the range of schedules faced by working families (including irregular as well as regular shifts) in implementing their prekindergarten programs. Approximately 21,800 children from moderate and low-income families participated in prekindergarten in 2001–02, roughly 13.5 percent of the state's 3- and 4-year-olds.

Hawaii's Preschool Open Door program funds full-day programs for all participating children, although only for 9 months a year. The state provided funds directly to parents, who could choose the program their children attended. This might be a prekindergarten program, although it could also be a child care program that met only child care licensing standards. Hawaii's program served approximately 800 3- and 4-year-olds from low-income families in 1999–00, roughly 2.5 percent of the relevant age group.

In all 3 cases, while the states provided funding for extended programs, they also required parents to pay fees on a sliding scale basis.

In 1998–99 several other states (California, Florida, and Maryland) reported providing some support for extended hours in their prekindergarten programs, although they did not require programs to offer extended hours.

SOURCE: Karen Schulman, Helen Blank, and Danielle Ewen, *Seeds of Success: State Prekindergarten Initiatives 1998–99* (Washington, D.C.: Children's Defense Fund, 1999), pp. 129–30; Nancy K. Cauthen, Jane Knitzer, and Carol H. Ripple, *Map and Track: State Initiatives for Young Children and Families, 2000 Edition* (New York, NY: National Center for Children in Poverty, Columbia University, 2000); unpublished information from *Education Week*.

funds on child care. The exact amount, especially the portion directed to preschool-age children, is hard to pinpoint. State and local spending on early care and education combined is estimated to have been about $8 to $10 billion in 1999.[19]

State child care spending tends to benefit low-income families and to take the form of vouchers or direct payments to providers. States sometimes draw on general revenues for child care funding but may also depend on a variety of other revenue sources. For example, Kentucky and Maine devote part of their tobacco settlement money to child care; and California uses funds raised by taxes on cigarettes and other tobacco products for a range of "early childhood development services," including child care. Massachusetts and Kentucky give individuals, when registering and licensing motor vehicles, the option of designating part of their fees to support child care. Missouri funds its Early Childhood Development, Education and Care Fund from gambling fees. Georgia funds its pre-K program, as well as college education, from a state lottery. Over half the states have tax credits or deductions for child and dependent care.[20]

Notes

a. Unlike the federal constitution, virtually every state constitution includes some kind of "education clause" specifying education as a government function and requiring legislatures to create public schools that provide education variously described as "thorough and efficient" or "ample" or "adequate." Many state school finance systems are under legal challenge for failing to support an "adequate" education for all students.

b. This figure compares to roughly 80,000 public elementary and secondary schools.

c. For example, some states exclude preschools and prekindergartens, which may be regulated by different agencies. Some states exclude religiously-affiliated centers from licensing requirements.

d. States have varying rules about which family child care homes must be regulated. Many exempt homes caring for a small number of children.

e. Head Start centers often provide a broader range of services to children and their families than do other early childhood centers or public schools, so annual per-child Head Start costs are not directly comparable to costs incurred by other early education providers.

f. Reliable data on enrollment rates in prekindergarten programs are not available. We have made rough estimates based on unpublished information provided to us by the staff of *Education Week*, who collected enrollment numbers from states. The problem in estimating enrollment rates is in knowing what denominator to use, since states may allow children younger than four to enroll but the extent of their eligibility to participate is difficult to determine.

Notes

1. *Hoke County v. State of North Carolina/State Board of Education,* 95 CVS 1158 (Hoke II, October, 2000); *Abbot v. Burke,* 748 A2d 82 (2000).

2. U.S. Department of Labor, *Report on the American Workforce* (Washington, D.C.: U.S. Department of Labor, 2001), pp. 126–127, tables 5–6.

3. R. Kent Weaver, *Ending Welfare as We Know It* (Washington, D.C.: Brookings Institution Press, 2000), p. 20.

4. State Policy Documentation Project, *Work Requirements: Exemptions as of October 1999,* available at <**http://www.spdp.org/tanf/exemptions.pdf**> Accessed June 21, 2001.

5. National Center for Education Statistics, *Digest of Education Statistics, 2000,* NCES-2001-034 (Washington, D.C.: U.S. Department of Education, January 2001), table 48.

6. The Children's Foundation, *Child Care Center Licensing Study Summary Data,* available at <**http://www. childrensfoundation.net**/ Accessed June 12, 2001.

7. The Children's Foundation, *Child Care Center Licensing Study Summary Data,* available at <**http://www. childrensfoundation.net/**> Accessed June 12, 2001. Estimate of the number of unregulated family care homes provided to CED by Children's Foundation staff.

8. U.S. General Accounting Office, *Child Care: State Efforts to Enforce Safety and Health Requirements,* GAO/HEHS-00-28 (Washington, D.C.: U.S. General Accounting Office, January 2000).

9. W. Steven Barnett, "Funding Issues for Universal Early Education in the United States" (draft, Center for Early Education, Rutgers University, March 30, 2001). Figures updated for CED by author.

10. U.S. Department of Health and Human Services, Head Start Bureau, *2001 Head Start Fact Sheet,* available at <**http://www2.acf.dhhs.gov/programs/hsb/about/fact2001.htm**>. Accessed July 5, 2001.

11. U.S. Department of Health and Human Services, Child Care Bureau, *FY 1999 CCDF Data Tables and Charts,* available at <**http://www.acf.dhhs.gov/programs/ccb/research/99acf800/**> Accessed July 12, 2001.

12. U.S. General Accounting Office, *Early Education and Care: Overlap Indicates Need to Assess Crosscutting Programs,* GAO/HEHS-00-78 (Washington, D.C.: U.S. General Accounting Office, April 2000), pp. 13–15.

13. U.S. GAO, *Early Education and Care,* pp. 13–15.

14. Karen Schulman, Helen Blank, and Danielle Ewen, *Seeds of Success: State Prekindergarten Initiatives 1998–1999* (Washington, D.C.: Children's Defense Fund, September 1999), p. 13.

15. Schulman, Blank, and Ewen, *Seeds of Success;* The Center for Career Development in Early Care and Education, Wheelock College, *Child Care Licensing: Qualifications and Training for Roles in Child Care Centers and Family Child Care Homes: 2000 Summary Sheet,* available at <**http://www.nccic.org/cctopics/cclicensing00.pdf**> Accessed September 13, 2001.

16. Schulman, Blank, and Ewen. *Seeds of Success,* p. 16.

17. Schulman, Blank, and Ewen, *Seeds of Success,* p. 87; The Center for Career Development in Early Care and Education, Wheelock College, *Child Care Licensing.*

18. Schulman, Blank, and Ewen, *Seeds of Success,* pp. 33–5.

19. W. Steven Barnett, "Funding Issues for Universal Early Education," p. 10.

20. Anne Mitchell, Louise Stoney, and Harriet Dichter, *Financing Child Care in the United States: An Expanded Catalog of Current Strategies 2001 Edition* (Kansas City, MO: Ewing Marion Kauffman Foundation, 2001).

Accountability Shovedown: Resisting the Standards Movement in Early Childhood Education

Mr. Hatch sees the proliferation of standards for early childhood settings as "accountability shovedown" that threatens the integrity of early childhood professionals and the quality of educational experiences for young children.

BY J. AMOS HATCH

DURING THE 1980s, early childhood educators waged a battle to resist attempts to require more and more of young children at younger and younger ages. This movement to push expectations from the primary grades down into kindergarten and preschool programs was characterized as "curriculum shovedown" by the mainstream early childhood educators, who argued that young children were not developmentally ready for the academic emphasis of such an approach. David Elkind, an articulate spokesperson for the early childhood community, argued that young children were being "miseducated" in settings where they were experiencing stress from academic pressure for no apparent benefit. In *The Hurried Child* and *Miseducation: Preschoolers at Risk,* Elkind provided powerful indictments of curriculum shovedown and related attempts to make children grow up faster.[1]

My view is that the standards movement—so pervasive across educational settings today—is threatening children in early childhood in the same ways as the curriculum shovedown movement did in the 1980s. The point of attack has changed from curriculum to outcomes, but the consequences for young children may be the same. Standards for such federal programs as Head Start are already in place, and the discourse in many states and across the early childhood field assumes the inevitability of standards.[2] After all, who could be against standards?

Who would have the nerve to say that standards are not important? Who would try to build an argument toward the conclusion that standards are somehow bad? Not I, certainly. I am all for standards in early childhood education, unless they fail to pass muster in the 10 areas discussed below.

1. *Pressure on children.* I support standards for early childhood programs—except when the implementation of those standards puts children as young as 3 and 4 at risk of feeling pressured in the classroom environment. Elkind noted that young children experience significant and sometimes debilitating stress when they are expected to perform at academic levels for which they are not ready. Further, he argued that waiting until they are ready puts children at no real academic disadvantage in the long run.[3]

It is axiomatic in early childhood that children develop at different rates. Some young children will be ready to meet the challenges of the new expectations associated with the standards movement; many will not. Holding all children to the same standard guarantees that some will face failure. And just setting up a situation in which failure is possible creates stress for even the most capable child, who might be wondering if he or she is achieving "high enough or fast enough."[4] Getting children to do more sooner sounds like a logical way to cure the ills of education. But ask someone who has comforted a child who cries because she cannot distinguish between a 3 and a 5 or who has coaxed a child to keep trying when he refuses to demonstrate (once again) his inability to match the letters with the sounds. Those who know young children understand that putting them under stress is an unacceptable by-product of accountability efforts designed to achieve dubious educational advantages.

2. *Pressure on teachers.* I see standards as vitally important in early childhood education—unless they are used in ways that put pressure on teachers to abandon their mission of teaching young children in favor of teaching a core set of competencies. The pressure to accelerate achievement gets translated to teachers as "Do a better job of getting your kids up to the standards—or else." If meeting the standards is what is valued in the school where they teach and if student performance provides the basis for how they are evaluated, teachers will feel pressured to meet the standards and to raise student performance. On its face, that kind of pressure may not seem so bad. Indeed, standards are set up to demand more of schools and teachers based on the belief that "demands will result in behavior that conforms to them."[5]

But pressuring early childhood professionals with demands and threats may work against the best interests of teachers and the children they serve. By training and disposition, teachers of young children are concerned with understanding and teaching the whole child. Teachers are motivated to know children's individual capacities and needs and to do whatever is necessary to develop those capacities and meet those needs, whether they are emotional, social, physical, or cognitive. It causes genuine anxiety when other domains of children's development are ignored or put at risk because of an overemphasis on something as narrowly defined as academic standards. In addition, early childhood teachers feel some anxiety when they see themselves as the agents of stress in their students' lives. When they are forced to implement standards-driven programs that focus on academic outcomes and put pressure on young children, teachers experience conflicts between what they believe to be best for their students and the accomplishment of what is required by their programs.[6]

Pressuring teachers to abandon practices that recognize the complexity of children's development is wrong. Demanding that they undertake practices that may ultimately harm children's chances for success in school and life is foolish.

3. *Narrowing of experiences.* I think standards are fine—except in cases where moving to a standards-based curriculum reduces a rich set of experiences to a narrow sequence of lessons. The consequences of implementing standards with older students are clear enough—when standards are in place, the curriculum is reduced to an emphasis on the content on which children, teachers, and schools will be assessed.[7] This narrow emphasis on easily measured objectives seriously limits what is being learned in elementary, middle, and high schools, and critics are not even convinced that the content on which the narrowed curriculum focuses is necessarily the right stuff.[8] Narrowing the preschool curriculum to accommodate standards such as those being promulgated by Head Start and promoted by the Bush Administration[9] not only limits the scope of what is

learned but will also take the life out of young children's initial experiences in classrooms.

The best early childhood programs are those that give children opportunities to explore meaningful content in meaningful ways. Skills and concepts—the same ones found in the standards-based approaches—are learned, but they are learned in the context of meaningful activity. Such programs are characterized by a sense of joyful discovery. Substituting a narrow, skills-based approach for a dynamic, child-responsive curriculum will rob young children of the joy of discovering how much they can learn and just how fulfilling school experiences can be.

4. *Accountability as punishment.* I believe standards are the centerpiece of reform in early childhood education—unless children, teachers, and programs are systematically identified as deficient in an effort to make them accountable. The logic of the accountability movement is based on the premise that students and teachers will not work hard unless they are afraid of the consequences of being found to be below the standard. What happens to 3- and 4-year-old children who are found to be below the standard? Kohn describes what happens in the primary grades:

> Skills develop rapidly and differentially in young children, which means that expecting everyone of the same age to have acquired a given set of capabilities creates unrealistic expectations, leads to one-size-fits-all (which is to say, bad) teaching, and guarantees that some children will be defined as failures at the very beginning of their time in school.[10]

It's wrong to label a 7-year-old second-grader a failure; it's criminal to do it to a 4-year-old preschooler. Using the threat of failure as a tool to motivate young children and their teachers is an absurd notion that characterizes a system designed to "punish rather than improve."[11] That some children will fail to meet a standard is inevitable.[12] That many who fail will come from groups that have historically been shortchanged by the system is highly likely.[13] While it may be politically expedient to join the call for tougher standards, systematically labeling large populations of our youngest students as failures is a price we should never agree to pay.

5. *Teacher deprofessionalization.* I am a proponent of early childhood standards—as long as teachers are not stripped of their roles as professional decision makers. Across the education landscape, the movement toward standards is a movement away from teacher responsibility and agency. As curricula, teaching strategies, outcomes, and evaluation techniques are standardized, teachers' opportunities to make decisions based on their professional judgment are systematically reduced. The implementation of standards-based programs signals students, parents, and society at large that teachers are not to be trusted or respected and that technical/managerial control is what is needed to fix problems that teachers helped create.[14]

For the past five years, I have been working with colleagues in Australia studying how early childhood teachers use child observation in their teaching. One of the striking findings from

14

our work is that teachers in the United States and Australia have reduced their use of child observation as a strategy for shaping curriculum and increased their use of observation as a device for monitoring student progress. Instead of studying children in an effort to better meet their needs and improve their learning opportunities, teachers are now filling out checklists so that they can chart the achievement of a narrow set of competencies. We (and the teachers we have interviewed) see this as evidence of teacher deprofessionalization in the areas of assessment and curriculum development.[15] Early childhood assessment appears to be becoming a form of "product control, closely tied to industrialization and the creation of an end product."[16] Early childhood teachers appear to be becoming what Jonathan Kozol calls "technicians of proficiency" whose task it is to monitor children's progress through a hierarchy of prescribed outcomes.[17] Something important is lost when the work of teachers is downgraded from professional to technical status.

6. *Performance over learning.* I support the standards movement—unless it teaches young children to value the attainment of certain objectives over their ability to learn. Why do children think they are in school? What do we teach them about why they are there? Systems set up on the premise that there are certain standards that everyone must attain teach students that meeting those standards is the reason they are in school. Children learn that doing the work that's put in front of them at a level that will get them by is the stuff of schooling.

In such a system, performance goals dominate learning goals. School tasks have no intrinsic value; they are only means to achieve the extrinsic rewards or avoid the punishments built into the system. Carol Dweck has contrasted performance goals and learning goals.[18] When learning goals are what's important, children are taught that learning itself has inherent value and that the reason they are in school is to learn. It's clear enough that performance-goal structures drive education from elementary through graduate school,[19] but preschools are just beginning to form their conceptions of what school is for and where they fit in. The goal in high-quality early childhood programs is to help students see themselves as able learners and see learning as an exciting adventure that has meaning and importance in their immediate experience. On the effects of standards, Eisner summaries, "In our desire to improve our schools, education has become a casualty."[20] If we continue down the road to standards-based reform in early childhood education, *learning* will be a casualty.

7. *Individual devaluation.* I like the idea of standards in early childhood education—except when their use encourages us to ignore the individual strengths and needs of young children. Susan Ohanian describes those who advocate standards as the cure-all for the ills of school and society as *standardistos,* who try to force their will on others in the form of one-size-fits-all curriculum plans. She argues that such an approach assumes that knowledge is pure and unrelated to the knowledge-seeker, so education can be prepackaged and delivered without regard for the individual needs and interests of the learners.[21] I agree with Ohanian and others who see standards-based approaches as systems that operate as if individual differences do not exist.[22] What is even more troubling for children is that ac-

countability systems operate as if individual differences *should not* exist; that is, if you don't fit the mold, there's something wrong with you.[23]

Such thinking turns contemporary best practices for teaching young children upside down. Knowing what individual children are like and providing the educational experiences they need are the cornerstones of sound early childhood programming. Anyone who has spent 30 minutes in a classroom full of 4- and 5-year-olds can tell you that children bring striking differences to their school experience. Imposing common standards on all students ignores individual differences, limiting the development of the most talented and jeopardizing the learning opportunities of those who need the most help and support.[24] In early childhood education, we should continue to have high standards for ourselves and for our students. But we should avoid implementing one-size-fits-all standards that devalue the uniqueness of the children we serve.

8. *Sameness versus diversity.* Standards seem like a good way to improve early childhood education—except in those instances where family and cultural differences are out of place because programs emphasize sameness. I am not surprised—but I am disappointed—that a tone of cultural elitism runs throughout the standards-for-accountability argument. It's clear that those who are making decisions about what should be taught are those who represent the dominant elite in our society. It's easy for those with cultural power to reach consensus about which knowledge is of the most worth: it's the knowledge they already have.[25] So small groups of privileged individuals are deciding what goes into children's heads based on an artificial consensus that may "underrepresent, misrepresent, or exclude groups of voices from the community."[26]

Children who are already excluded from access to the resources and supports of the mainstream will be further marginalized with the imposition of standards-based reform. They will be expected to perform at prescribed levels on prescribed tasks based on the false assumption that equal opportunities to learn exist.[27] In a model driven by an obsession with sameness, diversity becomes a problem, and children from diverse groups are likely to become casualties simply because of their differences. As a field, early childhood education has not been perfect in its attempts to recognize and celebrate the strengths that diversity brings to educational settings, but early childhood educators are well ahead of most segments of society. Moving to standards-based models that promote sameness and punish diversity is the wrong way to go if we are to continue to improve the life changes of every child in our society.

9. *Who benefits?* I will speak up for standards in my field—unless it is difficult to make a compelling case that young children actually benefit from this movement. There is little empirical evidence of a causal link between standard setting and enhanced student learning.[28] But even if we buy into the idea that young children's performance on academic tasks could be improved, it is reasonable to ask if those gains are worth the cost of the unintended consequences I have enumerated here. A number of respected researchers, educators, and social critics say the costs are too high.[29] So if students don't actually learn more or must pay dearly for improved performance on a nar-

rowly defined set of arbitrary standards, who benefits from the mania to implement standards?

Michael Apple calls the standards movement "reform on the cheap."[30] He and others point out that politicians and other individuals who use their power to influence educational change seek out simple and inexpensive strategies that give the appearance of providing solutions.[31] Politicians make political hay by offering quick fixes that put responsibility on others for their success. When the poorly thought out and inadequately funded reform strategies are unsuccessful, those in power are quick to blame educators, families, and children.

The standards movement is just such a strategy. It provides an opportunity for those in power to "get tough" with students and educators, spending small amounts of money developing outcomes without investing the large sums it would take to achieve significant change. If the standards are not met, you can be sure the victims, not the politicians, will be blamed. It's hard to see how our youngest and least powerful citizens will benefit from standards in early childhood education.

10. *Corporate mentality.* I am aboard the standards bandwagon—unless it means that the forces driving corporate America are being applied in early childhood classrooms. It amazes me that business executives and their political cronies are deciding how children ought to be educated. It makes my head spin to think that the "bottom line" mentality of giant corporations like IBM is having a profound influence on the lives of untold numbers of 3-, 4-, and 5-year-old children. Young children are not PCs to be efficiently assembled according to a set of profit-driven standards. Teachers are not "blue suits" who either meet corporate quotas or are fired. Education is not a commodity to be produced, marketed, and sold. Classrooms are not marketplaces where beating the competition at any cost is all that counts.[32]

It says something profound about what matters in our nation that folks who have committed their lives to caring for and educating young children are being told what to do by individuals whose expertise lies in running large companies or winning political elections. In spite of the rhetoric of those who have the media's attention, early childhood education has a long history of standard setting and accountability.[33] What's different is that our standards presume that young children are complex human beings who learn best when they are guided, nurtured, and cared for, not lifeless commodities that must meet standards of production. Our accountability comes from an ethical commitment to do what is right for every child, not from measuring productivity according to an arbitrary set of narrowly defined outcomes.

ACCOUNTABILITY SHOVEDOWN

In sum, I see the proliferation of standards for early childhood settings as "accountability shovedown" that threatens the integrity of early childhood professionals and the quality of educational experiences for young children. In spite of the seemingly unassailable logic of the standards movement, I believe educators and others interested in the well-being of our youngest citizens ought to mount a resistance movement to accountability shovedown that parallels the curriculum battles of 20 years ago. Elkind is publishing a new edition of *The Hurried Child.* The field needs to challenge aggressively the appropriateness of standards-based approaches to reforming early childhood education.

I don't see such resistance as a mindless defense of the status quo. Knowledge about how young children develop and learn is expanding rapidly, and the field is opening up to new thinking and expanding its perspective on what is appropriate in early childhood classrooms. I count this as forward movement, designed to improve the experiences of young children and maximize their chances for a rich, full life in school and beyond. Standards-based approaches represent backward movement, designed to force early childhood programs into molds that don't work with older students and are downright harmful for young children.

Kohn characterizes the dominant philosophy for fixing schools as a return to the methods of the past, only using them "harder, longer, stronger, louder, meaner."[34] This article constitutes a plea to resist adding "earlier" to the list. Let's continue to improve the quality of early childhood programs, but let's not do it by forcing children and teachers to suffer the consequences of implementing standards-based reform.

Notes

1. David Elkind, *The Hurried Child* (Reading, Mass.: Addison-Wesley, 1981); and *Miseducation: Preschoolers at Risk* (New York: Knopf, 1987).

2. Lawrence J. Schweinhart, "Assessing the Outcomes of Head Start: Where Is the Early Childhood Field Going?," *High/Scope Resource,* vol. 20, 2001, pp. 1, 9–11.

3. David Elkind, "Educating the Very Young," *NEA Today,* January 1988, p. 23.

4. Elkind, *The Hurried Child,* p. xii.

5. John Kordalewski, *Standards in the Classroom: How Teachers and Students Negotiate Learning* (New York: Teachers College Press, 2000), p. 5.

6. J. Amos Hatch and Evelyn B. Freeman, "Kindergarten Philosophies and Practices: Perspectives of Teachers, Principals, and Supervisors," *Early Childhood Research Quarterly,* vol. 3, 1988, pp. 158–59.

7. Elliot W. Eisner, "What Does It Mean to Say a School Is Doing Well?," *Phi Delta Kappan,* January 2001, pp. 368–69; and Robert L. Linn, "Assessments and Accountability," *Educational Researcher,* March 2000, p. 8.

8. John Goodlad, quoted in John Merrow, "Undermining Standards," *Phi Delta Kappan,* May 2001, p. 656; Alfie Kohn, "Fighting the Tests: Turning Frustration into Action," *Young Children,* vol. 56, 2001, p. 19; and Donald B. Gratz, "High Standards for Whom?," *Phi Delta Kappan,* May 2000, p. 687.

9. See Jacques Steinberg, "Bush's Plan to Push Reading in Head Start Stirs Debate," *New York Times,* 10 February 2001.

10. Kohn, p. 19.
11. Gratz, p. 685.
12. Linn, p. 11.
13. Anita Perna Bohn and Christine E. Sleeter, "Multicultural Education and the Standards Movement," *Phi Delta Kappan,* October 2000, p. 156; and Gratz, p. 682.
14. Gunilla Dahlberg, Peter Moss, and Alan Pence, *Beyond Quality in Early Childhood Education and Care: Postmodern Perspectives* (London: Falmer Press, 1999), p. 2; Bohn and Sleeter, p. 158; and Merrow, p. 655.
15. Susan Grieshaber, Gail Halliwell, J. Amos Hatch, and Kerryann Walsh, "Child Observation as Teachers' Work in Contemporary Australian Early Childhood Programs," *International Journal of Early Years Education,* vol. 8, 2000, pp. 50–53; and J. Amos Hatch, Susan Grieshaber, Gail Halliwell, and Kerryann Walsh, "Child Observation in Australia and the U.S.: A Cross-National Analysis," *Early Child Development and Care,* vol. 169, 2001, pp. 39–56.
16. Gaile S. Cannella, *Deconstructing Early Childhood Education: Social Justice and Revolution* (New York: Peter Lang, 1997), p. 103.
17. Jonathan Kozol, Foreword to Deborah Meier, ed., *Will Standards Save Public Education?* (Boston: Beacon Press, 2000), p. xii.
18. Carol S. Dweck, "Motivational Processes Affecting Learning," *American Psychologist,* vol. 41, 1986, pp. 1040–48.
19. Alfie Kohn, *The Schools Our Children Deserve: Moving Beyond Traditional Classrooms and "Tougher Standards"* (Boston: Houghton Mifflin, 1999), p. 26; and Eisner, p. 369.
20. Eisner, p. 370.
21. Susan Ohanian, *One Size Fits Few: The Folly of Educational Standards* (Portsmouth, N.H.: Heinemann, 1999), pp. 3, 14.
22. Ohanian, pp. 17–29; Kohn, "Fighting the Tests," p. 19; and Marion Brady, "The Standards Juggernaut," *Phi Delta Kappan,* May 2000, p. 650.
23. Rex Knowles and Trudy Knowles, "Accountability for What?," *Phi Delta Kappan,* January 2001, p. 392.
24. William E. Coffman, "A King over Egypt, Which Knew Not Joseph," *Educational Measurement: Issues and Practices,* Summer 1993, p. 8.
25. Brady, p. 649; Alan C. Jones, "Welcome to Standardsville," *Phi Delta Kappan,* February 2001, p. 463; and Lisa Delpit, *Other People's Children* (New York: New Press, 1995), p. 24.
26. Pamela A. Moss and Aaron Schutz, "Educational Standards, Assessment, and the Search for Consensus," *American Educational Research Journal,* vol. 38, 2001, p. 65.
27. Bohn and Sleeter, p. 157; and Kohn, *The Schools Our Children Deserve,* p. 55.
28. Bill Nave, Edward Miech, and Frederick Mosteller, "A Lapse in Standards: Linking Standards-Based Reform with Student Achievement," *Phi Delta Kappan,* October 2000, p. 128; and Gratz, pp. 683–84.
29. See, for example, Linn, p. 14; Ohanian, p. 23; and Michael W. Apple, *Cultural Politics and Education* (New York: Teachers College Press, 1996).
30. Apple, p. 157.
31. Gratz, pp. 683–84; Ohanian, p. 32; and Merrow, p. 657.
32. Brady, p. 651; Eisner, p. 370; and Kohn, *The Schools Our Children Deserve,* pp. 15–16.
33. Marilou Hyson, "Reclaiming Our Words," *Young Children,* vol. 56, 2001, pp. 53–54.
34. Kohn, *The Schools Our Children Deserve,* p. 16.

J. AMOS HATCH is a professor in the College of Education, University of Tennessee, Knoxville.

Too Soon to Test

*When it comes to kindergarten screening,
research raises warning signs*

By Susan Black

It's a rite of passage: Parents start calling in September to ask about preparing their 4- and 5-year-olds for kindergarten screening in the spring. "No matter how I reassure them and explain that screening is not a test," an elementary school principal told me, "many parents are anxious that their children won't be ready for kindergarten."

Parents have a right to be worried, and so do school boards and others involved in setting policies and determining practices for this annual event. On the surface, kindergarten screening appears innocuous—little more than greeting new students and their parents, checking their vision and hearing, and recording their knowledge of such things as numbers and letters.

But kindergarten screenings aren't always what they seem—or what they should be. In a recent large-scale study in New York state, Virginia Costenbader and her research team at the University of Rochester found that many schools are replacing developmental screening—used to identify possible problems in such areas as language, motor skills, and social-emotional growth—with readiness screening—used to determine whether or not children possess the cognitive and behavioral skills schools say they need to enter and succeed in kindergarten.

Especially troubling, says Costenbader, is the fact that the most commonly used standardized screening instruments are not psychometrically sound and do not accurately predict students' success in the early grades. The positive predictive value of many widely used screening measures hovers around 50 percent—meaning that only about half of the children with low scores on their screening actually turn out to have academic trouble. When I showed this finding to a superintendent, he said, with a hint of irony, "We could save a lot of money by rolling the dice."

Developmental or 'maturational'?

The National Education Goal that "all children will start school ready to learn," adopted as part of the national education agenda in 1990, outlined three objectives for schools and communities:

1. Provide disadvantaged and disabled children with access to high-quality and developmentally appropriate preschool programs designed to help prepare them for school.
2. Recognize that parents are their children's first teachers and encourage them to spend time daily to help preschool children learn; provide parents with training and support to teach their children.
3. Improve prenatal health systems to reduce the number of low-birth-weight babies and ensure that children receive the nutrition and health care they need to arrive at school with healthy minds and bodies.

But over the past decade, the concept of school readiness has drifted from the original goal and objectives, says Gilbert Gredler, a professor of school psychology at the University of South Carolina. Gredler's studies record a significant shift from a developmental perspective, in which schools adapt their curriculum to kindergartners, to a maturational perspective, in which schools insist that kindergartners must be ready for the curriculum.

"Readiness to learn" often implies that children aren't learners before they enter school, a concept that offends early childhood experts. In a commentary on school readiness, Lilian Katz describes the "spectacular learning" that occurs—especially in language and motor development—from birth to the time children reach school age. Most infants and children learn at astonishing rates, Katz contends, but she acknowledges that what they learn, how they learn, and how much they learn depend to a great extent on their physical and emotional well-being and their home environment.

Schools should not penalize children who spend their first years of life without benefits of stimulating developmental experiences, says Katz, who has written extensively about early childhood education and child development. Instead, she says schools should find ways to respond to the "wide range of experiences, backgrounds and needs of the children who are starting school."

Red-shirting kindergartners

IT'S HARD TO SAY what the "right" age is to begin kindergarten. According to the U.S. Department of Education, almost two-thirds of entering kindergartners are between the ages of 5 years and 5 years 8 months. About one-quarter are almost 6 years old; another 9 percent are still 4 years old, and 4 percent are over six.

And, the department says, 9 percent or more of the children eligible to enroll in kindergarten are "red-shirted"—that is, held out for a year to give them extra time for intellectual development and social maturity.

Some schools encourage red-shirting, especially for children they deem unready to sit still for long periods, follow complex directions, and complete considerable homework. Some parents request red-shirting, hoping that buying time for their children will ensure their success in kindergarten and later.

Who's being red-shirted? The 1997 National Household Education Survey, conducted by the National Center for Education Statistics (NCES), found that many children whose birth dates fall close to their school's cutoff date for kindergarten enrollment are granted delayed entrance.

But the statistics tell a more complicated story. Red-shirting is fairly common in affluent communities, especially among children attending private schools. Overall, boys and non-Hispanic white children are more likely to be red-shirted.

The benefits of red-shirting are mostly speculative, but a 1993 NCES study indicated that students whose school entrance was delayed for a year were less likely to receive negative evaluations from their teachers or to be retained in first or second grade. A repeat survey, conducted in 1995, found no differences between students, who were held out or retained and other first- and second-graders.

But Robert Byrd of the University of California, Davis, says delaying school entrance often leads to delayed problems.

Byrd's study, published in *Pediatrics,* found that students who started school later had more behavioral problems, especially when they reached adolescence. At age 17, Byrd reports, 16 percent of students with delayed kindergarten entrance demonstrated extreme behavior problems, compared to 7 percent of students who entered on time.

Red-shirting also affects the demographics of kindergarten, as Sandra Crosser points out in a 1998 ERIC Digest prepared for the Clearinghouse on Elementary and Early Childhood Education. In effect, Crosser says, red-shirting adds more 6-year-olds to the kindergarten classroom mix. As a result, the youngest children could be as much as two years younger than the oldest students.

This age spread, she says, presents "a real danger" that teachers will expect the youngest children to keep up to an advanced curriculum that's well beyond their reach. Crosser projects that red-shirting will lead to kindergarten programs that are developmentally inappropriate for the young children they are meant to serve.

Sources

Byrd, Robert et al. "Increased Behavior Problems Associated with Delayed School Entry and Delayed School Progress." *Pediatrics,* pp. 654-661, 1997.

Crosser, Sandra. "He Has a Summer Birthday: The Kindergarten Entrance Age Dilemma." ERIC Digest, 1998. www.ed.gov/databases/ERIC_Digests/ed423079.html.

West, Jerry, and others. "Children Who Enter Kindergarten Late or Repeat Kindergarten: Their Characteristics and Late School Performance." *Education Statistics Quarterly, 2001.* http://nces.ed.gov/pubs2001/quarterly/fall/elem_kindergarten.html.

Misusing readiness tests

Both the National Association for the Education of Young Children (NAEYC) and the American Academy of Pediatrics (AAP) have taken strong stands on the use—or misuse—of school readiness tests.

Misusing the concept of readiness NAEYC says, places the burden of proof on 5-year-olds instead of on the schools. NAEYC stands by its position statement on school readiness, issued in 1995, which advises schools to base readiness screening and kindergarten instruction on three factors: (1) diversity and possible inequity of children's early life experiences; (2) wide variation in young children's development and learning; and (3) the degree to which schools' expectations of children entering kindergarten are reasonable, appropriate, and supportive of their individual differences.

AAP's policy, also adopted in 1995, says school readiness tests often are used inappropriately. Children are most likely to be wrongly identified, AAP officials say, if schools administer screening instruments without adequate knowledge of child development and testing procedures, or if they use screening scores to diagnose children with learning disabilities or other problems. All children are entitled to an education in schools where the great variability in early childhood development is understood and supported, AAP's policy states.

New approaches

Some states and school districts are rethinking kindergarten screening and the notion of readiness. Maryland, for example, has begun collecting baseline information on all kindergartners' social, physical, linguistic, and cognitive skills. Baseline information for the 2001-02 school year shows that teachers judged 49 percent of entering kindergartners as "fully ready to do kindergarten work." Forty-four percent were rated as "approaching readiness" and in need of targeted support to meet expectations, and 7 percent were rated as "developing readiness" and in need of considerable support to succeed in kindergarten.

The Maryland Model for School Readiness—which focuses on helping pre-kindergarten and kindergarten teachers with family communication, curriculum, instruction, and assessment—avoids conventional readiness testing. Instead, teachers observe, record, and evaluate their students twice a year in seven areas: social and personal development; language and literacy; mathematical thinking; scientific thinking; social studies; the arts; and physical development and health. For each assessment area, teachers rate children as proficient, in process, or needing development.

Teachers are expected to use their observations to support and challenge children's learning by modifying instruction, grouping students according to learning needs, and providing support for individual students on an as-needed basis. But the observational data teachers collect is never used to place children in special programs.

Resistance to school readiness testing is also apparent in some local school districts. Wisconsin's Middleton-Cross Plains Area School District, for example, describes its all-day kindergarten as a "relaxed, unhurried experience" that allows children and teachers time for a variety of learning experiences, including music, art, and physical education, and ongoing screening and assessments. The district's policy, posted on its Web site (www.mcpasd.k12.wi.us/home.cfm), informs parents that children do not need to be ready for school—the school needs to be ready for the child. Screening includes mail-in packets, filled out by parents, that help determine which children might be eligible for support programs, and a number to call if parents have concerns about their child's development.

Are your schools ready?

About 4 million children will be eligible to enter kindergarten in 2003. They'll arrive at your school's doorway taking baby steps. But before they show up for kindergarten screening, I suggest that you and other school officials take a few giant steps to get ready for your youngest students:

1. Examine your kindergarten screening policies and practices and replace those that don't measure up to research on developmentally appropriate practice.

2. Study and review psychometric problems with standardized screening instruments.

3. Develop school-community partnerships for school readiness based on the three objectives attached to the national readiness goal.

4. Develop school readiness positions similar to those adopted in Maryland schools and in Shrewsbury and Middleton-Cross Plains.

5. Make sure your teachers will be ready for kindergartners with appropriate curriculum, instruction, and assessments that match students' developmental states.

Steps like these will help ensure that kindergarten, as it was originally conceived by Friedrich Wilhelm Froebel in the 1840s, lives up to its promise and remains a learning garden for all children.

Susan Black, an *American School Board Journal* contributing editor, is an education research consultant in Hammondsport, N.Y.

Selected references

Black, Susan. "The Children's Garden." *American School Board Journal,* September 1997, pp. 35-37.

"Children Entering School Ready to Learn: School Readiness Baseline Information." Executive Summary. Maryland State Department of Education, February 2002.

Costenbader, Virginia, and others. "Kindergarten Screening: A Survey of Current Practice." *Psychology in the Schools,* July 2000, pp. 323-332.

Gredler, Gilbert. "Issues in Early Childhood Screening and Assessment." *Psychology in the Schools,* 1997, pp. 98-106.

Gredler, Gilbert. *School Readiness: Assessment and Educational Issues.* Brandon Vt.: Clinical Psychology Publishing Co., 1992.

"The Inappropriate Use of School Readiness Tests." Policy Statement: American Academy of Pediatrics. *Pediatrics,* March 1995, pp. 437-438. www.aap.org/policy/00694.html.

Katz, Lilian. "Readiness: Children and Schools." ERIC Clearinghouse on Elementary and Early Childhood Education, 1991. http://ericeece.org/pubs/digests/1991/katz91.html.

"NAEYC Position Statement on School Readiness." National Association for the Education of Young Children, 1998. www.ed.gov/databases/ERIC_Digests/ed423079.html.

Zill, Nicholas, and Jerry West. *Entering Kindergarten: A Portrait of American Children When They Begin School: Findings from the Condition of Education, 2000.* U.S. Department of Education, National Center for Education Statistics, NCES 2001-035, 2001.

OVERBURDENED OVERWHELMED

Schools—and life—are more stressful than ever, and students are feeling the strain

By LAWRENCE HARDY

In the elementary and middle schools of Rockingham County, N.C., a rural district north of Greensboro, administrators have to discard as many as 20 test booklets on exam days because children vomit on them.

"Kids [are] throwing up in the middle of the tests," says Dianne Campbell, the district's director of testing and accountability. "They cry. They have to be removed. The stress is so much on the test that they can't handle it."

It's not just tests that are stressing students. Across the country, school nurses, psychologists, counselors, and others concerned about children's mental health say that schools in general have become more stressful places and that many students can't handle the pressure.

What are we doing to our children? Why are we making them sick? What is it about our families, our communities, and particularly our schools that has made their lives so stressful? And what can we do to help?

While there are few studies on stress among K-12 students, two recent surveys show a disturbing trend at the college level. In one of the studies, released in February by the journal *Professional Psychology: Research and Practice*, the counseling center at Kansas State University found that the percentage of students being treated for depression at the center had doubled between 1989 and 2001. The study, one of the most extensive of its kind, followed a 2001 national survey in which more than 80 percent of college counselors said they believed the number of students seeking help for serious psychological problems had increased over the past five years.

And the trend appears to be starting before college. At the K-12 level, school health experts say they are seeing more student stress, much of it coming from outside school. High divorce rates, a sluggish economy, and the rapid pace of society have all put unprecedented pressure on families—and on kids.

Fear of failure

These societal pressures are difficult enough without schools contributing to the problem, but some observers say that's exactly what's happening. Students are stressed by the climate of schools that have grown too large and impersonal and by the unintended effects of the nationwide effort to raise standards. Parents complain about a glut of homework in the early grades, about elementary school students having to sit through hours of testing, about kindergartens morphing from places where children learned to love school to the start of what could become a grueling 13-year marathon.

"Young children, even first-graders, know where they stand in the achievement hierarchy," says Rhonda S. Weinstein, a psychology professor at the university of California, Berkeley, and author of *Reaching Higher: The Power of Expectations in Schooling.* Rather than creating classrooms that develop talent, Weinstein says, "We magnify minor differences and make them salient."

This relentless sorting is not helping our students, Weinstein says: It undercuts self-esteem and increases the fear of failure. As the late John Holt, the eminent teacher and education writer, wrote in 1964, "Adults destroy the intellectual and creative capacity of children ... above all by making them afraid, afraid of not doing what other people want, of not pleasing, or making mistakes, of failing, of being *wrong.*"

Almost three decades later, that fear has not abated.

Intolerable levels of stress

In numerous interviews with professionals in education and mental health—including school nurses, counselors, and psychologists—*ASBJ* found near-unanimous agreement that too many students are suffering from intolerable levels of stress. Of course, much of this stress comes from family and societal factors that are beyond the school's control. But instead of creating schools that are refuges from outside stress, these professionals say, we have too often constructed environments that only add to them.

"It's about as rough as I've seen it in a number of years of talking to schools," says Randy Compton, executive director of the School Mediation Center in Boulder, Colo. "It's hard out there."

Adds Michael Klonsky, director of the Small Schools Workshop at the University of Illinois, Chicago: "The pressures on students are tremendous."

That's certainly the case in Rockingham County. In North Carolina, students are tested in grades three through eight as part of a process that can determine whether they will be promoted. For Rockingham, that's about 7,500 students. "I probably have, during a three-day period, about 15 or 20 cases where kids get sick during the test," Campbell says. "That's a pretty high rate. As the tests start, they literally fall apart. It would break your heart."

Campbell believes in testing as a diagnostic tool, and she says the teachers in Rockingham try their best not to transfer the pressure they feel to the kids. "Even though you feel the pressure, don't put it on your kids," she says. "There's a fine line between making them feel responsible and making them feel overstressed."

Stress and pressure—both external and self-imposed—affect kids all along the achievement spectrum. For high-achieving students, it's harder than ever to get into a top college or a state's flagship university. In part that's because of the sheer number of students competing for a limited supply of spots. At Berkeley, for example, where admissions officers refer to this generation as "Tidal Wave II," it's almost twice as hard to gain acceptance as it was 10 years ago, the admission rate having dropped from 42.9 percent in 1992 to 23.9 percent last year.

Increased anxiety

Low-performing students, especially those from poorer areas, face a different challenge—simply staying in school. And being held back a grade raises the stakes. Numerous studies show that grade retention doesn't help students' academic success and may even increase dropout rates, yet between 1980 and 1992 the number of students retained increased from about 20 percent to nearly 32 percent, according to a 1995 study by Melissa Roderick. Anecdotal evidence suggests the rates have increased further since 1992—and will continue to increase—as more states require high-stakes tests for promotion and graduation.

What impact is this retention—and the threat of it—having on students' emotional well-being? Without any national studies to draw on, we can't be sure, but some indications suggest it increases the level of anxiety. Consider a 1987 study in which Kaoru Yamamoto, of the University of Colorado at Denver, and Deborah A. Byrnes, of Utah State University, examined how stressful various events were in the lives of 558 elementary school children. For sixth-graders, fear of grade retention was the third-highest stressor, right behind losing a parent and going blind.

Rose Paolino is a counselor at Bailey Middle School in West Haven, Conn., where a large number of students receive free or reduced-price lunches. Lying just across the river from New Haven, the city shares many of the social and economic problems of its larger neighbor. Many of Paolino's students come from single-parent homes and don't have the emotional resiliency of their peers from intact families, Paolino says. She says her caseload has nearly doubled in six years.

"The social-emotional has to come before the academic, and it will always be that way," Paolino says. "Until a child is established socially and emotionally, you can forget about the academics."

Too much, too soon

How mulch of this stress can be blamed on schools and how much on our fast-paced, fractured society? It's hard to say. With anytime access to cable TV, the Internet, and other kinds of media, kids are no longer shielded from what goes on in the world. They're forced to grow up fast—or, at least, to appear to grow up fast. And a large part of that stepped-up pace of development is facing sexual pressures at an earlier age.

"Some girls will say, 'I'm a lesbian' to keep the boys off them and not be pressured so much," says Brenda Melton, a counselor at Alamo Achievement Center, an alternative school in San Antonio, and president of the American School Counselor Association.

A school may teach values or abstinence or problem-solving skills, but Britney Spears teaches something else. A generation ago, if you skipped school, your neighbor or your relative down the street might report you, and your parents and the teacher would have a talk. Now, your parents are both working, your neighbor doesn't know you, and there is no relative down the street.

Schools also can't control a child's reaction to world events, and the world of late has seemed a strange and treacherous place. Several school nurses and counselors say that Sept. 11, the war in Afghanistan, and the possibility of war in Iraq all cause stress for their students.

Sandra Gadsden, a school nurse in the Worthington Public Schools near Columbus, Ohio, tells of a fourth-grader who came into her office complaining of a stomach ache and saying his eyes were "feeling funny."

"His mother had the television on, and he heard all this rattling about war in Iraq," Gadsden says. "He told me he's afraid our country will go to war. He's 9 years old."

'A Complete Pressure Cooker'

AFTER MORE THAN 40 years as a psychologist in Philadelphia, Irwin Hyman is adamant about the stresses facing his patients, saying they are the worst he's ever seen.

"What we're doing is taking some of our brightest students and some of the most motivated and putting them through a complete pressure cooker," says Hyman, a Temple University school psychologist and coauthor of *Dangerous Schools: What We Can Do About the Physical and Emotional Abuse of Our Children.*

Hyman says the new education act has just added to the pressure. "No Child Left Behind puts pressure on school boards," he says "School boards put pressure on the superintendent. The superintendent puts pressure on the teachers. And the victims are the kids."

Some psychologists are particularly concerned about the stresses facing younger children and the consequences of such policies as reducing or eliminating recess and making kindergarten more academic.

"If you can't have a wonderful, joyous kindergarten experience, what's life all about?" asks Ted Feinberg, assistant executive director of the National Association of School Psychologists in Bethesda, Md.

Feinberg recalls an e-mail message he received from a mother whose daughter was in an accelerated kindergarten class. Noting that her child was having difficulty and had just been diagnosed with what Feinberg calls "a newly created syndrome," the woman asked if perhaps the problem might be that her daughter wasn't ready for such an intensive academic experience after all. When Feinberg stated the obvious—that, yes, the accelerated kindergarten might be causing the problem—the mother admitted, "I thought that all along."

Feinberg tells another story: About 12 years ago, when he was a school psychologist, he was conducting kindergarten screenings for 4-year-olds and was asked by a parent what was on the "test."

"She wanted to have a copy of the test so she could prep her child," Feinberg said. "God help us if we have to have test prep courses to prepare children for kindergarten."—*L.H.*

But most of her students' concerns are closer to home. They often involve their parents' expectations and the fear that they cannot meet them. "I've had children tell me, 'My mother says I won't get into a good college if I don't do well on the test,'" Gadsden says.

And these children are in elementary school.

Parent pressure

Sometimes, parental expectations and school pressure combine to put needless strain on children. More than a year ago, on a state testing day, a third-trader walked into Gadsden's office carrying with her a terrible odor of skunk. It turned out that the girl's dog had been sprayed by a skunk and then jumped on her.

"I had to come up with a plan very quickly to 'de-skunk' her" so she could take the test, Gadsden recalls.

The cafeteria didn't have any tomato juice, a common antidote for skunk musk, so Gadsden doused the girl with catsup, rinsed it off, and put a stocking cap over her wet head. She later recalled the note that had been sent home with the students, telling parents to make sure their children got a good night's sleep and a nourishing breakfast before the test. This test, the note seemed to say, was extremely important.

"This mother didn't have the confidence to say, 'Testing isn't all *that* important,'" Gadsden says.

Obviously, this mother thought the test was more essential than helping her daughter rid herself of an embarrassing and unpleasant odor. But other parents in Worthington are questioning the wisdom of frequent testing and the other academic demands being placed on their children. And they've asked Gadsden to lead a stress-reduction group for interested students.

One of those parents, Pam Nylander, was concerned about her 13-year-old daughter Brittany, a seventh-grader who has juvenile diabetes. A straight-A student, Brittany was staying up too late to finish her homework, and Nylander was worried about her health. She talked to other parents and found their children were also doing homework late into the night, so they approached the school about their concerns.

Of course, it's not all the school's fault. Parents need to limit their children's outside activities, Nylander says, but that, too, can be hard. There was a time a generation ago when students could do well in school, take up a sport, play an instrument, and participate in a youth group—and still have free time.

Not anymore. Noting that her daughter is an accomplished pianist, Nylander says, "If she wanted to, she could be in five music competitions in the next three months." The same is true of the increasingly competitive world of athletics, whether school sponsored or run by a club.

"Everybody has raised the bar on their expectations for these kids for everything," Nylander says, "and it's very difficult to strike a balance."

One school district that is trying to strike a balance is the Adams 12 Five Star Schools in Thornton, Colo. More than two years ago, the district convened the first of 89 focus groups to ask residents what they wanted for the school system and its students. What the district found, says Superintendent Jim Christensen, is "that they have higher expectations and more expectations than just the test scores."

The result is a plan for "Educating the Whole Child" in which students will be assessed according to eight traits. The district says students should be competent, creative, productive, healthy, ethical, successful, thoughtful, and good citizens.

Christensen, who has been working on ways to assess these traits, says the main goals are motivating students and involving their parents. "It really focuses on getting the students, the parents, and the teacher on the same page," Christensen says "so that [the student's] competence can be enhanced through these traits."

Measuring Results

There's a growing demand to assess the results of early-childhood programs, but what's appropriate?

By David J. Hoff

Somewhere, a 4th grader is gripping a No. 2 pencil in his sweaty palms, about to take a test that might determine his school's accreditation or future funding. At the very least, the results from the child's school will be posted on the Internet or printed in the newspaper.

Somewhere else, a high school senior may be reviewing the algebra she's learned, trying once again to pass an exam that will make or break her attempt to earn a high school diploma.

Meanwhile, a group of 4-year-olds is building a tower with blocks, playing a game, or telling a story to a teacher. Like the standardized or standards-based tests given to their older peers, the young children's play may be used to evaluate the program that they attend, inform parents whether their children are ready to move on to kindergarten, or help the teacher understand what challenges and experiences the pupils need to make the developmental leaps common in their age group.

But the experience will have none of the high pressure of entering a new situation and trying to master a set of skills that dominates testing in the K–12 arena.

The contrast demonstrates that assessment and accountability are completely different in preschools, Head Start, and other early-childhood programs that a majority of children experience before they enter the K–12 system.

Assessments in early-childhood programs must be different from the kinds of tests youngsters take after they're in school, experts say, because young children are especially subject to wide variations in their development. Their skills grow in fits and starts, so an assessment of their academic skills one month could be out of date the next.

Moreover, along with their cognitive skills, preschoolers are also working to develop their motor and social skills, which are best judged by observation rather than a formal assessment.

As state and local policymakers start to demand data that show the impact of their spending on early-childhood programs, assessment experts find themselves searching for ways to obtain that information accurately, fairly, and in a way that's best for children.

"It's very complex," says James H. Squires, a consultant in early-childhood education for the Vermont education department. "What we're grappling with is: How do you do it at all? How can you get meaningful, accurate results without doing damage?"

Some state officials are requiring local programs to evaluate themselves using whatever method they choose. Others specify the kinds of assessment tools to be administered. Still others are collecting statewide data by giving a specific assessment or a combination of them to a sample of children in the state's early-childhood programs.

So far, though, none has come up with a uniform or even widely accepted method for assessing young children.

> ## "There hasn't been something that people could call a standardized way to assess children this age for accountability."
>
> CATHERINE SCOTT-LITTLE
> Senior Program Specialist, Serve

"There hasn't been something that people could call a standardized way to assess children this age for accountability purposes," says Catherine Scott-Little, a senior program specialist for Serve, the Greensboro, N.C., federally financed research laboratory serving the Southeastern states.

The Foundation

As state leaders begin wading into testing young children, most are building their systems around the recommendations of a 1998 report issued by the National Education Goals Panel, a federally subsidized committee of state and federal policymakers.

The panel convened a group of early-childhood experts to define how states and districts should monitor progress to ensure that children enter school ready to learn—the first of the education goals set for the nation that were to be achieved by 2000. At the end of 1999, the goals panel reported that the goal had not been reached.

The 40-page booklet released by the panel in 1998 suggested that early-childhood programs evaluate individual children's skills, starting at age 3, and aggregate them as part of a formal appraisal of the programs. Not until children reach the 3rd grade, the report concluded, should high-stakes assessments be used to hold schools, students, and teachers accountable.

"Before age 8, standardized achievement measures are not sufficiently accurate to be used for high-stakes decisions about individual children and schools," the booklet said.

But early-childhood programs must conduct assessments for other purposes. Under federal special education law, districts and federal programs have been required to screen children who are suspected of having a disability. Head Start programs, for example, must assess children's physical and learning abilities within 45 days of their enrollment.

Such screening "helps to identify children who may be at risk for school failure," says Samuel J. Meisels, the president of the Erikson Institute for Advanced Study of Child Development, a Chicago graduate school. "It can be done simply, inexpensively, and fairly accurately."

According to the Erikson Institute, 15 states and the District of Columbia require diagnostic or developmental screening for children in prekindergarten.

Assessing youngsters to determine the success of the programs in which they're enrolled, however, is new territory for most states, Scott-Little of Serve says.

Of the statewide pre-K programs, "very few have begun to invest in assessment," says Meisels, one of the creators of the Work Sampling System, an assessment instrument that many states use in early-childhood programs and kindergartens.

Getting Started

Even those states in the forefront are just now getting started and searching for the best ways to evaluate children's progress and programs' success.

North Carolina, for example, collected data from 1,034 kindergartners in fall 2000. The study tried to determine, for the first time, how well a variety of early-childhood programs prepared children to enter school.

Researchers gave a representative sample of 10 percent of the state's new kindergartners assessments that gauged an assortment of skills, such as vocabulary, literacy, and social development. The research team selected portions of several different assessment batteries, including the Woodcock Johnson Test of Achievement-Revised Form A and the Social Skills Rating System, because the team couldn't find one product that fit all its needs, according to Kelly Maxwell, who headed the project.

"Some people thought there would be one magic test out there," says Maxwell, a research investigator at the Frank Porter Graham Child Development Center at the University of North Carolina at Chapel Hill. "It didn't work that way."

The study also surveyed parents, teachers, and principals about the school readiness of kindergartners.

In the end, the published report included only general findings and none of the specific score data that are common in accountability systems for the upper grades. For example, the study found that North Carolina's kindergartners "generally knew the names of basic colors," and that they had "demonstrated a wide range of social skills" that "were about as well-developed" as those of kindergartners nationally. Their language and math skills fell below the national averages.

Despite the generalities of the conclusions, the report has made a valuable contribution in the debate over how to improve early-childhood programs in North Carolina. "This is what we know about our children and our schools," Maxwell says. "It sets the stage for a discussion."

Maryland collected information on 1,300 kindergartners using portions of the Work Sampling System. In that system, teachers continually observe their students and note their progress in such areas as language, mathematical thinking, scientific thinking, physical development, and social and personal skills.

Even though scores from the Work Sampling System are based on teacher observations, the results are as reliable as older students' standardized-test scores, according to studies conducted by Meisels and his colleagues at the University of Michigan in Ann Arbor, where until recently he was a professor of education.

In a report published last year, Maryland concluded that about 40 percent of the state's kindergartners entered school "fully ready to do kindergarten work." Half needed "targeted support" so they could succeed in their first year of school, and 10 percent required "considerable support" from their kindergarten teachers.

In particular, the children needed the most help in mathematical and scientific thinking, language development, and social studies.

"I don't think we were surprised by anything," says Trudy V. Collier, the chief of language development and early learning for the Maryland education department. "There's a real need for children to be read to, talked to, and encouraged to participate in conversations."

Last fall, every kindergarten teacher evaluated every student using the same set of Work Sampling System indicators. The state hopes to use the results to continue tracking school readiness.

While the overall results are general, individual student outcomes help teachers design curricula to meet their classes' needs, Collier says. "They begin to establish very early what a child's specific needs and gifts may be," she says.

Other states are taking similar approaches, according to Scott-Little. She led a brainstorming session last fall for officials in the states that are furthest along in assessing early-childhood programs.

Missouri's School Entry Profile collects data from new kindergartners, and the state uses the results to shape policies for early-childhood programs. In Ohio, teachers are collecting data on 4-year-olds' skills so the state can evaluate the early-childhood programs. The process may also help teachers prepare curricula for their classes, Scott-Little says.

Do-It-Yourself Approaches

While some states are coming up with statewide ways of measuring young children's abilities, and the success of programs serving them, others are letting individual programs monitor themselves.

Michigan, for example, has a prekindergarten program serving more than 25,000 youngsters in 1,000 classrooms, but it has only three part-time consultants to evaluate them, according to Lindy Buch, the state's supervisor of curricular, early-childhood, and parenting programs.

The state has chosen to train local program directors to evaluate their own programs, using a tool created by the High/Scope Educational Research Foundation, a leading research and development group on early-childhood programs. In addition, the Ypsilanti, Mich.-based High/Scope is conducting in-depth reviews of randomly chosen programs to give a statewide snapshot of the program's success.

Evaluators score the program on a variety of measures, including the quality and size of the facility, the extent to which the curriculum is tailored for each child, and the amount of time teachers spend evaluating pupils' progress. In Georgia, local officials can choose from one of several approved assessment programs, including the High/Scope evaluation tool.

Meanwhile, school districts in Vermont are conducting school-readiness screenings of prekindergartners, says Squires, the state's early-childhood consultant. But the state is urging districts to conduct the evaluations in a nonstandardized way. Many local programs are inviting children in for a "play based" assessment. They enter a classroom and demonstrate their physical, language, motor, and cognitive skills while they play with toys, create art, and build structures.

"We did not want to create an individual assessment or a group assessment for every child where they were being asked to sit down and perform specific tasks," Squires says.

The federal Head Start program is taking a similar approach to complying with the 1998 law that requires every Head Start center to conduct evaluations based on performance indicators.

While many of the performance indicators are selected by federal administrators, local centers are required to do their own evaluations of children in the areas of language and literacy, mathematics, science, creative arts, social ability, interest in learning, and physical and motor skills.

The instruments they use must be validated for the way they're being applied. For example, a center may not rely on a test intended to individualize curriculum as part of its program evaluation.

Programs were collecting such information in various forms already, whether as part of the disabilities-screening requirement or their own curriculum planning. What's new to Head Start programs is tabulating the data to figure out the overall outcomes of participating children.

"This is—almost in every case—a new idea," says Thomas Schultz, the director of the program-support division of the federal Head Start bureau.

For all the activity aimed at assessing children to ensure that they received the services they needed or to communicate their abilities to parents, he says, "it was rare that programs would use that information at a management level. What we're talking about now is a new strategy."

Kindergarten: Stakes Rising?

While the evaluations conducted throughout early-childhood programs don't carry high stakes for the children involved, the nature of assessment changes once children enter kindergarten because of the nationwide goal to have every child reading at grade level by grade 3.

Still, such assessments are administered to drive instruction rather than reward or penalize the child. Michigan has devised a literacy assessment in which teachers evaluate a child's reading skills starting in kindergarten, with monitoring continuing through 3rd grade.

The one-on-one testing is designed to help teachers formally measure a child's skills and then determine what help he or she needs to take the next steps toward independent reading.

The state plans to expand the program so children in the pre-K program take it, too, says Buch, the Michigan education official.

The New York City public schools started a similar program—called the Early Childhood Literacy Assessment System, or ECLAS—in 1999.

The battery of tests assesses children on a wide range of literacy skills from kindergarten through 2nd grade.

The Early Childhood Literacy Assessment System "gives a complete knowledge of where the kids are and what they need."

CHARLIE SOULE, Associate Education Officer,
New York City Board of Education

"It gives a complete knowledge of where the kids are and what they need for literacy," says Charlie Soule, the city school official who runs the testing program.

Such programs can be great tools for helping children reach the goal of becoming independent readers, according to one reading expert.

In an evaluation of a California reading program, children in schools that conducted regular classroom assessments showed better reading results than those in other schools in the state, says Marilyn J. Adams, a Harvard University research associate specializing in reading.

"The best [an assessment] can do for you is say, 'You need to sit with this child and figure out if he's having trouble with this dimension,'" Adams says. Once teachers do that, they respond with individualized instruction.

"The pressure for results... may force early-childhood programs and administrators to adopt relatively simplistic methods."

SAMUEL J. MEISELS, President, Erikson Institute

But such programs also can eventually become a back door into high-stakes testing, some experts warn. If a child isn't reading well in the 2nd grade, and the teachers know that the pupil will face a state reading test in the 3rd grade, they may be tempted to hold the boy or girl back a grade.

"The literacy assessments," Meisels of the Erikson Institute says, "are only a problem if they are expected to accomplish more than they are intended to do—which, at least in the case of the Michigan profile, is to enhance teaching and learning."

But with the weight of accountability systems looming and a new emphasis on academic skills, early-childhood educators may be inclined to rely on assessments in ways that are unfair to young children, he adds.

"The pressure for results—both in skills and in accountability—may force early-childhood programs and administrators to adopt relatively simplistic methods of teaching and assessing that are not successful for young children," Meisels says.

From *Education Week*, January 10, 2002, pp. 48-52. © 2002 by Education Week. Reprinted by permission.

EARLY EDUCATION

Henry Petroski

Children are born engineers. Everything they see, they want to change. They want to remake their world. They want to turn over, crawl, and walk. They want to make words out of sounds. They want to amplify and broadcast their voice. They want to rearrange their clothes. They want to hold their air, their water, their fire, and their earth. They want to swim and fly. They want their food, and they want to play with it too. They want to move dirt and pile sand. They want to build dams and make lakes. They want to launch ships of sticks. They want to stack blocks and cans and boxes. They want to build towers and bridges. They want to move cars and trucks over roads of their own design. They want to walk and ride on wheels. They want to draw and paint and write. They want to command armies and direct dolls. They want to make pictures out of pixels. They want to play games—computer games. They want to talk across distance and time. They want to control the universe. They want to make something of themselves.

Grown-up engineering, which is as old as civilization, maintains the youth, vigor and imagination of a child. This is why, when presented to children on their own terms, the excitement of engineering is immediately apparent and fully comprehendible. No child is too young to play and therefore to engage in engineering, albeit of a primitive kind. We all did so as children ourselves, when we divided our own toys and games—and sometimes even imaginary friends to enjoy them with us. The idea of playfulness is embedded in engineering through the concepts of invention and design. Not that engineering is frivolous; rather, the heart of the activity is giving the imagination its head, reining it in only to check impossible or dangerous dreams and to turn ideas into reality.

Children do experience the essence of engineering in their earliest activities, yet there is seldom any recognition that this is the case. They may hear the word "engineer" only in connection with railroad locomotives and have no idea that their playful activity could become a lifelong profession. Engineers themselves are understandably reluctant to equate their professional activity with mere child's play. After all, they studied long and hard to master esoteric knowledge of atoms and molecules, stresses and strains, heat and power, currents and voltages, bits and bytes. They manipulate equations, not blocks. They use computers for serious modeling and calculation, not for fun and games. They design and build real towers and bridges that test the limits of reliability and safety, not toy ones that totter and fall down with little consequence.

These regimens learned in college and put into practice are important and serious, but they are still not essential to comprehending the profession's fundamental activity: design. Design is rooted in choice and imagination—and play. Thus the essential idea of engineering can readily be explained to and understood by children.

Sharing the Joy

Much has been said and written about the declining numbers of and disappointing lack of diversity among college students majoring in engineering. Among the factors cited to explain this paucity are the lack of exposure of high school students to the very idea of engineering and the fact that many have insufficient mathematics and science background to gain entrance to engineering school, even if they do identify the profession as a possible career. This is unfortunate, for the ideas of engineering should be integrated into the curricula not only of high schools but also of middle and primary schools. Our children are being done a disservice by not being exposed properly throughout their education to engineering activities identified as such. After all, even preschool children have the prerequisites in their play for appreciating exactly what engineering is: design. Indeed, design is ubiquitous throughout their school day, even in their before- and after-school activities. It need only be pointed out to them that they are designing something, and therefore being engineers of sorts, in virtually everything that they do.

According to Nicholson Baker in his novel, *The Mezzanine*, "Shoes are the first adult machines we are given to master." As children, we learn to tie our shoes even before going to school. This is no mean accomplishment, as most of us may remember, and its execution is by no means as rigidly codified among classmates as the alphabet they are drilled in school. There are different ways to tie a shoelace, as we readily learn when we help different children unknot theirs. This is a manifestation of the fact that the steps in tying a knot or bow can vary from family to family in ways that the order of the letters in the alphabet cannot. Most children learn from their parents how to tie a shoe, and in their teaching role the parents often have to relearn the process themselves from a different point of view. That there are different tying techniques is characteristic of the fact that tying a shoe is a design problem—and design problems seldom if ever have unique solutions. Each individual child may be taught to tie shoes in a prescribed way, but that is not to say that it is the only way or even the best way. The lessons that can come of such an observation are beneficial not only for introducing students to design but also for augmenting lessons in diversity.

Opportunities in the Everyday

The idea of tying a shoe, and the related problem of lacing one up, can be turned into playful educational activities that expose students to the idea of design and thereby to engineering. A recent article in the *New York Times'* "Science Times" described how Burkard Polster, a mathematician at Monash University, calculated that there are over 40,000 distinct ways to lace up a shoe with two rows of six eyelets each. In true academic mathematic fashion, Dr. Polster extended his research by viewing the laced shoe as a pulley system to determine which lacing pattern was most effective in performing its function. He also determined the lacing that could be effected with the shortest lace. The combinatorial mathematics used by Polster make the problem as he approached it unsuitable for school children, of course, but that is not to say that the practical problem itself cannot be used to advantage in the elementary-school classroom. How much fun could children have redesigning the lacings of their shoes into imaginative patterns and learning by dong that there is more than one way to solve a problem? Being told by the teacher that a mathematician calculated that there were exactly 43,200 different ways they could have solved the problem can only add to the wonder of the lesson.

Elementary school students might also be asked if they could imagine how Polster got the idea of counting how many ways there are to lace a shoe. Telling them that he did so after learning that two physicists from the University of Cambridge calculated how many ways there were to knot a necktie provides yet another opportunity to describe a commonplace problem in design. Even if the children are not in uniform—and the teacher, too, is dressed casually—the tie-knotting problem is at least one they might take home to tackle with their families. It would also expand the vocabulary of professions to which the children are exposed. To their knowledge that mathematicians can have fun counting shoe lacing patterns, the students can add the mental note that physicists can have fun counting tie knottings. To this can be added the observation that if mathematicians and physicists have such fun counting things, imagine how much fun engineers have in designing things that can be counted.

(As an aside to teachers and others, the word "science" is in fact a misnomer when it actually refers to engineering. Science, strictly speaking, does not include engineering, an activity distinguished by its domination by design. Engineers design things, such as patterns of shoe lacings; scientists analyze things, such as counting how many lacings can be designed. These are distinctly different activities, even though the object of their attentions can be common. Journalists and others often use the term "science" as a convenient shorthand to include "engineering," but it verbally subsumes engineering into an activity whose fundamental objectives are of another kind altogether. This use of "science" essentially keeps "engineering" out of the vocabulary of children, who consequently do not learn about all the possible ways there are to have fun with shoelaces, neckties, and so much more—including real towers, bridges, automobiles, airplanes, power plants, computers, and everything designed and made.)

An after-school snack provides further opportunities for children to learn that design means that there is not just one way to do something. Consider the problem of designing a method for eating an Oreo cookie with a glass of milk. Different children (and adults) employ different techniques. Those with big enough mouths might just pop the whole thing in. Most will eat the cookie in steps, some taking a bite at a time, as if it were a real sandwich. Others proceed by first twisting or prying off one side of the cookie to expose the cream. Some will eat the separated top right away; others put it aside and attack the cream first. Even this allows for variations: Some lick the cream off, and others scrape it off with their teeth; some use their top and others use their bottom teeth. After finishing the cream, those who put the top aside still have another choice to make: whether to eat the top or bottom next. All along, the glass of milk on the table has allowed for further variations on the process, for the cookie may be dunked or not before each bite. Countless everyday activities, in school or out, provide ample opportunities to introduce young children to design and therefore to engineering.

Invention—within Bounds

Design pervades the lives of children and adults alike; virtually nothing that we do goes untouched by it. We design our own approaches to the everyday things of life, such as lacing our shoes, knotting our ties, and eating our cookies. But we also design our own procedures for washing our hands, taking a shower, putting on our clothes. As I recall, in one episode of *All in the Family*, Archie Bunker's son-in-law, Mike, watches Archie put on his shoes and socks. Mike goes into a conniption when Archie puts the sock and shoe completely on one foot first, tying a bow to complete the action, while the other foot remains bear. To Mike, if I remember correctly, the right way to put on shoes and socks is first to put a sock on each foot and only then put the shoes on over them, and only in the same order as the socks. In an ironic development in his character, the politically liberal Mike shows himself to be intolerant of differences in how people do common little things, unaccepting of the fact that there is more than one way to skin a cat or put on one's shoes.

At times we do prescribe how certain everyday things are done, even though there might be countless ways to vary the procedure. This is especially the case in more formal social situations, where doing things too individually might detract from the formality or, in some instances, even prove to be repulsive to polite society. Thus, we have manners and social protocols. Arbitrary as they sometimes seem, such things as table manners and restraint in creativity at the table obviate distractions that otherwise might make eating with others, especially strangers, a less than pleasant experience. Imagine a business lunch where the group of people around the table ate with the individuality that children show when eating cream-sandwich cookies. As many ways to eat a sandwich as there might be, there are also practical reasons beyond decorum for following a customary procedure. By keeping the sandwich intact and bringing it to the mouth in the conventional way, we demonstrate one of the sandwich's design features: The fingers are kept free of mustard and mayonnaise, which in turn means that the outside of the drink glass remains relatively tidy throughout the meal and that after lunch the business associates can shake hands without feeling they are washing dishes.

We discover as children, sometimes with the guidance of an adult but often by our own devices, preferred ways to proceed with all sorts of social and recreational activities. There are many ways to design a ball game, and the plethora includes the supplemental use of bats, rackets, bases, baskets, goalposts, nets, and more. But when two or more people participate in any game, they must agree on which implements to allow and which rules to follow. Otherwise what transpired would hardly be a game as we know it. Imagine a player on a tennis court serving a foot-ball with a baseball bat across a volleyball net to an opponent with a lacrosse stick. Only an agreed-upon set of rules is likely to produce a recreational activity that is not chaotic. If the objective is to have a friendly, or even a fiercely competitive game, it must proceed according to rules of a rigid design. Even the game of solitaire is only truly played by sticking to the rules. Engineers must certainly stick to the rules of physics, chemistry, and the other sciences.

Putting together a jigsaw puzzle is an activity that can be done alone or in a group. Either way, it provides another fine example of how many ways there are to achieve an objective—forming a single picture out of hundreds of pieces of various colors and shapes. Theoretically, it is possible to solve the puzzle by arbitrarily choosing a piece and then trying to fit each of the remaining pieces to it. Systematically trying each piece in each orientation on each side of the starter piece would lead eventually to a match, and the procedure could be followed to completion. I know of no one who works jigsaw puzzles in this tedious and unimaginative way, however, because one of the implicit challenges is to finish the puzzle as efficiently as possible. Most people look for edge and corner pieces first, completing the periphery before tackling the more amorphous middle. If nothing else, this way there are fewer pieces to contend with. As many ways as there might be to complete a puzzle, the preferred way is the most efficient way.

Making Engineering Evident

Teachers cannot be faulted for failing to promote engineering if they have not been exposed to it themselves. Engineering is not taught in every teacher's college, and it is not a required field of study even in most full-service universities. It is certainly possible to get a bachelor of arts or science—and a teaching certificate—without appreciating that engineering is a profession every bit as noble, rewarding, and satisfying as medicine and law. The absence of even the playful rudiments of engineering in the curriculum is unfortunate, as I have learned from doctors and lawyers who have expressed a disappointment that they were not exposed more to engineering while in school themselves.

I compare engineering design to making sand castles or lacing up shoes or eating cookies or designing toys not to trivialize it but to humanize it. The conventional wisdom, among the general population, as well as among many teachers of children, is that engineering is a cold, dehumanizing and unsatisfying career. Those who hold such a view are not likely to have met or spoken with engineers who enjoy what they do. They are no longer children playing with blocks or building castles on the beach, of course, but many of them retain a certain childlike fascination with the elemental structure of the world and with what can be done with timber and concrete and steel—or with atoms and molecules and microbes. They know that what they have fun designing and building and overseeing is essential to the smooth working of civilization. We should all learn this as children.

Bibliography

Baker, Nicholson. 1990. *The Mezzanine: A Novel*. New York: Vintage Books.

Chang, Kenneth. 2002. Seeking perfection in shoe lacing, with 43,200 choices. *New York Times*, December 10, p. D3.

Fink, Thomas M., and Yong Mao. 1999. Designing tie knots by random walks. *Nature* 398:31–32.

Polster, Burkard. 2002. Mathematics: What is the best way to lace your shoes? *Nature* 420:476.

DOES UNIVERSAL PRESCHOOL PAY?

Support for the idea is growing, but the tab will be high

Two years ago, Vice-President Al Gore declared that if elected President he would spend $50 billion a year to offer pre-kindergarten to the country's 8.3 million three- and four-year-olds. With the U.S. at war and George W. Bush in the White House, odds are that Uncle Sam won't be paying to send toddlers to school just yet.

But just in the past month, early childhood education has suddenly moved to the political front burner again. In early April, Bush announced that his Administration would begin integrating early literacy skills into the curriculum of Head Start, the federal program that serves poor children. He also earmarked $45 million for research into the most effective techniques for teaching young children. Senators Edward M. Kennedy (D-Mass.) and George V. Voinovich (R-Ohio), meanwhile, want to parcel out $1 billion per year over five years to bolster state education programs aimed at kids from infancy to age five. Their goal: to accelerate a move already under way in the states, which have more than doubled their pre-kindergarten spending in the past decade, to $1.7 billion, according to the Children's Defense Fund, a Washington (D.C.) group. State pre-K programs now serve three-quarters of a million children.

The idea of exposing very young children to letters and numbers has been gaining momentum because of the ongoing school-reform movement. As experts search for ways to improve kindergarten through 12th grade (K-12), they have become increasingly convinced that many kids don't start school prepared to learn. This view has been bolstered by research showing that children absorb many basic cognitive skills between the ages of three

STARTING SCHOOL AT AGE THREE

Universal preschool education is on the political front burner again

NUMBER OF CHILDREN There are 8.3 million three- to five-year-olds in the U.S., many of whom get little formal exposure to reading or numbers.

COST Preschool would run $4,000 to $5,000 a year per kid, or $33 billion to $42 billion if every child were enrolled in a voluntary program. Head Start costs roughly $6,600 a year.

BENEFITS Studies show that early learning helps poor children, which experts say is evidence that middle-class kids would benefit as well, although less so. Poor three- to five-year-olds who get high-quality basic education consistently score about five percentage points higher on school tests through age 21 than those who get no early schooling. Only 30% repeat a grade, vs. 56% of those with no schooling. And some 35% attend college by age 21, vs. 14% of other poor kids.

WHO'S ON THE BANDWAGON President Bush wants to spend $45 million to study the best early-childhood teaching techniques. Senators Kennedy and Voinovich have proposed a $1 billion-a-year plan to fund state early education programs for all kids under five. The Committee for Economic Development, a business group, is pushing a national preschool program for all three- to five-year-olds.

and five. Transforming day care into preschool takes advantage of these crucial years, especially for poor children, who are most likely to fall behind in school. "You simply can't talk about closing the achievement gap without talking about pre-K," says Andrew Rotherham of the Progressive Policy Institute, a centrist think tank.

Proponents point out that most other developed countries guarantee an education to their three- to five-year-olds. France, Belgium, and Italy provide free preschool to everyone in this age group, including immigrants, who often lag other children. "A lot of children [in the U.S.] are starting school behind their peers, and in many cases they never catch up," says Isabel V. Sawhill, a senior fellow at the Brookings Institution.

Most of the hard evidence demonstrates that poor kids see the most enduring gains from preschool. Middle-class kids who attend pre-K show higher cognitive skills, including math and language abilities, as well as better social skills, says a 1999 study by a team of 10 researchers from the University of North Carolina and three other universities. But by age eight, which is as far as the study goes, most middle-class kids with no preschool have narrowed the gap. As a result, it isn't clear just how valuable widespread preschool would be for every American toddler. "The data on how much kids benefit is not very encouraging," says David F. Salisbury, an education expert at the libertarian Cato Institute, which opposes publicly funded pre-K.

Nonetheless, pre-K is gaining popularity in part because so many households these days face work-family conflicts. With more mothers working, 64% of three-to five-year-olds now go to some kind of day-care center, i.e., outside the home and not with a neighbor or family member. Most centers are private, and their quality varies widely. A recent study in four states found that 70% provide mediocre care, while one in eight is so inadequate as to actually endanger children's health or safety.

Still, the hodgepodge of nursery schools and child care that working families now use provides a platform on which a more comprehensive preschool system could be built. Rather than expanding K-12 schools to include pre-K, existing day-care centers could be upgraded, says Walter S. Gilliam, an education expert at the Yale University Child Study Center. Most of the state initiatives have involved improving existing programs rather than attempting to start new public preschools. Only one state, Georgia, now offers universal pre-K—but only to four-year-olds.

Another key building block for early childhood learning: lifting teacher skills. Currently, fewer than half of the states have minimum requirements for instructors in child-care centers. Low salaries are a big hurdle, too: Day-care employees earn about $16,000 a year, often less than a parking lot attendant. The result: a 30%-plus annual turnover rate, vs. 13% or so for K-12 teachers, who are paid more than

twice as much. A universal preschool system would make more money available for instructor pay.

The point on which there's strong consensus is that disadvantaged kids profit from early learning. As it is, Head Start serves more than 900,000 poor three- and four-year-olds. But the part-day program that focuses on health care and nutrition along with education is chronically underfunded. The $6.5 billion-a-year budget means it can't accommodate three of five eligible children. But those who do get in come out ahead. Only 30% of four-year-olds whose mothers are on welfare could count to 20 out loud or write their name correctly, according to an Apr. 16 study of kids in California, Connecticut, and Florida. By comparison, 53% of Head Start children—a comparable demographic group—could count to 20, and 66% could write their first names.

Programs that offer more education than Head Start reap even better results. The most thorough study, called the Carolina Abecedarian Project (after the ABCs), followed 111 disadvantaged North Carolina kids for 21 years. Half were enrolled in a high-quality educational program from infancy to age five, while the control group got only nutritional supplements. All the children attended comparable public

schools from kindergarten on. The result: Those who attended preschool were less likely to drop out of school, repeat grades, or bear children out of wedlock. By age 15, less than a third had failed a grade, vs. more than half of the control group. At age 21, the preschoolers were more than twice as likely to be attending a four-year college.

The big question about preschool, of course, is where to find the money. A universal program could be done for less than Gore's $50 billion proposal. But it still would run up to $42 billion a year, according to a new study by the Committee for Economic Development, a New York City-based group of blue-chip corporations. The price tag could be lower if some of the cost were borne by middle-class families, many of whom already are paying for day care.

Still to be debated is whether preschool is the best use of public funds for kids who aren't from poor families. No one has done a cost-benefit analysis to see if middle-class kids would be helped more by, say, extra money for K-12 schools instead. In the meantime, though, it's clear that as long as learning officially starts only in kindergarten, millions of children will fall behind before they even reach the schoolhouse door.

By Alexandra Starr in Washington

The 'Failure' of Head Start

By John Merrow

Head Start has failed. The federal preschool program for 4-year-olds was supposed to "level the playing field" for poor children, and it has not done that.

Educationally and linguistically, poor children are behind from the beginning. Parents with professional jobs speak about 2,100 words an hour to toddlers; those in poverty only about 600. Not surprisingly, a 5-year-old child from a low-income home has a 5,000-word vocabulary, while a middle-class child already knows 20,000 words.

One reason for its failure was the misguided practice at some Head Start centers, where teaching the alphabet was actually banned, in favor of teaching social skills. But the dominant reason for the persistent gap is the fervor with which middle- and upper-middle-class parents embrace preschool.

These parents enroll their own children in preschool because they know that 3- and 4-year-olds are ready and eager to learn. Seventy-six per cent of 4-year-olds from households with an annual income of more than $50,000 are enrolled. The National Center for Education Statistics reports that twice as many 3- to 5-year-olds from families with incomes above $75,000 are enrolled, compared with children whose parents make $10,000 a year.

By contrast, fewer than half of children whose families fall below the poverty line attend preschool, not because their parents don't want them to, but because we haven't created enough Head Start programs. To serve all the eligible children, we'd need twice as many as we have. Once again, we're talking the talk when it comes to helping poor children, but not walking the walk. And, largely for that reason, the gap will not only not disappear, it will grow.

We ought to be embarrassed about our approach to preschool. Most industrialized countries provide free, high-quality preschool for 3-, 4-, and 5-year-olds, regardless of family income. Almost all 4-year-olds in England, Luxembourg, and the Netherlands go to public school; 70 percent of German, Danish, and Greek 4-year-olds go to public school; and over 90 percent of 4- and 5-year-olds in Italy and Spain are in public school.

We're the opposite: a patchwork nonsystem with weakly trained, poorly paid staff members. The quality ranges from excellent to abysmal, the tuition from $15,000 to zero, the teachers' salaries from $45,000 a year with benefits to as low as $8 or $9 per hour, with no benefits.

I've just spent seven weeks driving around Europe, visiting lots of small towns and villages. Every small town I visited in France had a sign, prominently placed, pointing the way to the local école maternelle, the town's preschool. Had I stopped to look, I would have found every 3- and 4- year- old from the village at the school.

A few months earlier, I visited three écoles maternelles in very different neighborhoods in Paris. The school serving poor children was virtually identical to those serving middle-class and upper- middle-class children. All three schools were staffed with well-trained, well- paid teachers, because all école maternelle teachers must have master's degrees, and all are paid at the same rate as elementary school teachers. Today in France, 100 percent of children ages 3 through 5 attend preschool, most in public programs.

In the United States, preschool is a seller's market, and even well-off parents have to endure "preschool panic," because there's not enough quality to go around. One of the families in our forthcoming PBS documentary on the subject moved from New York City to France while we were filming. The parents had been forced to choose between career opportunities for themselves and a decent preschool for their sons. Today, while both parents are struggling to develop their careers in France, their children are in sound educational programs.

Today preschool is on a lot of state agendas. According to the Child Care Action Campaign, 42 states now have some form of "preschool initiative." However, that phrase encompasses everything from legislative proposals to real programs, and only Georgia, New York, Oklahoma, and the District of Columbia have genuine programs that provide free preschool for a substantial number of children.

Georgia is at the head of the preschool class. Its program currently serves more than 63,000 4-year-olds. In toto, 70 percent of Georgia's 4-year-olds are now in some form of publicly subsidized preschool. The Georgia program is the brainchild of former Gov. Zell Miller, now a U.S. senator, who believes that "preschool is more important than the 12th grade in high school." Georgia requires districts to offer prekindergarten and pays the bill—$240 million a year—with money from its lottery and with federal Head Start funds. New York and Oklahoma are leaving it up to school districts to decide whether they will provide such services, with the state paying the bills. But states are hard-pressed for funds these days, and so, for example, New York's legislature has put up less than half the money needed to establish programs across the state.

Creating high-quality programs is proving to be difficult. No state is starting from scratch, of course, which means that any new program must be grafted on to what exists. And what exists is a hodgepodge of programs: Some are run for profit, some are staffed with trained, well-paid teachers, some are storefront operations where a TV set is the caregiver, and so on. Some Head Start programs are excellent, but others are woeful. One evaluation of Head Start found that some children began knowing just one letter of the alphabet, A, and left nine months later without having learned B.

President Bush says he wants to change that, but his proposal is flawed. To improve literacy skills, he plans to give 2,500 Head Start teachers four days of training in early-literacy instructional techniques, after which they are supposed to pass on what they learned to the other 47,000 Head Start teachers. Critical reaction was immediate. A spokesman for U.S. Rep. George Miller, D- Calif., told reporters, "The idea that you would be able to create reading specialists among Head Start teachers with four days of training is absurd."

Moreover, the president's budget won't allow Head Start to grow, even though the program misses more than half of eligible children.

I BELIEVE THAT WE'RE OPERATING FROM THE WRONG PREMISE. Instead of relying on income-based programs like Head Start that are supposed to help the poor, we ought to be creating a system that would be good enough for the well-off. Create something that's good enough for those with money, but make it available to everyone. Design a preschool system the way we built our Interstate highway system. We didn't create separate highways for rich and poor. Instead, we built an Interstate system that was good enough for people behind the wheel of a Cadillac or a Lexus, a Corvette or a Mercedes, and there were no complaints from those driving a Chevy or a Ford.

We know that good preschools have long-term benefits for children, and we ought to recognize that as a nation.

Creating universal, free, high-quality preschool will be difficult, complicated, and costly: By one estimate, it would cost $30 billion a year to run programs just for those 3- and 4-year-olds from families making less that $30,000 a year. For all 3- and 4-year-olds, "The cost could easily be $100 billion," according to Ron Haskins of the Brookings Institution. However, we know that good preschools have long-term benefits for children, and we ought to recognize that as a nation.

It took 50 years for the United States to be able to compete as a peer in soccer's World Cup with Italy, Mexico, Portugal, France, Germany, Sweden, and other long-established powers. We cannot afford to take that long to catch up in the world of preschool education.

John Merrow's documentary "The Promise of Preschool" appeared on PBS. He is the author of Choosing Excellence *(Scarecrow Press, 2001) and an education correspondent for "The NewsHour with Jim Lehrer."*

Preschool: The Most Important Grade

Research findings confirm the long-term benefits of early education and offer some options for integrating the existing patchwork of U.S. public and private preK programs into a uniform system that provides a high-quality early education to all young children.

W. Steven Barnett and Jason T. Hustedt

The early education system in the United States has recently experienced tremendous growth, a trend that has enabled most children to gain access to some sort of early education program. Unfortunately, U.S. preschool education programs are generally mediocre and inconsistent, and the best programs are too expensive for most U.S. families to afford. A recent *USA Today* article declared that

> We can, and should, be creating a preschool system that would be good enough for everyone. Public preschools should be built the same way we constructed our highway system: the same road available to all Americans, rich and poor. (Merrow, 2002)

The Status of U.S. Early Education

Three-fourths of young children in the United States participate in a preschool program. These programs operate under a wide range of auspices, from private organizations to public schools and Head Start, a federal government education initiative that has provided children from low-income families with free access to early education programs since 1965. Until recently, most statewide early education programs followed Head Start's lead and targeted children of low socioeconomic status or children who were otherwise "at risk." In the past decade, however, states have developed more options for children from middle- and upper-income families to receive a free preschool education.

In 1995, Georgia introduced the first statewide universal preK program, a model that offers a free preschool education to all 4-year-old children, regardless of family income. New York and Oklahoma soon followed with their own universal preK programs, and in 2002, Florida voters approved a constitutional amendment stipulating that all 4-year-olds in the state be offered a free preK education by 2005. As the early education movement continues to gather steam and as universal preK programs take shape across the country, it is important to take stock of what we know about the long-term benefits and implementation of education for young children.

The Benefits of Early Education

Research has established that preschool education can produce substantial gains in children's learning and development (Barnett, 2002), but researchers disagree about whether such gains are permanent. Most research on early education has focused on its effects on the IQ scores of economically disadvantaged children and has found few preschool programs that have produced lasting IQ score gains (Barnett, 1998). Even the more effective programs tend to show positive results in the short rather than long term.

But studies also find that preschool education produces persistent gains on achievement test scores, along with fewer occurrences of grade retention and placement in special education programs (Barnett & Camilli, 2002). Other long-term benefits from preschool education include increased high school graduation rates and decreased crime and delinquency rates.

Recent research has shown that preschool education is a sound investment—academically, socially, and economically. Three studies—which examined the High/Scope Perry Preschool program, the Abecedarian Early Childhood Intervention program, and the Title I Chicago Child-Parent Centers—provide comprehensive evidence that academic and other benefits from preschool education can yield economic benefits that far outweigh the costs of intensive, high-quality preschool programs (Barnett, 1996; Masse & Barnett, 2002; Reynolds, Temple, Robertson, & Mann, 2002). These studies identified several long-term economic benefits of early education, finding that both former preschool participants and taxpayers can benefit from public investments in preschool education. For example, former preschool participants were less likely to cost taxpayers money in the long term for such public services as

- Schooling—Participants were less likely to be retained in grade or placed in special education.
- Welfare—As adults, participants were more likely to get better jobs and earn more money.
- The criminal justice system—Participants were less likely to break laws or participate in other delinquent acts.

These positive effects have far-reaching benefits. Although preschool education research has largely focused on the benefits of early education for children in poverty, several child care studies indicate that high-quality, effective early education programs improve the learning and development of all children (Shonkoff & Phillips, 2000). And problems that we tend to associate with students from low-income families—grade retention and high drop-out rates, for example—are more common among middle-class students than we often assume. For example, more than 1 in 10 children in the middle three quintiles of the U.S. income distribution are retained in grade, and the same proportion drop out of high school (National Center for Education Statistics, 1997). High-quality preschool programs might reduce such problems for middle-class students by 25 to 50 percent, again saving taxpayers' money in the long term.

The three successful programs discussed above, however, all had higher standards for education than do most typical early education programs today, many of which hire underqualified teachers and pay those teachers salaries that average less than half of a public school teacher's salary (Barnett, 2003). Teachers from each of the successful programs had credentials and received compensation equivalent to those of public school teachers. In addition, each program had relatively small class sizes and strong education goals. Unfortunately, current state child care standards are extremely low. Head Start requires that only half of its teachers have a two-year college degree, and even some state universal preK programs have lower standards for teacher qualifications than do public schools.

New Evaluations of Head Start

Head Start's research record shows consistent evidence of positive effects, but questions remain about the extent to which that research generalizes across variations both in different Head Start programs and in the children and families that Head Start serves. In recent years, research studies have attempted to provide more information on the services that these programs offer and on the progress of the programs' participants.

Shortly after the inception of Early Head Start—a program established in 1994 that seeks to improve the long-term outcomes of infants and toddlers in poverty by providing comprehensive services to both the children and their parents—the Administration on Children, Youth, and Families funded a multisite, randomized trial to evaluate Early Head Start and its effects on children and families. Recently released results (Love et al., 2002) comparing 2- and 3-year-old Early Head Start participants and their parents with a control group of demographically equivalent nonparticipant children and parents suggest that this program has a variety of positive im-

pacts. Participants earned higher scores on assessments of cognitive and language development and were less aggressive than were nonparticipants. Early Head Start parents achieved positive outcomes as well: They gained self-sufficiency through job training and education activities and improved on parenting assessments. Although effects were relatively small, the broad range of effects suggests that they might be important in the aggregate.

In 2002, data collection began for a large-scale, randomized experimental study to provide a similar look at the longitudinal effects of Head Start, mandated by the U.S. Congress as part of the program's 1998 reauthorization. The results of this study will provide stronger, more conclusive findings about Head Start's effects on children and families than current research such as the Family and Child Experiences Survey (FACES) (Zill et al., 2001). FACES tells us that Head Start children remain significantly behind their more advantaged peers, particularly in vocabulary. But FACES cannot tell us how much they gain from participating in Head Start.

Ongoing State Programs

As state initiatives for early education have grown, researchers have turned greater attention toward integrating existing preschool programs into more uniform state programs. Typically, universal preK and other broad state programs seek to build on and combine existing private and public programs into a more coordinated system with consistent standards. A recent study by the Center for the Child Care Workforce (Bellm, Burton, Whitebook, Broatch, & Young, 2002) examined large, publicly funded preK initiatives under way in Georgia, New York, Texas, California, and Chicago. Although only the Georgia program currently provides universal, statewide access to preK programs, comparisons across these programs help illuminate implementation issues that will become important as more states move toward universal preK.

Recent research has shown that preschool education is a sound investment—academically, socially, and economically.

The study found that a two-tiered system emerged wherever public and private programs participated together. Teachers in preK programs sponsored by public schools

were better educated, earned higher salaries, and had lower turnover in their jobs than teachers in privately operated programs. Private program providers voiced concern that teachers took private program positions only as stepping stones to more lucrative jobs in the public schools. Head Start directors frequently voiced similar concerns, because their teachers earn roughly half the salary of public school teachers. Substantial evidence shows that all of these advantages for public programs lead to higher education quality and improved learning and development for children (Barnett, 2003). States must face the challenge of successfully developing a universal preK program that delivers uniformly high-quality education services to all children by mixing publicly and privately operated programs funded with federal, state, and local government dollars.

Implications for the Future

As universal preK becomes more popular in the United States, we will need to clarify and refine the role of Head Start. With an annual budget of more than $6 billion, Head Start is by far the largest source of public funds for preschool education, employing one in five U.S. preschool teachers. Head Start has accumulated substantial expertise over the years in meeting the needs of at-risk children and families. But because Head Start targets children in poverty and is subject to an extensive list of federal standards regulating such factors as program governance, performance, and accountability, it will be difficult to integrate it into a state system serving all children.

To respond to the increasing availability of universal preK programs, Head Start could shift its focus to provide specialized services to children ages 3 and younger from low-income families. In states or communities that already provide all children with access to free universal preK, Head Start could use its resources more effectively by providing children in poverty with appropriate education preparation *before* they enter a preK program. This change can be accomplished within existing federal legislation; whereas current law mandates that Head Start provide a wide variety of services to low-income parents and their children, it does not mandate that the program focus primarily on 4-year-olds. In fact, Head Start already serves many 3-year-olds and even younger children.

Another option is for Head Start to merge with state universal preK programs. Such a move would permit states to incorporate Head Start funding, expertise, staff, and facilities into universal preK, thereby reducing costs to the state and making maximum use of existing resources. Local or state education agencies could make contracts with Head Start and provide a partial payment for each child eligible for Head Start (allowing Head Start to meet higher state requirements for teacher qualifications, for example) and a full payment for each child ineligible for Head Start (allowing Head Start to become a more socially integrated program).

Although some states already contract with Head Start as part of their state preK programs, others do not. Some modification or waiver of federal Head Start regulations is necessary to enable Head Start to effectively operate under contracts with state programs. For example, Head Start policy councils and local boards of education constitute potentially incompatible governance structures. To avoid such problems, the federal government could raise the education standards of Head Start and provide sufficient funds for Head Start to meet state preK standards. These changes could be conducted uniformly or on a state-by-state basis, and would allow Head Start to effectively "merge" without accepting state or local funds and governance.

Other ways to merge Head Start with state universal preK might provide even greater flexibility. One solution would be to allow Head Start dollars to follow the child to any program participating in universal preK (public or private) chosen by the parents. Another option would be for Head Start to begin providing supplemental services to Head Start-eligible children attending universal preK programs while withdrawing from the provision of direct classroom services. These children would then receive the advantages associated with participating in both Head Start and universal preK.

All of these approaches would address a longstanding issue for Head Start, which is that its eligibility requirements effectively isolate children in poverty from their more economically advantaged peers. A challenge for each of the approaches, especially the most flexible approach, is to ensure that Head Start and state preK standards are maintained or raised where necessary for more effective early education. These options would also require changes in federal legislation, and the 2003 reauthorization of Head Start provides an opportunity for creative thinking about how Head Start might best respond to the trend toward universal preK.

The Most Important Grade

Senator Zell Miller, the former governor of Georgia, has called preschool "the most important grade." The U.S. public agrees, judging from the steadily growing attendance rates and state movements toward universal preK, including the overwhelming support that passed Florida's universal preK ballot initiative in 2002. Many research studies have confirmed preschool's positive effects on school readiness and school success, especially for our most disadvantaged children.

Yet preschool will fulfill its promise only if educators take on the hard work of developing and implementing sound policy. This challenge will require higher standards, greater accountability, and increased public funding. It will also require creative new approaches to move from the current uneven patchwork of private and public programs to uniformly and highly effective universal preK programs that provide a high-quality early education for every child in the United States.

References

Barnett, W. S. (1996). *Lives in the balance: Age 27 benefit-cost analysis of the High/Scope Perry Preschool Program.* Ypsilanti, MI: High/Scope Press.

Barnett, W. S. (1998). Long-term effects on cognitive development and school success. In W. S. Barnett & S. S. Boocock (Eds.), *Early care and education for children in poverty: Promises, programs, and long-term results* (pp. 11-44). Albany, NY: SUNY Press.

Barnett, W. S. (2002). Early childhood education. In A. Molnar (Ed.), *School reform proposals: The research evidence* (pp. 1-26). Greenwich, CT: Information Age Publishing, Inc.

Barnett, W. S. (2003). Better teachers, better preschools: Student achievement linked to teacher qualifications. *Preschool Policy Matters* (No. 2). New Brunswick, NJ: National Institute for Early Education Research, Rutgers University.

Barnett, W. S., & Camilli, G. (2002). Compensatory preschool education, cognitive development, and "race." In J. M. Fish (Ed.), *Race and intelligence: Separating science from myth* (pp. 369-406). Mahwah, NJ: Erlbaum.

Bellm, D., Burton, A., Whitebook, M., Broatch, L., & Young, M. P. (2002). *Inside the preK classroom: A study of staffing and stability in state-funded prekindergarten programs.* Washington, DC: Center for the Child Care Workforce.

Love, J. M., Kisker, E. E., Ross, C. M., Schochet, P. Z., Brooks-Gunn, J., Paulsell, D., Boller, K., Constantine, J., Vogel, C., Fuligni, A. S., & Brady-Smith, C. (2002). *Making a difference in the lives of infants and toddlers and their families: The impacts of Early Head Start. Executive summary.* Washington, DC: Administration on Children, Youth, and Families, U.S. Department of Health and Human Services.

Masse, L. N., & Barnett, W. S. (2002). *A benefit-cost analysis of the Abecedarian Early Childhood Intervention.* New Brunswick, NJ: National Institute for Early Education Research, Rutgers University.

Merrow, J. (2002, July 17). European preschools should embarrass USA. *USA Today*, p. 15A.

National Center for Education Statistics. (1997). *Dropout rates in the United States: 1995.* Washington, DC: U.S. Department of Education.

Reynolds, A., Temple, J., Robertson, D., & Mann, E. (2002). *Age 21 Cost-benefit analysis of the Title I Chicago Child-Parent Centers.* Madison, WI: University of Wisconsin (Institute for Research on Poverty Discussion Paper #1245-02).

Shonkoff, J., & Phillips, D. (Eds.). (2000). *From neurons to neighborhoods: The science of early child development.* Washington, DC: National Academies Press.

Zill, N., Resnick, G., Kim, K., McKey, R. H., Clark, C., Pai-Samant, S., Connell, D., Vaden-Kiernan, M., O'Brien, R., & D'Elio, M. A. (2001). *Head Start FACES: Longitudinal findings on program performance. Third progress report.* Washington, DC: Administration on Children, Youth, and Families, U.S. Department of Health and Human Services.

W. Steven Barnett (sbarnett@nieer.org) is Director and **Jason T. Hustedt** (jhustedt@nieer.org) is an assistant research professor at the National Institute for Early Education Research, 120 Albany St., Ste. 500, New Brunswick, NJ 08901; http://nieer.org.

UNIT 2

Child Development and Families

Unit Selections

Key Points to Consider

- Why has childhood obesity become such an epidemic in our country today?

- What are some of the issues related to allergies facing school personnel?

- Describe the four types of emotional competence children can develop.

- What skills developed during the preschool years will be of most assistance as children grow and develop throughout life?

- Describe the role adults play in assisting children to develop a sense of right and wrong.

- What role do parents and the media play in gender identification?

- How do children benefit by having their fathers involved in their schools?

- Describe the effects on young children of viewing cartoon violence.

 **Links: www.dushkin.com/online/**
These sites are annotated in the World Wide Web pages.

Administration for Children and Families
http://www.dhhs.gov
Changing the Scene on Nutrition
http://www.fns.usda.gov/tn/Healthy/changing.html
Internet Resources for Education
http://web.hamline.edu/personal/kfmeyer/cla_education.html#hamline
The National Academy for Child Development
http://www.nacd.org
National Parent Information Network/ERIC
http://npin.org
Parent Center
http://www.parentcenter.com/general/34754.html

New trends related to the health of young children emerged this year. We have included articles that reflect the new interest in children's health and well being. The issue receiving the most attention this year was that of obesity in children. The editors considered seven articles on this subject and chose the one which is believed the best applicable to teachers working with young children and their families.

The issue of childhood obesity is noticeable every time one enters a fast food restaurant and hears a child order a meal by its number on the menu because they are so familiar with the selection at that particular restaurant. It is also evident on a playground where children just sit on the sideline not wanting to participate with their peers due to body image. In "Childhood Obesity: The Caregiver's Role", Bernadette Haschke provides many suggestions for educators to follow which will help children develop appropriate eating habits and an active lifestyle. Parents and educators must work together to promote healthy living. Teachers should also participate in healthy living activities. We are powerful role models in the lives of young children.

The next three articles in this unit deal with issues surrounding children who have severe health or behavior issues. Where it was once rare to find a child with a severe food allergy, it is common today to see signs posted in most schools noting a person with a severe food allergy is in the building. People are told not to bring peanuts, oranges, or certain beans into the school. One only needs to walk into an elementary school office at lunchtime and see the long line of children waiting to take their medication to know there are many children who depend on prescription drugs to control their behavior. These young children are so disruptive they are not able to function in a normal classroom setting without help. It is the job of teachers to carefully observe and determine when children are having behavior challenges that prevent them from being fully functioning members of a class.

Parents may want academic skills to be the focus of their child's early childhood learning experiences, but when asked what skills will best prepare their child to be successful in life, there may be a different answer. In "Skills for School Readiness—and Life", the Texas Workforce Commission outlines six important attitudes and behaviors for success throughout life. The teachers' role in providing for the development of independence, compassion, trust, creativity, self-control, perseverance, and resilience is critical. In a similar vein, "What's the Difference Between Right and Wrong?" examines the development of moral reasoning. Teachers, parents, and administrators, who focus solely on the development of the cognitive domains, ignoring the affective or social and emotional areas, are neglecting to educate the whole child.

Finally, after years of schools having "helping moms" or "room mothers," teachers are realizing the benefit of encouraging dads to participate in their children's education. "Encouraging Fathers to Participate in the School Experiences of Young Children: The Teacher's Role" by Barry Frieman and Terry Berkeley describes how fathers can become integral contributors to

children's education. In one Chevy Chase, Maryland, school, Lena is envied by her peers for her father's active participation in her school. Her dad will accompany the class on trips, document learning opportunities with photographs, or share art with the class. His contributions are greatly appreciated by a teaching staff that recognizes the importance of fathers in the classroom. Lena's father is encouraged by the teacher's use of "moms or dads" in her conversations about families helping in the classroom. The most striking evidence for supporting dads in their children's education comes in the form of a study from the U.S. Department of Education. The researchers recognized the contributions mothers make as essential to the social and emotional well-being of children, but they found that the involvement by fathers may be critical to academic achievement. Although this study was done with students in grades 6–12, it is important to note that parent participation in the later grades hinges on their involvement in their children's preschool and primary education. Our job as early childhood educators is to encourage all parents, but especially fathers, to come into the classroom and to feel comfortable and useful during their visits. Lorenza DiNatale provides suggestions for getting families involved in their children's early education in her article, "Developing High-Quality Family Involvement Programs in Early Childhood Settings." By getting parents off to a positive start with their initial school volunteer experience, we are doing a huge favor for our colleagues who work with older children. Then as children move through the grades, their families will be accustomed to contributing to their children's education.

The collaboration of families, the community, and school personnel will enable children to benefit from the partnership these three groups bring to the educational setting. Our hope is every child will have a strong network of support in their home, their community, and school.

Childhood Obesity:
The Caregiver's Role

by Bernadette Haschke

Children are getting fatter. Newspaper reports describe young children with weights in excess of 100 pounds. Recent surveys (U.S. Department of Health and Human Services, 2002) indicate that 10 percent of children ages 2 to 5 and 15 percent of children ages 6 to 19 are overweight.

Obesity is becoming a serious concern. Excessive weight impedes normal physical and psychological development of young children. Obesity is a detrimental cycle that gets progressively worse. Being overweight leads to inactivity, and inactivity contributes to obesity.

The cause is apparent: obesity begins when a child eats more calories than are used. However, other interrelated causes that begin in childhood have long-term consequences for a lifetime battle with obesity and health issues. For young children dealing with obesity is primarily a parental responsibility, but medical professionals, caregivers, and teachers play important roles.

Causes of childhood obesity

Limited physical activity. Obesity is a behavioral issue for all age groups and a direct consequence of lifestyle, even for young children. Young children readily adopt the lifestyle of their parents.

Today's families are increasingly busy with many activities pulling members in different directions. Such busyness does not mean physical activity. Most often young children follow along, riding in a car seat as family members drive from dance lesson to grocery store. As a result, children have little time for play and self-selected activities.

In many neighborhoods, safety is a concern. Parents keep children inside so they can watch them at all times.

Increased sedentary activity. The nature of inside activities for children today is an important factor in obesity. The amount of time children spend with television, computers, and video games has increased and is often the major childhood activity.

Such activities may or may not be harmful in themselves, depending on the nature of programs and games. The major concern is that these activities have replaced physically active play. Not only are young children burning few calories, but watching TV and playing video games often go hand in hand with snacking on high-calorie fat foods.

Eating habits. Snacking by both adults and children most often involves foods that are high in calorie, high in fat, and low in fiber. Children who snack shortly before meals are less likely to be hungry at mealtime. Families increasingly order delivery meals such as pizza or bring home prepared meals from a restaurant or grocery.

Because of busy schedules, families are increasingly choosing to eat meals away from home. They are likely to choose high-fat and high-calorie foods from fast-food restaurants.

All of these factors contribute to a lifestyle that increases the risk for childhood obesity.

The caregiver's role

Caregivers have a unique opportunity to provide nutrition education on a continuing basis, not just a weekly nutrition unit once or twice during the year. Ongoing discussion of nutrition and daily activities with a food and nutrition emphasis are important for teaching basic concepts. Ideally nutrition is an ongoing part of the curriculum and used to teach other concepts.

Nutrition education during the early childhood years is especially important because it is during this period that lifetime eating habits are formed. The quality of nutrition for children ages 2 to 5 is especially important because it affects growth and development. It is easier to develop healthy eating habits during this time than it is to change eating habits in adulthood. Habits established during childhood will last a lifetime.

Caregivers need to provide healthy foods that meet the recommended dietary guidelines and to offer only those food options for children to select. Children do not automatically make healthy food decisions. Without nutrition education and guidance, they tend to choose foods high in sodium, salt, sugar, and fat or those foods familiar to them. The goal is that children learn to self-regulate the intake of food and to realize when they are full.

The quality of nutrition for children ages 2 to 5 is especially important because it affects growth and development.

Don't fall into the trap of encouraging, forcing, or bribing children to eat more than they actually need. They will not starve if they don't eat everything on their plates. The goal is to encourage children to make wise choices and assume responsibility for those choices.

The caregiver's responsibility is to teach children to recognize the link between nutrition and physical well-being. Children need knowledge of the nutrients in foods and their effect on physical growth and development—not just for now, but for their future health and well-being.

Learning nutrition concepts

Piaget concluded that children ages 2 to 7 learn by actively participating in their environment, not by passively listening to instruction (Swadener, 1994). According to Piagetian theory, nutrition education for this age group involves interaction with food. Abstract concepts and stylized pictures have no place in nutrition education for young children. Because nutrition is an abstract concept for preschoolers, caregivers will use examples of real foods that are meaningful for children.

Research by Birch (1987) has found that early experience with food and eating is crucial to the food acceptance patterns children develop. Everyday experiences with food and eating affect food acceptance and intake.

Babies are born with a preference for sweets, but all other food preferences are acquired (Birch, 1994). The natural tendency for children is to reject anything that tastes new and unfamiliar. One study by Birch (1987) shows that the children 2 to 6 years old are initially reluctant to taste new or unfamiliar foods. However, the preference for a food increases with many exposures, regardless of one's age.

Other studies (Birch, 1990) indicate that young children must be exposed to a new food up to 15 times before they accept it. It is not surprising that the best time to introduce children to new foods is during the toddler period before they reach the negative 2-year-old stage in which the first response is usually "no."

Tips for parents

- Avoid having prepared high-sugar or high-fat snacks in the home. Instead, have plenty of fresh fruits and vegetables to choose from.
- Provide foods high in fiber such as fruits, vegetables, and whole-grain breads and cereals.
- Know your child's food patterns and needs. Don't force a bottle or require that your child finish a meal. Instead serve small portions and leave the decision about being full to your child.
- Don't use food as reward or punishment for behavior.
- Avoid using dessert and candy as a reward for eating other foods.
- Provide whole milk until age 2. After that, use 2 percent or skim milk.
- Limit television and computer time.
- Provide opportunities for active, physical play.
- Participate with your child in activities such as walking, swimming, and sports.

From Morgan, R. "Evaluation and Treatment of Childhood Obesity," *American Family Physician*, Feb. 15, 1999.

Preparing and serving healthy foods

Those who prepare and serve meals and snacks to young children need to examine how their practices may contribute to obesity. In a recent nutrition education workshop, a cook at a child care center said she didn't fry any foods that were served to the children. When participants were asked later to list the favorite foods served to children in their centers, this same individual volunteered "steak fingers." When the workshop leader pointed out this was a fried food, she replied, "I didn't fry the meat. I just warmed it in the oven." She didn't realize that the prepared steak fingers had been previously fried.

Serving a prepared food may be faster and easier, but it may also add calories to the meal. Serving prepared foods is increasing, despite their higher cost, because child care staff do not have the time, energy, or expertise to fully prepare foods themselves. Extra calories contribute to potential obesity, and serving unhealthy food leads to lifelong preferences and habits.

The caregiver's responsibility is to teach children to recognize the link between nutrition and physical well-being.

Portion size is an important factor in obesity (Young, 2002). Americans now "super-size" everything and expect to be served mounds of food at every meal. Caregivers need to help children learn to regulate their food intake and recognize the sensation of feeling full. Serving recommended portion sizes to young children is essential.

Start with an appropriate amount and give seconds only if the child wants more. Many caregivers report that children are now requesting third, fourth, and fifth servings of specific foods. An appropriate rule is to provide only one additional serving of a specific food, unless the child has a diet restriction and cannot eat other foods that are served. When children request a second helping, don't make them eat all other foods on their plates.

Encourage children to eat slowly, because the fullness sensation develops over time. Involving children in conversation about foods and eating preferences during snacks and mealtime helps to slow the intake rate and also provides an opportunity to discuss nutrition and foods on a daily basis. By allowing children time to acquire the fullness sensation, you may reduce requests for additional servings.

Serve meals and snacks at specific times and remove food when mealtime is over. Some children are naturally slow eaters and may need a few extra minutes to finish the meal. Eating should not become a stand-off between caregiver and child. If a child chooses not to eat, then remove the food and ask the child to move on to the next activity. Explain that the child will have another chance to eat at the next snack or mealtime.

Eating is a social behavior that is strongly influenced by the culture and traditions of society. The eating behavior of other children can serve as a role model and a social pressure for influencing a child's food preferences. Seating a child who refuses to eat corn with other children who love corn will likely increase the child's willingness to eat corn.

Model what you teach. Don't have coffee, a donut, or a can of soda in the room if you expect children to eat healthy foods at regular times.

Encouraging physical activity

Many caregivers might be surprised to learn that experts recommend an increase in physical activity for preschool children. Most of us spend much of the day trying to calm children and lessen their activity.

However, young children need to develop and practice motor skills. By incorporating active play and activities in the daily routine, we encourage an active childhood and lay the foundation for an active and productive adulthood. Research (Gabbard, 1998) indicates that the "window of opportunity" for acquiring basic motor movements is from the prenatal period to age 5. The development period for fine motor skills extends from infancy to around 9 years of age.

Childhood fitness and movement activity needs to be fun and appropriate for the age of the child. Remember that play is children's work and their way of exploring, learning, and exercising.

Children need early opportunities to climb, walk, run, kick, throw, and jump. They need to develop eye-hand coordination by participating in activities such as working puzzles, building blocks, and stringing beads. Development of eye-foot coordination depends on activities such as kicking large balls. Helping children acquire and practice these skills provides the foundation for physical abilities later in life.

What about children who are inactive and just sit on the playground? Consider a routine of rotating children through various areas such as swings, bikes, and sandbox to encourage more active participation. Encourage children to select or assign them to begin in a different area of the playground for the first few minutes each day before choosing their favorite play area. This encourages development of different types of motor play and helps children to develop proficiency and skills in many areas.

Working with parents

It's important to educate families about nutrition and preventing obesity. Here are suggestions for working with families and their children:

- Encourage parents to be involved in all areas of their child's life. Children need to know that parents love and care for them regardless of their physical qualities. Part of parents' love and care is encouraging a healthy diet and activities suitable for preschool children.

Some parents may need help in learning what is appropriate for children at a certain age. You can provide

---

Health consequences for obese children

- Risk factor for heart disease, high cholesterol, and high blood pressure
- Increased risk for Type II diabetes
- 70 percent chance of becoming an overweight adult if overweight as a teen
- Social discrimination
- Poor self-esteem

From "The Surgeon General's Call to Action to Prevent and Decrease Overweight and Obesity—Fact Sheet," www.surgeongeneral.gov/topics/obesity/calltoaction/fact_consequences.html.

What's an appropriate serving?

Grain group	1 slice of bread ½ cup cooked rice
Fruit group	1 piece of fruit ¾ cup of juice
Meat group	2–3 oz. cooked meat, fish, or poultry cup of cooked dry beans or pasta or 1 egg
Vegetable group	½ cup chopped raw or cooked vegetables 1 cup of raw leafy vegetables
Milk group	1 cup milk or yogurt 2 oz. cheese

Recommended for children ages 4 to 6. Offer 2- 3-year-olds less of all foods except milk.

Source: U.S. Department of Agriculture, Center for Nurtrition Policy, 1999.

information about your activities at the center and ways to follow up at home. Send home suggested activities for outside active play and for healthful snacks that children can help prepare.

Childhood fitness and movement activity needs to be fun and appropriate for the age of the child.

Nutrition information that reinforces food and cooking topics covered in the child's classroom is especially helpful. For example,"Chef Combo" nutrition materials distributed by the National Dairy Council (1998) include leaflets that you can copy and send home with parents.

- Be sensitive to the cultural backgrounds of parents. In some cultures a large child is considered healthy. Obese parents may feel an overweight child is not a problem. Be sensitive to such issues and approach obesity from the standpoint of long-term health and well-being. Emphasize the child's inability to participate in all activities and its effect on self-concept.

- Recommend a healthy diet to parents. Help parents to see the importance of healthy eating. Suggest healthy snacks children can eat on the way home at the end of the day. Recommend apples, carrots, and graham crackers instead of chips, fast foods and other high-fat foods that may seem more convenient to a hurried parent trying to get home with hungry children.
- Encourage parents to examine their own levels of activity and eating patterns as well as their need to set a healthy example. It is hard to keep children from eating while watching TV if the parents are having snacks. Parents may be unaware of how many calories they consume as they watch television.

Dealing with an obese child

These suggestions are primarily directed at preventing obesity in young children. What can you do about an obese child in the classroom.

Talk with parents in an effort to express concern and provide information. Describe how obesity is hampering the child's participation in activities and how that behavior is different from that of other children in the classroom. Discuss strategies for cutting back food consumption and for encouraging the child to become more active. Although most obesity is not caused by health-related problems, you might suggest that the parents contact their physician or public health staff in dealing with the problem.

Obesity has become a serious concern in this country. Preventing it in early childhood is much easier than trying to undo unhealthy eating habits and activity patterns in adulthood.

References

Birch, L. "Research Example 1: The Role of Experience in Children's Food Acceptance Patterns, " *Supplement to the Journal of the American Dietetic Association*, Vol. 87, No. 9, 1987, pp. S36–S40.
Birch, L.; L. McPhee; L. Steinberg; and S. Sullivan. "Conditioned Flavor Preferences in Young Children," *Physiology and Behavior*, Vol. 47, 1990.
Birch, L. "How Kids Choose Foods," research presented at International Conference of Gastronomy, Monterry, Calif., March 11, 1994.
Chef Combo's Fantastic Adventures in Tasting and Nutrition, National Dairy Council, Rosemont, Ill., 1998.
Gabbard, C. "Windows of Opportunity for Early Brain and Motor Development," *Journal of Health, Physical Education, Recreation and Dance*, Vol. 69, No. 8, 1998, pp. 54–30.
Morgan, R. "Evaluation and Treatment of Childhood Obesity," *American Family Physician*, Feb. 15, 1999.
The Surgeon General's Call to Action to Prevent and Decrease Overweight and Obesity—Fact Sheet. www.surgeongeneral.gov/topics/obesity/calltoaction/fact_consequences.html.

Swadener S. "Nutrition Education for Preschool Age Children: A Review of the Research," www.nal.usda.gov/fnic/usda/preschoolne.html.

U.S. Department of Agriculture, Center for Nutrition Policy and Promotion, 1999.

U.S. Department of Health and Human Services, "Obesity Still on the Rise, New Data Show," www.cdc.gov/nchs/releases/02news/obesityonrise/html.

Young, L. "The Contribution of Expanding Portion Sizes to the U.S. Obesity Epidemic," *American Journal of Public Health*, Vol. 92, No. 2, 2002, pp. 246, 49

About the author

Bernadette Haschke, PhD, is an associate professor in the Department of Family and Consumer Sciences at Baylor University in Waco, Texas. She has served as a teacher and director in early childhood programs. She is a trainer for the Texas Career Development System for Early Care and Education and conducts workshops on childhood obesity.

The Allergy Epidemic

We've conquered most childhood infections, but extreme reactions to everyday substances pose a new threat

By Jerry Adler

THE FIRST INDICATION THAT something was not quite right with David Adams was subtle, a mild rash around his mouth after nursing. Luckily, the second clue, at the age of 3 months, was not so subtle: angry hives that erupted over his entire body during a plane trip. After the family returned home to Georgia, a specialist determined that David was among the 6 to 8 percent of children under the age of 3 with an allergy to food—in his case, peanuts. His sensitivity was so acute that the hives may have been caused by the residue of peanuts on his parents' fingers, and the rash by his mother's eating a peanut-butter sandwich and excreting tiny amounts of peanut protein in her breast milk. What made the episode lucky was this: on a day two years later, when David began vomiting and gasping after chomping an energy bar that had escaped his parents' anti-peanut scrutiny, his mother could inject him with epinephrine and save his life. Implausible as it seems, David's condition is at the cutting edge of modern pediatric medicine, right up there with hay fever.

If a popular magazine had run a children's health issue a hundred years ago, the first article might have been about diphtheria or cholera—external threats that the West has largely conquered by antibiotics and sanitation. Instead we are examining allergies, a self-generated danger, the result of an immune system out of sync with its surroundings. These are among the leading challenges of the next century, a threat that may in part be an unintended consequence of our triumph over the infectious scourges of the past.

Speaking of hay fever, or "seasonal allergic rhinitis," the incidence of this annoying sensitivity to tree, grass or ragweed pollen has increased remarkably just since 1996—from 6 percent of American children 18 and under to 9 percent, according to the National Center for Health Statistics. All allergies seem to be on the rise, in fact, but "it's not just that more kids have allergies," says Dr. Marc Rothenberg, director of allergy and immunology at Cincinnati Children's Hospital. "The severity of those allergies has also increased."

An allergy is an overreaction by the immune system to a foreign substance, which can enter the body through a variety of routes. It can be inhaled, like pollen or dander, the tiny flakes of skin shed by domestic animals. It can be injected, like insect venom or penicillin, or merely touch the skin, like the latex in medical gloves. Or it can be ingested. According to the Food Allergy & Anaphylaxis Network, almost any food can trigger an allergy, although eight categories account for 90 percent of all reactions: milk, eggs, peanuts (technically, a legume), tree nuts, fin fish, shellfish, soy and wheat. (Allergies have nothing to do with the condition known as food intolerance; people who lack an enzyme for digesting dairy products, for instance, may suffer intestinal problems, but they are not allergic to milk.)

For reasons not fully understood, in some people these otherwise harmless substances provoke the same reactions by which the body attempts to rid itself of dangerous pathogens. These may include sneezing, vomiting and the all-purpose localized immune-system arousal known as inflammation. The lungs may be affected; allergies are a leading trigger for asthma attacks. In extreme cases, the reaction involves virtually all organ systems and proceeds to anaphylaxis, a dramatic drop in blood pressure accompanied by extreme respiratory distress that may be fatal without prompt treatment. Which is why, to this day—and possibly for the rest of his life—David Adams never sets foot outside his home without an emergency supply of epinephrine.

What can underlie such a self-destructive reaction? An infant who grows violently ill in the presence of as little as one hundredth of a peanut almost surely has some sort of genetic predisposition. Indeed, there is a strong inherited component in allergies. If one parent has an allergy, chances are one in three that the child will be allergic, according to the Asthma and Allergy Foundation of America. If both parents have allergies, the odds rise to 70 percent. But *the children aren't necessarily allergic to the same things as the parents*—strongly suggesting that some other factor must be at work as

The Itchy Sneezies: Kids & Allergies

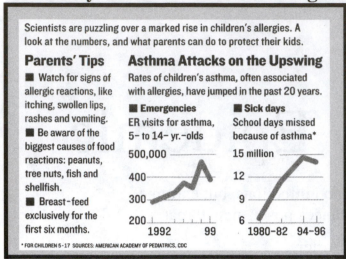

Scientists are puzzling over a marked rise in children's allergies. A look at the numbers, and what parents can do to protect their kids.

Parents' Tips

■ Watch for signs of allergic reactions, like itching, swollen lips, rashes and vomiting.

■ Be aware of the biggest causes of food reactions: peanuts, tree nuts, fish and shellfish.

■ Breast-feed exclusively for the first six months.

Asthma Attacks on the Upswing

Rates of children's asthma, often associated with allergies, have jumped in the past 20 years.

■ Emergencies
ER visits for asthma, 5- to 14-yr.-olds

500,000
400
300
200
1992   99

■ Sick days
School days missed because of asthma*

15 million
12
9
6
1980-82   94-96

* FOR CHILDREN 5-17 SOURCES: AMERICAN ACADEMY OF PEDIATRICS, CDC

well. And genetics cannot explain the rapid rise in allergies over the past few years or, for that matter, centuries. "The human race hasn't changed that much genetically in the last 200 years," since hay fever first came to the attention of doctors a single case at a time, says Dr. Andrew Saxon, chief of clinical immunology at UCLA.

So something must have changed in the environment—specifically, in the environment of developed nations, and especially their cities, where allergies are far more prevalent than in rural China and Africa. One obvious place to look is air pollution. Studies by Saxon and his colleague David Diaz-Sanchez have found a strong correlation between pollutants—diesel exhaust and cigarette smoke—and the development of allergies. Researchers don't believe pollution is the whole story, though; allergies have continued to climb even as smoking and air-pollution rates have fallen in recent decades. But industrialization has also brought about declines in infectious diseases and close exposure to farm animals. The "hygiene hypothesis" holds that it is precisely these (mostly desirable) trends that have contributed to the rise in allergies. The human immune system, which evolved in a natural environment teeming with hostile bacteria and parasites, finds itself uncomfortably idle in the antiseptic confines of the modern suburb, and, failing to mature properly, takes out its frustration on harmless peanuts and shrimp. Numerous studies have lent support to this general notion, notably one last year that showed a strong negative correlation between allergies and exposure to endotoxins, which are bacterial remains shed by farm animals. Research by Dr. Dennis Ownby of the Medical College of Georgia shows that children growing up with two or more pets, either cats or dogs, had a decreased risk of allergies—and not just to pet dander, but other unrelated allergens as well. But although many researchers accept the hygiene hypothesis in outline, the emerging picture is of "a complicated relationship, where dose and timing of exposure" play important but still uncertain roles, says Dr. Scott Weiss of Harvard.

So the hygiene hypothesis has yet to generate any concrete prescriptions (unless you count The New England Journal of Medicine's August 2000 editorial headlined PLEASE, SNEEZE ON MY CHILD). The eventual hope, says Ownby, is for a way to "artificially stimulate the immune system to reduce [allergy] risk without having all these diseases." Meanwhile, though, researchers are developing new drug therapies that go beyond epinephrine (for emergency treatment of anaphylaxis) and the growing array of over-the-counter antihistamines. (Histamine is a key substance in the cascade of biochemical events that constitute an allergic reaction.) Newer drugs, like Singulair and Xolair—just approved by the Food and Drug Administration in June for allergy-related asthma—block other chemicals in the chain. And even ordinary activated charcoal could be useful in blocking peanut allergies, according to a new study; if taken immediately it may neutralize the allergenic proteins in the stomach.

Pediatricians have also begun taking allergies more seriously. One key bit of advice to mothers is to breast-feed infants exclusively for six months. Delaying children's exposure to novel foods in this way is the "hallmark for food-allergy prevention," says the American Academy of Pediatrics. Nursing mothers should also be on the lookout for signs of a secondhand food reaction in their infants, including diarrhea, vomiting or itchy rashes (not counting diaper rash). If these rare reactions occur, the mother may want to avoid drinking milk, or eating eggs, fish, tree nuts and especially peanuts. Peanuts, in fact, are the one food the AAP recommends that a woman avoid, not only while nursing but also while pregnant, because of their allergic potential. For the same reason, the longer you can hold off feeding your child peanut butter, the better: the AAP suggests waiting until 3. Cow's milk, by contrast, is usually safe after the 1st birthday.

And once an allergy has been diagnosed, the only thing to do is what David Adams's parents did: draw a *cordon sanitaire* around the child. Again, this is especially important for peanut allergies. Unfortunately, peanuts and peanut butter are ubiquitous, found in many Asian and Mexican dishes, in baked goods—and in practically every other child's lunchbox. Peanut-free zones in school lunchrooms have become a vital amenity in many communities, but even so, parents with severely allergic children are constantly on alert—writing to food companies to double-check lists of ingredients, outlawing even innocuous bakery products (a spatula that came into contact with a peanut-butter cookie can transfer a dangerous dose of allergen to an oatmeal-raisin one) and equipping babysitters and teachers with dedicated cell phones and walkie-talkies for emergencies. Milk, another potentially potent allergen, is, if anything, even harder to avoid. "You're sitting at a [school] cafeteria table and someone across from you spills milk," says Denise Bunning, of suburban Chicago, describing her nightmare scenario; Bunning's two sons, Bryan, 9, and Daniel, 7, are both allergic to milk, along with several other foods. At the age of 4, Bryan went into anaphylaxis after eating a jelly worm from a dispenser that had previously held milk-chocolate candies.

Susan Leavitt of New York, whose 13-year-old son, David Parkinson, is allergic to milk products, eggs, fish, nuts and mustard, goes so far as to check out school art supplies; a fourth-grade teacher once mentioned adding eggs to tempera paint for a better texture. There's a lot he can't have—pizza, to start with—but a lot of it is stuff you wouldn't necessarily want your kid to have anyway. And thanks to her vigilance, her home-cooked and pre-frozen meals and New York's ubiquitous fruit and vegetable markets, David is a healthy, normal boy, an avid skier—and alive.

With Anne Underwood and Karen Springen

Preschool Meds

By SHERYL GAY STOLBERG

The first clinical trial examining the effects of generic ritalin on 3- to 5-year-old subjects raises questions not only about the safety of the drug but also about the ethics of testing on ever younger brains.

On a warm, breezy Friday in September, a parade of mothers in minivans arrived at a preschool in suburban Connecticut to drop off a collection of 4-year-olds. Among the young students was Sam G., a sturdy, big-eared boy with cheeks that flush easily and a personality that has earned him a reputation, politely speaking, as a handful.

Like most 4-year-old boys, Sam loves things that move—trains, planes and trucks, especially fire trucks—and is usually on the move himself. When he enters a room, his clear blue eyes dart about, as though he cannot take in the sights fast enough. His knees and elbows are perpetually scraped. When his teachers read stories aloud, Sam often wanders about.

This particular Friday was no exception. It was Bring-Your-Stuffed-Animal-to-School Day, and Sam burst through the door carrying a two-foot-tall black-and-white cow he calls Moo. Surveying the scene, he paused momentarily and then, as if someone had lighted a fuse underneath him, thrust his arms forward and began zipping around the room, the cow acting as his shield. During the next two hours, Sam tried to open the childproof window locks; he got into fights in the sandbox and repeatedly stood in the center of the room, swinging the cow by its tail. When his teacher finally put the animal on the shelf "for a nap," Sam burst into tears.

Time was, Sam's rambunctiousness would have been chalked up to childhood or, more precisely, boyhood. Today, Sam has a diagnosis—attention deficit hyperactivity disorder, and a potential treatment: methylphenidate, a drug better known by its brand name, Ritalin. Sam has been taking the drug, in various doses that are interspersed with dummy pills, since July as part of the three-year Preschool A.D.H.D. Treatment Study, known as PATS. This unusual clinical trial is financed by the National Institute of Mental Health and overseen by the New York State Psychiatric Institute in Manhattan. The institute, which is affiliated with Columbia Presbyterian Medical Center, is one of six academic medical centers around the country that have been recruiting children since January 2001. The aim is to enroll 314 children by February. Results are expected sometime in 2004.

The research may be the most controversial medical experiment the federal government has ever conducted in children: a study of the safety and effectiveness of generic Ritalin in preschoolers, ages 3 to 5. Experimenting on children is always delicate, especially when the children are barely out of diapers. Ritalin, marketed to help hyperactive students focus in school, is a stimulant, and though it is generally considered safe, scientists acknowledge they do not understand how it affects young children's developing brains. The drug is not approved for children under age 6. But doctors increasingly prescribe it to them "off label"—a worrisome trend, yet hardly surprising in an era when 3-year-olds are expected to know their numbers and 5-year-olds are being taught to read.

"We have an obsession with performance in our country," says Lawrence Diller, a behavioral pediatrician in Walnut Creek, Calif., and the author of two books on A.D.H.D. "We have a universal performance enhancer in Ritalin. It helps anyone, child or adult, A.D.H.D. or not, to perform better. It was inevitable that there would be this drift down to the 3- to 5-year-old set."

DARLENE AND BRIAN G., who insisted that their last names not be used to protect Sam's privacy, had struggled for years to have a child. Darlene, a compact 51-year-old woman with blond hair and jade-green eyes, was 39 when she married Brian, an engineer 13 years younger than she is. In 1997, having exhausted their emotional and financial resources on in vitro fertilization, they decided to adopt.

Sam was born Dec. 18 of that year to a 17-year-old. Only later would the couple learn that their son's biological mother, as well as some of her relatives, had been given the diagnosis of attention deficit hyperactivity disorder.

By the time Sam started walking, two things about him were clear: he was fearless and always on the go. When he was 2, Sam climbed onto the dining-room table and tried to swing from the ceiling fan. He switched on the electric stove, then stretched his little body across the burners. He tripped the latch on a sliding-glass door, then let himself out on the second-story balcony. Darlene yanked him back as he was about to topple over the rail.

Brian thought Sam was just being a boy, and the pediatrician seemed to concur. When Darlene asked about testing for hyperactivity, he told her to wait until Sam was 5 or 6, and in school. "If I live that long," she shot back.

When Sam was 3, the director of his preschool called to say that Sam had raised his fists to her "and we can't have that kind of behavior here." Darlene, upset yet relieved that someone else had seen what she

saw, called Brian in tears. "He's going to get kicked out of preschool," she told him. "He's only 3!"

A local psychologist diagnosed A.D.H.D. in Sam and recommended therapy. Darlene, a believer in holistic medicine, also took Sam to a naturopath, who tested him for food sensitivities and severely restricted his diet: no wheat, dairy, gluten, corn syrup or food additives. The entire family gave up pizza. At school birthday parties, Sam got soy ice cream.

By the time Sam turned 4, the family's insurance coverage for the therapy was running out. Then Darlene's cousin alerted her to an advertisement in The New York Daily News. "Is your preschooler just too active?" the ad asked. It promised "a comprehensive evaluation by our study team, as well as up to 14 months of treatment—*all at no cost.*"

THE MAN BEHIND the advertisement was Laurence L. Greenhill, a 61-year-old child psychiatrist at the Psychiatric Institute on Riverside Drive in New York City. Square-shouldered and stocky, with wire-rimmed glasses and dark wavy hair that he slicks down for speaking engagements, Greenhill is what pharmaceutical companies call a K.O.L.—key opinion leader—which means he conducts the cutting-edge drug research that shapes prescribing decisions for thousands of ordinary doctors who treat A.D.H.D. He is serious almost to the point of being humorless, a trait that colleagues say serves him well.

"Among people who do work like this, studies on the very young, the very sick, there is no shortage of cowboys," says Steven Hyman, who was the director of the National In-

stitute of Mental Health at the N.I.H., when the study was approved. "Larry Greenhill is not a cowboy."

Greenhill came of age in psychiatry at a time when medical experts were beginning to regard hyperactivity as not simply a behavioral disorder but a condition with a biological basis, akin to asthma or diabetes, that could be corrected with medicine. In 1998, having already helped lead a landmark study of Ritalin in school-age children, he turned his attention to preschoolers. In November 1999, the National Institute of Mental Health agreed to finance his preschool study.

But before the money was released, a scientific landmine exploded in the middle of the long-running Ritalin debate. In February 2000, The Journal of the American Medical Association reported a two-fold-to-threefold increase in the use of stimulant drugs, particularly methylphenidate, among 2- to 4-year-olds. The study, by Julie Magno Zito, a pharmacy professor at the University of Maryland, did not shock doctors who treat A.D.H.D. But it did shock the public.

"Those of us who have been prescribing medication since the 70's had been watching this huge increase," Lawrence Diller says. "Zito's piece put it on the front page of every newspaper."

Hillary Clinton, still first lady but running for Senate in New York, demanded to know what the government was doing about it. Hyman told her about Greenhill. Within weeks, the White House had announced a major initiative to reduce the use of stimulants among the very young. The preschool study was a central component.

One day, after Sam had been in the study for a few months,
he started to twitch. His parents agonized over whether
to stop giving him a drug that had helped him.

Critics argue that the trial may, in fact, increase stimulant use, legitimizing it for children who are not as closely monitored as Sam. But Hyman defends his decision to go ahead, given that so many pre-schoolers are already on the drug. "If we can do these trials right," he says, "we are damnable if we don't do them. Because if we don't do them, then every child becomes an uncontrolled experiment of one."

To Peter Breggin, the nation's best-known A.D.H.D. critic, the study marked "a tragedy for America's children." A soft-spoken, silver-haired psychiatrist, Breggin is the author of more than a dozen books, including "Talking Back to Ritalin." With his gentle manner and frequent television appearances, Breggin puts forth an appealing—and, Greenhill contends, troubling—message: attention deficit hyperactivity disorder is a figment of modern psychiatry's imagination.

Flipping through the fourth edition of the Diagnostic and Statistical Manual of Mental Disorders on a recent afternoon, Breggin read aloud from its list of A.D.H.D. symptoms: "Often fails to give close attention to details or makes careless mistakes in schoolwork. Often fidgets with hands or feet or squirms in seat. Often blurts out answers before questions have been completed." He scowled.

"There is no disease," he said flatly. "It's a list of behaviors that annoy adults."

ON JAN. 23, 2002, Sam and his parents made the first of what would become weekly visits to the psychiatric institute. They had come to meet Dr. Janet Fairbanks, the child psychiatrist and colleague of Greenhill's who would evaluate Sam.

Diagnosing A.D.H.D. is difficult with any child, but with preschoolers, who tend to be active and impulsive, it is especially hard. The medical literature suggests A.D.H.D. is often overdiagnosed and overtreated, which is one reason Breggin's arguments have gained so much currency.

Contrary to the perception that Ritalin is being used as a kind of "chemical handcuff" for inner-city kids, studies show the drug is most often prescribed to white suburban boys— in short, kids like Sam. Sensitive to the controversy, the mental-health institute insisted that Greenhill's team require parenting training: 10 weeks of classroom instruction in behavior modification. Children who show little or no improvement at the end of the 10 weeks then become eligible for medication.

The team also set strict limits on who can enroll, taking only the most severely affected children. Fairbanks knew right away Sam would qualify. The electric stove story, she says, was a big tip-off. "He has no sense of danger, which is characteristic of these kids, which is why they get hurt a lot. It's curiosity, combined with no impulse control."

By April, the psychiatric institute had recruited enough children, 13 in all, including a set of 3-year-old twins, to begin its next round of parent training. The course was led by Tova Ferro, a clinical psychologist who herself was expecting a child. On the night I sat in, the lesson was timeouts. Ferro popped a video into a recorder, and a man appeared on the television screen, begging his toddler to put away her toys amid lame threats of a timeout. Ferro asked what the father had done wrong. "He was a wimp," one mother piped up. Ferro agreed. She advised the parents to make a list of behaviors serious enough to warrant a timeout. Every family is different, she told them. "Think about what makes sense for you."

Although her goal is to help parents improve their children's behavior, Ferro is under no illusions. "Some children will need additional interventions," she said. Translation: Some will need drugs.

For Brian and Darlene, the parent training was mostly a review of what they had already picked up in parenting books, though they enjoyed the emotional support. But as with every other aspect of the PATS

clinical trial, the parent training, modeled on a Canadian program, has critics. Among them is William E. Pelham Jr., director of the Center for Children and Families at the State University of New York at Buffalo.

At his center, Pelham offers intensive training for teachers and summer camp for hyperactive kids— programs that he says help as many as 75 percent avoid medication. He says that Greenhill's less intensive training is set up to fail.

"I bet you 100,000 bucks I could tell you the results of that trial," Pelham said. "The results will be that kids need medication because parent training is not enough. I think that's dangerous. It is going to send a message to people that young children need medication."

But the cold truth, says Hyman, the former director of the mental-health institute, is that few Americans could afford the kind of help Pelham offers. "We were very concerned," he said, "that any behavioral therapy that came out of this trial had to be generalizable."

In Sam's case, the training was of little help, and the question of whether to put him on medication was much on his parents' minds throughout the 10-week session. On Sam's good days, Darlene was convinced she should hold out until he started school. On bad days, she was ready to cave. In the end, it was Brian who made the decision.

He liked the idea that Sam would be carefully monitored, that his medication would be increased only gradually until doctors determined the optimal dose, which he would take for 10 months. The father who once insisted his son was just being a boy had come to accept him as a boy with a problem.

"My eyes," Brian said, "have been opened."

SAM STARTED the medicine on the first Saturday in July. The following Friday, he strutted into the institute wearing one of his many fire truck shirts. His mother was glowing. "Today," Darlene announced, "was wonderful."

In keeping with the study requirements, Fairbanks started Sam on an extremely low dose, 1.25 milligrams of methylphenidate, once a day. Every two days, the dose went up; by Thursday, Sam was on 7.5 milligrams once a day, still much less than the study's maximum dose of 7.5 milligrams three times a day. Darlene had given him the medicine, a tiny white pill, in a bowl of applesauce at 10 a.m. At 10:45, she ran a little experiment. She offered Sam a spray bottle of pet deodorizer and asked him to help her spray the couch.

To his mother's astonishment, Sam did not run around the house squirting everything in sight. He stood in front of the couch and sprayed the cushions. Later, on a trip to the drug store, Sam asked if he could get a toy. When Darlene told him he would have to wait, he said, "O.K., Mom." She nearly burst into tears.

By 2 p.m., the magic was over. The medicine was wearing off. In the car on the way to their appointment, Sam was looking at a newspaper when Darlene heard the sound of paper crumpling. She asked Sam not to tear the paper, but he couldn't stop. Soon, his whole body was in motion, feet jangling, fingers wiggling.

That Friday, in Fairbanks's cramped office, the family squished next to one another on the psychiatrist's couch, all of Darlene and Brian's hopes and fears came spilling forth. They wondered aloud how they might channel Sam's impulsiveness and lack of fear. He could be an explorer, Darlene suggested. An astronaut, Fairbanks chimed in. "I want him to be a leader," Brian said finally. "I want him to follow his dreams."

Later, they took Sam out for pizza in the city, a rare treat. "I am starting to go on Ritalin," he announced. "They're these little tiny pills.

They're for to help me." Help you with what? I asked. "To help me with helping," he replied, as if this were the most obvious thing in the world. "With helping and listening." Then a bus rumbled by on Broadway, and Sam turned to look. Soon, he was out of his seat, darting for the door, his father calling out after him. It would be another 15 hours before his next little white pill.

IT WAS A difficult summer—"a roller coaster," in Brian's words. The trial followed a complicated double-blind crossover pattern, with the doses, and hence Sam's behavior, changing week to week. While outside experts charted Sam's responses, Sam's parents and doctors were kept in the dark. Darlene, though, wasn't fooled. The week Sam played Boggle Jr., a spelling game, for 30 minutes, was a high-dose week. The week he opened the childproof bottle of Clorox and accidentally doused himself in bleach ("I wanted to help you with the laundry," he told Darlene) was the placebo week.

By September, things had grown even more complicated. During a high-dose week, Sam developed a tic—a common and disconcerting side effect. It began subtly, an odd, occasional rolling of the shoulder, as though Sam were trying to wriggle out of his shirt. It didn't bother him, or his parents, until a few days after Labor Day, during a family trip to Cape Cod.

They were eating lunch when Darlene spotted Sam's arms going, first his left, then his right. His eyes grew big; his expression went blank. When she asked Sam to squeeze her hand, he couldn't; his own hand was curled up in a feeble knot. For two hours, Darlene and Brian watched their son deteriorate until, just as suddenly as it began, the twitching subsided. Frightened, they temporarily stopped the medication.

These kinds of reactions, Greenhill says, are just what his team is looking for, although the cause of Sam's tic remains unclear. It could be a side effect that goes away when the child stops taking the drug. Or Sam may have a tic disorder, which sometimes occurs alongside A.D.H.D. And there is also another, more troubling possibility, Fairbanks says: "Does the medicine somehow release something that was a vulnerability? And will it continue after the medication is stopped?"

The tic prompted Fairbanks to ask Sam's parents if they wanted to withdraw him from the trial. But Darlene and Brian, who once worried so much about putting their son on medication, did not want to take him off. "It's too soon to give up," Brian said. Today, Sam takes his optimal—and much lower—dose. The occasional shoulder roll remains.

Fairbanks has seen this kind of determination before. The parents of two of her patients were crushed when their children had to leave the trial because of appetite loss and insomnia, side effects of the medication.

In his own way, Sam seems to sense his parents' dilemma. On the drive back to Connecticut after a recent visit with Dr. Fairbanks, he pointed out the George Washington Bridge and talked about the pumpkin garden he had planted. Then he declared that he had become a parent. "I have a child," he said, in his serious, earnest way. "His name is Billy. He just turned 3. He knows all his alphabets. He knows at school when recess time is on. He knows when the bell rings, and they're going out. He listens to his teachers. He cleans up when he's supposed to." It did not take a child psychiatrist to figure out that, in his imagination, Sam had neatly created the boy he hopes to be.

Sheryl Gay Stolberg reports on medicine and health policy for The Times.

From the *New York Times* Magazine, November 17, 2002, pp. 58-61. © 2003 by Sheryl Gay Stolberg. Distributed by The New York Times Special Features. Reprinted by permission.

Troubled Souls

Mental illnesses are so complex in children that health-care professionals can't always detect them

By Claudia Kalb

Tyler Whitley, 7, is 4 feet 4 inches and weighs 75 pounds. He has blond hair, blue eyes, a generous spirit—and bipolar disorder, a serious mental illness. Highly irritable and angry one minute, he'll be laughing hysterically the next. Grand illusions kick in: he can leap to the ground from the top of a tall tree or jump from a grocery cart and fly. And then there are the heart-wrenching bouts of depression, when Tyler tells his parents, "I should never have been born. I need to go to heaven so people can be happy."

If only Tyler could be happy every day of his life.

The sobering reality is that mental illnesses, from depression to autism, do strike children. And they strike hard. In the United States, one in five children and adolescents has a mental disorder that causes at least some impairment. Many have more than one. The good news: kids' mental health is finally getting some attention. The Office of the Surgeon General has called for increased awareness and improved services for kids. Advocacy groups are battling stigma and demanding better detection. Scientists are learning more about genetic and environmental triggers—and about what the disorders look like in children, and how to treat them. "We've made major progress in the last 30 years," says Dr. Daniel Pine of the National Institute of Mental Health, but "we cannot ignore the fact that we have serious work to do."

The challenges are staggering. While pediatricians and school officials are at the front lines of children's health, not all are trained to see the warning signs. In kids, symptoms of mental disorders can be non-specific—stomachaches and irritability—and can blur from one disorder to the next. Parents and teachers often can't tell the difference between a normally rambunctious child and one who may be seriously ill. As a result, less than 20 percent of children with mental illnesses get the care they need. "The myth is it's a phase, they'll grow out of it," says Anne Marie Albano of the NYU Child Study Center. "A lot of them don't."

Mental-health professionals worry over how to treat their smallest patients: How young is too young to make a diagnosis? Are children being labeled and medicated too quickly? Are psychotropic drugs, most of which have not been specifically tested in kids, safe and effective? Researchers are working on the answers. The disorders, in the meantime, are very real. Left untreated, they can lead to academic failure, substance abuse and even suicide, the third leading cause of death in kids 10 to 19. Says Darcy Gruttadaro of the National Alliance for the Mentally Ill: "We're talking about very serious consequences."

ANXIETY DISORDERS

Anxiety disorders affect 13 percent of kids between 9 and 17. The category includes an array of conditions, from obsessive compulsive disorder (OCD) to social anxiety. OCD is among the easiest to spot. A child with the disorder might wash his hands repeatedly or perform a ritual—counting to 25 every time he gets on the bus. In very rare cases, children contract sudden and intense bouts of OCD from strep infections, but in general the condition appears to be triggered by a mix of genes and environment. One of the unique and challenging characteristics: "Kids know what they're doing doesn't make sense," says NIMH's Dr. Susan Swedo, "and they hide it from their parents."

Every parent knows about separation anxiety, and it's perfectly normal in infants and toddlers. But when a 9-year-old begins to fear that her mother is going to die and refuses to go to school, the condition may warrant treatment. Kids with social anxiety disorder want to avoid school for a different reason: they worry intensely about being judged. Even the simplest tasks, like eating in the cafeteria, can bring on intense embarrassment and sweating.

Not all anxiety is so specific. Kids who worry excessively about everything, from homework to earthquakes, may fall into the category of generalized anxiety disorder (GAD). One of the telling traits is incessant fears about the future. Like other anxiety disorders, which often clump together in kids and can be linked to depression, GAD must interfere significantly in a child's life and last for at least six months in order to fit the official psychiatric diagnosis. Treatment consists of cognitive behavioral therapy (coping strategies for parents and kids) and, in some cases, medication (typically antidepressants).

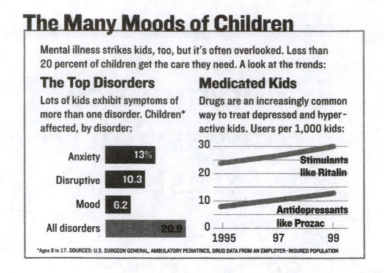

The Many Moods of Children

Mental illness strikes kids, too, but it's often overlooked. Less than 20 percent of children get the care they need. A look at the trends:

The Top Disorders

Lots of kids exhibit symptoms of more than one disorder. Children* affected, by disorder:

Anxiety 13%
Disruptive 10.3
Mood 6.2
All disorders 20.9

Medicated Kids

Drugs are an increasingly common way to treat depressed and hyperactive kids. Users per 1,000 kids:

Stimulants like Ritalin
Antidepressants like Prozac
1995 97 99

*Ages 9 to 17. SOURCES: U.S. SURGEON GENERAL, AMBULATORY PEDIATRICS, DRUG DATA FROM AN EMPLOYER-INSURED POPULATION

DEPRESSION AND BIPOLAR DISORDER

Depressed kids don't necessarily look like depressed adults: they're often irritable, rather than sad and withdrawn. Experts are now hunting for the disease's earliest footprints. In a study of preschoolers 3 to 5, Dr. Joan Luby of Washington University School of Medicine in St. Louis identified depression through play. Luby had children watch two puppets discuss their emotions, then asked the kids to point to the one that sounded most like them. The study found that depressed kids showed far less pleasure in play and some explored themes of death. "Preschoolers are inherently joyful beings," says Luby. Too often, "parents don't consider that a child is depressed." No one is suggesting that preschoolers be given Prozac. But given the disease's chronic effects, early recognition could ward off problems down the line.

Bipolar disorder, an ongoing cycle of depression and mania, used to be thought of as a disease that began in early adulthood. But psychiatrists are now detecting it much earlier, especially in kids with a family history since the disorder is so highly heritable. "These kids have always been there," says Martha Hellander of the Child & Adolescent Bipolar Foundation, an online support group. "They just ha-

ven't been properly identified." The illness is often confused with attention deficit hyperactivity disorder, but bipolar kids are more prone to elated moods, grandiose thoughts and daredevil acts. While bipolar adults have fairly well-marked periods of depression and mania, kids may have more rapid cycles. First-line treatment: mood stabilizers, and possibly antipsychotic or anticonvulsant drugs. "When children get properly treated, they feel better," says Dr. Jean Frazier of McLean Hospital in Belmont, Mass. "Parents will say, 'I finally have my child back'."

BEHAVIORAL DISORDERS

Concentration problems and hyperactivity can be symptoms of diagnosable disorders. ADHD, the most well known, affects 3 percent to 5 percent of school-age children, the majority of them boys. No, bad parenting isn't the cause, says Stephen Hinshaw, a child psychologist at the University of California, Berkeley. "Parents cause ADHD largely from the genes they pass on." While critics worry about an ADHD epidemic, experts say the condition may be underdiagnosed, especially in girls who are more likely to be daydreaming than hyperactive. The consequences can be disastrous: poor school performance, low self-esteem and substance abuse.

Oppositional defiant disorder can look like ADHD, and some kids have the inflammatory mix of both. But kids with ODD aren't necessarily inattentive. Instead, they exhibit a relentless and extreme pattern of defiance, anger and lashing out. The aggression is even more pronounced in a condition called conduct disorder, which tends to be diagnosed later, as kids enter adolescence. These children are not only unruly, they destroy property, harm animals and beat up other kids. While stimulants may be prescribed for ADHD, there are no specific drug classes for ODD and conduct problems. Behavioral therapy, including parent training programs, can make a world of difference.

There's still a long way to go in the quest to conquer children's mental illnesses. Tyler Whitley's mom, Leah, is taking it one step at a time. Early on, doctors said Tyler's moodiness was "just a little boy being a little boy." Finally, after several difficult years of searching for answers, her otherwise sweet and funny son has received a proper diagnosis. "This illness is nightmarish," says Whitley, but "with the help of our doctors, treatment and family support, we can get through it." And maybe one day Tyler can experience the happiness he—and every other child—deserves.

With JOAN RAYMOND

independence
compassion
trust
creativity
self-control
perseverance
Skills for school readiness—and life

Yes	No	
☐	☐	1. Children are ready for school when they know the letters of the alphabet and can sound out words.
☐	☐	2. Children entering kindergarten must know how to count to 20.
☐	☐	3. Children who are curious and creative will have lots of problems in school.
☐	☐	4. Children cannot be responsible for their own clothes, work, and lunch money in kindergarten.
☐	☐	5. Knowing how to make friends is less important in school success than knowing how to write your name.
☐	☐	6. Children cannot develop compassion until they reach high school.

If you answered yes to any of these questions, you may need to re-think your ideas about school readiness.

Too often early care and education teachers feel pushed to focus on academics. They may decide to drill letters and numbers. They may make flash cards and worksheets. They may order videos and computer programs that promise school readiness.

Let's take a step back and consider the skills children really need to succeed in school. Will 5-year-old Timmy succeed if he can count to 20 by rote on the first day of kindergarten? Or will he stand a better chance of success if he comes with a sense of self-confidence and trust? If he feels curious and creative? If he gets along well with others? If he has self-control and can finish what he starts? If he loves learning?

The truth is that if Timmy has the attitudes and behaviors that foster learning, he will likely learn what he needs to learn in every grade level. More than that, he will likely learn how to succeed in life.

The attitudes and behaviors children most need for school readiness are independence, compassion, trust, creativity, self-control, and perseverance. Our role as teachers is to create an environment where children can develop these traits.

Independence. Children begin learning independence as toddlers. They insist on doing things themselves one minute and wail in frustration the next. They say "no" and "mine" and resist taking a nap even when they can barely hold their eyes open.

Ideally by kindergarten, children are able to take some responsibility for their own success and failure. They discover that their actions have consequences and that they can influence those consequences by their actions. They learn to internalize motivation and don't

Readiness for life

Traits children need for school readiness extend throughout life.

Independence. We act independently when we make informed, competent decisions based on experience, information, and balanced judgment. We are willing to take reasonable risks, and look beyond "how we always do it" to improve a public or personal situation.

Compassion. Compassion enables us to recognize the humanity—and dignity—of all people. It is the characteristic that drives charity, volunteer work, tolerance, and mutual respect.

Trust. Trust allows us to accept our own worth, feel secure with friends, and have a positive, open outlook. We trust when we know the rules, want to abide by them, and expect consequences to certain behaviors.

Creativity. Creativity enables us to think through mental challenges and use negotiation techniques to solve social conflicts. It involves flexibility—not being locked into a routine for its own sake—and an eagerness to search for new answers and solutions.

Self-control. Self-control refers to the ability to think about a behavior and decide whether to act or not. Self-control enables us to be patient with ourselves and others.

Perseverance and resilience. We persevere by overcoming obstacles and solving problems. These qualities help us get to the bottom of the list—getting reports written, sweaters knit, cars manufactured, kitchens cleaned, and grass cut.

Compassion. Infants and toddlers regard themselves as the center of the universe. They are unable to understand the needs of others and can express only their own.

Ideally by kindergarten, children begin to empathize—to put themselves in another's place. Children begin to recognize the strengths and weaknesses of other people—and to share their sorrow or pride.

Encourage the development of compassion in the following ways:

- Talks about feelings. Give a name to pain, fear, anger, and joy, for example.
- Identify and encourage kindnesses, such as when Abby tries to console Abbot when he scrapes his knee.
- Make pet care more than routine by talking about feeling hungry, thirsty, or dirty.
- Encourage cooperative rather than competitive activities. Instead of challenging children to a foot race, plan an obstacle course that requires children to help each other squeeze through a cardboard box, for example.

Trust. When infants and toddlers have consistent, loving care they develop basic trust. They feel they are important members of the family or group and learn they can rely on adults for help in unfamiliar situations. Coupled with a desire for independence, trust enables children to feel the protection and support of adults as they explore, discover, and interpret the environment.

Ideally by kindergarten, children can understand the give-and-take of social situations. They are comfortable with the rules or "ways of doing" that keep them safe. They rely on our consistency to know what is expected of them and are eager to do things the right way.

Encourage the development of trust in the following ways:

- When a baby cries, respond as soon as possible.
- Follow daily routines for eating, play, and naps.
- Establish simple rules and enforce them consistently.
- Treat children fairly, with respect and consideration.
- Provide supervision to prevent biting, bullying, cruel teasing, and other violent behavior.

Creativity. Babies are born curious. They reach for objects and explore them with their mouths and hands. As toddlers, they get into everything and climb into interesting spaces.

Ideally by kindergarten, children are eager to work on and solve their own problems—in art and construction projects, computations, and social interactions. They approach ideas and tasks with initiative, playfulness, and inventive thinking. They ask lots of questions.

have to rely on rewards and praise to find success. They want to practice self-reliance—and show that they don't want or need the constant protection and supervision of adults. Encourage independence in the following ways:

- Give toddlers reasonable choices. "Do you want to read this book or that one?"
- Allow 18-month-old Jennie to use a spoon at mealtime but stand ready to help if she gets frustrated.
- Provide 3- and 4-year-olds with peanut butter, crackers, and plastic knives and let them prepare their own snack.
- Set up learning centers and let children choose activities within them. In the math center, for example, they might sort items by size, fit geometric shapes into a puzzle, or string beads in a pattern.

Encourage creativity in the following ways:

- Provide clay, paints, blocks, and other unstructured materials. Allow children time to explore the material without the need to make an object or paint a picture.
- Focus on the process, not the product. Avoid asking "What is it?" Rather say things like "Looks like you really enjoyed doing that" or "You worked hard on that."
- Ask open-ended questions. Instead of "Did you like the story?" ask "What did you like best about the story?"
- Notice and appreciate children's ideas. "Yes, Juan. We could take apart that old clock and see if we could make it work."
- Avoid rote learning and modeled projects that minimize individuality.

Self-control. Toddlers have little self-control. Ricky, for example, sees a truck and wants it. However, he does not have the intellectual or social skills to consider that Heddy is already playing with it and that he needs to wait for his turn.

Ideally by kindergarten, children understand and accept the need for rules—for their own sake and sake of others in community. They are learning the art of compromise and negotiation and can often see an event from someone else's point of view. Kindergarten children are usually able to identify their own property and respect the belongings of their peers. They are also able to take responsibility for simple tasks, have the self-control to stay focused, and follow through on a commitment.

Encourage self-control in the following ways:

- Model self-restraint. "I feel like eating a big bowl of ice cream right now, but I know I would feel too stuffed to move."
- Offer children choices.
- Consistently enforce simple rules.
- Offer to help children identify and deal with their frustrations. "Your face looks really angry, Jacob. Shall we take some deep breaths before we talk about the problem?"
- Be clear about appropriate and inappropriate ways to express anger. "You can stamp your feet, Hannah, but I can't let you use your feet to kick Hank."

Perseverance and resilience. Toddlers learn to walk only after lots of trials and tumbles. Determination to succeed helps them ignore bumps and falls, and find success. When preschoolers dig canals in the sand, they learn cause and effect—what works and doesn't work.

Ideally by kindergarten, children have experience with problem-solving, brainstorming, and evaluating decisions. They can often use these skills to evaluate what went wrong with a project—and find the courage and determination to try again.

Encourage perseverance and resilience in the following ways:

- Encourage children to finish projects they begin—work a puzzle, build a structure, paint a picture, or play a game before quitting.
- Let children extend their projects over time—a block construction or multi-piece puzzle, for example, could take several days.
- Provide storage space for unfinished art projects.
- Avoid the temptation to do something for, rather than with, a child.
- Teach negotiation skills. "Cole and Bryan, how can you both play with the trike without fighting?"

Independence, compassion, trust, creativity, self-control, and perseverance—these attitudes are the real signs of school readiness. These are also the attitudes children need to grow into successful, competent adults. With these qualities, they will find satisfying jobs, form loving families, and be respected in society.

From *Texas Child Care*, Fall 2002, pp. 40-42. © 2002 by Texas Workforce Commission.

WHAT'S THE DIFFERENCE BETWEEN RIGHT AND WRONG:
UNDERSTANDING HOW CHILDREN THINK

BY SANDRA CROSSER, PH.D.

"No! I can't share," shouted Ernie. Desperation could be heard in his voice as Ernie defensively attempted to gather all 147 blocks into his three-year-old arms. "I NEED them!" he protested. Ernie's sense of fairness—right or wrong—had been violated by a request to share. Is Ernie a selfish, naughty child? Has he been spoiled? Probably not. A more likely explanation is that Ernie is simply thinking and behaving normally in a way that exhibits his emerging sense of morality.

The experts tell us that morality involves thinking, feeling, and acting. Feelings of empathy and altruism and acts of sharing and compassion are coupled to and limited by the individual's cognitive development. How we feel, act, and think about good and bad are all parts of our morality.

A great deal has been written about emergent literacy and emergent numeracy as early childhood educators attempt to create and implement curricula that reflect developmentally appropriate practice in reading and mathematics. The young child is in the process of becoming a reader, a writer, or a mathematician. We try to understand those processes while realizing that they will be ongoing, continuing to develop in varying degrees over the child's lifetime.

In much the same way, preschoolers are emerging into the world of moral thought. How children think about right and wrong may be just as developmental as how children think about letters and numbers. Therefore, it is important to examine the young child's typical developmental progression of moral thought in order better to understand how to link emerging morality to developmentally appropriate practice. This article will focus on the young child's moral thinking. For that purpose, moral thought will be defined as thinking about right and wrong.

Is Taking off Your Hat Indoors a Moral Issue?

It is important to make the distinction between issues of morality and issues of social convention. While moral issues involve concepts such as justice, fairness, and human rights, issues that are conventions involve socially agreed-upon rules that are not moral in nature. Classroom rules such as taking off one's hat indoors, sitting on all four legs of a chair, or limits on the number of children allowed in a play area at any one time are all conventions which involve no moral issue. Even children as young as three years have been able to distinguish between moral and conventional issues (Nucci, 1981; Nucci & Nucci, 1982).

Developmental psychologists advise that it is important for teachers to discriminate between moral issues and issues of convention when dealing with discipline over rule infractions. When a child breaks a rule that is a convention, she is simply to be told that a rule was broken and to stop the action. No lectures, please. If, on the other hand, the infraction involves a moral issue, it is important for an adult to talk with the child about the implications of the action in regard to human rights and fairness. The wrong must be made right so that justice prevails.

Young children think of right and wrong in terms of...

Absolutes. Things are always good or always bad. It is unimportant whether an act was intentional or unintentional.

How much physical damage was done. The greater the damage, the worse the perception of the act.

Whether an act will evoke punishment. If an act will be punished then it is wrong.

Rules. Rules should never be broken. Breaking rules is viewed as wrong.

Their own perspective. Children have difficulty taking another person's view of an issue.

Piaget's View of Moral Development

Jean Piaget was perhaps the first to delve into the thought processes behind children's moral decision-making (Piaget, 1932/1965). While Piaget was not so concerned with what the child decided, he was interested in how the child arrived at the decision. In his wisdom, Piaget observed children playing games, told them stories involving moral dilemmas, and questioned them. He arrived at the conclusion that young children differ from older children in the ways they think about moral issues. The child's individual level of cognitive development, enhanced by informal interactions with other children, determines how the child characteristically thinks about right and wrong. Though Piaget's work was done many years ago, subsequent investigations have generally supported his findings.

Are You a Good Guy or a Bad Guy?

According to Piaget, preschoolers are in a stage called Morality of Constraint. In this stage, children tend to think of right and wrong in black and white terms. That is, an act is always right or always wrong. There are no shades of gray and there is no room to negotiate. People are good people or

people are bad. Good guys are always good and bad guys are always bad.

Typically, the young child will define the rightness or wrongness of an act in terms of whether or not it will evoke punishment. For example, it is wrong to take your brother's toy car because you will have to sit in the time-out chair. There is sure to be punishment, even if there is no one to witness the wrong, because the child in the Morality of Constraint stage believes in imminent justice. Accordingly, the child might believe that she fell and skinned her knee because she told a lie. The child believes justice will be served. There is always a payback.

Children in the Morality of Constraint stage are convinced of the sacred nature of rules. Rules must not be changed, even if they are simply rules for playing a game. However, it is right and fair to ignore rules if they interfere with one's individual benefit. This egocentric focus is termed relativistic hedonism and is evident when Ernie says, "I can't share the blocks. I need them!" However, Ernie would be incensed by the injustice of another child's hoarding of the blocks. Relativistic hedonism enables the child to take from others without feeling guilt because, "I need it." The child is not being bad or immoral. He is simply demonstrating normal moral development.

Step on a Crack, Break Your Mother's Back

The young child's egocentric nature is also evident as she mentally connects her own actions with unrelated events because she is not always accurate in her understanding of cause/effect relationships. Remember the old rhyme, "Step on a crack, break your mother's back"? Didn't we all avoid those cracks in the sidewalk and feel a twinge of guilt when we accidentally stepped on one? The young child's immature concepts of cause/effect relationships may link up with her natural egocentrism for sometimes emotionally devastating feelings of guilt as the child mistakenly blames herself for a divorce, illness, or other catastrophe.

This natural egocentrism is also tied to the preschooler's cognitive difficulty in taking another person's mental perspective, or thinking about how the other person feels. The child in the Morality of Constraint stage typically considers only one perspective... his own. It is not until the child is in elementary school that he can easily put himself in another person's shoes. And it is not until much later that he can comprehend multiple perspectives (Selman, 1980).

How Boys and Girls Differ in Moral Decision-Making

Carol Gilligan, a student of Kohlberg's, took issue with his finding that males tend to think in higher moral stages than do females. Gilligan (1982) embarked on research that led her to conclude that females think about moral issues in a manner that is different from, but not inferior to, males. In resolving moral dilemmas, females are typically less concerned with justice and more concerned with caring and maintaining relationships, even to the point of self-sacrifice.

Gilligan's point can be seen in children's free play. When boys are confronted with a conflict involving fairness they tend to argue it out or take their ball and go home. On the other hand, girls faced with conflict over fairness will try to resolve the issue through compromise. But if compromise fails, girls will generally change the activity rather than disband the group (Cyrus, 1993).

Preschoolers' typical level of cognitive development places other constraints on their moral thinking, as well. They tend to think about the wrongness of an act in terms of how much physical damage has been caused, without regard for whether or not the act was intentional or accidental. If Sammy spills water while trying to clean up the art table, he will be considered naughty regardless of his intention to help. The wrongness of the act is judged in direct proportion to the amount of damage, regardless of motive.

In the same way, it is difficult for the preschooler to understand the concept of an accidental wrong. It may be impossible to convince the young child that a classmate accidentally knocked down her block building or stepped on her toe because the area was crowded (Vasta, Haith & Miller, 1995).

Children in Piaget's Morality of Constraint stage tend to look at adult authority in a manner that is different from children who are a few years older. While older children evaluate whether or not an adult has earned or deserves respect, young children tend to think that it is wrong to disobey an adult simply because the person is an adult. Age and status confer authority. This, of course, is one factor that makes young children so vulnerable to sexual abuse.

How children think about right and wrong may be just as developmental as how children think about letters and numbers.

Kohlberg's View of Moral Development

Several decades after Piaget described his work in the area of children's moral development, a young graduate student, Lawrence Kohlberg, began what would be a lifetime study of human moral development. Defining the concept of morality as justice, or fairness, he asked people to respond to a series of moral dilemmas. Based upon their reasoning, Kohlberg classified moral development into stages, which he believed were invariant and hierarchical. That is, we all pass through the stages in sequence, reaching higher levels of moral thought. However, some of us get stuck somewhere in the progression and never reach the highest levels of moral thinking (Kohlberg, 1984).

Like Piaget, Kohlberg believed that in order to move up the staircase of moral thought, we must possess the cognitive abilities to think about moral issues in more and more abstract ways. That is, cognitive development sets parameters around our ability to reason morally. However, moral development can be facilitated if the person is regularly exposed to reasoning that is slightly higher than the level on which he is thinking. This exposure resolves cognitive conflict and helps moral thinking to advance.

In Kohlberg's scheme, the preschool child is probably judging right and wrong based on the same factors Piaget described earlier. However, Kohlberg expanded the work of Piaget to include three levels: Preconventional, Conventional, and Postconventional. Preconventional and conventional levels of thought pertain to children and are described here. The postconventional level of thought is not described because it is beyond the grasp of children.

Preconventional Thought

When preschool children make moral decisions, Kohlberg would predict that those decisions would be based on avoiding punishment and satisfying one's immediate desires, from an egocentric perspective, and probably on the basis of a whim. This level is called preconventional thought.

Conventional Thought

At the intermediate level, conventional thought, development takes a turn from concern with egocentric morality to consideration for the needs of working and living together. The child begins to think in terms of pleasing others and doing what is helpful. The emphasis is on being a good boy or a good girl. Concern starts to move beyond self-interest to the good of the group. While this level of conventional moral thought is beyond that of most preschool children, it is the level toward which they are growing. According to Kohlberg, children should be exposed to moral thinking at this next higher level in order to facilitate that growth.

Kohlberg's theory remains strong but open to some criticism (Kurtines & Gewirtz, 1995). While the theory appears to hold true for Western culture, some Eastern cultures are not based on the same justice criterion posed by Kohlberg as the ultimate morality (Huebner & Garrod, 1991).

How to Help Children Develop Moral Thought and Action

1. Deal with problems appropriately.

When dealing with discipline problems, determine whether the infraction involves a moral issue or a social convention, and deal with the situation accordingly. If a moral issue is involved, be sure to talk with the child so that she understands the reasons her actions were wrong, lead the child to consider that the other person also has a perspective, and help the child decide how to right the wrong. Use reasoning rather than punishment. "I'm sorry" should be spoken only from the child's heart, never upon command.

2. Allow children to experience moral conflict. Schedule large blocks of free play time so that children may experience natural moral conflicts and practice working out their solutions.

3. Discuss moral dilemmas. Select stories involving moral dilemmas and talk about the perspectives of the various characters. Emphasize that people make mistakes. We are not always good or always bad.

4. Encourage children to change the rules. When playing a favorite game, encourage children to change the rules. Play the game in different ways, emphasizing that if all the players agree, it is OK to change the rules.

5. Involve children in making some classroom rules. Emphasize what is good for the group. Avoid having children decide on punishments because they will most likely prefer harsh, unrealistic punishments that do nothing to change behavior.

6. Encourage dramatic play and role playing. Dramatic play and role play enable children to stand in another person's shoes and promote the development of perspective-taking.

7. Explore the concept of intention and motive. Use stories and puppet skits. Discuss the character's motivations. Did Goldilocks try to break the Little Bear's chair? Why did it break? How did Little Bear feel? What could Goldilocks do to help Little Bear feel better?

8. Praise moral behavior. Make it a point to comment on the helpful nature of an act that promotes or assists other individuals within the group. Praise children for putting the needs of the group ahead of their own needs. Recognize children for being kind, fair, and helpful.

9. Use real dilemmas. Use real dilemmas and concrete classroom situations to discuss moral issues. Avoid the use of fables and maxims as they are too abstract for young children to comprehend fully.

Conclusion

Because young children are emerging moral thinkers constrained by their cognitive characteristics, the early childhood curriculum should provide opportunities for children to deal with moral issues and think about right and wrong in developmentally appropriate ways. Preschool teachers can promote children's moral development by dealing with issues of fairness, justice, human rights, and caring. In addition, the teacher who understands normal moral development will be aware of the reasons young children sometimes appear to be selfish and will recognize opportunities to promote the development of moral thinking in ways that match the child's cognitive level of functioning.

References

1. Cyrus, V. (1993). *Experiencing race, class, and gender in the United States.* Mountain View, CA: Mayfield Publishing Company.

2. Gilligan, C. (1982). *In a different voice: Psychological theory and women's development.* Cambridge, MA: Harvard University Press.

3. Huebner, a. & Garrod, a. (1991). Equilibration and the learning paradox. *Human Development, 34,* 261–272.

4. Kohlberg, L. (1984). *Essays on moral development, Volume II: The psychology of moral development.* San Francisco, CA: Harper & Row.

5. Kurtines, W. & Gewirtz, J. (Eds.) (1995). *Moral development: An introduction.* Boston: Allyn and Bacon.

6. Nucci, L. (1981). The Development of Personal Concepts: A Domain Distinct from Moral or Societal Concepts. *Child Development, 52,* 114–121.

7. Nucci, L. & Nucci, M. (1982). Children's Responses to Moral and Social Conventional Transgressions in Free Play Settings. *Child Development, 53,* 1337–1342.

8. Piaget, J. (1932/1965). *The moral judgment of the child.* (M. Gabain, Trans.) New York: Free Press. (Originally published 1932.)

9. Selman, R. (1980). *The growth of interpersonal understanding: Developmental and clinical analysis.* New York: Academic Press.

10. Vasta, R.; Haith, M.; & Miller, S. (1995). *Child psychology: A modern science.* New York: John Wiley & Sons, Inc.

Sandra Crosser, Ph.D., is a Professor at Ohio Northern University, Ada, Ohio.

From *Earlychildhood News,* May/June 2002, pp. 12-16. © 2002 by Excelligence Learning Corporation. Reprinted by permission.

The Role of Emotional Competence in the Development of the Young Child

BY RUTH WILSON, PH.D.

Jeremy and Maria are busy experimenting at the water table in Jodie Snell's preschool classroom. While Jeremy plays with funnels, cups, and an eyedropper, Maria floats small pieces of bark. Meredith walks over to join Jeremy and Maria, but she trips and falls as she approaches the table. Her arm hits the side of the water table and she begins to cry.

As Meredith gets up from her fall, Maria pushes her hard and almost knocks her down again. Then Maria yells at Meredith and tells her to go away. Jeremy, concerned about Meredith and the ensuing fight, calls Ms. Snell for help. He then tells Maria to stop hitting Meredith.

What Is Emotional Competence

There may be a number of reasons why Maria and Jeremy respond so differently to Meredith's "intrusion" at the water table. Some research, however, suggests that their reactions may be related to their different levels of emotional development and competence (Garner & Estep, 2001; Denham, 2001). Jeremy realizes that Meredith may have hurt herself during her fall and is concerned about her feelings. Maria, however,

doesn't even notice Meredith's distress and focuses only on protecting her own play space.

In terms of emotional development, Jeremy's response suggests competence in several related skills. He's aware of Meredith's feelings and expresses sensitivity to her plight. By calling to the teacher for help and telling Maria to stop hitting, he also actively intervenes to help Meredith in this stressful situation. In other words, Jeremy demonstrates skill in recognizing the feelings of others and responding appropriately to others in distress. In this way, he seems to be more emotionally competent than Maria. This article will discuss the four types of emotional competence, examine competence and behavior, and offer suggestions for guiding young children in the development of emotional competence.

Emotional Competence Versus Social-Emotional Development

While social-emotional development was at one time viewed as a single developmental domain, emotional competence is now being recognized as an area of development that is separate from, yet related to social competence (Garner & Estep, 2001). Emotional competence, as

an area of child development, "has long been underrated in both psychology and early childhood education, but no longer" (Denham, 2001, p. 6). New understandings about the impact of emotional competence to other areas of development are emerging. For example, we're learning that "when developmental milestones of emotional competence are not negotiated successfully, children are at risk, both at the time and later in life" (Denham, 2001, p. 5). Related areas of concern include behavioral difficulties, the development of a sense of well-being (Denham, 2001), and the ability to learn (Roffey & O'Reirdan, 2001). Emotionally competent children know how to vary their behavior to correspond with the thoughts, feelings, and situations of those around them. They are also less likely to be involved in angry disputes with peers and to use constructive strategies in response to potentially conflicting situations. We saw this in the case of Jeremy and Maria.

Types of Emotional Competence

Research on emotional competence suggests that there are four different types of emotional competence: situation knowledge, explanations of emotions, positivity of emotional expression, and emotional intensity (Garner & Estep, 2001). Situation knowledge and explanations of emotions represent children's knowledge of emotions, which can be defined as an awareness of one's own and others' emotions. Children who have developed knowledge of emotions can usually: 1) infer the thoughts and feelings of others, 2) justify their own behavior to peers, and 3) express sensitivity to the emotions of others. The other two types of emotional competence—positivity of emotional expression and emotional intensity—focus on children's expressivity. Expressivity refers to how emotions, both positive and negative, are expressed. Emotionally competent children are able to modulate emotional expressions and behavior (Garner & Estep, 2001), while children lacking such competence tend to be more explosive and demonstrative in expressing how they feel.

To help young children grow in emotional competence, early childhood educators should be aware of the four different areas of this developmental domain and have an understanding of related social implications. The following discussion provides a brief overview of each of these areas.

Situation Knowledge

Situaiton knowledge relates to children's understanding of contextual clues that can be used to infer the cause of an emotional display. Situation knowledge also relates to children's decisions about how to respond to emotionally charged situations. Children who are knowledgeable about emotions tend to have fewer negative exchanges with peers and, when disagreements do occur, they seem better able to use reasoned arguments to resolve conflicts than children who are not knowledgeable about emotions (Garner & Estep, 2001). Therefore, it is not surprising to find that children high in emotional knowledge experience a greater number of positive peer interactions than other children (Garner & Estep, 2001).

Explanations of Emotions

Children's ability to talk about the causes and consequences of others' emo-

tions falls under the explanations of emotions category. Such emotional discourse skills are often used to negotiate conflicts and misunderstandings with peers. Children's discussions about different emotions also provide a constructive way to convey their own feelings and to elicit feedback about those feelings. Research studies indicate that young children's ability to talk about emotions leads to greater peer-rated likeability and ease in initiating social contact and having others initiate contact with them (Denham, 2001).

Positivity of Emotional Expression

Positivity of emotional expression deals with emotion management skills. Such skills are used to initiate and maintain peer interactions, to offer comfort, and to minimize negative interactions. Related research indicates that children who have difficulty managing the expression of emotion are less likely to respond appropriately during highly charged negative interactions with peers than other children (Garner & Estep, 2001).

Emotional Intensity

The ability to control the expression of emotion describes the emotional intensity category. Examples of items on a questionnaire used by Garner and Estep (2001) to assess emotional intensity include: 1) "This child shows strong reactions to things, both positive and negative," and 2) "The child reacts strongly (cries or complains) to a disappointment or failure." In the case of Maria, we saw a strong reaction to a situation, suggesting a high level of emotional intensity on her part. Emotionally competent children tend to have greater control over the intensity of how they express their emotions.

Social and Other Developmental Implications

It seems obvious that children who are knowledgeable about their emotions and who can control the expression of emotion have a better chance of being successful in negotiating complex interpersonal exchanges with their peers

than children who are not as emotionally competent. Current research supports this hypothesis and found, for example, that emotional competence plays an important role in establishing and maintaining satisfying peer relationships (Garner & Estep, 2001). In the research, children who were adept at understanding expressive and situational cues of emotion were more popular with their peers than other children. Children who were deficient in emotional knowledge often misinterpreted social and emotional cues. Such misinterpretations interfered with their ability to initiate and maintain positive social interactions with peers.

Certain aspects of children's emotional competence, then, are considered to be prerequisites or "fundamental supports" for their growing social competence (Denham, 2001). The lack of emotional competence, on the other hand, tends to "promote spiraling difficulties" in children's ability to interact and form relationships with others (Denham, 2001, p. 6). A close connection between emotions and behavior also seems fairly obvious. Emotions tend to regulate both inter- and intrapersonal behaviors, and the literature on behavior disorders repeatedly addresses emotional factors (Denham, 2001).

As previously stated, there is also a connection between children's emotional competence and their ability to learn and be successful in a classroom setting. Research studies have shown that deficiencies in the area of emotional competence include disruptive behaviors and poor school performance (Roffey & O'Reirdan, 2001; Shields, Dickstein, Seifer, Giusti, Magee, & Spritz, 2001). Children who are unable to monitor and modulate their emotional arousal usually find it very difficult or impossible to maintain an optimal level of engagement within the school context (Shields, et al., 2001). They tend to have trouble adjusting to classroom structure, complying with rules and limits, and negotiating cooperative relationships with their peers. As a result, children who are able to control the expression of emotions in the classroom are more likely to perform better on cognitive tasks than other children (Garner & Estep, 2001).

Other research studies found that pre-schoolers' emotion regulation at the start of the school year was associated with school adjustment at year's end, whereas early emotional liability predicted poorer outcomes (Shields, et al., 2001). Such findings support school-based interventions, which will be discussed in detail below.

Helping Young Children Develop Emotional Competence

To appropriately guide young children in the development of emotional competence, teachers need to be aware of related expectations at different stages of development. A list of skills and abilities that can be expected of most preschool children who are developing emotionally at an optimum rate may be helpful. These skills and abilities, as developed by Roffey and O'Reirdan (2001), include:

- Being enthusiastic and motivated to learn
- Experiencing a wide range of feelings (but not necessarily able to identify them clearly)
- Being aware of feelings and able to relate these to wants
- Using a range of varied, complex and flexible ways of expressing emotions
- Using language for emotional control and expression
- Having increasing emotional control (but not able to hide feelings completely)
- Using play to work out emotional issues
- Demonstrating a growing sensitivity to the feelings of others
- Caring for and about pets and younger children
- Comforting distressed peers
- Identifying what is right and wrong in relation to family and cultural values
- Testing behavioral boundaries from time to time.

Recommended Children's Literature for Fostering Emotional Competence

Young children can feel overwhelmed by their emotions. At times, they may even be frightened by the power of their emotions. Carefully selected children's books can be used to help young children understand different emotions and ways of expressing their feelings in appropriate ways. The following list represents a small sample of the many books you can use to help children grow in emotional competence.

Anholt, C. and Anholt, L. (1994). *Makes Me Happy*. Cambridge, MA: Candlewick Press. A question and answer format is used to talk about different feelings (including being scared, sad, shy, excited, mad, proud, and jealous). While the answers as to what causes these different feelings vary from individual to individual, the book ends with a statement about what makes us all happy (such as playing in the sun, singing a song, and being together).

Anholt, C. and Anholt, L. (1991). *What I Like*. New York: Putnam's Sons. Different ideas about what individual children like and dislike are presented in this book. While one theme of the story is that we all have different tastes, another theme focuses on the idea that most of us feel the same about some things in life (such as friends).

Baker, L. (2001). *I Love You Because You're You*. New York: Scholastic. This book describes in rhyming text a mother's love for her child through all kinds of moods and behaviors. At different times, the child is sad, sleepy, frisky, silly, happy, and frightened—and through it all the mother's love remains constant.

Evans, L. (1999). *Sometimes I Feel Like a Storm Cloud*. Greenvale, NY: Mondo Publishing. *Sometimes I Feel Like a Storm Cloud* is about a child who describes how it feels to experience a variety of emotions. Different similes are used to describe the wide-ranging ups and downs of childhood: there's the rain cloud ready to burst into a shower of tears; a balloon that grows larger and larger with excitement and then becomes deflated as the air woooshes away; there's winter snow which is silent, cold, and alone; and there's a tornado that goes around bashing and smashing things to the ground.

Leonard, M. (1999). *Scared*. Lake Forest, IL: Forest House Publishing. *Scared* is an interactive book focusing on different things that scare some children, including the dark, thunder, bugs, strange dogs, and climbing up high. The text invites readers to identify some of the things that scare them. The text also offers some suggestions for dealing with fears, such as learning more about what scares you and talking to parents when you are scared. A special introductory page, written for adults, offers suggestions on how to encourage further discussion about things that children fear. It also presents several ideas for follow-up activities. *Scared* is one of four books in a "How I Feel" series published by Forest House Publishing Co. (P.O. Box 738, Lake Forest, IL 60045–0738. 1–800–394–READ). The other three titles in the series are *Angry, Happy,* and *Silly*.

Modesitt, J. (1992). *Sometimes I Feel Like a Mouse*. New York: Scholastic. Animal images are used to represent different feelings in this wonderful book. There's the shy mouse, the bold elephant, the happy canary, the scared rabbit, the excited squirrel, etc. The book ends with an important statement about feelings—that is, that everyone has feelings and that there is no such thing as a right or wrong feeling. The book encourages children to listen to their own feelings and to be comfortable with the idea that we have many different feelings.

As in other areas of development, intervention should start with prevention and a focus on building strengths. As Denham (2001) states, "We owe our children more than a mere lack of disorder, more than averting tragedy. We need to study not just weakness, but also strength, not just fixing what is broken, but nurturing what is best within our children" (p. 5). Preventive interventions are based on the premise that teachers can play a key role in fostering children's emotional competence (Denham, 2001). Examples of specific interventions include coaching students in areas such as recognizing emotions, coping with frustrating situations, understanding different situations, and developing perspective-taking skills (Shields, et al., 2001).

While "coaching" interventions (which tend to be somewhat didactic) have proven effective, studies examining teachers' naturally occurring influences indicate that preschoolers' secure emotional attachments to their teachers also impact children's display of emotions in school. Preschool children who develop secure attachments to their teachers are less likely to engage in unregulated anger and behavior problems. They are also more likely to exhibit positive emotions in the school setting (Shields, et al,

2001). A warm, close relationship between student and teacher, then, can positively influence young children's emerging emotional competence.

While theory strongly supports a "prevention-first" approach to fostering emotional competence, research indicates a lack of curricular attention to this area of development. "In the majority of preschool contexts ... emotion socialization does not have an easily defined place in the curriculum, and emotional issues are likely to receive sustained attention from school personnel only during crisis situations" (Shields et al., 2001, p. 90). For a more preventive approach, teachers should act as "emotion coaches" and models in even routine situations during an average school day (Shields et al., 2001). They recommend that teachers use the everyday situations in the classroom to help children identify emotions and develop effective coping skills.

There are many naturally-occurring opportunities for children to learn how to deal with the frustration of mastering a new academic skill, how to negotiate the complex behaviors involved in sharing and cooperative interactions with peers, and how to manage angry feelings when limits are placed on their behaviors. While teachers should certainly capital-

ize on these naturally-occurring situations, they should also consider the importance of establishing strong relationships with young children as a vehicle for fostering emotional competence.

Ruth Wilson, Ph.D., is a Professor Emeritus of Special Education at Bowling Green State University in Ohio. Dr. Wilson's expertise is early childhood special education, and much of her research has focused on early childhood environmental education. She retired from teaching and now devotes much of her time to writing.

References

Denham, S.A. (2001). Dealing with feelings: Foundations and consequences of young children's emotional competence. *Early Education and Development,* 12(1), 5–9.

Garner, P.W. & Estep, K.M. (2001). Emotional competence, emotion socialization, and young children's peer-related social competence. *Early Education & Development,* 12(1) 29–46.

Roffey, S.A. O'Reirdan, T. (2001). *Young children and classroom behavior.* London: David Fulton Publishers.

Shields, A.; Dickstein, S.; Seifer, R.; Giusti, L.; Magee, K.D.; & Spritz, B. (2001). Emotional competence and early school adjustment: a study of preschoolers at risk. *Early Education & Development,* 12(1), 73–90.

Encouraging Fathers to Participate in the School Experiences of Young Children: The Teacher's Role

Barry B. Frieman and Terry R. Berkeley

INTRODUCTION

Female teachers share the gender experience with the mothers of their students and as such they have some insight into how other women have developed into the role of mother. It is not as easy for female teachers, the overwhelming majority of early childhood educators, to relate to fathers. Teachers can maximize the participation of fathers in the school experiences of young children by understanding how men learn what it means to be a father, being sensitive to working fathers, trying to involve absent fathers, and encouraging positive parenting skills.

LEARNING HOW TO FATHER

Fathers, like mothers, do not start out with all the insights and skills needed to be an effective parent. Many begin with the first model they see, which is the behavior of their own parent. Using one's own fathering as a template for behavior can be growth enhancing or potentially destructive.

Teachers can play a key role by understanding that many fathers have not learned positive skills from their own fathers and by providing fathers with information about positive fathering. A teacher cannot assume that all men know how to father, just as they cannot assume that all women know how to mother. Many men have grown up with deficient models or absence of models of fathering in their families....

Teachers cannot assume that men know how to father. They can help by making educational materials about fathering available. Newsletters can include a column about fathering as well as one about mothering. The columns can be written by a male faculty member, counselor, or administrator with a female counterpart, preferably a father and a mother, or they can be reprinted from one of the many Internet sites that include material on fathering, mothering, and parenting. Even if parents are divorced, school personnel should send the newsletter, via mail if necessary, to the noncustodial parent.

Teachers can lobby with their school counselors to run an "informational" group for fathers, who are either custodial or noncustodial. These groups can help fathers explore their feelings about fathering with a skilled facilitator. Counselors will have a better chance of recruiting fathers to participate if the group is labeled as "educational" rather than a group "to share feelings" (Frieman, 1994).

Teachers need to be cautious when asking children to get information from their fathers. A child with a noncustodial father can often talk to his parent on the telephone, but children with absent fathers are put in a very embarrassing position when asked about their fathers.

WORK AND FATHERING

The traditional role of the father is that of the provider of the family. Fathers thought of their role as working hard to provide their children with the financial means to buy the necessities of life (LaRossa, 1997). Many men grew up with fathers who made sure that work obligations were satisfied, often at the expense of child obligations (McKenry, Price, Gordon, & Rudd, 1986). Men of the twenty-first century who want to place their child first and their work second are facing the reality that working women have had to deal with for decades. It is not easy, and often people have to make hard choices between their children and their careers.

Some men and women have no choice. Those working lower on the career ladder are faced with the ultimatum of "show up for work or lose your job." These parents often figure out ways to spend time with their children when they are out of work. Often, this might mean giving up personal time and devoting significant time outside of work to being with one's children....

People in professions are more likely to have choices about work hours. As college professors, the authors of this article have more flexible schedules. For example, one can teach at night and have a few hours during the afternoon to watch a field hockey game, or one can work late or on weekends to make up time that has been spent with children. However, even in the professions fathers may be faced with conflicts....

Teachers should be able to make provision for fathers who cannot take time off from work to be involved in their child's school experience. One way to do this is to have flexible times for fathers to visit the school. A pot of coffee brewing early in the morning can lure a father to drop his child off at school a few minutes early and stay for a cup of coffee and discuss his child's schooling and development. Other possibilities include making sure fathers know that they are important by providing time to speak with fathers either in person or communicating via e-mail or telephone. Also, teachers and administrators can make time to communicate to fathers via letters and newsletters (paper or electronic) that they are very welcome in their children's schooling, not just relegated only to special projects involving manual labor.

Working fathers would also benefit from early morning or late afternoon or evening conference hours so they could keep connected with their child's education. Fathers with flexible schedules could be invited to school to have lunch with their child or to share some time reading to a child's class, or tutor children in their child's class.

Anton found that he could not attend his daughter's evening violin concert at her elementary school. When he told this to his daughter's teacher, she invited Anton to come to the special day program that was presented to the other children in the school so he would still be able to see the performance. He was the only parent there. Because of the teacher's actions, he was able to watch his daughter play.

Teachers could also provide fathers with a list of low-cost weekend educational activities. Lists of suggested field trips, such as an excursion to the library, along with a list of possible books to read together, are particularly appreciated by fathers who see their children only during scheduled visitations. Suggested lists of good educational toys could be given to fathers to aid in birthday and holiday gift giving.

ABSENT FATHERS

It is an unfortunate fact that many fathers choose not to make themselves a part of the lives of their children....

Fathers can be physically absent from the home for reasons of divorce, remarriage, military service, incarceration, or work that requires travel. Some fathers although physically present are emotionally absent from their children. This includes the father who lives in the same home as his children but never emotionally connects with them. Other men choose to be both physically and emotionally absent from their children, have children and, then, take no interest in fathering. Often, these are the men or boys who have children but do not intend to live with the child's mother and their child as a family. They might occasionally visit their children or provide them with money, but they don't take part in the process of fathering. They are fathers in title only (Frieman, 2000).

Teachers can help children with absent fathers by involving males to serve as role models in the classroom, arranging for services for physically absent or noncustodial fathers, and altering the curriculum to make it male friendly (Frieman, 2000). Female teachers, aware that children need males in their lives, can involve surrogate "fathers" in the classroom lives of father-absent children. Volunteers can come from the ranks of retired

community members or volunteers from civic organizations. Of course, great care must be taken to ensure that any person entering the classroom to work with children is safe. Criminal background checks are one way to ensure that volunteers will do no harm to children. Male volunteers, similar to classroom helpers, will first have to be trained in how to relate appropriately to young children.

Routine phone calls reporting positive behaviors of their children, newsletters mailed home, and report cards mailed home are other ways to ensure that noncustodial fathers are involved in the school process. Children's books and stories used in the classroom can also help to present fathering in a positive light to children who have no active fathers. Many books present positive images of men and confront issues involving absent fathers. This literature represents the great diversity found in today's schools.

TEACHING POSITIVE PARENTING SKILLS

Teachers can play an important role in teaching positive parenting skills to all fathers. Some important issues that fathers need to learn are how to praise their children, how to put their children's needs first, and how to deal with mistakes.

Praising Children

Fathers need to learn how to give their children praise for accomplishments. It is easy to be supportive of a child when she or he does something so spectacular that others acknowledge the child's accomplishments. But it is just as important for a father to praise his children when they do ordinary things. The key is to let the child own the accomplishment and all of the resulting praise. Bill's story illustrates this point.

> After a wonderful singing performance by my daughter, one of the people in the audience came up to me and said, "Congratulations! She was wonderful." I replied, "Yes, I know. She works very hard at her music and deserves a great deal of credit for what she has accomplished."

Bill recognized that his daughter deserved the praise and not him. Similarly, when his younger daughter led her field hockey team to the playoffs, Bill quickly pointed out to other parents who congratulated him that it was his daughter who deserved the recognition for her hard work and leadership.

After each of his son's high school football games, Rodney would meet his coworker, Sam, very early before work for coffee. During this session, he would proudly give his colleague a complete description of his son's hard work and actions on the field, noting that he was proud of his son but was clear that the accomplishments belonged to his son.

Learning to praise their children might not be a natural thing to do for all fathers. Teachers can help fathers learn the appropriate responses to their child's victories and appropriate responses to other child actions. This can be modeled by praising daily "victories" that all children have in school when speaking to the child's father. An occasional phone call home or e-mail to the father to report that the child performed well, or worked especially hard during the day, can be helpful. In this way fathers can see a model that praises desirable behavior.

Ms. Rogers, a fifth-grade teacher, gave fathers a few file cards and asked them as they watched their child participate in the school play to note everything that their child did that was positive. Fathers were encouraged to write down these things and share them with their child after the performance. This exercise helped teachers to train fathers to look for the good in their own children.

Putting Children's Needs First

Many things that men need to learn in order to become more effective fathers run counter to the way men are normally socialized, especially being socialized to think that fathers are the most important members of the household. Particularly when a father has younger children and has to make a choice between whose needs get met—his or his child's—he needs to learn to value the child's needs above his own. The situations of two fathers illustrate this point:

Harry came home after a particularly hard day at work. He was physically exhausted having spent the day doing hard work. He wanted nothing more to enjoy the dinner his wife was making that night and then lie down and rest. As soon as he walked in the door, his first-grade daughter jumped on him and excitedly reminded him that this evening was the school skating party and that she would have a chance to have a special skate with her dad. Harry forgot about how tired he was and concentrated on how excited his daughter was to go skating with him.

Paul recalled, "At two in the morning I received a phone call from my daughter noting that she was stuck at a club in town and needed a ride home." The fact that he was tired did not matter. Most important to him was that his daughter called him and knew that he would be there for her. These fathers have placed their children's needs as first as a "way of life." They saw it as a regular part of fathering.

Weekly newsletters can highlight important events to children. A first-grade teacher, for example, sent a letter home announcing the annual parent-child "Olympics" in the school gym. Also with the announcement, she wrote a note home letting parents know how important the event was to their child and noting to fathers that their children were excited about participating together with their fathers. After the event all fathers who attended were issued a special "badge," which recognized their contributions to the school by attending the event. Fathers who attended other events and contributed to the classroom were also recognized in the school newsletter. Another teacher contacted the local community newspaper and had them write an article about the contributions that fathers were making to her classroom.

Concerned that some fathers might not be able to attend the traditional Thanksgiving lunch, one teacher in a neighborhood in which most of the men worked in the same factory contacted the factory manager and asked if the company would donate 1 hour of time so the men would be able to extend their lunch hour to be with their children. There were benefits to the students, the fathers, the school, and the factory.

Making Mistakes

Many men have a hard time accepting the fact that they can make mistakes in their fathering or parenting. Fathers may feel their authority is compromised if they back down from a decision. This is not true. Children respect a father who makes mistakes and corrects them, and they have greater respect for fathers who are this honest and sensitive with them.

Most caring men have done their share of insensitive things as fathers. Speaking as fathers ourselves, we usually figure out pretty quickly that we have made mistakes from the reactions of our children. When we make mistakes, we have learned to apologize and to ask our children what we could do next time to make sure that things work out differently. We also try to forgive ourselves. It is easy to berate oneself for making a mistake, but it serves no purpose. As fathers we try to learn from our mistakes. A parent is continually learning. The fact that fathering is a developmental process has allowed us to be even more excited about our children, about fathering, and about our growth as individuals.

When necessary, a father has to put his pride on the shelf and think of his child first. One might have to accept verbal abuse from someone in order to protect one's child. Divorced fathers have to maintain a business-like co-parenting relationship with their former wives, even if pride gets in the way when dealing with the "other" parent. Also, fathers should stay focused on the importance of protecting their children physically and psychologically. If it means getting psychologically punched, a father needs to take that punch rather than let it land on one's child. It is important to take the time to listen, to admit mistakes, to find better ways to do things, and then, to acknowledge to one's child how what they have said has been helpful to them.

Teachers must work to protect the pride of fathers by giving divorced fathers the chance to deal with the school independently of their former wives (Frieman, 1998). By understanding that one's pride might get in the way of involvement, teachers need to treat divorced fathers as if they were single parents, providing them with all information about their child independent of that given to mothers. This does not mean a teacher gets in the middle of parents; rather, the teacher offers information to each parent just to be sure everyone is appropriately informed.

CONCLUSION

If teachers, especially female teachers, understand the uniqueness of fathers, they will be better able to increase father involvement in their child's educational experience. By understanding the unique paths to fatherhood that many men take, teachers will be better able to engage fathers as allies in the educational experiences of their children. The benefits of such understanding will accrue to fathers, their children, their teachers, and the school community in which all participate.

REFERENCES

Frieman, B. B. (1994). Children of divorced parents: Action steps for the counselor to involve fathers. *Elementary School Guidance and Counseling, 28,* 197–205.

Frieman, B. B. (1998). What early childhood educators need to know about divorced fathers. *Early Childhood Education Journal, 25,* 239–241.

Frieman, B. B. (2000). *What teachers need to know about children at risk.* Boston: McGraw-Hill.

LaRossa, R. (1997). *The modernization of fatherhood: A social and political history.* Chicago: University of Chicago Press.

McKenry, P., Price, S., Gordon, P., & Rudd, N. (1986). Characteristics of husbands' family work and wives' labor force involvement. In R. Lewis & R. Salt (Eds.), *Men in families* (pp. 73–84). Beverly Hills, CA: Sage.

Barry B. Frieman and Terry R. Berkeley are from the Department of Early Childhood Education, Towson University.

Correspondence should be directed to Barry B. Frieman, Department of Early Childhood Education, Towson University, 8000 York Road, Towson, MD 21252; e-mail: bfrieman@towson.edu.

From *Early Childhood Education Journal,* Spring 2002, pp. 209-213. © 2002 by Early Childhood Education Journal.

Developing High-Quality Family Involvement Programs in Early Childhood Settings

Lorenza DiNatale

> **Tell me, I'll forget. Show me, I may remember. But involve me, and I'll understand.**

These words, paraphrased from Confucius, form the motto of the Even Start Program at Cane Run School in Louisville, Kentucky. Educators have long understood the primary role of parents in the physical, moral, and emotional development of their young children. More recently, they have also acknowledged the importance of families' involvement in the education of their children.

When parents are involved, they have a better understanding of their role as their child's primary educators. Moreover, parents and teachers get to know and learn from each other, which results in children receiving more individual attention and curricula becoming more rich and varied.

Although I use the word *parent* in this article, I recognize that family members and other adults also hold responsibility for raising a child. Therefore, references to parents should be construed to include any adults who play an important role in a child's development and upbringing.

The need for strong partnerships

Many preschool and primary teachers understand the vital role parents play and the need for developing strong partnerships with families. Parents are the primary teachers and nurturers of their children. They provide appropriate environments and interactions that promote learning and help their children develop the skills and values needed to become healthy and successful adults. Two of the main purposes of an early childhood program are to support and strengthen the parent in this role and to provide the foundation for a family's ongoing involvement in their child's education.

NAEYC's revised statement on developmentally appropriate practice states that programs should support strong ties between child and family (Bredekamp & Copple 1997). Head Start is a national, federally funded, community-based program for children from families with low incomes and their parents. Head Start grantees are required to develop goals for children in collaboration with families and to involve parents in making decisions about both education and program management.

Research findings

Decades of research have shown that one of the most accurate predictors of achievement in school is not family income or parents' education level, but the extent to which parents believe they can be key resources in their children's education and become involved at school and in the community (Henderson & Berla 1994; Lewis & Henderson 1997;

Powell 1998). Parent involvement in education benefits not only children and parents, but also teachers and overall program quality. When parent involvement is strong, teachers and program administrators are more likely to experience improvement in self-esteem, have higher morale, feel more job satisfaction, and hold greater respect for their profession (Epstein et al. 2002). Schools and programs with a high degree of consistent and meaningful parent involvement usually outperform similar programs without family involvement. Such schools tend to have more support from families and more respect in the community (Cavarretta 1998; Hatch 1998).

> **One of the most accurate predictors of achievement in school is the extent to which parents believe they can be key resources in their children's education and become involved at school and in the community.**

In this technological age, we are all realizing how the school, the home, and the community are connected to each other and to the world at large. Kibel and Stein-Seroussi (1997) believe that a community can truly exist only when its members acknowledge their importance to each other, come together, and identify themselves by joint efforts to achieve mutual goals. An early childhood program is a community of families, teachers, and neighborhood residents accepting mutual responsibility for sustaining and enhancing relationships that promote children's success.

Basics of Family Involvement

Recruit volunteers. Provide parents with calendars listing special events or classroom projects, so they can plan ahead—and take off work, if necessary—for specific days and times to volunteer during the month.

Make volunteers feel welcome. Create a special place for parents to put their belongings. Greet volunteers as they enter the classroom and introduce them to the children.

Plan ways to involve volunteers. Survey parents about their interests and talents. Match volunteer assignments to parent interests when possible. Develop job descriptions that outline and clarify volunteer responsibilities.

Supervise volunteers. Set aside a regular time to talk to volunteers in person, on the phone, or through e-mail each week to plan and evaluate activities. Provide positive feedback and encouragement, and discuss concerns as they arise.

Steps to establishing quality parent involvement programs

If research has found that educators and parents agree that collaboration can be effective and beneficial and bring added resources to the classroom, then why are there not more successful parent involvement programs in early childhood settings? Barriers range from teachers' concerns over the ability of parents to maintain confidentiality to not knowing how to effectively recruit, use, or supervise volunteers. Parents often feel they do not have the time to volunteer or do not know what they can do to help. Teachers often feel they do not have the time to

prepare activities for volunteers. Although time and planning are needed to begin a program, the long-term results are well worth the initial investment.

Assessing needs

Establishing a successful family involvement program begins with assessing your program's volunteer needs. Develop a short survey or meet with other staff to determine where, besides the classroom (for example, the office, the kitchen, on the bus, the playground, at home), parents can make contributions and in what ways.

Planning for success

If you do not have a parent/volunteer coordinator on staff, work with the program administrator to seek the assistance of a volunteer coordinator from the local school district or another professional with a background in developing volunteer programs. This person could provide workshops or consultation on the basics of creating and maintaining a successful family involvement program (see "Basics" at left).

A first step in building a bridge between the culture at home and the one at school is for parents and teachers to talk often and get to know and understand each other's perspectives, behaviors, and interactions.

Supporting cultural differences

Early childhood programs reflect the racial, ethnic, and cultural diversity of our society. When designing parent involvement programs that are inclusive of all families and respectful of cultural differences, it is important to consider parents' views of their children's development and behavior as well as their own roles and responsibilities as parents. A first step in building a bridge between the culture at home and the one at school is for parents and teachers to talk often and get to know and understand each other's perspectives, behaviors, and interactions. Teachers can ask parents how the

school can complement a family's beliefs and values rather than always expecting parents to adapt. Translators—friends, family members, or even other parents who are native speakers—can help foster communication if necessary.

Policies and practices should promote respect and appreciation for the cultures of all children and families.

Policies and practices should promote respect and appreciation for the cultures of all children and families. One way to show respect is to ask parents to help create signs that hang on each entrance of the school and each classroom that say "Welcome" in all the languages spoken by families in the program. Written materials for families should be translated into languages spoken at home. Holiday celebrations should likewise be respectful and inclusive of the cultures of all families.

Respect for differences should be part of the planning and implementation of volunteer experiences. Some cultures prize cooperation and obedience within the group more than competition or individual achievement. Teachers should respect all parents' cultural values.

Orientation is the key

A well-planned orientation eases anxiety and confusion, alleviates fears, and increases the chances of parents maintaining a long-term relationship with the program. Orientation sets the tone and helps create the environment in which families will participate. An effective orientation familiarizes the parent or community member with the school's facilities and staff, the program's philosophy and curriculum, and relevant policies and procedures on confidentiality, discipline, and attendance, as outlined in a family handbook. Orientation should focus on volunteer job descriptions and expectations, how volunteers are supervised, and how volunteers should check in and record their hours, as required by Head Start.

INVOLVING PARENTS AT THE CENTER

Teachers and administrators know that the selection of toys and materials and the way the early childhood environment is organized are designed to accomplish the goals of the curriculum and enhance the child's social, emotional, cognitive, and physical development. It is important for parents to understand this as well and to know how their interactions with children in each area of the classroom facilitate learning and development. Here are some ways parent volunteers can support children in the classroom and outdoors.

Art

- Sit at the table and offer help, as needed, to children using scissors, glue, or clay.
- Talk to children about their artwork and show an interest in their creations.
- Help children write their names on their work.
- Replace paper at the easel and help children put on and take off smocks.
- Help children develop sensory abilities by exploring the concepts of color, pattern, texture, size, and shape.

Woodworking

- Show children the proper and safe way to use materials.
- Make sure children wear safety goggles and follow safety rules.
- Supervise the use of tools.
- Help children pound nails, steady a piece of wood, or hold a saw or hammer.

Blocks

- Help children start a building project and then encourage them to complete it on their own.
- Allow children to knock down their own buildings but not those of others.
- Help children explore basic math concepts such as *larger* and *smaller* and skills such as counting and grouping.

Dramatic play

- Join in the children's play, if invited, and make comments or ask questions to expand the play.
- Help children learn self-help skills such as grasping, snapping, buttoning, zipping, and tying so they can put on and take off clothes.
- Help children group objects in categories, such as separating cups and plates at cleanup time.
- Help children understand measurement by cooking a "make believe" family dinner by following recipe directions that call for adding ingredients by teaspoons, cups, and so on.

Manipulatives

- Sit at the table with children and assist them with puzzles and other table toys. Encourage children to try to complete more complex puzzles if they are ready.
- Sort and group materials with the children by color, shape, size, and other characteristics.
- Help children build eye-hand coordination as they thread beads or build with table blocks.

Music

- Sit on the floor and sing and/or play instruments with the children.
- Dance and do movement activities with children during group time.
- Imitate fingerplay actions with the children.
- Encourage children to share their favorite songs and fingerplays.

Library

- Hold up books while reading to children so they can see the pictures.
- Invite children to help turn the pages of big books.
- Use the felt board and felt pieces to lead children in retelling a story.
- Read to individual children during playtime.
- Talk with children about the pictures in books.
- Encourage children to join in with repetitive sounds and phrases from a story as they read it together.

Writing

- Write children's dictated stories and help them create their own books.
- Help children practice writing their names and individual letters.
- Read to children.

Science

- Let children help to fill or empty the water and sand tables.
- Encourage children to choose and add new materials to the area.

- Work with children as they pour and fill containers and notice the differences in weight of empty containers versus containers filled to different levels.
- Encourage children to discover what kinds of materials float and sink in water and discuss the possible reasons why.
- Help children with blowing bubbles, feeling different textures, or smelling mystery substances.

Outdoor Play

- Throw balls and play catch with children to help them coordinate eye and hand movements.
- Encourage children to look around the playground and talk about changes in plants and other living things outside as the seasons shift. Ask children to tell you what they are seeing and smelling.
- Help children climb on outdoor equipment and push children on swings.
- Set up and supervise an obstacle course with tires, boxes of different sizes, and so on. As children move through the course, point out when they are going "around," "over," "through," and "under" things.

Parents can also lead an art project, tell a story, teach a song or dance, or cook with the children using a recipe from their culture or a family favorite. They can help serve meals, assist at naptime by putting important notes in cubbies or comforting children who cannot sleep. They can assist on the playground, in the planning and chaperoning of field trips, and in developing events such as open houses, parent workshops and seminars, and book and health fairs.

It is also important to give families a voice in program development and decision making. Open access to teachers and the program's administrator, regularly scheduled family meetings, and the formation of committees to address specific issues or program concerns should be part of any family involvement program.

Involving families at home

Some parents cannot come to the center during the day to volunteer; however, there are many ways they can contribute from home. A parent with access to a computer might design and update the center's Web page, create a newsletter, or design forms and stationery. Other tasks a family might do at home include creating homemade learning games and toys for the classroom, reading and tape-recording stories or music, sewing costumes and uniforms for the dramatic play area, or making curtains for a puppet theater.

Teachers can support all children and families at home by preparing exploration kits for use at home. These kits can contain videos, books, learning toys or games, and index cards with parent-child activity ideas that focus on a particular topic. Circulate the kits until all families have had a turn. Teachers can also start a book- or toy-lending program with reading tips for parents and suggestions for using a toy to develop different kinds of skills.

> **To develop and sustain a feeling of camaraderie, belonging, and satisfaction, provide ongoing parent training, treat parents with respect, and provide activities throughout the year that demonstrate appreciation for their work.**

Assessing progress

It is important to evaluate family involvement strategies on a regular and on-going basis. This can be done informally through regular observation and conversations with parents. Use more formal surveys or interviews to assess the overall quality and success of a family involvement program. As a part of the evaluation process, recognize parents for their contributions both personally and publicly. To develop and sustain a feeling of camaraderie, belonging, and satisfaction, provide ongoing parent training, treat parents with respect, and provide activities throughout the year that demonstrate appreciation for their work.

What parents take with them

As children transition out of the early childhood environment, parents bring away with them the experiences and skills they learned from the child's initial exposure to school. Most important, parents also have a commitment to helping their child succeed in school. By investing in parents, we invest in children.

References

1. Bredekamp, S., & C. Copple, eds. 1997. *Developmentally appropriate practice in early childhood programs.* Rev. ed. Washington, DC: NAEYC.
2. Cavarretta, J. 1998. Parents are a school's best friend. *Educational Leadership* 55 (8): 12–15.
3. Epstein, J. L., M. G. Sanders, K. Clark Salinas, B. Simon, N. Rodriguez Jansorn, & F. L. VanVoorhis. 1997. *School, family, and community partnerships: Your handbook for action.* Thousand Oaks, CA: Corwin/Sage Publications.
4. Hatch, T. 1998. How community action contributes to achievement. *Educational Leadership* 55 (8): 15–16.
5. Henderson, A. T., & N. Berla. 1994. *A new generation of evidence: The family is critical to student achievement.* Columbia, MD: National Committee for Citizens in Education.
6. Kibel, B., & A. Stein-Seroussi. 1997. *Effective community mobilization: Lessons from experience.* Rockville, MD: U.S. Department of Health and Human Services.
7. Lewis, A. C., & A. T. Henderson. 1997. *Urgent message: Families crucial to school reform.* Washington, DC: Center for Law and Education.
8. Powell, D. 1998. Reweaving parents into the fabric of early childhood programs. *Young Children* 53 (5): 60–67.

For further reading

1. Campbell-Lehn, C. 1998. Finding the right fit: Creating successful volunteer job descriptions. *The Journal of Volunteer Administration* 26 (3): 22–29.
2. Coleman, M. 1997. Families and schools: In search of common ground. *Young Children* 52 (5): 14–21.
3. Diffily, D., & K. Morrison, eds. 1996. *Family-friendly communication for early childhood programs.* Washington, DC: NAEYC.
4. Goldberg, S. 1997. *Parent involvement begins at birth: Collaboration between parents and teachers of children in the early years.* Boston: Allyn & Bacon.
5. Harms, T., R. Clifford, & D. Cryer. 1998. *Early Childhood Environment Rating Scale.* Rev. ed. New York: Teacher's College Press.
6. Herr, J., & Y. Libby-Larson. 2000. *Creative resources for the early childhood classroom.* 3d ed. New York: Delmar.
7. Lee, L., & E. Seiderman. 1998. *Parent Services Project.* Cambridge, MA: Harvard Family Research Project.
8. Mulcahey, C. 2002. Take-home art appreciation kits for kindergartners and their families. *Young Children* 57 (1): 80–87.
9. U.S. Department of Education. 1996. *Reaching all families: Creating family-friendly schools.* Washington, DC: Author.

Lorenza DiNatale, M.S., is the parent involvement program coordinator for National PTA. She has taught preschool, supervised early childhood teachers, administered early childhood programs, and written a book for National PTA on how to develop a quality parent involvement program.

Cartoon Violence: Is It as Detrimental to Preschoolers as We Think?

Kristen M. Peters and Fran C. Blumberg

INTRODUCTION

What impact does television content, specifically the violence presented in children's cartoons, have on 3- to 5-year-old children? Whether cartoons provide primarily good entertainment or bad examples of conflict resolution is difficult to readily determine. Policymakers and television networks acknowledge possible negative effects of cartoon violence on child viewers, as evidenced by the following initiatives:

1. The Children's Television Act (CTA) of 1990, which requires broadcasters to provide informative and educational programming for children;
2. V (Violence)-chip legislation that allows for the insertion of electronic blocking devices for adults to screen out shows rated for high violent and objectionable content; and
3. The National Cable Television Association's TV Parental Guidelines, a television program rating system that provides parents with information about violence, sexual situation, coarse language, and suggestive dialog in the programs (Banta, 2001; Federal Communications Commission, 1996; National Cable Television Association, 1996; Wright, 1995).

The necessity of these measures is questionable given preschoolers' fairly sophisticated understanding of moral violations, such as physically harming another individual (Wainryb & Turiel, 1993). The present research review critically examines the effects of cartoon violence on children's moral understanding and behavior for the purposes of enabling early childhood educators and parents to make informed decisions about what constitutes potentially harmful television viewing (Huston & Wright, 1998; Huston, Wright, Marquis, & Green, 1999).

HOW VIOLENT IS CHILDREN'S TELEVISION PROGRAMMING?

According to Huston and Wright (1998), preschoolers watch up to 30 hours of television per week. Four-year-olds, on average, watch 50-70 minutes of television a day, most of which is animated cartoons (Huston et al., 1999). This finding is noteworthy, as cartoon shows have been characterized as containing some of the highest levels of violent and aggressive content on television (Calvert, 1999; National Television Violence Study, 1997; Potter, 1999). For example, Gerbner, Morgan, and Signorielli (1993) examined television programming from 1973 to 1993 and found that 92% of children's Saturday morning programs contained some form of violence, as compared with 71% of prime time programs; the average number of violent scenes per hour was 23.0 as compared with 5.3 on prime time programs.

The National Television Violence Study (NTVS), funded by the National Cable Television Association, assessed television violence with the "goal of encouraging more responsible television programming and viewing" (1997, p. 1). The NTVS found that nearly two-thirds of serials for children contained violent acts. This situation may be further exacerbated by the current popularity of the Japanese cartoon genre called "anime" (e.g., *Cardcaptors, Batman Beyond*). This genre is characterized by fast action animation featuring numerous violent fight scenes (Rutenberg, 2001). As Rutenberg noted, anime is vastly popular among young viewers.

WHAT DO WE MEAN BY VIOLENCE AND HOW DO YOUNG CHILDREN RESPOND TO IT?

Clearly, violence sells—even among young children. Despite its widely perceived egregious effects, there is disagreement about how violence should be defined. One standard definition, adopted by the Cultural Indicators Project that was charged in 1967–68 with investigating television violence, is "the overt expression of physical force, with or without weapon, against self or other, compelling action against one's will on pain of being hurt or killed, or actually hurting or killing" (Gerbner, Gross, Jackson-Beeck, Jeffries-Fox, & Signorielli, 1978, p. 179). This definition excludes violence that is implausible or reflected in threats, verbal abuse, and comic gestures (Potter, 1999; Signorielli, Gerbner, & Morgan, 1995). Other researchers, such as Williams, Zabrack, and Joy (1982), distinguished between aggression and overt violence. Specifically, they characterized aggression as a "behavior that inflicts harm, either physically or psychologically, including explicit or implicit threats and nonverbal behaviors" and violence as "physically aggressive behaviors that do, or potentially could, cause injury or death" (p. 366).

Given differing conceptions of violence, it remains unclear as to whether aggressive acts committed by cartoon characters are truly violent (Condry, 1989). Given their fantasy-based content and unrealistic character actions, cartoons create a "gray world" as far as violence is concerned. In fact, adult television viewers perceive fantasy and cartoons as devoid of violence and not particularly disturbing or frightening (Potter, 1999). Major television networks (e.g., Kids WB) also characterize cartoon episodes as reflecting themes of good-versus-evil that emphasize the reinforcement of loyalty and punishment for selfishness (Rutenberg, 2001). Accordingly, violence and conflict between "good" and "evil" characters are appropriate because the end is justified by the means.

Not all television networks, however, adhere to a positive view of cartoon violence, as in the case of Nickelodeon's refusal to show anime cartoon genre (Rutenberg, 2001). Research shows that children perceive comic cartoons, in which the victim remains uninjured, as more violent and less acceptable than violence depicted without comic intent (Haynes, 1978). Bjorkqvist and Lagerspetz (1985) reported that preschoolers showed fear when they viewed violent cartoon scenes and were asked to recall scenes that were most anxiety producing. Paik and Comstock (1994) also suggested that cartoons might be harmful because young children have difficulty distinguishing reality from fantasy.

A longstanding concern in the study of children's social and emotional development is the nature of the relationship between television violence and aggressive behavior (Simmons, Stalsworth, & Wentzel, 1999). According to the American Psychological Association's review of research examining the effects of television violence (1985), when children watch programs with violent content, they demonstrate increases in aggressive attitudes, values, or behavior. Numerous studies have shown that preschoolers demonstrate increased aggressiveness after watching cartoon characters engaged in violent behavior (Bandura, Ross, & Ross, 1963a, 1963b; Paik & Comstock, 1994; Potts, Huston, & Wright, 1986; Sanson & DiMuccio, 1993).

These findings are theoretically consistent with Bandura's social learning perspective (Bandura & Walters, 1963), which contends that children learn behaviors by observing others' actions and the consequences of those actions. Actions resulting in a reward are presumably more likely to be learned than those resulting in punishment. Findings from Bandura and Huston (1961) indicate that for preschoolers, observation of aggressive models is a "sufficient condition for producing imitative aggression" (p. 317), regardless of the nature of the relationship between the model demonstrating the behaviors and the child. Similarly, preschool children may demonstrate overt aggressive behavior in their play and interactions with peers and adults after viewing cartoons containing violent and aggressive content (Bandura et al., 1963a, 1963b; Friedrich & Stein, 1973; Sanson & DiMuccio, 1993). Bandura et al. (1963a) concluded

that children modeled their aggressive behavior after video-taped characters and generalized this behavior to other forms of aggressive acts (i.e., aggressive gun play). Thus, the behavior of popular cartoon characters may serve as models for children with the accompanying message that aggressive behavior is justified, especially when the behavior is rewarded (Bandura et al., 1963b; Bjorkqvist & Lagerspetz, 1985).

The models that children view on cartoon programs, such as "superheroes," are often highly attractive and aggressive in their behaviors (Liss, Reinhardt, & Fredriksen, 1983; NTVS, 1997). The NTVS reported that for all types of programs, about a third of the perpetrators of violence demonstrated some good qualities, such as considering the needs of others, with which viewers might identify. For preschoolers, the actions of cartoon heroes are clearly visible on the screen and likely to be imitated in play (Liss et al., 1983). In cartoons, the characters' actions seldom result in negative consequences. For example, the NTVS reported that nearly 70% of the violent interactions depicted on children's programs revealed no pain on the part of characters. Of those violent interactions, nearly 60% featured unrealistic harm, or no harm. Additionally, less than half of these programs featured negative consequences for violent interactions. Thus, cartoon violence may provide young viewers with a faulty impression of the impact of violence and aggression in real-life situations.

There are also questions about the long-term effects of specific types of violence on children's behavior (Van Evra, 1998). Different theoretical perspectives have examined these effects. For example, Zillmann's excitation transfer or arousal theory (1971) contends that watching television violence and aggression arouses individuals who subsequently direct or "transfer" their energies into another activity, perhaps in behavior that may be inappropriate in their social environment. Berkowtiz's cognitive neoassociation or cue theory (1984) suggests that ideas or "cues" portrayed in television violence (e.g., guns, particular kinds of characters and settings) send a signal to individuals, which increases the likelihood that they will behave aggressively when they experience the aggressive-eliciting cues in real-life situations (Potter, 1999). According to the Gerbner et al.'s cultivation theory (1978), heavy television viewing facilitates a mainstreaming effect in which children may regard what they see as an accurate representation of real-life situations (Calvert, 1999). Accordingly, children may acquire a distorted view of violence in the real world (Gerbner et al., 1978; Lometti, 1995). Drabman and Thomas (1974) suggested that by the time children are in elementary school, they may have become desensitized to the effects of violence on victims. This claim is best examined in the context of children's understanding of television content in general.

PRESCHOOLERS' INTERPRETATION OF TELEVISION CONTENT

Research has consistently indicated that preschoolers' comprehension of television content is relatively poor and may remain poor through age 8 (Bjorkqvist & Lagerspetz, 1985;

Condry, 1989). Four-year-olds recall more of the story line than peripheral television content, but may have difficulty identifying and differentiating central from incidental content (Van den Broek, Lorch, & Thurlow, 1996). Central content refers to content that is important to understanding a given story whereas incidental content refers to information that may embellish but not advance the understanding of a given story. Even 6-year-olds experience programs such as cartoons in a "fragmentary manner rather than a continuous story" (Bjorkqvist & Lagerspetz, 1985, p. 77). Hodapp (1977) found that 5- and 6-year-olds failed to transfer what they learned from educational programs to solving similar problems in real-life situations. Thus, preschoolers also may be unable to incorporate actions based on the violent behaviors of cartoon characters into their repertoire of social behaviors.

One contributing factor to this inability to transfer knowledge from media to daily life is children's understanding of reality versus fantasy. In general, researchers have found that when violent scenes are interpreted as real, they have a greater likelihood of resulting in subsequent aggressive behavior than when they are interpreted as unrealistic (Berkowitz, 1984; Huesmann, Lagerspetz, & Eron, 1984). Individuals tend to use cues such as animation to help them distinguish reality from fantasy (Condry, 1989). However, according to Flavell (1986), preschoolers may possess little or no understanding of the distinction between reality and fantasy, indicating that what they view on television may be perceived as "real." Even 6- and 7-year old children "appear to have difficulty understanding television conventions that violate real-world possibilities," for example, in understanding scene cuts and instant replays (Huston & Wright, 1998, p. 1020).

The character's motive and the consequence of violent actions may help the child viewer interpret events seen on television. According to Roberts and Bachen (1981), the portrayal of aggression on television, combined with a moral verbal message, may be too sophisticated for young children. Collins, Berndt, and Hess (1974) found that kindergarten children recalled the consequences of the characters' aggressive actions but were less able to identify the characters' motives for those actions. Children typically need adults' help to understand relationships between social acts portrayed on television and cues such as motives and consequences (Collins, Sobol, & Westby, 1981). Heroes or protagonists in cartoons, however, often use aggression while delivering moral lessons (Liss et al., 1983). Thus, children believe that there are immediate rewards for the antisocial behavior, especially when there is a lag between the violent behavior and subsequent punishment. This perception may promote inappropriate beliefs about the consequences of harming others.

PRESCHOOLERS' INTERPRETATION OF THE MORALITY OF VIOLENT ACTIONS

Consideration needs to be made of the preschoolers' perception of the portrayed violence and their understanding of con-flict resolution in terms of its underlying morality. Simply observing a preschooler's aggressive behavior following the viewing of violent television does not provide information about how the child behaves in the context of real-life moral dilemmas. Situations presented in the world of cartoons may be specific to the domain of cartoons and, therefore, may be interpreted differently than violence in the domain of reality. Bjorkqvist and Lagerspetz (1985) found that 5-, 6-, and 9-year-olds tended to base their moral judgments of the "goodness" or "badness" of a cartoon character's behavior on their ability to identify with that character. Research findings indicate that preschoolers' moral reasoning abilities may be relatively advanced (Wainryb & Turiel, 1993). Bandura et al., (1963b) found that preschoolers could indicate the consequences of a character's actions, for example, that the character acted aggressively (e.g., engaged in a fight) to receive a reward (e.g., toys). They also tended to criticize that character's actions as morally wrong (e.g., selfish, mean).

Current views on the development of moral reasoning contend that young children are able to identify moral transgressions and breaches of social conventions. Moral transgressions, or violations of moral rules, are those actions that infringe on the rights, duties, or welfare of others (Wainryb & Turiel, 1993). Social-conventional rules pertain to acceptable behaviors within a specific social system (Wainryb & Turiel, 1993). Preschoolers may be able to identify and make distinctions between moral transgressions and social-conventional transgressions (Cassidy, Chu, & Dahlsgaard, 1997). In fact, preschoolers were found to recognize real-life dilemmas as well as identify, differentiate, and make inferences about the features of moral and social-conventional interactions presented in story form (Oppenheim, Emde, Hasson, & Warren, 1997; Smetana, 1981, 1985). Additionally, preschoolers conceptualized hypothetical and actual moral transgressions as more serious in nature and worthy of punishment than personal rules (i.e., those pertaining to an individual's subjectively perceived rights) or social-conventional violations (Smetana, Schlagman, & Adams, 1993; Tisak, 1993). Thus, researchers believe that preschoolers may be able to differentiate between moral and social-conventional transgressions and consider both in evaluating situations in real-life and hypothetical scenarios (Cassidy et al., 1997; Weston & Turiel, 1980). This understanding also may help preschoolers mediate between the effects of cartoon violence on the screen and in their lives beyond the screen.

CONCLUSION

To pinpoint the effects that the viewing of cartoon violence has on preschool children, it is essential to determine what children interpret and learn from what they watch. The bottom line is whether preschoolers understand that the consequences of cartoon transgressions differ from those of real-life transgressions. Accordingly, if preschoolers can differentiate between the appropriateness of cartoon actions versus similar actions in the real world, then the influence of cartoon violence may not be as detrimental as commonly accepted. Similarly, young children's imitation of cartoon characters' behaviors may be more situation-specific than an incorporation of the characters' actions into a long-term repertoire of social skills. These conclusions, while supported in our literature review, remain controversial.

What is less controversial is adults' role in helping young viewers interpret the violent content that they see in popular cartoons. This effort involves monitoring how violence is used to resolve interpersonal conflicts and the message communicated to the viewer about the appropriateness of this violence. For example, a superhero that always conquers her enemies through violent means that inflict minimal physical harm may leave children with the message that violent behaviors are justified and inconsequential. This type of message can be characterized as an informational assumption. According to Wainryb and Turiel (1993), informational assumptions influence how children and adults evaluate the morality of a given behavior or action. These assumptions are largely based in societally mandated beliefs, one's current understanding of the world, and interactions with significant others. For children, these significant others include adult caregivers. Accordingly, parents and educators play vital roles in influencing children's impressions of violent actions, violent actions as a means of conflict resolution, and the moral acceptability of that means of resolution.

Children's spontaneous impressions can be addressed in a variety of contexts, most notably, that of adults and children watching programs together, or co-viewing. Research indicates that co-viewing helps improve children's recall of the television program content (Watkins, Calvert, Huston-Stein, & Wright, 1980). Co-viewing also has been used as an instructional vehicle for adults to comment on program content as it is presented and to address children's potential questions about character motives and actions (Wright, 1995). Adults should use the co-viewing situation to not only address questions but also to model and discuss morally acceptable alternatives to resolving conflicts in both cartoon and real-life situations.

Clearly, cartoon watching will continue to be a popular and enjoyable preschool-age activity. The most frequently watched cartoons will continue to contain high levels of violent content. Our goal as early childhood educators and those interested in young children should be to use conflicts on cartoons as a learning opportunity to teach invaluable moral lessons applicable to real-life situations.

REFERENCES

1. American Psychological Association. (1985). *Violence on television.* Washington, DC: APA Board of Ethical and Social Responsibility for Psychology.
2. Bandura, A., & Huston, A. C. (1961). Identification as a process of incidental learning. *Journal of Abnormal and Social Psychology, 63,* 311–318.
3. Bandura, A., Ross, D., & Ross, S. (1963a). Imitation of film-mediated aggressive models. *Journal of Abnormal and Social Psychology, 66,* 3–11.
4. Bandura, A., Ross, D., & Ross, S. (1963b). Vicarious reinforcement and imitative learning. *Journal of Abnormal and Social Psychology, 67,* 601–607.
5. Bandura, A., & Walters, R. H. (1963). *Social learning and personality development.* New York: Holt, Rinehart, & Winston.
6. Banta, M. (n.d.). The V-(Violence) chip story. Retrieved on January 15, 2001, from National Coalition on Television Violence Web site: http://www.nctvv.org.
7. Berkowitz, L. (1984). Some effects of thoughts on anti- and prosocial influences of media events: A cognitive-neoassociationist analysis. *Psychological Bulletin, 95,* 410–427.
8. Bjorkqvist, K., & Lagerspetz, K. (1985). Children's experience of three types of cartoons at two age levels. *International Journal of Psychology, 20,* 77–93.
9. Calvert, S. L. (1999). *Children's journeys through the information age.* New York: McGraw-Hill College.
10. Cassidy, K. W., Chu, J. Y., & Dahlsgaard, K. K. (1997). Preschoolers' ability to adopt justice and care orientations to moral dilemmas. *Early Education and Development, 8(4),* 419–434.
11. Collins, W. A., Berndt, T. J., & Hess, V. L. (1974). Observational learning of motives and consequences for television aggression: A developmental study. *Child Development, 45,* 799–802.
12. Collins, W. A., Sobol, B. L., Westby, S. (1981). Effects of adult commentary on children's comprehension and inferences about a televised aggressive portrayal. *Child Development, 52,* 158–163.
13. Condry, J. (1989). *The psychology of television.* Hillsdale, NJ: Lawrence Erlbaum Associates.
14. Drabman, R. S., & Thomas, M. H. (1974). Does media violence increase children's toleration of real-life aggression? *Developmental Psychology, 10,* 418–421.
15. Federal Communications Commission. (1996). Children's Educational Television. Retrieved on February 8, 2001, from http://www.fcc.gov.
16. Flavell, J. H. (1986). The development of children's knowledge about the appearance-reality distinction. *American Psychologist, 41(4),* 418–425.
17. Friedrich, L., & Stein, A. H. (1973). Aggressive and prosocial television programs and the natural behavior of preschool children. *Monographs of the Society for Research in Child Development, 38* (4, Serial No. 151).
18. Gerbner, G., Gross, L., Jackson-Beeck, M., Jeffries-Fox, S., & Signorielli, N. (1978). Cultural indicators: Violence profile no. 9. *Journal of Communication, 30(3),* 176–207.
19. Gerbner, G., Morgan, M., & Signorielli, N. (1993, December). *Television violence profile No. 16: The turning point from research to action.* Unpublished manuscript, Annenberg School of Communication, University of Pennsylvania, Philadelphia.
20. Haynes, R. B. (1978). Children's perceptions of "comic" and "authentic" cartoon violence. *Journal of Broadcasting, 22,* 63–70.
21. Hodapp, T. V. (1977). Children's ability to learn problem-solving strategies from television. *The Alberta Journal of Educational Research, 23(3), 171–177.*
22. Huesmann, L. R., Lagerspetz, K. M. J., & Eron, L. D. (1984). Intervening variables in the television violence-aggression relation: Evidence from two countries. *Developmental Psychology, 20,* 746–775.
23. Huston, A. C., & Wright, J. C. (1998). Mass media and children's development. In W. Damon (Series Ed.) & I. E. Siegel & K. A. Renninger (Vol. Eds.), *Handbook of child psychology: Vol. 4. Child psychology in practice* (5th ed., pp. 999–1058). New York: John Wiley & Sons.
24. Huston, A. C., Wright, J. C., Marquis, J., & Green, S. B. (1999). How young children spend their time: Television and other activities. *Developmental Psychology, 35(4),* 912–925.
25. Liss, M. B., Reinhardt, L. C., & Fredriksen, S. (1983). TV heroes: The impact of rhetoric and deeds. *Journal of Applied Developmental Psychology, 4,* 175–187.
26. Lometti, G. E. (1995). The measurement of televised violence. *Journal of Broadcasting & Electronic Media, 39,* 292–295.
27. National Cable Television Association. (1996). TV Parental Guidelines. Retrieved on January 21, 2001, from http://www.ncta.com/tv.html.

28. National Television Violence Study (Vol. 1). (1997). Thousand Oaks, CA: Sage.

29. Oppenheim, D., Emde, R. N., Hasson, M., & Warren, S. (1997). Preschoolers face moral dilemmas: A longitudinal study of acknowledging and resolving internal conflict. *International Journal of Psychoanalysis, 78,* 943–957.

30. Paik, H., & Comstock, G. (1994). The effects of television violence on antisocial behavior: A meta-analysis. *Communication Research, 21,* 516–546.

31. Potter, W. J. (1999). *On media violence.* Thousand Oaks, CA: Sage.

32. Potts, R., Huston, A. C., & Wright, J. C. (1986). The effects of television form and violent content on boys' attention and social behavior. *Journal of Experimental Child Psychology, 41,* 1–17.

33. Roberts, D. F., & Bachen, C. M. (1981). Mass communication effects. *Annual Review of Psychology, 32,* 307–356.

34. Rutenberg, J. (2001, January 28). Violence finds a niche in children's cartoons. *New York Times* (CL 51, 647), A1, A19.

35. Sanson, A., & DiMuccio, C. (1993). The influence of aggressive and neutral cartoons and toys on the behavior of preschool children. *Australian Psychologist, 28,* 93–99.

36. Signorielli, N., Gerbner, G., & Morgan, M. (1995). Violence on television: The Cultural Indicators Project. *Journal of Broadcasting & Electronic Media, 39,* 278–283.

37. Simmons, B. J., Stalsworth, K., & Wentzel, H. (1999). Television violence and its effects on young children. *Early Childhood Education Journal, 26(3),* 149–153.

38. Smetana, J. G. (1981). Preschool children's conceptions of moral and social rules. *Child Development, 52,* 1333–1336.

39. Smetana, J. G. (1985). Preschool children's conceptions of transgressions: Effects of varying moral and conventional domain-related attributes. *Developmental Psychology, 21,* 18–29.

40. Smetana, J. G., Schlagman, N., & Adams, P. W. (1993). Preschool children's judgments about hypothetical and actual transgressions. *Child Development, 64,* 202–214.

41. Tisak, M. S. (1993). Preschool children's judgments of moral and personal events involving physical harm and property damage. *Merill-Palmer Quarterly, 39(3),* 75–390.

42. Van den Broek, P., Lorch, E. P., & Thurlow, R. (1996). Children's and adults' memory for television stories: The role of causal factors, story-grammar categories, and hierarchical level. *Child Development, 67,* 3010–3028.

43. Van Evra, J. (1998). *Television and child development* (2nd ed.). Mahwah, NJ: Lawrence Erlbaum Associates.

44. Wainryb, C., & Turiel, E. (1993). Conceptual and informational features in moral decision making. *Educational Psychologist, 28(3),* 205–218.

45. Watkins, B., Calvert, S., Huston-Stein, A., & Wright, J. C. (1980). Children's recall of television material: Effects of presentation mode and adult labeling. *Developmental Psychology, 6,* 672–674.

46. Weston, D. R., & Turiel, E. (1980). Act-rule relations: Children's concepts of social rules. *Developmental Psychology, 16(5),* 417–424.

47. Williams, T. M., Zabrack, M. L., & Joy, L. A. (1982). The portrayal of aggression on North American television. *Journal of Applied Social Psychology, 12,* 360–380.

48. Wright, J. C. (1995). Child viewers, television violence, and the First Amendment. *The Kansas Journal of Law and Public Policy, 4(3),* 33–38.

49. Zillmann, D. (1971). Excitation transfer in communication-mediated aggressive behavior. *Journal of Experimental Social Psychology, 7,* 419–434.

Kristen M. Peters and Fran C. Blumberg are from the Division of Psychological & Educational Services, Fordham University.

Correspondence should be directed to Fran C. Blumberg, Division of Psychological & Educational Services, Fordham University, 113 West 60th Street, Room 1008, New York, NY 10023; e-mail: kpeters@fordham.edu.

From *Early Childhood Education Journal,* Spring 2002, pp. 143-148. © 2002 by Early Childhood Education Journal.

UNIT 3

Care and Educational Practices

Unit Selections

Key Points to Consider

- What are some steps teachers can take to counteract negative aspects of toys and materials in the classroom?

- What steps has your state taken to improve child-care staffing ratios, funding, regulations, and employee turnover this past year?

- Make a brief listing of the components of developmentally appropriate practice that you believe are vital.

- What is *redshirting*?

- How does the compensation for early childhood teachers in preschool programs in your area compare with neighboring states?

 **Links: www.dushkin.com/online/**
These sites are annotated in the World Wide Web pages.

Canada's Schoolnet Staff Room
http://www.schoolnet.ca/home/e/

Classroom Connect
http://www.classroom.com/login/home.jhtml

The Council for Exceptional Children
http://www.cec.sped.org/index.html

National Resource Center for Health and Safety in Child Care
http://nrc.uchsc.edu

Online Innovation Institute
http://oii.org

The passage of No Child Left Behind legislation by Congress in 2002 has many implications for early childhood care and educational practices. As academic assessment and accountability measures are implemented, the impact on children's play is becoming quite clear; preschool children are spending more and more time preparing for and taking tests and less time in developmental play. Several of the articles in this unit address the issues in protecting children's right to play as an avenue of cognitive, emotional, and academic growth. However, to be beneficial to growth and development, play needs to be channeled and supported. In "Let's Just Play," the author emphasizes the importance of fostering cooperative, non-violent play. And in "The Importance of Being Playful," teachers are encouraged to provide appropriate props and materials to foster the type of play that extends learning.

A hallmark of quality childcare is strong home-school partnerships, and parental involvement in a wide variety of activities is the way to develop partnerships. When parents are engaged in school activities, children are better able to learn and grow and their teachers gain respect and appreciation of family cultures. "Creating Home-School Partnerships" gives valuable strategies for understanding family diversity as the beginning point for working closely with parents.

Another implication of No Child Left Behind is an alarming increase in the number of children, particularly boys, whose entry into kindergarten is being delayed by parents and teachers. The reason most frequently cited for delaying entry is the child's lack of readiness or maturity. With schools under pressure to meet higher annual yearly progress goals, some districts are raising entrance age for kindergarten. The issues involved in delayed entry, or redshirting, are discussed in "Opportunity Deferred or Opportunity Taken? An Updated Look at Delaying Kindergarten Entry."

Appropriate practice in early childhood education depends on the teachers' own learning opportunities. As teachers grow to understand a wide range of educational practices, they are better equipped to provide effective education and care for young children. The foundation of early childhood care and education is constructivism, an approach that views learning as an interac-

tive experience. When teachers adopt elements of constructivist practice, they begin to view children as active learners. Two divergent yet sound approaches to constructivist practice are discussed in this unit. "Different Approaches to Teaching: Comparing Preschool Program Models" presents the basics of Montessori and High/Scope.

The final two articles in this unit deal with issues of quality. Across the country, more states are supplementing federal early childhood programs and paying for full-day kindergarten. Yet quality remains very uneven. Of all the issues facing early childhood education and childcare today, none is as important as eliminating the barriers to quality. The trend in many states is toward a mediocre level of childcare services, coupled with underpreparation and low wages of caregivers. When the press for higher (and possibly inappropriate) standards is added to the situation, this trend is one that needs to be reversed. Standards and accountability and quality do not automatically add up to a developmentally appropriate education for young children. Early childhood educators, have the obligation to carefully examine these trends and act on behalf of the young children in their care.

LET'S JUST PLAY

Preserve a child's right to create and explore

BY JANET SCHMIDT

> *"[Participating countries] recognize the right of the child to rest and leisure, to engage in play and recreational activities appropriate to the age of the child and to participate freely in cultural life and the arts."* ARTICLE 31, PART 1, OF THE UN CONVENTION ON THE RIGHTS OF THE CHILD

"I like the pink ranger!"

"My favorite is red."

"Mine, too!"

The *Mighty Morphin Power Rangers* captured the imaginations of the 3- and 4-year-olds in my suburban Boston public preschool class. For one little girl, whose language development was delayed, even the experience of naming her first few colors fell "captive" to the Rangers' original color scheme—pink, blue, red, yellow and black. Although I was pleased with the child's growing vocabulary, it disturbed me that her grasp of color concepts was connected to a violent TV show.

I should not have been surprised.

The plot of a typical *Power Rangers* episode features several fight scenes, complete with high kicks, powerful weapons, loud yells and grunts. Frequent commercial breaks promote other violent shows and toys. In the span of just one TV show, a child's vision is captivated and dominated by violence. And away from the screen, related action figures, lunch boxes, sheets, underwear and books ensure that Power Rangers images are ever present.

Children have a right to play. The idea is so simple it seems self-evident. But a stroll through any toy superstore, or any half-hour of so-called 'children's "programming on commercial TV,

makes it clear that violence, not play, dominates what's being sold.

The problem got much worse in 1984, when the Federal Communications Commission deregulated children's television, paving the way for program-length commercials and massive marketing to children. In *Remote Control Childhood? Combating the Hazards of Media Culture* (1998), Diane Levin, professor of education at Wheelock College in Boston, writes that, within one year of deregulation, nine of the 10 best-selling toys were linked to TV shows and seven of these shows were violent.

Another study offers further proof.

The National Television Violence Study (*see Resources*) examined 10,000 hours of programming between 1994 and 1997 and found that 60 percent of all shows contained some kind of violence. The study also found that a preschool child watching two hours of cartoons each day will witness nearly 10,000 acts of violence each year.

Kathy Roberts, co-founder/director of the Dandelion School in Cambridge, Mass., from 1971 to 2002, has been following the evolution of children's play as a parent, grandparent and educator. In the 1970s, she and her colleagues observed that "children who watched little or no TV were more self-sufficient and creative in their play."

As the video culture boomed, however, violent TV and movie plots began to dominate the content of child's play, displacing the influence of children's imaginations and literature.

Roberts and her colleagues also observed an economic change. As marketing began to dominate children's entertainment, some families simply couldn't afford clothes and accessories tied to the latest media characters.

At the Dandelion School, Roberts and her colleagues worked against such influences. Parents and children alike understood that media-linked toys, clothes and backpacks stayed at home, and the school community could focus on topics from nature, children's own experiences and literature.

The policy got good reviews from parents.

As Roberts said, "When their children move on to public elementary school, they're bombarded with the media culture, and they feel like they have a grounding to deal with it."

CREATIVE PLAY, WITH DIRECTION

Teachers like Roberts and others promote creative play by providing a well-planned environment with engaging open-ended materials such as blocks, dolls, animal figures, paper, paint, glue, scissors, sand boxes and water tables. Children can create and explore, and teachers can be directly involved.

That direct involvement is especially important when children imitate what they've seen on TV and movie screens.

ACTIVITY

Making Shoe Box Gifts

Usually, for children, gift giving means buying manufactured toys at a store. Here is an alternative gift idea: Shoe Box Gifts are collections of small, familiar items that are organized around a play theme. They also show that expensive toys in fancy packages aren't necessarily the best.

Decorate an empty shoe box (or a larger box if needed) and gather items related to the chosen theme. Build dividers into the box or use small containers or zip-lock bags to keep things organized. Note that some suggested items might require adult supervision. Have fun!

Here are two suggestions to get you started:

Garden Box	Creating with Play Dough
• Plastic lining	• Buy some or make your own
• Potting soil	• Garlic press
• Seed packets	• Plastic knife
• Small watering can	• Popsicle sticks
• Popsicle sticks	• Plastic lids
• Garden tools	• Small tray/plate
• Gardening gloves	• Plastic animals

Adapted with permission from TRUCE (Teachers Resisting Unhealthy Children's Entertainment).

Tricia Windschitl and her colleagues at the Preucil Preschool in Iowa City, Iowa, take advantage of teachable moments that arise during play to interject ideas to make play more peaceful and respectful, while setting limits on pretend fighting. "Anything that makes someone feel uncomfortable or scared" is not allowed, Windschitl explains.

So if the boys are interested in Batman, Windschitl will encourage them to build a Batmobile, challenging their creativity and fostering cooperation.

"The focus goes away from the fighting and into more creative play," she says. "But if we completely ban superhero play, there is no opportunity to guide it."

Beyond preschool, recess becomes a testing ground for such play.

At first-grade teacher Sandra Rojas' school in Cambridge, Mass., students staked out part of the schoolyard as "Martian Land" in the 1980s. It has continued ever since, with boys and girls of various ages using rocks for money and setting up inventive trading-and-selling scenarios. "Real" toys are nowhere to be found.

"When there are no gadgets to play with," Rojas says, "they do really well coming together as a group."

Children's creativity in the absence of "store-bought play" is the core concept of WorldPlay, a grassroots project based in Atlanta that showcases toys made from found materials by children all over the world (*see Resources*). The group has also created Internet and videoconferencing opportunities that allow children to teach each other how to make such toys.

While adults can help by providing materials, suggesting safety guidelines and offering ideas, children have the right to bring their own ideas and experiences, even challenging ones, to life through play. Denise Jansen, a second-grade teacher in Madison, Wis., believes that denying children the opportunity to play is "taking away a right as necessary as eating or sleeping."

In support of that right, teachers and parents share responsibility to protect children from the onslaught of violent and scripted play ideas brought by TV, movies, video games and the vast collection of media-linked products.

CHOOSING GOOD TOYS

Choosing appropriate toys can go a long way toward improving play opportunities for children.

The Good Toy Group (*see Resources*), currently made up of more than 50 U.S. toy retailers, emerged at the 2000 American Specialty Toy Retailers Association convention. Colleen Pope, owner of The Dollhouse Shop in Montgomery, Ala., was part of the original group and contributes to the production of a catalogue that features toys chosen on the basis of creative play value, cultural sensitivity and nonviolence.

"We go to the annual Toy Fair and work in teams, looking for the best new stuff. Then we meet, compare notes and decide what to put in the catalogue," Pope explains.

TRUCE (Teachers Resisting Unhealthy Children's Entertainment), founded in 1995, also promotes creative and constructive play.

The group's Shoe Box Gifts (*see Activity*) provide an antidote for the aggressive marketing of media-linked toys. Parents and teachers can help children discover ways to channel their interests into creative dramatic play, using simple props and collective imagination.

The TRUCE *Media Violence Guide* (*see Resources*) provides suggestions for adults who seek to minimize the effects of media culture and violence on children.

SCREENING OUT VIOLENCE

According to The Lion and Lamb Project's short film *Video Games: The State of the "Art"*:

- 145 million Americans play video games;
- 65 million are under the age of 17;
- 20 million are 12 years old or younger;
- And 92 percent of 2- to 17-year-olds play video or computer games.

In addition, three different studies found that approximately 75 percent of youths between the ages of 13 and 16 who attempted to purchase M-rated (mature) video games were able to do so. Such M-rated games, including *Duke Nukem* and *Grand Theft Auto: Vice City,* depict graphic violence, complete with blood, vomit, sickening sounds and sexual images of women with exaggerated figures and scanty clothing. They include scenes of men beating prostitutes and encourages the player to shoot naked women who call out, "Kill me!"

While the First Amendment allows for the production of such violent material, adults are responsible for protecting children from exposure to it. Parents can't accomplish this alone; teachers, retailers and others need to monitor the video game world and take action to keep children safe from such images. Even E-rated (everybody) games include violent images, cautions Lion and Lamb's executive director Daphne White.

Also, be wary of videos and computer games with misleading terms such as "educational" and "interactive." Although such computer activities offer young users exciting choices and individualized responses to mouse clicks or screen touches, these are still no substitute for face-to-face interactions.

Children can learn to see the negative messages presented through entertainment and the manipulation involved in advertising. Teachers and parents can talk with children about what they see, and help them understand the realities that may conflict with the images on the screen.

Recently, for example, at the neighborhood video store, I heard a 5-year-old ask, "Dad, do all video games have violence?" Another 5-year-old, Morgan (*see In Focus*), persuaded his friends to play regular tag instead of Power Rangers tag at school.

'FIGHTING' BACK

Recently, Lion and Lamb's White, seeing the need for heightened awareness and powerful, nationwide collaboration in order to reduce the marketing of violence to children, has organized a working group of representatives from several organizations.

WEB EXCLUSIVE

Visit our Web site for a collection of resources about mass-marketed toys and creative play. Log onto www.teaching tolerance.org/magazine; click on "Let's Just Play."

Lion and Lamb also promotes community events such as Violent Toy Trade-Ins and Peaceable Play Days. Merle Forney, along with Jane and Dan Bucks, organized the first Trade-In in Columbia, Md., in 1995. Children who turned in a violent toy received a peacemaker certificate to use at a local specialty toy store. A team of sculptors helped attach the 300 collected toys to a serpent-shaped steel framework.

"A serpent sheds its skin, and the kids were also going through a transformation," recalls Forney, who now lives in Amesbury, Mass.

The first Trade-In took place on a Saturday, followed on Sunday by a "New Ways to Play Day," where parents and children participated together in a variety of creative, nonviolent play activities.

As Denise Janssen sees it, we have to find ways to work with children to build peaceful classrooms and to counteract the negative messages they get through TV and other media. Janssen and her teaching partner, Sue Harris find time in the busy school day to learn what their young students think and feel, through role-playing, reading and discussion of good literature, and talking about good role models from the past and present.

"When we talk about real people who have made a difference in the world, the children are fully involved and enthusiastic. These are the best discussions of the day," she says.

The challenge lies in channeling these positive images into their play.

"Kids don't know how to turn off the TV," Janssen says, "so they learn that most people who look good *are* good, that people who are not good-looking are bad, and that the good guys usually win."

While these simplistic associations permeate play, teachers can remind their students of the real, multidimensional people who captured their attention during classroom discussions. With adult guidance, children can think more critically about the images they see on TV and movie screens.

"Play," asserts Janssen, "represents not only the culture in which the children live, but also the process through which they develop the skills and behaviors needed to live as conscientious adult citizens within their communities."

Play is a child's right, and protecting it is everyone's responsibility.

RESOURCES

Two books by Diane Levin support teachers' efforts to promote peace and safety in children's lives. *Remote Control Childhood? Combating the Hazards of Media Culture* ($15) offers practical background information and concrete suggestions for working with parents and children to counteract negative aspects of toys, entertainment and advertising. The second edition of *Teaching Young*

Children in Violent Times ($24) is a guide to creating peaceful classrooms for children in preschool and Grades K-3.

**National Association for the
Education of Young Children
(866) 424-2460
www.naeyc.org**

TRUCE (Teachers Resisting Unhealthy Children's Entertainment) is a network of early childhood professionals that fosters adult collaboration to promote positive play and to resist negative effects of media culture on children's lives.

**TRUCE
www.truceteachers.org**

The Lion and Lamb Project works to reduce the marketing of violence to children through parent workshops, community events and outreach to government officials and leaders in the toy and entertainment industries. Resources include a *Parent Action Kit* ($15) and the manual *Toys for Peace: A How-to Guide for Organizing Violent Toy Trade-Ins* ($12).

**The Lion and Lamb Project
(301) 654-3091
www.lionlamb.org**

The Good Toy Group, made up of 58 independent toy retailers across the U.S., offers an online catalogue of high-quality, culturally-sensitive toys and a listing of nearly 90 stores.

**The Good Toy Group
www.goodtoygroup.com**

Through their Web site, traveling exhibits, how-to books, videos and CD-ROMs, WorldPlay introduces children from all over the world to each other's cultures through their handmade toys.

**WorldPlay
www.worldplay.org**

The National Television Violence Study, conducted between 1994 and 1997, is the largest ongoing study on the topic. Executive summaries and further information are available online.

**The Center for Communication and Social Policy
University of California, Santa Barbara
www.ccsp.ucsb.edu/ntvs.htm**

Janet Schmidt, an educator in Wellesley, Mass. and member of TRUCE, was the 2002-03 Teaching Tolerance Research Fellow.

The Importance of Being Playful

With the right approach, a plain white hat and a plate full of yarn spaghetti can contribute to a young child's cognitive development.

Elena Bodrova and Deborah J. Leong

Educators have always considered play to be a staple in early childhood classrooms. But the growing demands for teacher accountability and measurable outcomes for prekindergarten and kindergarten programs are pushing play to the periphery of the curriculum. Some proponents of more academically rigorous programs for young children view play and learning as mutually exclusive, clearly favoring "serious" learning and wanting teachers to spend more time on specific academic content. But do play and learning have to compete? Research on early learning and development shows that when children are properly supported in their play, the play does not take away from learning but contributes to it (Bergen, 2002).

As researchers studying the ways to scaffold the development of foundational skills in young children, we have never met a teacher—preschool, Head Start, or kindergarten—who disagreed with the notion that young children learn through play. At the same time, many teachers worry that children's play is not valued outside of the early education community. These teachers must increasingly defend the use of play in their classrooms to principals, parents, and teachers of higher grades.

Early childhood teachers admit that the benefits of play are not as easy to understand and assess as, for example, children's ability to recognize letters or write their names. Teachers also tell us that they feel obligated to prove that play not only facilitates the development of social competencies but also promotes the learning of pre-academic skills and concepts. We believe that a certain kind of play has its place in early childhood classrooms and that the proponents of play and academic learning can find some much-needed common ground.

Effects of Play on Early Learning and Development

Play has been of great interest to scholars of child development and learning, psychologists, and educators alike. Jean Piaget (1962) and Lev Vygotsky (1978) were among the first to link play with cognitive development. In a comprehensive review of numerous studies on play, researchers found evidence that play contributes to advances in "verbalization, vocabulary, language comprehension, attention span, imagination, concentration, impulse control, curiosity, problem-solving strategies, cooperation, empathy, and group participation" (Smilansky & Shefatya, 1990). Recent research provides additional evidence of the strong connections between quality of play in preschool years and children's readiness for school instruction (Bowman, Donovan, & Burns, 2000; Ewing Marion Kauffman

Foundation, 2002; Shonkoff & Phillips, 2000). Further, research directly links play to children's ability to master such academic content as literacy and numeracy. For example, children's engagement in pretend play was found to be positively and significantly correlated with such competencies as text comprehension and metalinguistic awareness and with an understanding of the purpose of reading and writing (Roskos & Christie, 2000).

How Play Evolves

Make-believe play emerges gradually as the child moves from infancy to preschool. In the beginning, children are more focused on the actual objects that they use when they play. Later, they focus on the people who use the objects in social interaction. Whereas a toddler might simply enjoy the repetitive action of rocking a baby doll, an older child engaged in the same activity would call herself "Mommy" and add other mommy behaviors such as using baby talk when talking to the doll. These preschoolers depend heavily on props and may even refuse to play if they think that the props are not sufficiently realistic.

By the time most children turn 4, they begin to develop more complex play with multiple roles and symbolic uses of props. Many preschool- and even kindergarten-age children, however, still play at the toddler level. We define this kind of repetitive, unimaginative play as "immature play" to distinguish it from the "mature play" that is expected of older preschoolers and kindergartners. Mature play contributes to children's learning and development in many areas that immature play does not affect (Smilansky & Shefatya, 1990).

As children grow older, they tend to spend less time in pretend play and more time playing sports and board or computer games. In these activities, children have to follow the established rules and rarely have a chance to discuss, negotiate, or change those rules—an important skill that contributes to the development of social competence and self-regulation. When learning to play games takes its natural course (see Piaget, 1962; Vygotsky, 1978) and builds on the foundation of well-developed pretend play, children get an opportunity to both develop and apply their social and self-regulation skills. When pretend play is completely replaced by sports or other organized activities, however, these important foundational skills might not develop fully.

Characteristics of Mature Play

Teachers often disagree about what constitutes mature play. Some think that the play has to have more sophisticated content, such as playing archaeological dig or space station; others believe that children play in a mature way when they don't fight with one another. We, however, consider play to be mature only when it has the following characteristics, which we have extracted from research and best practices.

Imaginary situations. In mature play, children assign new meanings to the objects and people in a pretend situation. When children pretend, they focus on an object's abstract properties rather than its concrete attributes. They invent new uses for familiar toys and props when the play scenario calls for it. Sometimes children even describe the missing prop by using words and gestures. In doing so, they become aware of different symbolic systems that will serve them later when they start mastering letters and numbers.

Multiple roles. The roles associated with a theme in mature play are not stereotypical or limited; the play easily includes supporting characters. For example, playing "fire station" does not mean that the only roles are those of firefighters. Children can also pretend to be a fire truck driver or a phone dispatcher.

When children assume different roles in play scenarios, they learn about real social interactions that they might not have experienced (not just following commands but also issuing them; not only asking for help but also being the one that helps). In addition, they learn about their own actions and emotions by using them "on demand." (I am really OK, but I have to cry because I am playing a baby and the doctor just gave me a shot.) Understanding emotions and developing emotional self-control are crucial for children's social and emotional development.

Clearly defined rules. Mature play has clearly defined rules and roles. As children follow the rules in play, they learn to delay immediate fulfillment of their desires. A child playing "customer" cannot take an attractive toy if the toy—a scale or a cash register—is the prop for the role of the "checker." Thus, mature play helps young children develop self-regulation. To stay in the play, the child must follow the rules.

Flexible themes. Mature play usually spans a broad range of themes that are flexible enough to incorporate new roles and ideas previously associated with other themes. When children play at a more mature level, they negotiate their plans. For example, when playing "hospital" or "store," children can create a new play scenario in which a doctor goes to the grocery store to buy medicine for the hospital or a cashier in a grocery store gets sick and is taken to the hospital. By combining different themes, children learn to plan and solve problems.

Language development. A mature level of play implies an extensive use of language. Children use language to plan their play scenario, to negotiate and act out their roles, to explain their "pretend" behaviors to other participants, and to regulate compli-

ance with the rules. In doing so, they often need to modify their speech (its intonation, register, and even choice of words) according to the requirements of a particular role or as they switch from talking in a pretend way to talking for real. As the repertoire of roles grows, so do children's vocabulary, mastery of grammar and practical uses of language, and metalinguistic awareness.

Length of play. Mature play is not limited to one short session, but may last for many days as children pick up the theme where they left off and continue playing. Creating, reviewing, and revising the plans are essential parts of the play. Staying with the same play theme for a long time allows children to elaborate on the imaginary situation, integrate new roles, and discover new uses for play props.

How Teachers Can Support Imaginative Play

In the past, children learned how to play at a mature level simply by being part of an extended multi-age group within their own family or in their neighborhood. Unfortunately, with children spending more time in age-segregated groups, that is no longer the case. TV shows and computers, even with carefully selected educational content, cannot replace live play mentors. The teacher needs to take the primary role in helping children develop and maintain mature play.

Some teachers go overboard and become too involved so that the play loses its spontaneous, child-initiated character and changes into another adult-directed activity. Other teachers prefer to limit their interventions in play to the situations in which children get into fights or fail to communicate. They do not intervene when children's play remains stereotypical and unexciting day after day. Thus, children miss opportunities to expand the scope of their play. Teachers can maintain a balance between supporting mature play and keeping it truly child-initiated. To do so, they need to provide specific support for each of the key characteristics of mature play.

Create Imaginary Situations

A good way to guide children in the development of imaginary situations is to provide multipurpose props that can stand for many objects. For example, instead of placing specific dress-up costumes in the dramatic play area, stock it with bolts of differently colored and textured fabrics. Children can then use the same piece of lace to play Sleeping Beauty and Cinderella, wear the same white hat when playing a nurse or a chef, and drape themselves in a piece of fabric with an animal print when playing different animals. Instead of buying plastic food for a pretend restaurant, teachers might use generic paper plates and have children draw food on them or use other objects to represent food (for example, packing peanuts look like marshmallows, and pieces of yarn make great spaghetti).

Some children may not be ready to make their own props and will not play without realistic props. If many children are at this stage, teachers can combine multipurpose props with realistic ones to keep play going and then gradually provide more unstructured materials. At the same time, teachers can use additional strategies to help children create and maintain the imaginary situation. During small-group time, teachers can show the children different common objects and brainstorm how they can use them in different ways in play. For example, a pencil can be a magic wand, a thermometer, a space ship, a stirring spoon, or a conductor's baton. Teachers should always encourage children to use both gestures and words to describe how they are using the object in a pretend way.

Integrate Different Play Themes and Roles

Left to their own devices, children rarely come up with truly imaginative play scenarios because they lack knowledge about the roles and the language needed. As a result, play themes in most classrooms are limited to family, hospital, or store, with few roles to play.

Teachers should use field trips, literature, and videos to expand children's repertoire of play themes and roles. Children rarely incorporate the new themes into their play scenarios, however, if these resources are not used properly and the teacher focuses children's attention on the "things" part of the field trip or video—what is inside a fire station or what happens to the apples when they become apple cider. Instead, teachers should point out the "people" part of each new setting—the many different roles that people have and how the roles relate to one another. Learning about the new roles, language, and actions will help children reenact them later in their play.

Sustain Play

Teachers can support mature play by helping children plan play in advance. Planning helps children communicate about the roles and describe what the person in each role can and cannot do. Children benefit most from advance planning when they record their plans by drawing or writing them. By using these records later as reminders of their play ideas, they may be stimulated to create new developments in their play scenario.

TV shows and computers, even with carefully selected educational content, cannot replace live play mentors.

Children who put effort into planning their future play tend to stay longer with their chosen play theme and get less distracted by what is happening in other areas of the classroom. Teachers see fewer fights in the classrooms when children draw pictures of what they want to play first. For instance, when Monica wants to be the cashier in a pretend bakery, Isabella shows her the plan in which she drew herself at the cash register, so Monica agrees to choose a different role.

Positive Effects of Mature Play

As we worked with preschool and kindergarten teachers on scaffolding children's literacy development (Bodrova & Leong, 2001; Bodrova, Leong, Paynter, & Hensen, 2002; Bodrova, Leong, Paynter, & Hughes, 2002), we noticed that teachers achieved the best results when they focused on supporting mature play. Children in these classrooms not only mastered literacy skills and concepts at a higher rate but also developed better language and social skills and learned how to regulate their physical and cognitive behaviors (Bodrova, Leong, Norford, & Paynter, in press). By contrast, in the classrooms where play was on the back burner, teachers struggled with a variety of problems, including classroom management and children's lack of interest in reading and writing. These results confirm our belief that thoughtfully supported play is essential for young children's learning and development.

References

Bergen, D. (2002). The role of pretend play in children's cognitive development. *Early Childhood Research and Practice, 4*(1). [Online]. Available:http://ecrp.uiuc.edu/v4n1/bergen.html

Bodrova, E., & Leong, D. J. (2001). *The Tools of the Mind Project: A case study of implementing the Vygotskian approach in American early childhood and primary classrooms.* Geneva, Switzerland: International Bureau of Education, UNESCO.

Bodrova, E., Leong, D., Norford, J., & Paynter, D. (in press). It only looks like child's play. *Journal of Staff Development, 2*(24), 15-19.

Bodrova, E., Leong, D. J., Paynter, D. E., & Hensen, R. (2002). *Scaffolding literacy development in a preschool classroom.* Aurora, CO: Mid-continent Research for Education and Learning.

Bodrova, E., Leong, D. J., Paynter, D. E., & Hughes, C. (2002). *Scaffolding literacy development in a kindergarten classroom.* Aurora, CO: Mid-continent Research for Education and Learning.

Bowman, B., Donovan, M. S., & Burns, M. S. (2000). *Eager to learn: Educating our preschoolers.* Washington, DC: National Academies Press.

Ewing Marion Kauffman Foundation. (2002). *Set for success: Building a strong foundation for school readiness based on the social-emotional development of young children.* Kansas City, MO: Author.

Piaget, J. (1962). *Play, dreams, and imitation in childhood.* New York: Norton.

Roskos, K., & Christie, J. F. (Eds.). (2000). *Play and literacy in early childhood: Research from multiple perspectives.* Mahwah, NJ: Erlbaum.

Shonkoff, J. P., & Phillips, D. A. (Eds.). (2000). *From neurons to neighborhoods: The science of early childhood development.* Washington, DC: National Academies Press.

Smilansky, S., & Shefatya, L. (1990). *Facilitating play: A medium for promoting cognitive, socio-emotional, and academic development in young children.* Gaithersburg, MD: Psychological and Educational Publications.

Vygotsky, L. (1978). *Mind in society: The development of higher psychological processes.* Cambridge, MA: Harvard University Press.

Elena Bodrova is a senior consultant with Mid-continent Research for Education and Learning, 2550 S. Parker Rd., Ste. 500, Aurora, CO 80014, and a research fellow for the National Institute for Early Education Research; ebodrova@mcrel.org. **Deborah J. Leong** is a professor of psychology at Metropolitan State College of Denver, P.O. Box 173362, Denver, CO 80217, and a research fellow for the National Institute for Early Education Research; leongd@mscd.edu.

creating home-school partnerships

BY KERI PETERSON

"Home-school partnerships command a lot of attention these days. The federal government has issued documents to help schools organize parent participation programs. Major reform efforts and educational interventions list parental involvement as an important ingredient. Scholarly writing on the topic abounds, and various publications offer guidance to schools or describe exemplary programs" (Finn, 1998, p. 20). "Early interventionists have recognized for many years that the most powerful, efficient, and effective system for making a lasting difference in the life of a child has always been the family" (Gage and Workman, 1994, p. 74). Schools often recognize this, but teachers all too frequently get discouraged and don't spend the needed energy to establish and nurture partnerships with parents. This article will explain what home-school partnerships are, discuss the benefits that home-school partnerships create, present barriers for effective home-school partnerships and, finally, offer suggestions for improvement of home-school partnerships.

WHAT DO HOME-SCHOOL PARTNERSHIPS LOOK LIKE?

Parental involvement can simply be categorized in two ways: parental engagement in school activities and parental engagement at home. Traditionally, parental engagement in school activities "has encompassed a variety of activities such as volunteering in the classroom, participating in parent conferences and home visits, communications between parent and teacher via phone, and written means, assisting with fundraising and special events, and participating on advisory boards. Essentially, parents have been invited and welcomed to be involved in the established structure of a program for their child" (McBride, 1999, p. 62). Parents engaged at home may look differently from one family to another, but may include "actively organizing and monitoring the child's time, helping with homework, discussing school matters with the child, and reading to and being read to by their children" (Finn, 1998, p. 20).

WHO BENEFITS FROM HOME-SCHOOL PARTNERSHIPS?

All of those involved (teacher, child, and parent) in home-school partnerships stand to gain from the relationship that is created between the school and the family. In a study conducted of nine kindergarten children who seemed headed for reading difficulties in first grade, Goldenberg concluded that "the earlier in a child's school career his/her parents become involved, and that involvement is sustained, the bigger the payoff" (Eldridge, 2001, p. 65).

Parental involvement benefits children both academically and in their behaviors and feelings about school. "The benefits for young children begin with greater gains in reading for those children whose parents are encouraged by the teacher to help with reading activities at home" (Eldridge, 2001, p. 65). In an elementary school in Oakland, CA, four classrooms piloted a Home-School Connections project in their classrooms. "Activities included frequent information updates, via phone and mail, family homework projects that encouraged reading at home, and a series of family seminars on such topics as homework help and reading. Parents felt free to visit the classrooms and to communicate with the teacher by phone. Although it is difficult to assess the direct impact of this close family connection, students in the pilot classrooms had some of the highest reading scores in the school" (Cohn-Vargas and Grose, 1998, p. 45). "Extensive research reviews find that the home environment is among the most important influences on academic performance" (Finn, 1998, p. 20). Simply put, the amount of time parents spend monitoring their children's activities and assisting their children with homework has a dramatic effect on how successful their children are academically. "Additionally, children of parents who are involved have a more positive attitude about school, improved attendance, and show better homework habits than do children whose families are less involved" (Eldridge, 2001, p. 65).

Parents that become involved in their child's schooling can benefit significantly from the experience. "Parents involved with school in parent-related activities show increased self-confidence in parenting, more knowledge of child development, and an expanded understanding of the home as an environment for learning" (Eldridge, 2001, p. 66). Involved parents report that they feel they should help their child at home, that they understand more about what the child is being taught, that they know more about the school program, and that they support and encourage their child's school work (Eldridge, 2001, pp. 65–66). "Additionally, involved parents show an increased appreciation for a teacher's merits and abilities and are more likely to view positively a teacher's interpersonal skills" (Eldridge, 2001, p. 66).

Parental involvement also affects the teacher. "A teacher who involves parents in children's learning is more likely to report a greater understanding of families' cultures, an increased appreciation for parental interest in helping their children, and a deeper respect for parents' time and abilities" (Eldridge, 2001, p.

66). Teachers who are committed to parental involvement tend to reap significant positive benefits in terms of parental perceptions of their merits. When parents and teachers connect, both will see significant and lasting effects in their appreciation and understanding of each other's efforts (Eldridge, 2001, p. 66).

BARRIERS TO HOME-SCHOOL CONNECTIONS

There are several barriers that prevent effective home-school connections from happening in many schools across our nation. Most of these barriers involve the school and the parents. In my experience as a primary classroom teacher, children have always enjoyed their parents' involvement and have, in fact, shown much enthusiasm for it.

One barrier to home-school connections is the lack of knowledge and training teachers have regarding parental involvement. "Despite the strong evidence supporting the importance of home-school collaborations, prospective teachers receive little training, information, or experience working with parents. Surprisingly few in-service programs have been designed to support teachers in expanding or improving their parent involvement efforts" (Brand, 1996, p. 76). Many teachers feel uncomfortable and awkward around parents and have had little training on how to overcome their feelings, let alone truly support and encourage home-school partnerships.

Another barrier to home-school partnerships is that many parents do not fully understand how valuable and important their interactions with their children are. Parents also don't feel they have the ability to truly help their child academically. "Many parents express a belief that their assistance is not needed by the schools or teachers" (Eldridge, 2001, p. 66). "Well-designed school opportunities and incentives for parent involvement may have only limited success if they do not also address parents' ideas about their role in children's education and their self efficacy for helping their children succeed in school" (Powell, 1998, p. 64). Researchers have discovered that children succeed in school more often when the home is emotionally supportive, when parents provide reassurance when their

child encounters failure and when parents accept responsibility for assisting their children (Finn, 1998, p. 20). Barriers are created when homes and parents do not closely resemble these ideas.

"The reason some families don't become more involved in schools stems in part from parental perceptions of school. Menacker, Hurwitz, and Weldon (1988) reporting on home-school relations in inner-city schools, noted that most of the adults in these families had had unsuccessful or negative school experiences themselves, which contribute to their perception of the school as unresponsive" (Eldridge, 2001, p. 66).

Timing of home-school connections often creates a barrier for parents as well. "Time constraints and work schedules of parents have been found to be problems in involvement efforts" (Eldridge, 2001, p. 67). When schools do not offer programs that are flexible, such as evening events, participation levels decrease.

"Family circumstances also need to be addressed in attempts to remove barriers to participation in meetings" (Powell, 1998, p. 64). Schools that do not take into account child care arrangements and transportation barriers, for example, experience less parental involvement in home-school partnerships, especially with low-income families. In a recent study in 12 Baltimore schools, parental involvement increased by 10 percent when a high level of support (transportation to workshops, child care, meals, two meeting times) was offered to families. "It appeared that the additional 10 percent was a higher-risk group as measured by children's reading achievement and teacher ratings of the home educational environment" (Powell, 1998, p. 64). It is likely that there are many other barriers to effective home-school partnerships. It is important for schools to identify as many barriers as possible so that they may be eliminated in hopes of creating stronger partnerships with the families it serves.

SUGGESTIONS FOR IMPROVING HOME-SCHOOL PARTNERSHIPS

"Across all populations and programs, a major challenge is to develop ways of engaging parents that respond to a family's interests and life circumstances"

(Powell, 1998, p. 63). "Our understanding of parent involvement needs to be on a continuum that allows for parent participation on a variety of levels and through a wide variety of activities" (Gage and Workman, 1994, p. 77).

"First and foremost, a teacher should create a classroom climate that is open and accepting of parents and is based on a partnership approach. In this way the barriers of parental reluctance and awkwardness are lowered, and those parents who know the school to be unresponsive can begin to experience the classroom in another way" (Eldridge, 2001, p. 67). In order to do this, more universities and school districts need to be better training teachers on parental involvement concepts so that home-school partnerships are natural for teachers. "The currently weak attention to teachers' demonstrated skills in relating to parents must be strengthened in professional education and state certification requirements. It appears that, among the many competencies required for effective work with parents, special emphasis should be given to skills in learning and appreciating the perspectives of families" (Powell, 1998, p. 66).

One important thought to remember that may help improve home-school partnerships is the idea of what home-school partnerships "look like."

"Teachers pay more attention to students whose parents are involved in school" (Finn, 1998, p. 23). Often, educators dismiss the work that families do at home with their children—forgetting that the "home environment is among the most important influences on academic performance" (Finn, 1998, p. 20). One suggestion for improvement, then, would be for educators to recognize the work that families do at home. "The most powerful form of parent involvement has the parent actively involved with the child at home in all ways that relate to optimal learning and growing" (Gage and Workman, 1994, p. 77).

Research indicates that as educators we need to be telling parents about how important their job is and how much what they do with their children at home affects their achievement in the classroom. "Many parents feel they lack, or do lack, the skills to guide their children's reading or schoolwork" (Finn, 1998, p. 22). Sup-

BARRIERS TO POSITIVE FAMILY-TEACHER PARTNERSHIPS

BY AMY SUSSNA KLEIN, ED.D., AND MARIAN MILLER, M.ED.

There are a number of barriers that can prevent positive family-teacher relationships from forming. Some of these common obstacles include:

- **Differences in backgrounds.** The family and teacher come from different cultures, languages, and socio-economic statuses.
- **Stress.** There is stress for both families and teachers. For example, long hours and little flexibility at work reduce the time available for teachers to work on family communication and for parents/caregivers to relate to school.
- **Differing Values.** The family and teacher lack a mutual set of values.
- **Differences in viewing roles.** Differing views of the role of the school for the child between the teacher and the parent or caregiver.
- **Types of experiences.** Prior experiences with families/teachers have set up differing expectations.
- **Notions of openness.** Lack of openness to outsiders entering their territory (home or school).
- **Differences in experiences.** A parent's experience in school (positive or negative) sets up some expectations for their own interactions with school/teacher for their own child.

- **Communication abilities.** Teachers or families lack the ability to identify and communicate key experiences, ideas, or issues.
- **Communication discomfort.** Families or teachers are uncomfortable about communicating their needs, or do not have enough fluency in the language.
- **Need to feel valued.** Parents and teachers perceive that their perspective and opinions are not valued.
- **Differences in viewing child's needs.** The school views the child (her learning and development) differently than the family does. The school's philosophy differs from the family's view of appropriate child rearing. For example: The family equates teaching with telling, and the teacher equates learning with doing. Or, behavior issues are handled one way at home and another at school (spanking at home, explaining at school). When the school clearly explains philosophy, families get a better sense of the match between home/school expectations.

Amy Sussna Klein, Ed.D., is President of ASK Education Consulting. She can be reached by email at Askeducation@cs.com.

Marian Miller, M.Ed., is a faculty member at Lesley College

porting and encouraging parents in their role as their child's first teacher is vital to their child's success.

"To serve the needs of diverse children and families, teachers often must seek support for children and families beyond the traditional walls of the school" (Hurd, Lerner and Barton, 1999, p. 74). Schools need to continue to rely on community agencies to help in the effort of educating our children. "Dryfoos (1990) finds that when collaboration occurs between the school and the youth- and family-serving agencies and the community programs in which the school is embedded, an integrated and comprehensive community-wide system is established" (Hurd, Lerner and Barton, 1999, p. 74). Head Start is a well-known leader of an integrated services model.

CONCLUSION

"Teaching, nurturing, and caring for children is a community process. When most effective, many constituents—parents, teachers, extended family, neighborhoods, agencies, and community partners—are engaged. In the best of worlds, all parties work together to support children in the context of their families" (Hurd, Lerner and Barton, 1999, p. 74).

REFERENCES

Brand, S. (1996). Making parent involvement a reality: Helping teachers develop partnerships with parents. *Young Children,* 51(2), 76–80.
Cohn-Vargas and Grose, K. (1998). A partnership for literacy. *Educational Leadership,* 55(8), 45–48.
Eldridge, D. (2001). Parent involvement: It's worth the effort. *Young Children,* 56(4), 65–69.
Finn, J. (1998). Parental engagement that makes a difference. *Educational Leadership,* 55(8), 20–24.
Gage, J. and Workman, S. (1994). Creating family support systems: In head start and beyond. *Young Children,* 49(7), 74–77.
Hurd, T., Learner, R., and Barton, C. (1999). Integrated services: Expanding partnerships to meet the needs of today's children and families. *Young Children,* 54(2), 74–79.
McBride, S. (1999). Family centered practices. *Young Children,* 54(3), 62–68.
Powell, D. (1998). Reweaving parents into the fabric of early childhood programs. *Young Children,* 53(6), 60–67.

Keri Peterson is a teacher in the four-year-old program at Early Learning Center, Tiffany Creek Elementary School, in Boyceville, WI. She is currently enrolled in the M.S. program at the University of Wisconsin-Stout.

Opportunity Deferred or Opportunity Taken?

An Updated Look at Delaying Kindergarten Entry

Hermine H. Marshall

Many families find themselves in a quandary about whether their child is ready for kindergarten, even though he or she is legally eligible to enroll. They often seek the advice of the preschool or kindergarten teacher concerning their child's readiness. One family may wonder whether their child is mature enough. Another family may consider keeping their child out of school an extra year because the family wants to give the child an extra advantage. This practice has been labeled *redshirting*, analogous to the deferment procedure in high school and college sports. Teachers themselves may have concerns about certain children in their class, and therefore need to be aware of the latest research regarding the consequences of keeping eligible children out of school an extra year.

Parent concerns often are based on outdated beliefs and assumptions about the meaning of readiness. In the following sections, I discuss these assumptions and accompanying pressures as well as teachers' and parents' beliefs about prerequisites for kindergarten success. Then I summarize recent research on the effects on both the academic and social domains of delaying children's entry into school.

To ensure the quality of the research reviewed, I began with research that was published only in peer-reviewed journals. I then eliminated studies that were inadequate in terms of such factors as (a) reliability, validity, meaningfulness, and bias of the measures and (b) equivalency of control groups. I added a book-length interview study of the meaning of readiness (Graue 1993b) that provides insights regarding beliefs not available from other sources. I conclude the article with suggestions for early childhood educators to help families in their decisions.

What is *Redshirting*

The term *redshirting* refers to the practice of keeping students off a varsity athletic team on the assumption that in the following year their more mature bodies and skills will enable them to be better athletes.

Assumptions and pressures

Unexamined assumptions about the meaning of readiness held by families and teachers as well as pressures on administrators for accountability influence decisions about whether to recommend holding children out of kindergarten. Assumptions based on beliefs about the relative importance to development and learning of maturation versus interactive stimulation and teaching are elaborated on, followed by a discussion of the effects of accountability pressures on kindergarten entry decisions.

The meaning of readiness

Maturationist assumptions. For many years readiness for school was conceptualized in terms of the maturation of cognitive, social, and physical abilities. These abilities were perceived as developing essentially on their own according to a child's own time clock, without regard to stimulation from the outside environment. The idea that development proceeds in a linear and automatic manner has been interpreted to mean that certain levels of maturity need to be reached before children can succeed in school.

Maturationists believe that the passage of time will produce readiness. They generally advise delaying school entry for some children, especially those whose birthdays occur near the cutoff date and those considered not ready for kindergarten by teachers, caregivers, and parents who believe that with the simple passage of time, children will achieve higher levels of development and greater readiness to participate in kindergarten.

Interactionist assumptions. An alternate conception of readiness derives from interactionist and constructivist views. The work of Piaget is often mistakenly interpreted as supporting the view that children must reach a certain level of development before they are ready to learn new strategies or skills. Frequently overlooked, however, is Piaget's view that development results from the interaction between a child and the physical and social world (see Liben 1987).

Piaget did not believe that development is automatic. Rather, he believed that development must be stimulated by children's interactions with the world around them and the people with whom they come in contact. A child may handle an object in a new way and make new discoveries that lead to higher levels of thinking. Or children may watch other children do something they had not thought of, and this may cause them to try new actions. Or a peer or teacher might ask a question that stimulates new ways of thinking. According to this interactionist view, interactive stimulation rather than age or maturation alone contributes to development and to readiness for new tasks.

> The only legally and ethically defensible criterion for determining school entry is whether the child has reached the legal chronological age of school entry.

Extending this view further, Vygotsky (1978) described how learning, development, and readiness for new learning often require guidance and instruction, not just the passage of time. In Vygotsky's view, learning and often teaching precede development. New knowledge and skills result from support or *scaffolding* by an adult or a more expert peer. According to this view, the point is not that children need to be

ready for school, but that schools need to be ready to guide, support, and instruct each child, regardless of the skills or knowledge a child brings. Age is largely irrelevant. In fact, research in countries with different age requirements for school entry shows that the oldest entrants in one country would be the youngest in another (Shepard & Smith 1986).

Countering a maturationist perspective, the National Association for the Education of Young Children (NAEYC) points out that believing that children need basic skills before they can proceed is a misconception. For example, children can compose stories that are far more complex than those they can read. In other words, learning does not occur according to a rigid sequence of skills (NAEYC 1990).

Pressures

Accountability pressures have led some school districts to raise the age of school entry, with the goal of ensuring that children are ready for tasks formerly found in first grade. With older, supposedly more mature children at each grade, administrators in districts in which children enter at an older age hope for higher average achievement scores. However, raising the entrance age provides only a temporary solution. A more academic kindergarten curriculum increases the number of families who hold out their children (Cosden, Zimmer, & Tuss 1993). When families delay their children's school entry, the children who have been redshirted require a more advanced curriculum—thereby boosting the spiral upward.

The need for appropriate support and stimulation for children and the futility of increasing school entry age form the basis for the position of NAEYC: "The only legally and ethically defensible criterion for determining school entry is whether the child has reached the legal chronological age of school entry" (NAEYC 1990, 22). Kagan (1992) adds that in addition to "a clear defensible standard, the flexibility to individualize ... services according to children's needs after entry" (p. 51) is necessary. It is the

school's responsibility to meet the needs of the children who are legally eligible. Similar concerns are expressed in the position statement on kindergarten trends developed by the National Association of Early Childhood Specialists in State Departments of Education, and endorsed by NAEYC, "Not only is there a preponderance of evidence that there is no academic benefit from retention in its many forms, but there also appear to be threats to the social-emotional development of the child subjected to such practices" (NAECS/SDE 2000).

Beliefs

The beliefs of families, preschool and kindergarten teachers, school administrators, and pediatricians concerning the prerequisites for kindergarten influence decisions about school entry. These include beliefs concerning skills and attitudes important to school success and beliefs underlying families' consideration of delaying kindergarten for their children.

Beliefs about prerequisite resources and skills

For children to start school ready to learn, experts on the National Education Goals Panel emphasized five interrelated dimensions of development:

- physical well-being and motor development
- social and emotional development
- approaches to learning
- language use
- cognition and general knowledge (Kagan, Moore, & Bredekamp 1995)

On a more specific level, in the National Household Education Survey—a nationally representative sample of families of four- to six-year-olds not yet in school—parents rated taking turns, sitting still and paying attention, and knowing letters as important (Diamond, Reagan, & Bandik 2000).

In a mostly African American and Latino urban district that had high rates of poverty as well as high drop-out, grade retention, and special education placement rates, parents of both ethnicities agreed with teachers that health and social competence were important prerequisites (Piotrkowski, Botsko, & Matthews 2000). However, parents of both ethnicities emphasized academic skills and compliance with teacher authority to a greater extent than did teachers. Regardless of their educational level, parents believed that children's knowledge was more important than their approach to learning. Preschool teachers in this study, like those in a sample from a less impoverished community (Hains et al. 1989), had higher expectations for entry level skills than did kindergarten teachers.

What Teachers Can Do

What can you do if you are concerned about the readiness of any of the children in your preschool or kindergarten class?

Explore resources for screening for suspected problems in speech, hearing, vision, communication, or motor development. Discuss your concern with the family, prefacing your remarks with the caveat that children develop at different rates. Emphasize that to avoid problems in the future, it might be wise to have expert guidance.

Be sure your program includes opportunities for children to develop social and communication skills along with cognitive and motor skills. Model appropriate ways to enter a group, to ask for a desired object, to solve problems. Use stories and puppets to raise social dilemmas. Have the children suggest ways to solve the dilemma. Discuss with the family ways to enhance their child's social and communication skills.

If your concerns relate to parenting skills, include good parenting practices in your parent education meetings or recommend parenting classes.

Teachers' beliefs, program implementation, and effects on parents

Teachers' and administrators' beliefs as well as pressures from other teachers affect teachers' perceptions of children's readiness for school. These beliefs also affect how they deliver programs for children. Graue's (1993b) fascinating study of conceptions of readiness in kindergarten classrooms in three different schools within the same school district shows contrasting views and practices.

Fulton. The kindergarten teacher at Fulton, a school in a working class community, saw readiness as comprised of both the child's maturational level and an environmental component that the teacher provided through appropriate activities and feedback. The teachers in this school "tended to work on an interventionist model of readiness ... [to] allow precise remediation of problems" (Graue 1993b, 236). For example, an extended-day kindergarten program was developed with the goal of encouraging all children to learn the skills needed to leave kindergarten on an equal level. Families in this school relied on the staff to gain an understanding of the meaning of readiness. Consistent with an interactionist approach in which teachers see their role as providing needed learning materials and stimulation, holding children out was not a popular idea at Fulton.

Rochester. An interventionist approach was also in place in one kindergarten at Rochester, a school with children from different socioeconomic backgrounds and ethnicities in a community with a large bilingual population. The teacher in the extended-day bilingual class that Graue studied believed that provision of environmental stimulation was critical to enhancing the readiness of the children because they lacked the kinds of preschool experiences from which other children benefited. The bilingual families in this class, like the families at Fulton, counted on the teacher to interpret the meaning of readiness

for them. They entered their children when they were eligible, whereas affluent families at Rochester were more likely to hold their children out.

Parents rated taking turns, sitting still and paying attention, and knowing letters as important.

Norwood. In contrast, the teachers at Norwood, a school in a primarily Anglo, middle-class community, held a maturationist model of readiness. As opposed to schools where teachers worked together to understand and meet the needs of individual children, the kindergarten teachers at Norwood felt pressured by the first grade teachers to produce students who could meet fairly rigid standards for first grade entry. The kindergarten teacher in the class studied believed that readiness was related to age. She expected younger children to be less ready.

Not surprisingly, the parents at Norwood also conceived of readiness "in terms of age, maturity, and social behaviors necessary to do well in school" (Graue 1993b, 230). They worried about whether their children had the necessary skills for kindergarten success. They were also aware of the expectations of the first grade teachers.

More parents at Norwood delayed kindergarten entry for their children, especially boys, apparently to ensure success—although these parents were not necessarily concerned about their children's academic readiness. Fourteen percent of kindergarten boys in the school and close to 40 percent of the boys in the class studied had been held out an extra year. (Other studies, e.g., Graue & DiPerna 2000, also show that boys are more frequently held out.) Various extra-year programs were tried in attempts to provide children with more time to develop readiness.

Clearly, the beliefs and practices of the Norwood administration and teachers influenced not only their

What We DO Know about Holding Children Out

1. Some families delay their child's kindergarten entry because of maturity concerns. Often these concerns are influenced by the culture of the school or community.
2. On average, delaying kindergarten entry has no long-term effect on academic achievement. By about third grade, any early differences disappear. However, the combination of youngness and low ability may have negative consequences for achievement.
3. Holding children out deprives them of instruction that, regardless of age, promotes learning of many skills.
4. Holding children out does not result in any social advantage. There are no differences in peer acceptance or self-concept. On the contrary, some children who are redshirted worry that they have failed and develop poor attitudes toward school. They are more likely later to have behavior problems and to drop out.
5. Children who have been held out are more likely to receive special education services later. Enrolling children when they are eligible may lead to their receiving help earlier.
6. In developmentally appropriate kindergartens, children's age or maturity should make no difference. In kindergartens that are pressure-cookers influenced by the demands of achievement-oriented teachers, families may have greater cause for concern.

practices, but also the beliefs and decisions of parents. The beliefs in this school were similar to those of parents and teachers in another high achieving school studied by Graue (1993a).

Parents' beliefs related to delaying kindergarten entry

Very little research is available about parents' reasons for delaying kindergarten entry. In making their decisions, parents of four- to six-year-olds in the National Household Education Survey expressed concern about their children's preacademic skills rather than about reports of their behavior (Diamond, Reagan, & Bandik 2000). Although Anglo parents were less likely than other parents to be concerned about their children's readiness (how-

ever, 13.5 percent were)—even with level of parent education controlled—these parents and parents with higher education levels were more likely to suggest delaying their child's kindergarten entry.

Only the study by Graue (1993b), noted earlier, specifically sought information about parents' actual decisions prior to the beginning of school. Graue conducted interviews with the parents of the five or six oldest and youngest children scheduled to enter kindergarten in each school about what they thought about kindergarten entrance. Parents at all three schools expressed concerns about maturity, which they saw in terms of personal and social characteristics, rather than academic knowledge. Many also emphasized wanting their children to have a good start. The culture at Norwood

and of the more affluent parents at Rochester seemed to encourage parents to hold their children out. For example, of the six parents interviewed at Norwood, three had kept their age-eligible children (two boys and one girl) out the previous year. Greg's mother wondered about his emotional readiness. She was the only parent to state that the major reason for holding her child out was to give him an advantage in high school sports (reflecting the traditional meaning of redshirting). She commented, "Plus, everyone says how boys are so much later blooming in a lot of ways" (Graue 1993b, 128). The decision of one parent at Rochester to hold out her son was influenced by the fact that her own brother had been held back in third grade and did better following retention.

What We DON'T Know about Holding Children Out

1. Little information is available about why parents hold their children out. The one interview study included only a small number of families. We do not know if parents suspect that their child has some problem, which they hope will disappear with the passage of time, that could prevent him (or occasionally her) from being successful in kindergarten.
2. There are no longitudinal studies that follow individual children over their school career that include information about why each child was held out and whether they received special services during the extra year. The research results reported are based on averages. Therefore, we cannot predict under what circumstances which children might encounter negative consequences nor which children might benefit from being held out and provided with what types of special services.
3. We do not know whether children's progess differs depending on whether the decision to delay was based on family concerns or whether it was the result of district screening.
4. There is no way of knowing whether children who were held out might have fared more poorly if they had not been held out (Stipek 2002). Controlled studies to investigate this possibility would be difficult to conduct.

Even among those whose children entered Norwood when eligible, parents expressed reservations. Typical was Alyson's mother, who worried that Alyson's September birth date put her at a disadvantage, although both mother and preschool teacher thought she was ready. However, the mother's desire for her child to be at the top of her class made her consider keeping her out an additional year. Families of older children often stated that they were glad their children were more mature and would feel stronger about themselves.

Effects of delaying school entry

Maturationists predict that children whose kindergarten entry is delayed will fare better in school. However, as we will see, research does not substantiate the predicted beneficial effects on achievement, self-concept, or social development. The research results are summarized below according to their focus on academic or social effects.

Academic effects

The classic review of the literature by Shepard and Smith (1986) indicates that although the oldest children in a class on average are more successful than their younger peers in the first few grades (in first grade by about 7–8 percentile points), these differences are of little practical significance and usually disappear by grade three. Most of the differences are almost entirely attributable to children who fall below the 25th percentile in ability. That is, it seems that the combination of young age and low ability has negative consequences for achievement. Moreover, the validity of those studies in which differences were found can be questioned on the basis of criteria that are subject to teacher bias. The influence of teacher expectations regarding age can also be seen in teachers' tendencies to retain more younger than older students even if their skills are equally deficient.

> **Research does not substantiate the predicted beneficial effects on achievement, self-concept, or social development.**

Many studies have been conducted over the past 15 years that shed further light on the issue but essentially uphold Shepard and Smith's basic findings. For example, in a study of African American and Caucasian urban children, older children performed slightly but significantly better academically in grade one, but these differences disappeared four years later (Bickel, Zigmond, & Staghorn 1991; see also Cameron & Wilson 1990). In a study of children in families with very low incomes from a predominantly Anglo rural community, a predominantly African American urban community, and a predominantly Latino urban community, the oldest children scored higher than the youngest in reading and math in kindergarten, but these differences disappeared by grade three. Similarly, for upper-middle-class children, performance differences decreased by grade five (Sweetland & DeSimone 1987).

A comparison of children in a transitional (readiness) first grade classroom with children who were selected but not placed in that classroom, remaining in first grade, showed no significant differences in second grade achievement (Ferguson 1991). That is, having an extra year with a "dumbed-down curriculum" and attaining an older age had no positive effect on children's achievement or need for other services. A recent review of the empirical literature concludes that delayed entry as well as retention and transition class practices are not effective (Carlton & Winsler 1999).

Schooling vs. allowing time to mature. Among the advantages of children entering when eligible is that some skills, such as those needed for reading readiness, require instruction. A well controlled study of more than 500 children in a

district with developmentally appropriate kindergartens compared young first-graders (whose birthdays fell within two months of the cutoff date) with older kindergartners (whose birthdays fell within two months following the cutoff date) and older first-graders (who were one year older than the older kindergartners). At pretest, the reading and math achievement scores of younger first-graders were lower than those of older first-graders but higher than those of older kindergartners. The same was true at posttest. The differences between older kindergartners and younger first-graders on pretest indicate that a year in kindergarten has instructional benefits.

> **Children whose entry into school has been delayed do not seem to gain an advantage socially.**

Moreover, there was no difference in the progress of younger and older first-graders from fall to spring. That is, each group achieved one year's growth. In addition, younger firstgraders' progress exceeded that of older kindergartners, suggesting that age is an insufficient criterion for benefiting from reading and math instruction in first grade (Morrison, Griffith, & Alberts 1997).

Other studies comparing same-age children in different grades showed that by the end of first grade, younger children's reading ability was no different from their older classmates' (Crone & Whitehurst 1999), and math achievement scores were higher than those of their same-age peers who were still in kindergarten (Stipek & Byler 2001; see also Morrison, Smith, & Dow-Ehrensberger 1995). After reviewing the research literature, Stipek (2002) concluded that for math and most reading and literacy skills, the effects of schooling seem to be more potent than the effects of time to mature; whereas for certain tasks, such as conservation and story recall and production, general maturation and

What to Advise Families

What advice can preschool teachers and early childhood caregivers give to families who question whether their child is ready for kindergarten?

First, it is wise to become familiar with what the kindergartens in your area expect in terms of abilities and whether they are prepared to meet the needs of all children. If kindergartens are overly academic and competitive, advocate for developmentally appropriate classes. Help families understand what this means so they also can advocate for kindergartens that are prepared to receive, support, and stimulate all children.

Second, find out why families are considering holding their child out. If it is due only to a late birthday, tell them that although we cannot predict for individual children, research shows that any early achievement differences generally disappear by third grade and that children who are held out may worry that they have failed. These children are also more likely to have behavior problems by high school and to drop out of school. Some evidence suggests that children placed in readiness programs are also more likely to drop out. Encourage families to take the long view and think about what they would like their child to be like in 10 to 15 years.

For families concerned about their child's social skills, let them know that delaying kindergarten does not provide children with a social advantage. Focus on finding ways to enhance children's social skills through your curriculum. Suggest things that a family can do, like arranging for the child to play with another compatible child.

If a family is concerned about communication skills, suggest activities the family can do with the child or refer them to a specialist. Tell them that if special services are needed, the child's entry at the eligible age might provide these services earlier.

Although parents are unlikely to admit it, some may want to keep their child out because of their own needs and fears of separation. If you suspect that this is the case, reassure them that this is not uncommon. Refocus them on their long-term goals for their child.

You can also present information about readiness concerns and the development of skills at a parent education meeting.

---

experience are likely to contribute to skill acquisition. Other work suggests that instruction in school may contribute to the development of children's working-memory strategies (Ferreira & Morrison 1994).

Factors other than age. An additional point to consider is that a substantial number of redshirted and retained children have above average IQ scores (Morrison, Griffith, & Alberts 1997). The number of younger and older students who qualified for a gifted program was similar, although more older students were sent to be evaluated (De Meis & Stearn 1992)—perhaps exemplifying teacher expectations. Even though the oldest children in a large nationally representative study were more likely than the youngest to score in the highest quartile in reading, math, and general knowledge, some of the youngest also scored in the highest quartile and some of the older children scored in the lowest quartile (West, Denton, & Germino-Hausken 2000). Many other factors, such as mother's education and marital status, had similar relationships. Hence, it is not age alone that contributes to children's achievement.

It is important to note that parents who hold their children out for social reasons may be disappointed by the lack of academic content and challenge in some kindergartens. They often discover that their children encounter what appears to be largely a repeat of preschool (Graue 1993a).

Social effects

Contrary to popular belief, children whose entry into school has been delayed do not seem to gain an advantage socially. In fact, more drawbacks than advantages are evident. Many children who have been redshirted worry that they have failed or been held back (Graue 1993b) and often have poor attitudes toward school (Shepard & Smith 1989; Graue & DiPerna 2000). Furthermore, students who are too old for grade are less likely to graduate from high school. However, according to Meisels (1992), "[i]t is possible that middle- to upper-income students who have been held out will form a subgroup of overage students who will not be at risk for dropping out in the same way as other students, but this is yet to be demonstrated" (p. 167).

Social development. Reviews of the literature have found no difference in self-concept, peer acceptance, or teacher ratings of behavior (Graue & DiPerna 2000; see also Stipek & Byler 2001). In one study of social adjustment and self-perceptions in a mostly Anglo and Latino sample, the few correlations found between social functioning and age were subject to teacher bias; and most of these differences disappeared by grade one (Spitzer, Cupp, & Parke 1995). No differences were found in self-reported school adjustment, loneliness, perceptions of competence, or acceptance. However, although younger children were no more likely than older children to be rejected or neglected, they were less likely to be nominated by peers as well liked and as showing prosocial behavior.

Children who were deemed unready according to the Gesell Test (Ilg & Ames 1965) and placed in a developmental kindergarten or pre-first-grade class showed no difference in ratings for social development in first grade when compared to a matched control group (Matthews, May, & Kundert 1999). Those who were identified as immature but who did not attend readiness programs were no more likely to miss school or receive poor social development ratings in grade one than those who had attended the readiness classes. However, a greater number of students identified as unready to enter school but who were not placed in readiness programs were retained at some point in their school career, and half of these retentions were made in kindergarten.

These results raise several questions: How many of the decisions to retain children have been based on a screening test with questionable reliability and validity? Were kindergarten teachers more likely to retain those children whose parents did not follow through on recommendations? Or were parents and teachers reluctant to retain those already overage from earlier developmental placement? More important, would special help during the kindergarten year have obviated the need for retention?

For more on redshirting…

Go to the academic redshirting information page of the ERIC Clearinghouse on Elementary and Early Childhood Education: `http://ericeece.org/faq/redshirting.html`.

Challenging behaviors. Those who advocate the benefits of delaying kindergarten entry predict fewer behavior problems for children who are unready and whose entry is delayed. With the exception of a study by Bickel, Zigmond, and Staghorn (1991), studies have found an increase in behavior problems for children held out or those placed in a transition class (Ferguson 1991; Graue & DiPerna 2000). Note, however, that although the study of urban African American and Caucasian children by Bickel and associates found no difference in report card ratings of conduct, referrals, and retentions when controlled for socioeconomic level, preschool attendance, and race, the measure

used in the study is subject to teacher bias.

Moreover, a large crosssectional survey of more than nine thousand children at different ages shows that by adolescence, the overage children, even those who had not been retained, had higher rates of parent-reported behavior problems, such as bullying, trouble getting along with others, depression, losing temper, feeling inferior; and after age twelve, hanging out with kids who get in trouble—even though these children had low scores for being at risk when they were younger (Byrd, Weitzman, & Auinger 1997). This was especially true for the Caucasian youth. Children who have been redshirted were also found to need more special services, not fewer (Graue & DiPerna 2000; see also Matthews, May, & Kundert 1999).

These findings suggest that there may be adverse behavioral consequences associated with the decision to delay kindergarten entry that may not appear until later years. It is not clear whether these problems derive from the effects of holding children out or from some preexisting condition that influenced parents' decisions; however, the latter is unlikely since many problems do not emerge until adolescence.

Influenced by maturationist thinking, parents often believe that with additional time, their child will outgrow a possible problem. What they fail to realize is that the sooner the nature of the problem is identified, the sooner the child can receive special services that may help the child overcome the problem (see also Maxwell & Eller 1994). When children who may have problems enter at the eligible age, they may actually benefit—assuming the school district makes services available and that their teachers refer them for these services rather than advising families to keep these children out an extra year.

Suggestions for advising families

Many families are under the mistaken impression that holding their child out will be beneficial, that it

will give the child the gift of time. But families need to be aware of the possibility of too little challenge and the potential negative effects of holding children out. They need to know about the advantages of enrolling children when they are eligible.

In the cases of children whose entries were not delayed and who were later retained, it is important to consider whether the stimulation provided by the next year's teacher and/or remediation would have allowed the child to catch up without retention. Families also need to consider what would have happened had the child received extra help during the year before he or she was retained. Growth and skill learning are not linear. Some teachers and administrators encourage families to delay kindergarten entry for a number of reasons. Not only might they be unaware of current research on the negative effects of delaying school entry, but they often see only the progress children make during an extra year. They do not consider that similar or greater progress might occur if the child were to enter school and receive stimulation, instruction, and intervention services.

Nor do teachers see the negative consequences, which might not appear until high school. Moreover, pressured administrators frequently believe that if younger children are held out, the achievement scores of the older children remaining will be higher.

Conclusions

Families concerned about their child's maturity and whether to enroll their child in kindergarten when he or she is eligible have often been advised to give the child the gift of time. Research does not support this practice. In fact, delaying kindergarten entry often has negative effects. Families need to consider that by holding their child out, they may in fact be depriving the child of important opportunities for learning—what Graue and DiPerna (2000) refer to as *theft of opportunity*.

Reference

Bickel, D., N. Zigmond, & J. Straghorn. 1991. The effect of school entrance age to first grade: Effects on elementary school success. *Early Childhood Research Quarterly* 6 (2): 105–17.

Byrd, R., M. Weitzman, & P. Auinger. 1997. Increased behavior problems associated with delayed school entry and delayed school progress. *Pediatrics* 100 (4): 651–61.

Cameron, M.B., & B.J. Wilson. 1990. The effects of chronological age, gender, and delay of entry on academic achievement and retention: Implications for academic redshirting. *Psychology in the Schools* 27 (3): 260–63.

Carlton, M., & A. Winsler. 1999. School readiness: The need for a paradigm shift. *School Psychology Review* 28 (3): 338–52.

Cosden, M., J. Zimmer, & P. Tuss. 1993. The impact of age, sex, and ethnicity on kindergarten entry and retention decisions. *Educational Evaluation and Policy Analysis* 15 (2): 209–22.

Crone, D.A., & G.J. Whitehurst. 1999. Age and schooling effects on emergent literacy and early reading skills. *Journal of Educational Psychology* 91 (4): 604–14.

Diamond, K.E., A.J. Reagan, & J.E. Bandyk. 2000. Parents' conceptions of kindergarten readiness: Relationships with race, ethnicity, and development. *Journal of Educational Research* 94 (2): 93–100.

Ferguson, P.C. 1991. Longitudinal outcome differences among promoted and transitional at-risk kindergarten students. *Psychology in the Schools* 28 (2): 139–46.

Ferreira, F., & F.J. Morrison. 1994. Children's metalinguistic knowledge of syntactic constituents: Effects of age and schooling. *Developmental Psychology* 30 (5): 663–78.

Graue, M.E. 1993a. Expectations and ideas coming to school. *Early Childhood Research Quarterly* 8 (1): 53–75.

Graue, M.E. 1993b. *Ready for what? Constructing meanings of readiness for kindergarten*. Albany: State University of New York Press.

Graue, M.E., & J. DiPerna. 2000. Redshirting and early retention: Who gets the "gift of time" and what are its outcomes? *American Educational Research Journal* 37 (2): 509–34.

Ilg, F.L., & L.G. Ames. 1965. *School readiness: Behavior tests used at Gesell Institute*. New York: Harper & Row.

Hains, A.H., S.A. Fowler, I.S. Schwartz, E. Kottwitz, & S. Rosenkotter. 1989. A comparison of preschool and kindergarten teacher expectations for school readiness. *Early Childhood Research Quarterly* 4 (1): 75–88.

Kagan, S.L. 1992. Readiness past, present, and future: Shaping the agenda. Young Children 48 (1) 48–53.

Kagan, S.L., E. Moore, & S. Bredekamp, eds. 1995. *Reconsidering children's early development and learning: Toward common views and vocabulary*. National Educational Goals Panel. Goal 1 Technical Planning Group. Washington, DC: U.S. Government Printing Office.

Liben, L.S. 1987. *Development and learning: Conflict or congruence*. Hillsdale, NJ: Erlbaum.

Matthews, L.L., D.C. May, & D.K. Kundert. 1999. Adjustment outcomes of developmental placement: A longitudinal study. *Psychology in the Schools* 36 (6) 495–504.

Maxwell, K.L., & S.K. Eller. 1994. Children's transition to kindergarten. *Young Children* 49 (6): 56–63.

Meisels, S.J. 1992. Doing harm by doing good: Iatrogenic effects of early childhood enrollment and promotion policies. *Early Childhood Research Quarterly* 7 (2): 55–74.

Morrison, F.J., E.M. Griffith, & D.M. Alberts. 1997. Nature-nurture in the classroom: Entrance age, school readiness, and learning in children. *Developmental Psychology* 33 (2): 254–62.

Morrison, F.J., L.K. Smith, & M. Dow-Ehrensberger. 1995. Education and cognitive development: A naturalistic experiment. *Developmental Psychology* 31 (5): 789–99.

NAECS/SDE (National Association of Early Childhood Specialists in State Departments of Education). 2000. Still unacceptable trends in kindergarten entry and placement. Online: http://www.naeyc.org/resources/position_statements/psunacc.htm.

NAEYC. 1990. Position statement on school readiness. *Young Children* 46 (1): 21–23.

Piotrkowski, C.S., M. Botsko, & E. Matthews. 2000. Parents' and teachers' beliefs about children's school readiness in a high need community. *Early Childhood Research Quarterly* 15 (4): 537–58.

Shepard, L.A., & M.L. Smith. 1986. Synthesis of research on school readiness and kindergarten retention. *Educational Leadership* 44 (3): 78–86.

Spitzer, S., R. Cupp, & R.D. Parke. 1995. School entrance age, social acceptance, and self-perception in kindergarten and first grade. *Early Childhood Research Quarterly* 10 (4): 433–50.

Stipek, D. 2002. At what age should children enter kindergarten? A question for policy makers and parents. *Social Policy Report* 16 (2): 3–17.

Stipek, D., & P. Byler. 2001. Academic achievement and social behaviors associated with age of entry into kindergarten. *Journal of Applied Developmental Psychology* 22 (2): 175–89.

Sweetland, J.D., & P.S. DeSimone. 1987. Age of entry, sex, and academic achievement in elementary school children. *Psychology in the Schools* 24 (4): 406–12.

Vygotsky, L. [1930–35] 1978. *Mind in society: The development of higher psychological processes*, eds. & trans. M. Cole, V. John-Steiner, S. Scriber, & E. Souberman. Cambridge, MA: Harvard University Press.

West, J., K. Denton, & E. Germino-Hausken. 2000. America's kindergartners: Findings from the early childhood longitudinal study, kindergarten class of 1998–99: Fall 1998. *Education Statistics Quarterly* 2 (1): 7–13.

Hermine H. Marshall, Ph.D., is emerita professor at San Francico State University, where she was coordinator of the early childhood education and master's degree programs. She has conducted research on self-concept, self-evaluation, and classroom processes. She thanks Susanna S. Marshland, M.S.W., for comments on an earlier version of this article.

This is one of the regular series of Research in Review columns. The column in this issue was edited by journal research editor **E. Dianne Rothenberg**, codirector of ERIC Clearinghouse on Elementary and

Early Childhood Education at the Early Childhood and Parenting Collaborative, University of Illinois at Urbana-Champaign.

10 Signs of a Great Preschool

Is your child learning or just playing? Here's what makes for an excellent early education.

What an adventure awaits your little one as he heads off to preschool—new friends, new experiences, and new kinds of fun. Though you certainly want your child to enjoy himself, he'll also be practicing important skills that will prepare him for kindergarten and beyond.

"Your 3- or 4-year-old will learn the fundamental building blocks of reading, writing, math, and science, as well as how to interact with teachers and classmates," says Barbara Willer, Ph.D., deputy executive director of the National Association for the Education of Young Children (NAEYC), in Washington, D.C. "However," she says, "the overarching goal of any preschool should be to help a child feel good about himself as a learner and to feel comfortable in a school-like setting."

Chances are you chose your child's school carefully and can rest assured that he's in good hands. However, as you look around the classroom, here's what you should see.

By Irene Daria-Wiener

1 The Right Student-Teacher Ratio

There should be one teacher for every seven to ten students and no more than 20 children per classroom, according to the NAEYC. State laws vary, however, and some permit even higher ratios. Choosing a school that follows the NAEYC guidelines will ensure that your child receives enough attention and that her teachers will get to know her as an individual.

2 Daily Circle Time

During this group meeting, children practice important social skills, such as taking turns, listening to each other, and sitting still. They'll also hone their language skills by listening to stories and singing songs. In fact, singing is very important in pre-

school. "As kids get older, they can link song words to written words, and that encourages literacy," Dr. Willer says. Songs also help children recognize rhythms and count beats, which enhances their understanding of math.

3 A Language-Rich Environment

Children should be read to every day. The classroom should have plenty of books available, as well as words posted all over the walls: signs labeling objects, weather charts, and posters describing the children's activities. Even preschoolers' artwork can be used to promote literacy; teachers should write the children's dictated descriptions ("Here is my brown dog.") on the bottom of their pictures.

4 An Art Center

This should be stocked with easels, chunky paintbrushes, and other materials, such as crayons and clay. While art—and getting messy—is certainly fun, it also allows children to express their thoughts in a way they might not yet be able to in words. In addition, art helps kids develop fine motor control and a basic understanding of science concepts, such as seeing what happens when colors are mixed and how different media create varying textures. It also gives children a sense of how things change as time passes—paint dries and clay hardens.

5 A Block Corner

Building with large blocks has been shown to help children develop crucial spatial and problem-solving skills. For example, your preschooler will learn that two of the small square blocks equal one of the longer rectangular blocks—a fundamental principle of geometry. Boys tend to gravitate to the block corner more than girls do. To help interest girls, some teachers have found it helpful to place dollhouse furniture in the block corner, because girls like to play house with the buildings that they create.

6 Rotating Chores

Besides developing a sense of responsibility and accomplishment, many chores your child will be asked to help out with in preschool foster math basics. For instance, handing out cups, paper plates, or napkins to each child at snack time introduces the key math concept of one-to-one correspondence.

7 Manipulatives

These items build the fine motor skills that are necessary for writing. In addition, puzzles strengthen spatial skills; sorting and counting buttons or beads help develop early math skills; and Peg-Boards and stringing beads require hand-eye coordination, which is also an important part of learning how to write.

8 A Water Table and a Sand Table

Not only are both of these materials fun, but children can explore so much with them—space, size, weight, force, pressure,

terrific teachers

Of course, no matter how good a school is, your child's experience there will depend on whether he has an engaging and energetic teacher. According to Barbara Willer, Ph.D., deputy executive director of the National Association for the Education of Young Children, teachers should:

• Have a bachelor's degree or a formal credential in early-childhood education. "The research is very clear that a teacher with a degree makes a big difference in the quality of the program," Dr. Willer says.
• Come over and kneel down to talk to the children at their eye level and not call to them from across the classroom.
• Greet your child by name and with a smile each morning.
• Structure the daily curriculum around the children's interests and questions and give kids freedom to choose at least some of the activities in which they participate.
• Keep parents informed of the day's activities and of any issues that their child may be having.

and volume, says Lilian Katz, Ph.D., codirector of the ERIC Clearinghouse on Elementary and Early Childhood Education at the University of Illinois at Urbana-Champaign. "Of course, 3- and 4-year-olds will

understand these concepts only on a very rudimentary level, but when they're older, they'll be able to build on their preschool experience," Dr. Katz says.

9 Physical Activity Every Day

Your child's class will probably go to the playground when the weather is nice. But the school should also have equipment (mats, climbing apparatus, tricyles, or other riding toys) and space for the kids to play actively indoors. "Three- and 4-year-olds are still developing their coordination, and need a chance to practice their basic physical skills," Dr. Katz says.

10 New Materials Introduced Frequently

Some classrooms have an official "discovery table" for displaying items such as autumn leaves or beach glass. "Bringing in new items for the children to explore leads to discussion as well as longer-term projects," Dr. Katz says. For example, an assortment of leaves may prompt a discussion of different types of trees and plants and then inspire the class to plant seeds to see how plants grow, as well as gain an appreciation for the living world around them. "Kids need the chance to wrap their mind around a topic in depth," says Dr. Katz, "and to know that there's something they can come back to and explore the next day."

Study: Full-Day Kindergarten Boosts Academic Performance

By Debra Viadero
New Orleans

A study of 17,600 Philadelphia schoolchildren suggests that full-day kindergarten programs may have both academic and financial payoffs.

The study found that, by the time they reached the 3rd and 4th grades, former full-day kindergartners were more than twice as likely as children without any kindergarten experiences—and 26 percent more likely than graduates of half-day programs—to have made it there without having repeated a grade.

Moreover, the researchers calculated, the lower retention rates for graduates of Philadelphia's full-day classes shave close to 19 percent off of the cost of providing them, which in 1999 came to about $2 million for every 1,000 kindergartners.

"A lot of research suggests that how students are doing those first few years is very telling of what they'll do later on," said Andrea del Gaudio Weiss, the lead researcher on the study, which was conducted by the research office of the 208,000-student district. "If we can show we're saving money, that's all to the better."

She presented her report here this month during the annual meeting of the American Educational Research Association, a 23,000-member group based in Washington.

The study's cost-benefit information comes at a critical time for the debt-ridden Philadelphia school system. Taken over by the state of Pennsylvania in December, the district faces a projected budget shortfall of $105 million by 2005. (*See* "Takeover Team Picked in Phila.," *Education Week, April 3, 2002.*) The popularity of full-day kindergarten programs has been growing nationwide—with or without evidence of their economic and educational effectiveness.

Although only eight states and the District of Columbia now require schools to provide full-day kindergarten, nationwide surveys suggest that close to half of 5-year-olds attend them. And parents in some cities, such as Seattle, are even willing to ante up the money for their local public schools to provide them.

In her search for studies on the long-term benefits of the full-day programs, however, Ms. Weiss came across only one other study that tracked former full-day kindergartners through the 3rd grade, and few that focused on the programs' effects for poor, minority students in cities like Philadelphia.

Better Scores, Attendance

For her study, Ms. Weiss gathered data on groups of children who started school two years before the district made the move to all-day kindergarten in the fall of 1995 and two years after. Before the policy change, schools offered a mix of options for 5-year-olds, including full- and half-day programs; some schools provided no kindergarten at all.

Even though the results for the full-day programs were more dramatic, both kinds of kindergarten classes seemed to increase the likelihood that pupils would be promoted to the next grade on time. Compared with pupils who had never been to kindergarten, for example, the half-day graduates had a 70 percent better chance of reaching 3rd grade on schedule.

Among just those students who made it to 3rd grade on time, the full-day graduates were also likely to score higher on standardized reading and math tests, get better grades, and come to school more often, compared with youngsters who hadn't been full-day kindergartners. That was true, the researchers said, even after they adjusted the numbers to account for any differences between the groups in age, gender, and family income.

The former half-day students in that group were likely to score higher on standardized tests in science, however, according to the report.

The academic edge that the full-day kindergartners enjoyed in 3rd grade dissipated a little the following year. Compared with all the students who had made it to 4th grade on time, the former full-day pupils were more likely to have better outcomes that year in just two areas: attendance and science.

But Ms. Weiss, a senior research associate in the district's office of research and evaluation, said the apparent drop-off was not a cause for concern, since the former full-day kindergartners were not lagging behind any group of their peers.

What the study did not show was how teachers of the full-day kindergarten classes used the additional time. Other researchers have pointed out, for example, that some full-day classes offer a double dose of playtime, while others increase the time children spend learning academic material.

"More research is needed," the authors conclude, "to determine whether full-day students' higher long-term achievement is related to greater instruction or to qualitative differences in the curriculum, or to a combination of the two."

DIFFERENT APPROACHES TO TEACHING:

Comparing

Three* Preschool Program Models

AMY SUSSNA KLEIN, ED.D.

As early childhood educators, we all have our own philosophies and approaches to education. Our approach to teaching is created from a multitude of resources and probably includes knowledge from early childhood theorists, an understanding of child development, and our experiences with children in different learning environments. Whether you are a new teacher about to embark on an early childhood career or a well-seasoned professional, it is helpful to know what other educators are doing in different types of programs. New approaches to teaching and learning can be adapted within our own environment and information about how your philosophy of education compares or differs from others can be shared with parents considering your program for their children.

- **What is the program's history?**
- **What are its main components?**
- **What is unique about the program?**
- **How can one tell if a school is truly following the model?**

THE MONTESSORI METHOD

Maria Montessori, Italy's first woman physician, opened her first school in 1907. The first Montessori school in the United States opened in 1911, and by 1916 the Montessori method was found in locations across the world.

The use of *natural observation* in a *prepared environment* by an objective teacher led Montessori to consider her method scientific. After Montessori completed her direct study of children, she specified every particular detail of how the school should be operated to ensure accurate replication. The teacher's role in a Montessori school is to observe in order to connect the child with suitable materials (Goffin, 2001).

Two main branches of Montessori method have developed: the Association Montessori Internationale (AMI) and the American Montessori Society (AMS). The Association Montessori Internationale was founded in 1929 by Montessori, herself, to maintain the integrity of her life's work and to ensure that it would be perpetuated after her death. Nancy Rambush attempted to Americanize the Montessori method and founded the American Montessori Society (AMS) in 1960. What is most important to note about the two branches is that both are currently in preschools throughout the United States, and both have excellent programs with credentials for teachers. Also, both AMI and AMS support the use of Montessori materials. These learning materials are "self correcting;" they can only be used by a child in one way, thus avoiding the possibility of the child learning the wrong way to use them.

What Are Montessori's Main Components?
Social

- The link between family and school is important.

- Most Montessori classrooms have multiple age groups, which is intended to give children more opportunity to learn from each other.
- Montessori advocated that children learn best by doing.
- In order to help children focus, the teacher silently demonstrates the use of learning materials to them. Children may then choose to practice on any material they have had a "lesson" about.
- Once children are given the lesson with the material, they may work on it independently, often on a mat that designates their space.

Curriculum

- There is a belief in sensory learning; children learn more by touching, seeing, smelling, tasting, and exploring than by just listening.
- The child's work as a purposeful, ordered activity toward a determined end is highly valued. This applies both to exercises for practical life and language.
- The main materials in the classroom are "didactic." These are materials that involve sensory experiences and are self-correcting. Montessori materials are designed to be aesthetically pleasing, yet sturdy and were developed by Maria Montessori to help children develop organization.

- Evans (1971) summarized the preschool curriculum in a Montessori program as consisting "… of three broad phases: exercises for practical life, sensory education, and language activities (reading and writing)." (p. 59)

Environmental Set-Up

- Montessori believed that the environment should be prepared by matching the child to the corresponding didactic material.
- The environment should be comfortable for children (e.g., child-sized chairs that are lightweight).
- The environment should be homelike, so child can learn practical life issues. For example, there should be a place for children to practice proper self-help skills, such as handwashing.
- Since Montessori believed beauty helped with concentration, the setting is aesthetically pleasing.
- In the setting, each child is provided a place to keep her own belongings.

What Is Unique About the Program?

The environment is prepared with self-correcting materials for work, not play. The Montessori method seeks to support the child in organization, thus pretend play and opportunities to learn creatively from errors are less likely to be seen in a Montessori classroom. Chattin-McNichols (1992) clarifies how Piaget, often called the "father of constructivism," and Montessori both agreed that children learn from errors, yet the set-up in which errors may occur is controlled differently in the Montessori classroom. The didactic, self-correcting materials assist in controlling error versus an adult correcting the child.

How Can One Tell If a School Is Truly Following the Montessori Method?

The first step to ensure whether a school truly practices the Montessori method is making sure that its teachers are AMI or AMS credentialed. Not every Montessori school has teachers with Montessori training.

Although Montessori schools are sometimes thought of as being elitist institutions for wealthy families, this is not true. There are many charter and public Montessori schools. Nor, despite the fact that Montessori began her work with poor special needs children in Rome, are Montessori schools reserved for low-income children with disabilities.

THE HIGH/SCOPE® APPROACH

High/Scope® was founded in 1970 and emerged from the work Dave Weikart and Connie Kamii did on the Perry Preschool Project. This project, initiated in 1962, involved teachers working with children (three and four years old) a few hours a day at a school, attending staff meetings, and making weekly home visits. The program was developed with the idea that early education could prevent school failure in high school students from some of the poorest areas in Ypsilanti, MI (Kostelnik, 1999). The Perry Preschool Program is one of the few longitudinal studies in the early childhood field and had significant findings. For instance, compared with a matched control group, the children that were part of the Perry Preschool Program had significantly more high school graduates and fewer arrests.

The High/Scope Foundation is an independent, nonprofit research, development, training, and public advocacy organization. The Foundation's principal goals are to promote the learning and development of children worldwide from infancy through adolescence and to support and train educators and parents as they help children learn.

The High/Scope Approach has roots in constructivist theory. Constructivists believe that we learn by mentally and physically interacting with the environment and with others. Although errors may be made during these interactions, they are considered just another part of the learning process.

Although both Constructivism and the Montessori Method involve learning by doing, there are significant differences. In Montessori, for instance, the didactic, self-correcting materials are specifically designed to help prevent errors. Children learn by repetition, instead of by trial and error. The role of pretend play is also different in the two methods. In High/Scope, children's creative exploration is encouraged, and this sometimes leads to pretend play, while in Montessori, "practical life work" that relates to the real world is stressed.

Although Constructivism is a theory of *learning*, as opposed to a theory of *teaching*, High/Scope has exemplified an approach of teaching that supports Constructivist beliefs. Thus, children learn through active involvement with people, materials, events, and ideas.

What Are High/Scope's Main Components?
Social

- One of the fundamental points in the High/Scope approach is that children are encouraged to be active in their learning through supportive adult interactions.
- The High/Scope approach includes times for various grouping experiences in the classroom. There are specific periods in each day for small group times, large group times, and for children to play independently in learning centers through out the classroom.
- Children are encouraged to share their thinking with teachers and peers.
- Social interactions in the classroom community are encouraged. Teachers facilitate work on problem resolution with children as conflicts arise.
- When a child talks, the teachers listen and ask open-ended questions; they seek to ask questions that encourage children to express their thoughts and be creative rather than a "closed" question that would elicit more of a yes/no or simplistic answer.
- Each day the High/Scope teacher observes and records what the children are doing. During the year, teachers complete a High/Scope Child Observation Record from the daily observations they have collected.

Curriculum

- "Key experiences" were designed specifically for this approach. The following is a brief summary of key experiences taken from Kostelnik, Soderman, & Whiren (1999, p. 32). The key experiences for preschool children are:

  -**Creative representation**
  -**Classification**
  -**Language and literacy**
  -**Seriation**
  -**Initiative and social relation**
  -**Number**
  -**Movement**
  -**Space**
  -**Music**
  -**Time**

- "Plan-do-review" is another major component of the High/Scope framework. Children are encouraged to: 1) **plan** the area, materials, and methods they are going to work with; 2) **do**, actually carry out their plan; and 3) **re-**

view, articulate with the classroom community what they actually did during work time. The review time helps children bring closure to their work and link their actual work to their plan.

- Cleanup time is a natural part of plan-do-review. Children are given a sense of control by cleaning up. Representative labels help children return materials to appropriate places (Roopnarine & Johnson, 1993).

- The High/Scope classroom has a consistent routine. The purpose of the resulting predictability is to help children understand what will happen next and encourage them to have more control in their classroom.

Environmental Set-Up

- The High/Scope® classroom is a materials-rich learning environment. Usually, the locations for classroom materials are labeled to help children learn organizational skills.

- Materials are set-up so that they are easily accessible at a child's level. This helps facilitate children's active exploration.

- Teachers set up the classroom areas purposefully for children to explore and build social relationships, often with well-defined areas for different activities.

How Can One Tell If a School Is Truly Following the High/Scope Approach?

Teachers new to the High/Scope curriculum sometimes find work confusing be-cause they are not sure of their roles (Roopnarine & Johnson, 1993). Sometimes, a list of the key experiences is displayed in the classroom, but then most of the day is spent in teacher-directed activities. This is not what was meant by key experiences! Key experiences in which the children have plenty of time for active exploration in the classroom, is a major component of the High/Scope approach. Furthermore, the teacher is not just passively facilitating while the children play. Rather, teachers in High/Scope classrooms are interactive (though not interruptive of peers playing). Often the role of a High/Scope teacher is to be actively observing and setting up problem solving situations for children.

Plan-do-review was developed to help play become meaningful. There are many ways of implementing the review piece of plan-do-review. One example of successful review is when the children draw a picture of what they worked on. However, it is not usually successful for children to each individually recall during a long large-group time. For example, when children sit for a long period of time through large-group time and each child is asked to say something (sometimes anything). These group times can grow long and the children get restless or drift off.

What Is Unique About High/Scope?

"Key experiences," "plan-do-review," and the High/Scope Child Observation Record are all unique components of the High/Scope framework.

References

Chattin-McNichols, J. (1992). *The Montessori controversy*. New York: Delmar.

Evans, E. (1971). *Contemporary influences in early childhood education*. New York: Holt, Rinehart, and Winston, Inc.

Goffin, S., & Wilson, C. (2001). *Curriculum models and early childhood education appraising the relationships*. New Jersey: Prentice Hall.

Kostelnik, M. Soderman, A., & Whiren, A. (1999). *Developmentally appropriate curriculum best practices in early childhood education*. New Jersey: Prentice Hall.

Roopnarine, J. & Johnson, J. (1993) *Approaches to early childhood education*. NY: Macmillan Publishing Company.

Website Resources
Montessori

www.montessori-ami.org
www.americanmontessorisociety.org

High/Scope®

www.highscope.org

*The second installment of this two-part article, which covers Reggio Emilia, is available at www.earlychildhoodnews.com

Amy Sussna Klein, Ed.D., is President of ASK Education Consulting. She can be reached by email at Askeducation@cs.com.

In Early-Childhood Education and Care: Quality Counts

State interest in early learning is growing, but large gaps in access and quality remain.

Most Americans think education begins at age 5—with kindergarten.

But children are learning from the moment they're born. And for millions of youngsters, the reality is that their early learning is a joint enterprise between parents and early-childhood educators.

Today, 11.9 million children younger than 5 in the United States—or about six in 10—spend part of their waking hours in the care of people other than their parents: relatives, caregivers operating out of their homes, workers in child-care centers, Head Start staff members, and teachers in state-financed prekindergartens among them. The quality of the early care and education that young children receive in such settings sets the tenor of their days and lays the building blocks for future academic success.

Studies conclude that early-childhood education makes a difference. Young children exposed to high-quality settings exhibit better language and mathematics skills, better cognitive and social skills, and better relationships with classmates than do children in lower-quality care. Evaluations of well-run early-learning programs also have found that children in those environments were less likely to drop out of school, repeat grades, need special education, or get into future trouble with the law than similar children who did not have such exposure.

Quality Counts 2002: Building Blocks for Success examines what states are doing to provide early-learning experiences for young children; to ensure that those experiences are of high quality; to prepare and pay early-childhood educators adequately;

and to measure the results of early-childhood programs. The report also examines states' commitment to kindergarten, the transition point into the formal public education system. The report is based on the premise that when it comes to early learning, quality counts, just as it does in K–12 education.

Increasingly, states are getting that message. Today, every state subsidizes kindergarten in at least some districts or for a portion of the school day, according to a survey conducted by *Education Week* for *Quality Counts.* Twenty-five states pay for kindergarten for the full school day, at least in districts that opt to offer such services. So does the District of Columbia.

But nine states—Alaska, Colorado, Idaho, Michigan, New Hampshire, New Jersey, New York, North Dakota, and Pennsylvania—still do not require districts to offer kindergarten.

Thirty-nine states and the District of Columbia provide state-financed prekindergarten for at least some of their 3- to 5-year-olds, up from about 10 in 1980. Annual state spending for such programs now exceeds $1.9 billion.

In 2000, 21 states and the District of Columbia supplemented federal aid to serve additional children through Head Start, one of the nation's largest preschool programs for disadvantaged 3- to 5-year-olds. Thirty-one states underwrite one or more programs for infants and toddlers, up from 24 in 1998.

In addition, every state helps at least some low-income families buy child care through a combination of state and federal

money under the Child Care and Development Fund block grant and Temporary Assistance for Needy Families. Twenty-six states, the District of Columbia, and the federal government also help families pay for child care through tax credits or deductions. But only 10 states made the credits refundable in the 2001 tax year so that the lowest-income families could benefit.

Despite federal and state efforts, access to high-quality early-childhood education remains out of the reach of many families. None of the federal programs reaches more than a fraction of the newborns to 5-year-olds who could benefit from such services. And states' financial commitment to early-childhood education varies widely, as do eligibility requirements and the number of children who actually receive services.

Most states focus their prekindergarten efforts on the neediest youngsters. Twenty-six target children from low-income families; 15 of those also look at other risk factors, such as having a teenage parent. And nine states leave it up to local districts to determine which risk factors they will consider.

Only three states—Georgia, New York, and Oklahoma—and the District of Columbia are phasing in prekindergarten for any 4-year-old whose parent wants it, regardless of income.

Similarly, although all states provide child-care subsidies for at least some poor families, wide variations exist in the income limits that families must meet to qualify, the actual dollar amount of the subsidies, and the percentage of eligible children served.

Families with low incomes, particularly the working poor, have the least access to high-quality early-childhood services.

Traditionally, "quality" in early-childhood education has meant ensuring that children are cared for in a safe and nurturing environment. State licensing standards commonly address group size, the number of children per caregiver, and such physical features as the height of playground equipment. Licensing standards rarely, if ever, address the learning aspects of early care and education.

Even those minimal protections often fail to safeguard children adequately. In many states, certain settings are exempt from licensure entirely: family child-care homes that serve a small number of children, preschools that operate only a few hours a day, or sites run by religious organizations.

New research about the importance of early learning, however, has led some states to describe the quality of instruction that should occur in preschool settings, at least for programs that receive state money. While almost all states have standards for students in elementary school, only 19 states and the District of Columbia lay out specific expectations for kindergartners. Fifteen states and the District have specific standards for prekindergarten. Five more states are working on such standards. Only six states—California, Connecticut, Georgia, Maryland, Michigan, and Washington—require preschool programs to adhere to the standards. In addition, seven states require their state-financed prekindergartens to satisfy federal Head Start standards.

States also are mounting efforts to improve the quality of early-childhood pro-grams. Seven require their prekindergarten programs to earn accreditation from the National Association for the Education of Young Children. Twenty-six states and the District of Columbia offer tiered reimbursement rates that provide higher child-care subsidies to providers that earn national accreditation or meet other quality criteria.

But states still have a long way to go to ensure that those who work with young children are well-educated and well-compensated.

As a nation, the United States pays about as much to parking-lot attendants and dry-cleaning workers as it does to early-childhood educators, according to data from the federal Bureau of Labor Statistics. The average annual salary of child-care workers in 1999 was $15,430. Preschool teachers, who typically work with 3- to 5-year-olds, had annual salaries of $19,610, less than half what the average elementary school teacher earned.

Not surprisingly, given those numbers, turnover among early-childhood workers is high, and education requirements are minimal. Every state, for example, requires kindergarten teachers to have at least a bachelor's degree and a certificate in elementary or early-childhood education. But only 20 states and the District of Columbia require teachers in state-financed prekindergartens to meet similar requirements. In 30 states, teachers in child-care centers can begin work without having any preservice training.

Recently, states and the federal government have begun to get more serious about the preparation of early-childhood educators.

Congress has ordered that by 2003, 50 percent of a Head Start program's teachers must have an associate's degree in early-childhood education. A growing number of states also have initiatives either to help providers acquire more education or to supplement their wages. The TEACH Early Childhood Project, which began in North Carolina in 1990, provides scholarships to child-care workers to attend school and bonuses or raises from their employers when they complete their programs of study. Seventeen additional states have since adopted the program. Nine states have programs to improve the compensation of early-childhood educators.

States' growing investments in the early years, and their concerns about school readiness, also have led them to revisit the question of how to measure the success or failure of their early-childhood initiatives. Today, 17 states mandate readiness testing of kindergartners as a first step in identifying children with special needs or to help plan instruction. Six states use kindergarten testing to gauge school readiness statewide. Fifteen states and the District of Columbia require diagnostic or development testing of prekindergartners. At the federal level, new performance measures are being used to evaluate Head Start programs, including their impact on children's math and literacy skills.

Efforts also are under way to rethink how states pay for early care and education. Many states, for instance, are seeking new sources of money to support their efforts, such as beer and cigarette taxes or state lottery proceeds.

Despite the economic downturn, many believe that the continued push for better academic performance in the elementary years could well compel states to pay more attention to early learning for years to come.

Concern Turns to Preschool Facilities

BY LINDA JACOBSON
San Francisco

With no playground of its own, the Tenderloin Childcare Center sometimes has its 36 preschoolers walk past boarded-up buildings and homeless men sleeping in doorways to reach a subway station, where the youngsters catch a ride to a city playground.

Traveling back and forth from the playground to the child-care center—located on the first floor of a brick apartment building that used to be a YMCA hotel—is not something the children or the teachers look forward to. But there is no alternative.

"It can be one of the most challenging parts of the day," Graham Dobson, the administrative coordinator of the center, said of the trek.

Efforts are growing to pay for preschool facility improvements

The lack of a playground is just one of the many facility needs that this center, and others like it around the country, have to go without. And the potential dangers and depressing physical characteristics of many such centers have some early-childhood policymakers saying it's time to start focusing more attention on improving the quality of the nation's child-care and preschool facilities.

The Tenderloin Childcare Center, for instance, is housed in the former YMCA hotel's ballroom on the building's first floor. Once an ornate hall with high ceilings, it's now just a large room with peeling paint that has been turned into three makeshift classrooms like cubicles in an office.

The old stage in the ballroom has children's climbing structures and soft mats behind a floor-to-ceiling safety net, which keeps the youngsters from falling off the stage. In the large room, voices echo across the open space, and children playing loudly in one area can drown out the voices of teachers trying to talk or read books to other children.

"We have to juggle the space around a huge amount," Mr. Dobson said as he tried to talk over the sound of small toilets flushing outside the cluttered office he shares with another director.

'An Invisible Issue'

The condition of facilities for preschool-age children rarely receives the same emphasis from advocacy organizations as the call for qualified and well-compensated early-childhood teachers, said Cheryl D. Hayes, the executive director of the Finance Project. The Washington-based policy-research and technical-assistance organization focuses on services for children and families.

"It's a little bit of an invisible issue," Ms. Hayes said.

Efforts are growing, however, to bring not only attention to the issue, but new financing to help programs find higher-quality facilities or upgrade their current buildings and classrooms.

For example, the Tenderloin center, which serves poor children, some of whom are from homeless families, was a prime candidate for help from the Child Care Facilities Fund, a nonprofit lender based in Oakland, Calif. The fund works with the San Francisco mayor's office and private donors to improve and expand early-childhood-education facilities in that city.

Early this year, the center will move to a fully renovated site a few blocks away that has two floors of classrooms, office space, a staff meeting room, a gathering room for parents—and finally, an outdoor playground.

It's a step other directors of early-childhood facilities would like to take, but can't because of budget constraints.

In many centers, teachers and classroom assistants have to walk children to other parts of the building to use the restroom because no such facilities are nearby. That is frustrating for teachers, especially those in understaffed centers, where it is difficult to take one child to the restroom while also monitoring the other youngsters.

And preschool teachers rarely have break rooms, where they can unwind and compare notes, or adequate storage space, which means that supplies are often scattered all over the place.

"You need at least a healthy and safe space, if not stimulating and developmentally appropriate," said September Jarrett, the director of the Child Care Facilities Fund.

Experts say better facilities raise teacher morale.

Beyond those basics, some experts say better facilities can significantly improve the attitudes of early-childhood educators toward their work and toward the children they teach.

"I think there is growing evidence that facilities are more important than were previously thought," said Carl Sussman, who runs a Boston-based community-development consulting group. He is a founding member of the National Children's Facilities Network, an organization working to improve early-childhood facilities throughout the country.

Finding the Money

The San Francisco city government, which already had a history of providing financing for child-care facilities, approached the Low Income Housing Fund, a national financial institution based in San Francisco that focuses on community development, about operating such a program specifically for such facilities.

With what Ms. Jarrett now describes as a "layered cake" approach, the Child Care Facilities Fund pieces together a variety of different sources of public and private money to pay for anything from heating repairs to brand-new buildings.

In a pioneering move, the city secured its primary source of funding for major child-care construction and renovation projects from the U.S. Department of Housing and Urban Development. The money is loaned to child-care providers, who have to repay 20 percent of the debt over 10 years. The other 80 percent is paid for by San Francisco's department of human services.

About $8.6 million in what is known as Section 108 funding—federal dollars that can be used for community development projects—is being used to develop child-care space that will eventually serve almost 600 more children, according to Ms. Jarrett.

San Francisco, where real estate costs are among the highest in the United States, is also among the most unlikely places for a wave of child-care construction to be taking place.

In fact, shortly after the fund was created, real estate costs in the city "went through the roof," Ms. Jarrett said. Even churches that had been renting space to child-care providers for years were saying they could make more money by leasing the space to someone else or developing it as something other than a child-care center.

Many of the new facilities are now part of larger subsidized-housing developments throughout the city, such as the new Heritage Homes community in the Visitacion Valley, which is the southernmost part of the city and county. When complete, the development, which includes townhouses for low-income families, will also have a new center for 45 children attached to a senior housing facility.

"If you're going to build low-income housing, you've got to have a child-care angle," Ms. Jarrett said.

Providers in need of smaller improvements are not left out. The facilities fund also provides smaller grants of up to $20,000 for needs such as playground improvements or emergency equipment purchases.

One such provider is Cruz Fernandez, who runs a home-based Montessori program on the first floor of her house in the Oceanview neighborhood here. She opened her business in 1999, using borrowed materials. A $4,500 grant from the facilities fund has allowed her to buy new child-size furniture and the expensive, durable materials that are an essential part of a Montessori education.

"When I first heard about [the grants], I couldn't believe it," Ms. Fernandez said. And, she added, the children are proud of the new equipment. "They take care of it," she said.

Beyond San Francisco

Other places around the country also have come up with different ways of paying for early-childhood facilities.

The facilities fund in the San Francisco area was modeled after work done by the Illinois Facilities Fund, a community-development financial institution in Chicago that began making real estate loans to nonprofit organizations, including child-care centers, about 12 years ago.

It wasn't until 2000, however, that Chicago officials agreed to put a significant amount of money—$25 million—into

building child-care facilities to serve children from low-income families. That, combined with a $25 million match being raised by the fund, has helped pay for 16 building projects.

Like the Child Care Facilities Fund used in San Francisco, the Illinois fund also has smaller "loan products" for providers who need to make minor improvements.

Back east in Connecticut, school readiness legislation passed in 1997 fostered a much greater demand for classroom space. But unlike other states, Connecticut is financing preschool construction in much the same way that school districts build schools—by issuing 30-year revenue bonds. That approach has generated more than $40 million for the construction of 19 new facilities in the state's 21 "priority," or high-need, districts.

The state also appropriated $2.5 million to pay 80 percent of the interest on the bonds. Providers were responsible for 20 percent. That funding has now been exhausted, and supporters are hoping the legislature will renew the program.

On the other hand, in New Jersey—where the state supreme court in 1998 ordered the state education department to provide early-childhood programs in 30 needy districts—advocates for early-childhood education say the state has been a stumbling block rather than a supporter on facilities issues.

> "... some [facilities] are
> in parking lots, some
> are on school grounds,
> taking up playground space."

The poor condition of facilities in those districts has become a key part of the debate over how to improve the quality of preschool facilities across the state.

"There is a major problem with the amount of facilities and the quality of these facilities," said Joan M. Ponessa, the director of research at the Education Law Center in Newark, which represents all the children in the 30 districts that were part of the state supreme court ruling.

While funding for school construction, including preschool facilities, has been passed by the New Jersey legislature, districts have not been given permission from the state to build permanent buildings for early-childhood programs. Instead, the state ordered districts to use trailers to house the programs. But many of the urban schools, Ms. Ponessa said, don't have space for trailers.

As a result, she said, some programs "are in parking lots," and "some are on school grounds, taking up playground space."

Policymakers Interested

The quality of child-care facilities is an issue that is beginning to attract attention from policy-makers at the federal level, too. Last year, the Department of Health and Human Services awarded $2.5 million to 10 different organizations around the country—from Alaska to Maryland—that will provide technical assistance to providers to help them renovate or build child-care facilities.

> *Research on how facilities affect what happens in early childhood classrooms is almost nonexistent*

But Sens. Christopher J. Dodd, D-Conn., and Mike DeWine, R-Ohio, would like the federal government to do much more. Last year, they introduced a bill that would provide $250 million over five years to improve and build child-care facilities. The proposed Childcare Facilities Financing Act would be targeted toward low-income areas.

The bill did not move out of committee last year, though, and Ms. Jarrett acknowledged that even though many policymakers agree that more public money is needed to improve child-care programs, it's hard to predict when money might be available.

Many of those concerned with improving facilities also would like to see more included on the issue as part of the accreditation process for early-childhood programs.

But Alan Simpson, a spokesman for the National Association for the Education of Young Children, a Washington-based organization that accredits early-childhood programs, said that while the association "might like more programs to be in facilities that were designed for that purpose, we're not in a position to demand it."

Moreover, because local building codes vary tremendously, it would be hard for the NAEYC or other organizations to write one set of facility standards for the whole country, said Trinita Logue, the president of the Illinois Facilities Fund.

'Out of the Basement'

Research on how facilities affect what happens in early-childhood classrooms is almost nonexistent.

A landmark 1995 study by researchers from four universities, known as the "Cost, Quality, and Outcomes" study, found, however, that many classrooms—especially those for infants and toddlers—did not meet basic sanitary requirements and were even dangerous to children.

And child-care experts emphasize that the physical features of a facility can have an effect on how the teachers do their work.

"We really believe that if you respect the adult, that trickles down to the children," Ms. Logue said.

A recent example to support her belief comes from the School for Young Children, a laboratory preschool at St. Joseph College in West Hartford, Conn.

When students in a child-study course observed youngsters at play at the school, they found that the adults in the school, which

was in the basement of a college building, were interacting with the children during only about 3 percent of the observations.

While that figure was comparable to earlier research on adult involvement in play, the college students and their faculty adviser, Carlota Schechter, were still disturbed by the results. So they observed the children again. But this time, the program was in a new facility, an old elementary school that was renovated to serve the needs of young children. This time, the percentage of observations in which teachers were interacting with children during playtime jumped to 22 percent.

Astounded by the increase, Ms. Schechter and the director of the program met with the teachers, who attributed the difference to their move to the new site. In the old facility, the children's spots for storing their personal items, the restrooms and sinks,

and the phones were all down the hall, which forced the teachers to leave the room frequently.

"In the new space, teachers do not need to leave the room to monitor these activities, and thus there is much more time for teachers to be interacting with children in the classroom," Ms. Schechter wrote in a proposal for a similar study that is now being conducted at a preschool in Hartford.

The teachers also noted that because the rooms in the new facility were larger, the children had more room to play—and, as a result, there seemed to be fewer disputes between children than there were in the other location.

"The feeling of coming out of the basement—literally out of the basement—raises teacher morale so much," Ms. Schechter said.

From *Education Week*, January 16, 2002, pp. 14-15. © 2002 by Education Week. Reprinted by permission.

UNIT 4

Guiding and Supporting Young Children

Unit Selections

Key Points to Consider

- What role should preschool children have in making classroom rules?

- How can a teacher address the needs of boys in making the program more developmentally responsive?

- Make a list of some of the school-related "stressors" that primary-grade children may experience.

- Why do you think young children bring violent content and themes into their play?

- What are the reasons young children bully other children?

- How should early childhood educators help young children deal with death and grief?

 **Links: www.dushkin.com/online/**
These sites are annotated in the World Wide Web pages.

Child Welfare League of America (CWLA)
http://www.cwla.org

Early childhood teaching is all about problem-solving. Just as children work to solve problems, so do their teachers. Every day, teachers make decisions about how to guide children socially and emotionally. In attempting to determine what could be causing a child's emotional distress, teachers must take into account a myriad of factors. They consider physical, social, environmental, and emotional factors, in addition to the surface behavior of a child. Whether it is an individual child's behavior or interpersonal relationships, the pressing problem involves complex issues that require careful reflection and analysis. Even the most mature teachers spend many hours thinking and talking about the best ways to guide young children's behavior: What should I do about the child who is out of bounds? What do I say to parents who want their child punished? Should intrinsic motivation be taught to every child or are tangible reinforcers appropriate for some? How do I guide a child who has experienced trauma and now acts out violently?

Our first article in this unit provides a useful process for involving children in solving classroom problems. "When Children Make Rules" is a detailed description of a constructivist approach to engaging children in forming classroom rules, discussing problems, and finding solutions. The benefit is that when children share in the process, they also take more ownership by following it.

Teachers and caregivers who find that boys have a more difficult time adjusting to classroom life than girls may find helpful suggestions in "Building an Encouraging Classroom with Boys in Mind." The authors give a number of recommendations for expanding children's opportunities for physical movement and exploratory play. In general, they encourage teachers to make the learning environment more active, to support the needs of children who need to explore and experiment.

A technique that is traditionally used in early childhood classrooms is "time out", yet its appropriateness has rarely been questioned. In "Guidance and Discipline Strategies for Young Children: Time Out is Out," Preuesse presents a clear argument that time-out is actually a punishment strategy. Better guidance strategies than time-out should be considered if the goal is for young children to learn self-control.

The themes in children's play tell a lot about what they watch on TV, the kind of games they play, and the type of toys their parents give them. Violence has always been a theme of children's play, and many experts say that children need to express the pressures of life. But instead of simply declaring war and superhero play off limits, teachers can use specific approaches to promote creative play. "Beyond Banning War and Superhero Play" includes suggestions for guiding children to positive themes and open-ended toys.

At some point, every early childhood teacher will need to deal with a child who bullies other children in the classroom or on the playground. While it may be easy to identify the bullying behaviors, it is more difficult to understand the reasons behind such aggressive actions. "Bullying Among Children" is an in-depth look at what may be causing some children to bully others and provides teachers with effective strategies for guiding these children.

Helping children cope with stress can be difficult for teachers in these times of upheaval and trauma. Children today—and their teachers—are learning that terrorism is a fact of life. With acts of violence occurring randomly across the nation, teachers must be very alert to the effects of stress on young children. These are times that call for teachers to demonstrate care and concern as they teach children to cope. "Children and Grief: The Role of the Early Childhood Educator" is an article worth keeping for future reference. Many children experience the death of someone close to them. This article describes young children's stages of grieving and gives suggestions for supporting them as they deal with death.

Determining strategies of guidance and discipline is important work for an early childhood teacher. Because the teacher-child relationship is foundational for emotional well-being and social competence, guidance is more than applying a single set of discipline techniques. Instead of one solitary model of classroom discipline strictly enforced, a broad range of techniques is more appropriate. It is only through careful analysis and reflection that teachers can look at children individually, assessing not only the child but the impact of family cultures as well, and determine what is appropriate and effective guidance.

When Children Make Rules

In constructivist classrooms, young children's participation in rule making promotes their moral development.

Rheta DeVries and Betty Zan

Sherice Hetrick-Ortman's kindergartners were passionate about block building. These children at the Freeburg Early Childhood Program in Waterloo, Iowa, lavished care on their complex structures and felt justly proud of their creations. Some of the children were concerned, however, about problems in the block area. They discussed the matter at group time and came up with some new rules to post in the block-building area:

- Keep hands off other people's structures.
- No knocking people's structures down.
- Four friends in the block area at one time.

When children care about a classroom problem such as this one and take part in solving it, they are more likely to view the resulting rules as fair. Having *made* the rules, they are more likely to observe them. Just as important, participating in the process of rule making supports children's growth as moral, self-regulating human beings.

Rules in schools have traditionally been made by teachers and given to children. Today, many teachers see the benefits of allowing children to have a voice in developing classroom rules. But if we are not careful, this involvement can be superficial and meaningless. How can we best involve children in making classroom rules?

Morality and Adult-Child Relationships

We speak from a constructivist point of view, inspired by the research and theory of Jean Piaget. In constructivist education, rule making is part of the general atmosphere of mutual respect, and the goal is children's moral and intellectual development (DeVries & Zan, 1994).

Piaget (19832/1965) identified two types of morality that parallel two types of adult-child relationships: one that promotes optimal moral and intellectual development, and one that retards it. *Heteronomous* morality consists of conformity to external rules without question. Overly coercive relationships with adults foster this type of morality and can impede children's development of self-regulation. *Autonomous* morality, by contrast, derives from an internal need to relate to other people in moral ways. Cooperative relationships with adults foster this type of morality and help children develop high levels of self-regulation.

Obviously, children and adults are not equals. However, when the adult respects the child as a person with a right to exercise his or her will, their relationship has a certain psychological equality that promotes autonomy.

Piaget, of course, did not advocate complete freedom, and neither do we. Although constructivist teachers minimize the exercise of adult authority or coercion in relation to children, *minimize* does not mean *eliminate* (DeVries, 1999; DeVries & Edmiaston, 1999; DeVries & Kohlberg, 1987/1990). Rather, we strive for a balance that steadily builds the child's regulation of his or her own behavior.

Norms and Rules in Constructivist Classrooms

To investigate how constructivist teachers use external control and how they develop classroom norms and rules, we interviewed the teachers at the Freeburg Early Childhood Program, a laboratory school serving children ages 3–7 in a predominantly low-income neighborhood. The school's aim is to demonstrate constructivist practices.

Norms Established by Teachers

We define *norms* as specific expectations that teachers establish for children's behavior—ways of behaving that everyone takes for granted as part of the culture of the classroom. A norm is usually unwritten and sometimes unspoken until someone violates it and the teacher takes corrective action. The Freeburg teachers' reflections revealed three kinds of norms that existed in their classrooms:

- *Safety and health norms* ensure children's well-being. Our teachers articulated these as non-negotiables. Examples include "No hurting others," "Lie down at rest time," "Keep shoes on outside," "No crashing trikes or other vehicles," and "Don't throw sand."
- *Moral norms* pertain to respect for people and animals. They often relate to fair treatment or distribution of goods. Examples of these are "Take fair turns," "Talk through a conflict until there is a resolution," "If you bring a live animal into the classroom, try to make it comfortable," and "No hurting animals."
- *Discretionary norms* consist of routines and procedures to make the classroom run smoothly and make learning possible. Kathy Morris, the teacher in the 3-year-olds' class, pointed out that

young children do not like chaos, and they need adults to figure out routines that work so that events run smoothly. Discretionary norms also include societal norms for politeness and individual responsibility that children need to know. Examples include "Sit with the group at group time," "Wait until all are seated at lunch before eating," and "Clean up your place after lunch."

All teachers must sometimes exert external control.

All teachers have safety and health norms, moral norms, and discretionary norms. These norms are acceptable and necessary uses of external authority in a constructivist classroom. But constructivist teachers carefully evaluate their reasons for norms and attempt to minimize the use of external control as much as possible.

Rules Made by Children

We define rules as formal agreements among teachers and children. Constructivist teachers often conduct discussions of problems that relate to their norms and engage children in making classroom rules that arise from these norms.

When teachers first suggest that children make rules, children often parrot such adult admonitions as "Never talk to strangers" or "Raise your hand and wait to be called on." This occurs especially when children are unaccustomed to a sociomoral atmosphere in which they feel free to express their honest opinions. Children may view rule making as another exercise in trying to figure out the right answer or say what they think the teacher wants to hear. The rules that they suggest may not reflect a real understanding of the need to treat others in moral ways. When children only mindlessly restate adults' rules, they have not engaged in true rule making.

Children who engage in true rule making sometimes reinvent rules that elaborate on already established norms. Although these elaborations are not entirely original, they still give the children feelings of autonomy in their power to create rules. For example, Gwen Harmon's 4-year-olds, working within the classroom norm "Don't hurt animals," developed the following practical and concrete rules regarding the chicks that they hatched in the classroom:

- Pick them up safely.
- Don't push them.

- Don't squeeze them.
- Don't put things in their box.
- Don't punch them.
- Don't put them on the light bulb.
- Don't drop them.
- Don't throw them.
- Don't pick them up by their wings.
- Don't color on them.
- Don't pull their heads off.

Reinvented rules demonstrate children's understanding of the moral norm because they translate the norm into children's own words and provide elaborations that make sense to them. Sometimes the elaborations are novel, dealing with situations that the teacher had not considered discussing. For example, in Beth Van Meeteren's 1st grade classroom, where the norm is to treat others with respect, children made the rule, "When people pass gas, do not laugh, or they will be upset or embarrassed."

Sometimes children develop entirely original rules. Unlike reinvented rules, invented rules reflect children's power to make decisions in the classroom. For example, Dora Chen's class of 4-year-olds invented a new rule in response to a problem they saw during one of their classroom routines. One day during clean-up, a child saw another child finishing a snack and felt that no one should eat snacks during clean-up time. He told the teacher, who raised the issue at group time. She asked, "What should our rule be?" After a 17-minute discussion in which the children suggested various possibilities, the teacher clarified the choice between "No snack during clean-up: throw it away" or "Finish snack before going outdoors." The children voted to throw away their unfinished snacks when clean-up started.

The new rule, driven by children's interest and concern, went beyond the teacher's concerns. Although the teacher preferred giving the children more time to finish their snacks, she believed that the children's solution was fair given the one-hour activity time in which to eat snacks.

Guidelines for Exerting External Control

Some people have the misconception that constructivist teachers are permissive and that external control never occurs in constructivist classrooms. In fact, all teachers must exert external control sometimes. From our discussions with teachers and our understanding of research and theory,

we have derived four general guidelines for the use of external control.

Provide a general and pervasive context of warmth, cooperation, and community. We draw inspiration for this guideline from the work of Jean Piaget, especially from *The Moral Judgment of the Child* (1932/1965). Many others, however, have come to this same conclusion starting from different theoretical perspectives (Nelson, 1996; Watson, 2003). In fact, almost all of the recent classroom management programs on the market, with the exception of Assertive Discipline, stress the importance of cooperation and community (Charles, 2002).

Act with the goal of students' self-regulation. A developmental perspective leads us to focus on the long term. We want to contribute to the development of autonomous, self-regulating human beings who can make decisions based on the perspectives of all involved. Therefore, compliance is not our primary goal. Of course, we all wish sometimes that children would be more compliant. But we constantly remind ourselves and one another that developing self-regulation takes time, and we celebrate significant events, such as when an aggressive child actually uses words for the first time to tell another child what he wants instead of slugging him.

Minimize unnecessary external control as much as is possible and practical. Constructivist teachers do use external control; in fact, they use it quite a bit. As Piaget states, "However delicately one may put the matter, there have to be commands and therefore duties" (1932/1965, p. 180). Teachers in constructivist classrooms, however, use external control of children consciously and deliberately, not impulsively or automatically. The teachers with whom we work constantly ask themselves whether the external regulation is absolutely necessary.

Through discussions with teachers Gwen Harmon, Shari McGhee, and Christie Sales, we have identified several situations that can lead to unnecessary control of children. Avoidable control-inducing situations occur when

- The classroom arrangement invites rowdy behavior.
- Children do not know the classroom routine.
- Too many transitions lead to too much waiting time.
- Crowding in a part of the classroom leads to conflicts.

Use mistakes as teaching tools.

Treat mistakes, errors, and accidents as steps to learning—everyone makes them as they try new things. Share some of your mistakes—"Oops, I mixed too much water into the paint. Next time I better measure more carefully." In doing so, you help children know that adults too have accidents and can still learn. Build a learning environment that discourages failure and promotes success.

Example	Encourages failure	Promotes success
• After a water table activity, the floor is slippery and children's clothes are wet.	Fuss about the mess and children's carelessness--without offering solutions.	Anticipate the mess by covering the floor under the table with newspaper, having towels nearby, and providing smocks.
• Yetta has a hard time completing a puzzle or another project.	Make Yetta sit in one place to "finish what you have started."	Accommodate Yetta's needs by letting her finish the puzzle on the floor or stand to paint.
• The toddler room floor is covered with toys, making Ben and Laurie reluctant to practice walking.	Leave the disorder until naptime "since it will just get messy again" and the children can crawl to what they want.	Arrange furniture and materials so that there is always a clear path for new walkers.

Give children limits—and security.

Everyone needs to have boundaries defined. You, for example, rely on speed-limit signs, price tags, and recipes to guide some of your activities. Children need to know limits and, within those limits, need the freedom to practice making appropriate decisions. They need adults to help draw the line between not enough and too much decision-making freedom.

Children also must know behavior limits will be enforced consistently—what's OK today will be OK tomorrow. Look at your own behavior for mixed messages. Did you have children finger paint with pudding yesterday and then get frustrated at lunch today when children smeared the pudding on the table?

Set behavioral limits to reflect the safety of children, the safety and well-being of others, and the protection of community property. Rules that are few, enforceable, and essential give children the freedom and responsibility to make good behavioral choices. Evaluate limits—or rules—regularly. Ask: Is the rule still necessary, or have the children outgrown it? Is the rule for my convenience alone? Does the rule restrict experimentation or keep a child from trying new things? Can the rule be enforced? Make sure you understand the reason for the rule—the children will surely ask for it.

Example	Invites conflict	Offers security and reassurance
• On the playground you monitor 5-year-olds climbing the old oak tree.	No climbing above that branch.	I know you want to go higher. I'll be here if you feel like you're getting into trouble.
• In the classroom you use a timer to remind children to give up a place at a favorite activity.	Because I say so.	We have this rule so that every child has a chance to play with the train. Would you like to read the train book while you wait?
• At naptime you help children settle on their mats.	Go to sleep. Close your eyes right now and quit wiggling.	Sometimes it's hard to sleep. Would you like to choose a book to look at during rest time?

Use logical consequences.

Respond to inappropriate behavior with logical consequences—the natural result of a particular behavior. A logical consequence for an adult, for example, may be a stomach ache after eating spicy food. For a child, a logical consequence may be feeling cold after going outside without a sweater.

This kind of learning goes on all the time. In some cases, we can set up a logical consequence if one doesn't occur naturally. If a 3-year-old spills milk, for example, one logical consequence is to have the child help with cleanup. The consequence is not punishment and it always relates to the original behavior. It's not logical, therefore, to deny time in the art center to a child who spills milk—the two things don't relate to each other.

The consequence must also be reasonable. If a child's behavior poses danger—picking up broken glass or running into the street, for example—stop it immediately. Avoid extremes. If 9-year-old Josh breaks a baseball bat by swinging it against a brick wall, don't say, "You can never play baseball here again." Show children that you trust them to change and learn. "Here's a glove for you to practice catching. You can try batting later this afternoon."

For a logical consequence to be effective, you must respond immediately. Make it clear that it's the behavior—not the child—that is objectionable.

Example	Illogical punishment	Logical consequence
• Benny runs on the playground and knocks Jena over.	Make Benny sit in the sandbox for the rest of outdoor time. (Not related.)	Have Benny help Jena up and walk with her to clean her hands and knees.
• Toddler Mike scribbles on a wall with crayon.	Remove crayons from the classroom for six weeks.	Help Mike scrub off the wall with a soapy rag.
• Laura misuses a book and tears several pages.	Take the book away from Laura and tell her she has ruined it. (Not related.)	Show Laura how to use tape to repair the book.

Set an example.

Children learn by watching you. They observe your interactions with children and other adults and are likely to model their behavior on yours. For example, if you consistently talk to children rudely in a loud voice, you're teaching them that this is the way to treat others. If you tell the director that you are out of glue and then produce a hidden bottle from the closet, you'll have a difficult time convincing children that it's not right to lie.

Instead, show concern for others, work out conflicts, and respect the dignity of others—both adults and children. In this way, you model behaviors children need to learn for their social and emotional success.

Example	Negative role model	Positive role model
• At lunchtime	You watch the children eat their lunch while you have a snack of soda and chips.	You sit with the children and model sound nutritious and social mealtime habits.
• On the playground	You scream across the yard to tell Hank his dad is ready to go home.	You wave to Hank's dad, walk across the yard to tell Hank it's time to leave for the day, and help Hank say goodbye to his friends.
• In the art center	Mirabelle spatters paint on the floor and wall. You tell her that it doesn't matter because the custodian is paid to clean up.	You let Mirabelle get the sponge and help her wipe down the wall and floor. When she's finished you congratulate her for helping make the classroom a pleasant place to work and play.

Tips for handling common behaviors

The child	It may mean the child	So don't	Instead try to
becomes angry.	• does not feel successful with an important task. • has been told *stop, no*, and *don't* too many times. • is being forced to do something. • feels frustrated by too many demands from adults.	• become angry. • allow an out-of-control tantrum.	• remember anger is normal and sometimes appropriate. • evaluate and modify the environment to minimize frustration. • help the child express anger in ways that don't hurt anyone. • provide an outlet for strong emotions.
won't share.	• is too young (under 3 years) to understand sharing. • needs experience and guidance in owning and sharing.	• snatch an object from the child. • scold the child. • say you don't like the child.	• help the child feel more secure. • teach problem-solving skills. • provide duplicate toys and materials.
bites other children.	• is teething. • is using the mouth for learning. • communicates through biting rather than words. • doesn't understand that biting hurts. • feels frustrated but hasn't learned more appropriate coping skills.	• bite the child back. • encourage biting back. • make the child bite soap. • force the child to say, "I'm sorry."	• provide toddlers with alternative and soothing objects to bite. • supervise closely to prevent biting. • help children develop other communication skills. • evaluate and modify schedule, environment, or materials to reduce children's stress. • comfort victims. • teach children that biting hurts. • share information with parents, stressing how typical biting is.
is jealous.	• feels replaced by a new person in the family. • has been unfairly compared with others. • has been treated unfairly.	• shame the child. • ignore the child.	• provide warmth, love, and understanding. • discuss the child's feeling one-on-one. • help children feel competent and successful with tasks. • make available books that deal with jealousy. • ignore the incident.
uses foul language.	• doesn't know any better. • is imitating someone. • is trying something new. • is trying to get your attention. • is letting off steam.	• show shock or embarrassment. • get excited. • over-react. • wash out the child's mouth with soap. • put hot pepper on the child's tongue.	• offer a substitute word. • teach children new, extra-long words. • evaluate and modify materials to be stimulating but not overwhelming.

Tips for handling common behaviors

The child	It may mean the child	So don't	Instead try to
hurts you or other children.	• is too young to understand the pain. • is inexperienced in social relationships. • is angry. • is frustrated.	• get angry. • hurt the child. • force the child to say, "I'm sorry." • say you don't like the child. • ignore the child.	• attend the hurt person first and involve the child who did the hurt in the comforting. • quietly separate the children. • divert the children's attention. • take away hurting objects —calmly and firmly. • offer different ways to express feelings.
destroys materials.	• is curious about how things work. • does not understand the correct way to use the materials. • has had an accident. • feels excited or angry. • finds the materials too difficult or frustrating.	• scold, yell, or shout. • tell the child "You're bad." • hurt the child.	• teach and model the proper ways to handle materials. • examine fragile items with the child. • remove broken materials from the area. • teach the difference between valued and throw-away items. • involve the child in repair work.
refuses to eat.	• is showing a normal decrease in appetite. • is not hungry. • does not feel well. • dislikes a particular food, flavor, or texture. • is imitating someone. • is trying to be independent. • is trying to get attention.	• make a scene. • reward or bribe the child. • threaten the child. • scold the child. • force the child to eat. • withhold other foods or drink.	• remain calm and casual. • make food interesting and attractive. • introduce new foods a little at a time. • help children learn to serve and feed themselves. • serve small portions. • involve children in food preparation.
demands attention.	• is tired, hungry, or not feeling well. • feels left out, insecure, or unloved. • really likes you and is jealous of the attention you give other children. • hasn't yet learned to play creatively and independently.	• ignore or isolate the child. • shame the child. • scold or punish the child.	• attend to the child's physical needs. • show interest in the child's ideas and discoveries. • offer interesting activities for the child to do with other children. • recognize the child's efforts and successes.

Adapted from "Tips for Handling Common Situations With Children," *Texas Child Care*, Winter 1983.

From *Texas Child Care*, Spring 2002, pp. 10-16. © 2002 by Texas Workforce Commission.

GUIDANCE & DISCIPLINE STRATEGIES FOR YOUNG CHILDREN:
TIME OUT IS OUT

BY KATHY PREUESSE

In a typical early childhood classroom, children engage in a variety of behaviors—some appropriate and some inappropriate. Early childhood teachers need to deal with all behaviors, but of course it is the inappropriate ones that are the subject of so much study! And even more than the inappropriate behaviors themselves, our response to the behaviors is weighed, measured, and quantified by a wide range of early childhood experts. The question remains: how do teachers react to children's behavior, and how does that reaction impact the child in later incidents? Through the years, styles of discipline have changed. "Spare the rod and spoil the child"—the in vogue punishment over perhaps a hundred years—gave way to time out sometime in the late 1970s. And now time out, the "strategy of choice" for 20 years or so, seems to be falling out of favor. What is time out, why has it been so popular, and what strategy will replace it if indeed it is on the way out?

What Is Time Out?

Sheppard and Willoughby (1975) define time out as the "removal of an individual from a situation which contains minimal opportunity for positive reinforcement." According to Schreiber (1999) the intent of time out is to "control and extinguish undesirable behaviors." When you say time out to a classroom teacher, many times the image evoked is that of a chair in the corner of the classroom where a child is put when she has "misbehaved." The length of time that child needs to "think about what she has done wrong" is many times determined by the child's age. The rule of thumb generally has been one minute per year.

The Use of Time Out as a Discipline Strategy

Time out was originally used in institutional settings with people who had a variety of mental or emotional disorders (Marion, 2001). In that setting, time out might have been used to ensure the safety of other residents by removing a dangerous or disruptive resident from a setting. It might also have been used as a consequence, when a resident refused to comply with requests of the staff. In such a setting, time out was considered a legitimate guidance strategy.

At some point during the 1970s, time out made its way into schools as a discipline technique. As corporal punishment declined, time out arose to fill the void with what seemed as a more caring, humane, and non-violent method. In an early childhood classroom, time out has seemingly been used as a discipline strategy to control and extinguish undesirable behaviors. Well-meaning teachers might use it to cope with non-compliance in young children, or to give a consequence for unsafe behavior. In some situations time out may be viewed as a logical consequence to inappropriate behavior or the loss of self-control (Gartrell, 2001).

How effective is time out in the typical early childhood environment? *Two-and-half-year-old Ben runs over to giggling two-year-old Jack and pushes him. The teacher says, "Ben! I told you not to push Jack! Use your words!" Ben tries again to push Jack. The teacher shouts, "Ben! That is not okay! You need to sit in the time-out chair!" She leads Ben to the chair and sits him down. In the time-out chair, Ben might be thinking, "I'm sitting in the chair... What is that noise?... I'm sitting in the chair... I want my mommy... I'm sitting in the chair." Ben is probably not thinking, "Wow! I guess I'll never push Jack again! I'm really sorry I did that!" Jack might be thinking: "What happened? I was giggling and then I was pushed down!"* (Schreiber, 1999, p. 22).

Should the Use of Time Out be Questioned?

Although many teachers view this technique as discipline, the lost opportunities and deprivation of positive interactions move this technique into the punishment category. The NAEYC Code of Ethical Conduct, P-1.1, states, "Above all, we shall not harm children. We shall not participate in practices that are disrespectful, degrading, dangerous, exploitative, intimidating, psychologically damaging, or physically harmful to children. This principle has precedence over all other in this code." Marion and Swim (2001) point out that "punishment has great potential for doing harm to children because it often serves as a model of negative, hurtful and aggressive measures."

Teachers may view time out as discipline rather than punishment, but children view these strategies as painful. When two-, three- and four-year-old children were asked in a study about time out, they expressed sadness and fear, as well as feeling alone, feeling disliked by the teacher and feeling ignored by peers (Readdick and Chapman, 2000).

Many early childhood experts agree with Readdick and Chapman. For example, Montessori (1964) sees these external controls that reward and punish as an opportunity lost to teach children how to self-regulate (Gartrell, 2001). The removal period can be confusing to the child because he lacks the cognitive ability to understand the process (Katz, 1984; Gartrell, 2001). Schreiber (1999) calls the practice of using time outs "undesirable" for five reasons: 1) external controls overshadow the need to develop internal controls; 2) adult needs are met at the expense of the child's needs; 3) a negative effect can be seen in the child's self-worth and self-confidence; 4) confusion arises over the connection between the action and the consequence; and 5) the lost opportunity for learning. These "undesirable" aspects of time out, along with the others mentioned above, make this strategy developmentally inappropriate. The needs of the child are not met, thus, causing harm to the child.

Guiding Children's Behavior

Time out needs to be revisited under the broader umbrella of guidance. Guidance can be defined as "Everything adults deliberately do and say, either directly or indirectly, to influence children's behavior, with the goal of helping them become well-adjusted, self-directed, productive adults" (Hildebrand and Hearron, p. 4, 1999). Using this definition, it is obvious that teachers have a re-

sponsibility to guide interactions towards a meaningful end. It is through positive actions or techniques that learning takes place. Today many positive techniques are available to early childhood teachers. Let's look at three areas: 1) managing the environment, 2) demonstrating developmentally appropriate practices, and 3) fostering the development of self-regulation in children.

Managing the Environment

Managing the environment must start with safety as the first priority. Consider the child who seems to be always running in the classroom. The teacher says, *"John, stop running before you hurt yourself. I've told you many times that if you run you will have to sit on a chair and slow down."* A positive alternative to this would be to take a look at the environment. Is there sufficient space for large muscle or active play? Instead of changing the child's behavior with negative consequences, add a tunnel for crawling through, steps for walking up and down or change your schedule to provide outdoor play earlier in your morning routine. Schreiber (1999) lists several ways to minimize conflicts such as keeping group sizes small so each child gets more attention and minimize crowding of play spaces to minimize disruptions. Classrooms need personal spaces and social spaces. Personal space refers to an area where children put belongings or spend time when privacy is needed. Social space refers to an area around the child that the child feels is his such as a seat at the art table, or a section of the sand box (Hildebrand & Hearron, 1999). Teachers need to provide enough social spaces in their classrooms so children feel comfortable while playing. Take a look around your room. Is there adequate play space? Consider having 50 percent more play spaces than the number of children present.

Developmentally Appropriate Practices

Developmentally appropriate practices and positive guidance strategies go hand in hand. As teachers, we must make sure

our expectations are in line with the developmental levels of the children.

Giving children choices is one of Eaton's (1997) suggestions for positive guidance techniques. For example, *if a two-year-old is having difficulty coming to the snack table, the teacher can say, "It is time to sit down for snack now Jody. You may sit on the red chair or this blue chair."* Choices allow the child to have control over her environment within the boundaries set by the teacher.

Teaching expected behavior is another positive guidance strategy (Marion & Muza, 1998). As teachers we model behavior continuously. As a toddler teacher, I find myself modeling appropriate behaviors in the house area in my room especially at the beginning of the year. The children love to set the table and serve food. They also love to put everything in their mouths as they play and pretend to eat. In order to keep the toys clean (and out of the sanitizing container), I need to model how to hold the food inches from my mouth and move my lips as if I was eating. I tell them what I am doing and why. I label it by saying, "I'm pretending to eat the spaghetti." They love to watch and then repeat the modeled behavior.

Redirecting behavior takes on many forms—diverting, distracting, substituting (Marion, 1999). Consider having two of some items in your room so that substituting can easily happen such as in this example: *Sydney is playing with a doll when Michael tries to take it away. The teacher redirects by substitution when he hands Michael the second doll and replies, "Michael you may use this doll. Sydney is feeding that doll now."*

Setting limits in a preschool classroom provides boundaries for the children and teacher. Limits are set to assure the safety of children, adults, and materials. They also provide a framework in which trust, respect, equality, and accepting responsibility can flourish. Routines and transition times are ideal opportunities to apply positive guidance strategies. Use phrases such as, "It's time to (wash hands, go outside, rest quietly,)" "It's important to (use soap to remove germs, stay where a teacher can see you)," and "I need you to (wait for me before you go outside, pick up those two blocks)." (Reynolds, 2001).

Using action statements to guide behavior in young children. Telling children what to do, such as "we walk inside," takes the guesswork out of the situation. The child knows exactly what is expected of him. Hildebrand and Hearron (1999) point out that putting the action part of the statement at the beginning of the sentence is an effective method. For example, saying, "Hold on to the railing" is better than, "You might fall off the slide, so be sure to hold on." This allows the important part to be stated before it's too late or the child loses interest in your comments.

Demeo (2001) suggests when using positive guidance strategies a teacher must also take into account the variables that affect compliance. When advocating for behavior change in young children we should:

- Use statements
- Give the child time to respond
- Use a quiet voice, don't give multiple requests
- Describe the behavior we want to see
- Demonstrate and model
- Make more start requests than stop requests (do vs. don't)
- Be at the child's eye level and optimal listening distance of three feet.

Fostering the Development of Self-Regulation in Children

Self-regulation allows children to control their actions. They must develop the ability to know when to act, when to control their impulses and when to search for alternative solutions. This is a learned, ongoing process that can be fostered by teachers who use an integrated approach that considers the whole child and the developmental level of that child. "To support developing impulse control [in toddlers], caregivers can use responsive guidance techniques that emphasize individual control over behavior, provide

simple cause-and-effect reasons for desired behaviors, use suggestions rather than commands, and use language to assist self-control" Bronson (2000, p. 35). When we teach problem-solving skills, we help children take responsibility for their actions, see a situation from another point of view, and develop decision-making skills (Miller, 1984). These internal processes help children think of alternative solutions and possible outcomes. As teachers we can start the thought process by asking children, "How can you...?" or "What could we do to...?" As children develop these skills they will soon generate their own solutions and gain control of their actions.

Conclusion

Time out is out! As early childhood professionals, we must abide by the code of Ethical Conduct laid out by NAEYC, which states that "Above all we shall not harm children." The use of time out as a discipline strategy can harm children and must not be used in our classrooms. It is our responsibility to help "children and adults achieve their full potential in the context of relationships that are based on trust, respect, and positive regard" (NAEYC, 1990). As teachers we influence children daily. We can choose to affect children in positive ways by managing the environment, using developmentally appropriate practices, and fostering self-regulation. An effective teacher uses a mix of several techniques. One strategy may work one day while another may be best another day. It takes forethought and reflection. Positive guidance strategies help children develop into caring, respectful human beings.

References

Bronson, M. (2000). Recognizing and supporting the development of self-regulation in young children. *Young Children,* 55 (2), 33–37.

Demeo, W. (2001). Time-out is out: Developing appropriate alternatives for helping difficult young children develop self-control. Presentation at NAEYC Conference, Anaheim, CA.

Eaton, M. (1997). Positive discipline: Fostering the self-esteem of young children. *Young Children,* 52 (6), 43–46.

Gartrell, D. (2001). Replacing time-out: Part one—using guidance to build an encouraging classroom. *Young Children,* 56 (6), 8–16.

Hildebrand V. & Hearron P. (199). *Guiding young children.* Upper Saddle River, NJ: Prentice-Hall, Inc.

Katz, L. (1984). The professional early childhood teacher. *Young Children,* 39 (5), 3–10.

Marion, M. (1999). *Guidance of young children.* Upper Saddle River, NJ: Prentice-Hall, Inc.

Marion, M. & Muza, R. (1998). Positive discipline: Six strategies for guiding behavior. *Texas Child Care,* 22, (2), 6–11.

Marion, M. & Swim, T. (2001). First of all, do no harm: Relationship between early childhood teacher beliefs about punitive discipline practices and reported use of time out. Manuscript, under review.

Marion, M. (2001). Discussion information.

Miller C. (1984). Building self-control: Discipline for young children. *Young Children,* 39 (6), 15–19.

Montessori, M. (1964). *The Montessori method.* New York: Shocken Books.

NAEYC Code of Ethical Conduct and Statement of Commitment (1990).

Readdick & Chapman, P. (2000). Young children's perceptions of time out. *Journal of Research in Childhood Education,* 15 (1).

Reynolds, E. (2001). *Guiding young children: A problem-solving approach.* Mountain View, CA: Mayfield Publishing Company.

Schreiber, M. (1999). Time-outs for toddlers: Is our goal punishment or education? *Young Children,* 54 (4), 22–25.

Sheppard, W. & Willoughby, R. (1975). *Child behavior: Learning and development.* Chicago: Rand McNally College Publishing Company.

Kathy Preuesse is currently a lab school teacher in the two-year-old toddler class at the Child and Family Study Center at the University of Wisconsin-Stout in Menomonie, WI.

Beyond Banning War and Superhero Play

Meeting Children's Needs in Violent Times

Diane E. Levin

Four-year-old Jules is particularly obsessed. Telling him no guns or pretend fighting just doesn't work. When he's a good guy, like a Power Ranger, he thinks it's okay to use whatever force is needed to suppress the bad guy "because that's what a superhero does!" And then someone ends up getting hurt. When we try to enforce a ban, the children say it's not superhero play, it's some other kind of play. Many children don't seem to know more positive ways to play or play the same thing over and over without having any ideas of their own. I need some new ideas.

THIS EXPERIENCED TEACHER'S ACCOUNT captures the kinds of concerns I often hear from teachers worried about how to respond to war play in their classrooms (Levin 2003). These expressions of concern about play with violence tend to increase when violent world events, like 9/11 and the war against Iraq, dominate the news.

Play, viewed for decades as an essential part of the early childhood years, has become a problem in many classrooms, something even to avoid. Teachers ask why is play deemed as being so important to children's development when it is so focused on fighting. Some are led to plan other activities that are easier to manage and appear at first glance to be more productive. Reducing playtime may seem to reduce problems in the short term, but this approach does not address the wide-ranging needs children address through play.

Why Are Children Fascinated with War Play?

There are many reasons why children bring violent content and themes into their play. They are related to the role of play in development and learning as well as to the nature of the society in which war play occurs (Cantor 1998; Carlsson-Paige & Levin 1987, 1990; Katch 2001; Levin 1998a & b, & 2003).

Exposure to violence.

From both therapeutic and cognitive perspectives, children use play to work out an understanding of experience, including the violence to which they are exposed. Young children may see violence in their homes and communities as well as entertainment and news violence on the screen. We should not be surprised when children are intent on bringing it to their play. Children's play often focuses on the most salient and graphic, confusing or scary, and most aggressive aspects of violence. It is this content they struggle to work out and understand. Typically, the children who seem most obsessed with war play have been exposed to the most violence and have the greatest need to work it out.

Need to feel powerful.

Most young children look for ways to feel powerful and strong. Play can be a safe way to achieve a sense of power. From a child's point of view, play with violence, especially when connected to the power and invincibility of entertainment, is very seductive. Children who use war play to help them feel powerful and safe are also the children who feel the most powerless and vulnerable.

Open-ended toys, like blocks, stuffed animals, and generic dinosaurs, can be used in many ways that the child control.

Influence of violent, media-linked toys.

Children's toys give powerful messages about what and how to play. Open-ended toys, like blocks, stuffed animals, and generic dinosaurs can be used in many ways that the child controls. Highly structured toys such as play dough kits with molds to make movie characters and action figures that talk tend to have built-in features that show children how and what to play. Many of today's best selling toys are of the highly structured variety and are linked to violent media. Such toys are appealing because they promise dramatic power and excitement and then they channel children into replicating the violent stories they see on screen. Some children, like Jules, get "stuck" imitating media-linked violence instead of developing creative, imaginative, and beneficial play.

Why Are Teachers Concerned about Today's War Play?

There are many reasons why teachers are concerned about war play and why they seek help figuring out how to deal with it.

Lack of safety in the classroom.

Play with violence tends to end up with children out of control, scared, and hurt. Managing the play and keeping everyone safe can feel like a never-ending struggle and a major diversion from the positive lessons we want children to learn.

Old approaches not working.

Many veteran teachers say that the bans they used to impose on war play no longer work. Children have a hard time accepting limits or controlling their intense desire or need to engage in the play. And children find ways to circumvent the ban—they deny the play is really war play (i.e., learning to lie) or sneak around conducting guerilla wars the teacher does not detect (i.e., learning to deceive).

Worries about the limited nature of the play.

Like Jules, some children engage in the same play with violence day after day and bring in few new or creative ideas of their own. Piaget called this kind of behavior "imitation," not "play" (Carlsson-Paige & Levin 1987). Such children are less likely to work out their needs regarding the violence they bring to their play or benefit from more sustained and elaborated play.

Concerns about lessons learned from the play.

When children pretend to hurt others, it is the opposite of what we hope they will learn about how to treat each other and solve problems. Children *learn* as they play— and what they play affects what they learn. When children are exposed to large amounts of violence, they learn harmful lessons about violence whether they are allowed to play it in the classroom or not.

> *When children are exposed to large amounts of violence, they learn harmful lessons about violence, whether they are allowed to play it in the classroom or not.*

At the same time, children do not think about the violence they bring into their play the same way adults do. Jules focuses on one thing at a time—the bad boy is one dimensional and bad, without thinking about what makes him bad. He thinks good guys can do whatever hurtful things they want because they are "good." Except when he gets carried away and hurts another child, Jules probably does know that at some level his play is different from the real violence he is imitating.

Approaches to Working with Children's Violent Play

- **Address children's needs while trying to reduce play with violence.** Banning play rarely works and it denies children the opportunity to work out violence issues through play or to feel that their interests and concerns are important. Trying to ban media-controlled imitative play, or even just to contain it, can be an appropriate stopgap measure when problems become overwhelming. However, a total ban on this kind of play may leave children to work things out on their own without the guidance of adults.
- **Ensure the safety of all children.** Involve children in developing rules for indoor and outdoor play that ensure safety. Help children understand the safety issue and what they can do to prevent injuries (physical and psychological) to themselves and others. Encourage children to paint, tell stories, and write (as they get older) to deal with issues of violence in ways that are safe and easier to control than play.
- **Promote development of imaginative and creative play (rather than imitative play).** To work through deep issues and needs in a meaningful way, most children require direct help from adults. How you help depends on the nature of children's play (Levin 1998b). Take time to observe the play and learn what children are working on and how. Use this information to help children move beyond narrowly scripted play that is focused on violent actions. Help children gain skills to work out the violent content they bring to their play, learn the lessons you aim to teach, and move on to new issues.

Approaches to Working Outside Violent Play

- **Encourage children to talk with adults about media violence.** As children struggle to feel safe and make sense of violence—regardless of the source—they need to know that we are there to help them with this process (Levin 2003). Start by trying to learn what they know, the unique meanings they have made, and what confuses and scares them.

  When a child raises an issue it is helpful to start by using an open-ended question like "What have you heard about that?" Respond based on what you learn about their ideas, questions, and needs. Keep in mind that children do not understand violence in or out of play as adults do. Try to correct misconceptions ("The planes that go over our school do not carry bombs"), help sort out fantasy and reality ("In real life people can't change back and forth like the Power Rangers do"), and provide reassurance about safety ("I can't let you play like that because it's my job to make sure everyone is safe").

- **Try to reduce the impact of antisocial lessons that children learn both in and out of play.** It can be helpful to encourage children to move from imitative to creative play so they can transform violence into positive behavior. Then talk with them about what has happened in their play ("I see Spiderman did a lot of fighting today. What was the problem?"). Help children to connect their own firsthand positive experiences about how people treat each other to the violence they have seen ("I'm glad that in real life you could solve your problem with Mary by..."). These connections can help diffuse some of the harmful lessons children learn about violence.

  Talking with children about violence is rarely easy, but it is one of our most powerful tools. It is hard to predict the directions in which children might take the conversations and teachers will often find it challenging to show respect for the differing ways families try to deal with these issues.

- **Work closely with families.** Reducing children's exposure to violence is one essential way to reduce their need to bring violence into their play. Most of young children's exposure occurs in the home, so family involvement is vital. Through parent workshops and family newsletters that include resource materials such as those listed below, teachers can help families learn more about how to protect children from violence, help children deal with the violence that still gets in, and promote play with open-ended toys and non-violent play themes (Levin 1998a, 2003). In addition, families can learn about how to resist the advertising for toys linked to violence in ways that keep the peace in the family (Levin 1998; Levin & Linn in press).

Reconcile Children's Needs and Adults' Concerns

In our society children are exposed to huge amounts of pretend and real violence. There are no simple or perfect solutions that simultaneously address children's needs and adults' concerns (Carlsson-Paige & Levin 1987). However, there is much teachers can do working with and outside of the play to make it better for everyone (see "Approaches to Working with Violent Play" and "Approaches to Working Outside Violent Play").

More Important Now Than Ever

There is no perfect approach for dealing with children's play with violence in these times. The best strategy is to vastly reduce the amount of violence children see. this would require adults to create a more peaceful world and limit children's exposure to media violence and toys marketed with media violence.

Given the state of the world, including the war against Iraq, children now more than ever need to find ways to work out the violence they see. For many, play helps them do so. We have a vital role in helping meet their nneds through play. We must create an approach that addresses the unique needs of children growing up in the midst of violence as well as concerns of adults about how play with violence contributes to the harmful lessons children learn.

References

Cantor, J. 1998. *"Mommy, I'm scared!" How TV and movies frighten children and what we can do to protect them.* NY: Harcourt Brace.

Carlsson-Paige, N. & Levin, D.E. 1987. *The war play dilemma: Balancing needs and values in the early childhood classroom.* NY: Teachers College Press.

Carlsson-Paige, N. & Levin, D.E. 1990. *Who's calling the shots? How to respond effectively to children's fascination with war play and war toys.* Gabriola Island, BC, CAN: New Society.

Katch, J. 2001. *Under dead man's skin: Discovering the meaning of children's violent play.* Boston: Beacon Press.

Levin, D.E. 1998a. *Remote control childhood? Combating the hazards of media culture.* Washington, DC: NAEYC.

Levin, D.E. 1998b. Play with violence. In *Play from birth to twelve: Contexts, perspectives, and meanings,* eds. D. Fromberg & D. Bergin. New York: Garland.

Levin, D.E. 2003. *Teaching young children in violent times: Building a peaceable classroom.* 2d ed. Cambridge, MA: Educators for Social Responsibility & Washington, DC: NAEYC.

Levin, D.E. & Linn, S. In press. The commercialization of childhood. In *Psychology and the consumer culture,* eds. T. Kasser & A. Kanner. Washington, DC: American Psychological Association.

Bullying Among Children

Most teachers are aware that bullying begins early, yet many appear to believe the myth that children "picking on" or teasing one another is a "normal" part of childhood.

Janis R. Bullock

Six-year-old Sam is barely eating. When asked by his dad what is wrong, he bursts into tears. "The kids at school keep calling me a nerd, and they poke and push me," he sobs.

"There's a kid at school no one likes," 7-year-old Anika shares with her parents. "We all tease her a lot. She is a total dork. I would never invite her to my birthday party."

Bullying is a very old phenomenon; European researchers have studied its effects for decades (Olweus, 1991). Until recently, however, the issue has received less attention from researchers in the United States, perhaps because of the prevailing belief that bullying among children is inevitable. Considering that bullying often is a sign that aggressive or violent behavior is present elsewhere in children's lives—young children may be acting out at school what they have observed and learned in the home—and the fact that bullying among primary school-age children is now recognized as an antecedent to progressively more violent behavior in later grades (Saufler & Gagne, 2000), it behooves teachers to take notice.

Unfortunately, teachers have differing attitudes toward children who bully. Most teachers are aware that bullying begins early, yet many appear to believe the myth that children "picking on" or teasing one another is a "normal" part of childhood. They also may believe that these conflicts are best resolved by the children themselves. Consequently, some teachers do not intervene.

CHARACTERISTICS OF BULLIES AND THEIR VICTIMS

Bullying refers to repeated, unprovoked, harmful actions by one child or children against another. The acts may be physical or psychological. Physical, or direct, bullying includes hitting, kicking, pushing, grabbing toys from other children, and engaging in very rough and intimidating play. Psychological bullying includes name calling, making faces, teasing, taunting, and making threats. Indirect, or less obvious and less visible, bullying includes exclusion and rejection of children from a group (Olweus, 1991).

Children who bully are impulsive, dominate others, and show little empathy. They display what Olweus (1991) defines as an "aggressive personality pattern combined with physical strength" (p. 425). Without intervention, the frequency and severity of the bullying behaviors may increase. Even more disturbing, it appears that the patterns of bullying learned in the early years can set children on a course of violence later in life (Batsche & Knoff, 1994; Baumeister, 2001).

Although a longstanding characterization of children who bully points to their low self-esteem, there is little empirical evidence to support this view. In fact, more recent research (Baumeister, 2001; Bushman & Baumeister, 1998) suggests that an inflated self-esteem increases the odds of aggressive behavior. When a bully's self-regard is seriously threatened by insults or criticisms, for example, his or her response will be more aggressive than normal. Furthermore, bullies often report that they feel powerful and superior, and justified in their actions.

Research on family dynamics suggests that many children already have learned to bully others by preschool age. Many young children who bully lack empathy and problem-solving skills, and learn from their parents to hit back in response to problems (Loeber & Dishion, 1984; Vladimir & Brubach, 2000).

Children who are bullied, on the other hand, are often younger, weaker, and more passive than the bully. They appear anxious, insecure, cautious, sensitive and quiet, and often react by crying and withdrawing. They are often lonely and lack close friendships at school. Without adult intervention, these children are likely to be bullied repeatedly, putting them at-risk for continued social rejection, depression, and impaired self-esteem (Schwartz, Dodge, & Coie, 1994). A smaller subset of these children, known as "provocative victims," have learned to respond aggressively to perceived threats by retaliating not only against the aggressor, but also against others (Olweus, 1993).

INCIDENCES OF BULLYING AMONG CHILDREN

Evidence suggests that, in the United States, the incidence of bullying among children is increasing and becoming a nationwide problem. One out of five children admits to being a bully (Noll & Carter, 1997). In general, boys engage in more physical, direct means of bullying, whereas girls engage in the more psychological and indirect bullying, such as exclusion. Roland (1989) reported that girls may be involved in bullying as much as boys, but are less willing to acknowledge their involvement. In addition, because indirect bullying is often less apparent, girls' bullying may be underestimated. Girls tend to bully less as they get older. The percentage of boys who bully, however, is similar at different age levels (Smith & Sharp, 1994).

Twenty-five to 50 percent of children report being bullied. The great majority of boys are bullied by other boys, while 60 percent of girls report being bullied by boys. Eight percent of children report staying away from school one day per month because they fear being bullied. Forty-three percent of children have a fear of being harassed in the school bathroom (Noll & Carter, 1997). Children report that many incidents of bullying occur in situations that are difficult for the teacher to monitor, such as during playground activity.

THE EFFECTS OF BULLYING ON CHILDREN

To succeed in school, children must perceive their environment as being safe, secure, and comfortable. Yet, for many children, bullying and teasing begins as soon as children first form peer groups. For some children, this is a time when patterns of victimizing and victimization become established. Consequently, the victims perceive school as a threatening place and experience adjustment difficulties, feelings of loneliness, and a desire to avoid school. These feelings may linger even when bullying ceases (Kochenderfer & Ladd, 1996).

Children desire and need interaction with peers, physical activity, and time outdoors. Consequently, they often consider outside recess to be their favorite part of the school day. Sadly, however, many children who are bullied report that problems occur on the playground and view the playground as a lonely, unhappy, and unsafe environment.

If children are fearful or feel intimidated, they cannot learn effectively. They may react by skipping school, avoiding certain areas of the school (the bathroom or the playground), or, in extreme, yet increasingly common, cases, they may bring weapons to school (Noll & Carter, 1997). Olweus (1991) reminds us that "every individual should have the right to be spared oppression and repeated, intentional humiliation in school, as in society at large" (p. 427). As early exposure to bullying can produce both immediate and delayed effects in children's ability to adjust to school, school staff need to intervene as soon as problems are detected.

RECOMMENDATIONS FOR TEACHERS TO SUPPORT CHILDREN

A comprehensive plan to address the problems of bullying and teasing must involve school personnel, teachers, children, and families. Intervention must occur on three levels: school-wide, in specific classrooms, and with individuals.

School-wide Intervention

School personnel must recognize the pervasiveness of bullying and teasing and its detrimental effects on children's development. Inservice training can be developed that outlines a clear policy statement against bullying and intervention strategies for addressing it. The school also can develop a comprehensive plan geared to teach children prosocial behaviors and skills. The children may be involved in the development of such policies and strategies, providing their input on what behavior is appropriate and identifying sanctions against bullies (Lickona, 2000; Olweus, 1997).

School personnel could enlist families' support and involvement by sharing details of the policy through parent-teacher conferences and newsletters. Families need to be aware of the specific sanctions that will be imposed on children who bully, and they need opportunities to offer feedback and suggestions. It is important to encourage parents to talk with their children about bullying. Children who are bullied often believe that their parents are unaware of the situation, and that their concerns are not being addressed or discussed. Children *do* want adults to intervene, however (Gropper & Froschl, 1999). If families are kept informed, they can work as a "team member" with school counselors and teachers to change the school environment.

Additional sources of school-wide support for children who are bullied and teased may be developed, including mentoring programs. Teachers can identify children who need support, and find them a mentor. Children may feel more at ease and less anxious when they have a "buddy," such as an older student, who can help intervene (Noll & Carter, 1997). Counselors at one elementary school selected, trained, and supervised high school students to teach the younger children how to deal with bullying and harassment. After implementation of this program, the teachers observed a decline in reports of harassment (Frieman & Frieman, 2000).

Bullying frequently occurs on the playground (Whitney, Rivers, Smith, & Sharp, 1994), yet many children believe that teachers do little to stop it. Consequently, "play-time… is more of a prison sentence than an opportunity to play and socialize" (Slee, 1995, p. 326). Therefore, school personnel may need to review playground design and space, children's access to these spaces, teacher supervision, and the role of the school in early intervention on the playground (Lambert, 1999). Yard monitors and lunch time supervisors can be trained to watch for signs of bullying. In addition, children can be asked to identify those places where bullying most frequently occurs.

Intervention in Specific Classrooms

Clearly, bullying and hurtful teasing affects children's ability to learn and enjoy play, as well as the teacher's ability to teach. Within the classroom, teachers can begin addressing the problem by creating times for children to talk about their concerns. Interestingly, one study showed that when children ages 5 to 7 years of age were asked about assisting someone who was being bullied, 37 percent replied that it was none of their business to help (Slee & Rigby, 1994).

Teachers can ask children to talk about what makes them feel unsafe or unwelcome in school. The teacher then can make a list of the children's responses, discuss them (e.g., "I don't like it when someone hits me or calls me a name"), and create corresponding rules (e.g., "Hitting and name calling are not allowed in the classroom"). When necessary, the discussions can be continued during class meetings so that the rules can be reviewed, revised, and updated. The teacher can also show children what to do to help themselves or other children, and remind them of the consequences of breaking the rules. Teachers can reduce children's anxiety by setting firm limits on unacceptable behavior (Froschl & Sprung, 1999).

If the bullying continues, teachers may need to make referrals to school counselors who will work with children, either individually or in groups, to talk about concerns, discuss solutions and options, and give suggestions on how to form friendships. Children without close friends are more likely to be victimized and may benefit from specific suggestions for building friendships (e.g., invite a friend to your house, work together on a school project, share a common interest, play a favorite game together).

Certain types of curricula, especially those that provide opportunities for cooperative learning experiences, may make bullying less likely to flourish. Children need to be engaged in worthwhile, authentic learning activities that encourage their interests and abilities (Katz, 1993). When they are intellectually motivated, they are less likely to bully. For example, project work (Katz & Chard, 2000) involves children's in-depth investigations into topics of their own choosing. As they explore events and objects around them in the classroom, in the school yard, in the neighborhood, and in the community, they learn to cooperate, collaborate, and share responsibilities. Project work can be complemented by noncompetitive games, role playing, and dramatization to raise awareness of bullying and increase empathy for those who experience it. Some teachers use children's literature to help create caring and peaceful classrooms (Morris, Taylor, & Wilson, 2000).

Intervention With Individuals

Developing both immediate and long-term strategies for identifying and working with bullies may be necessary. When teachers observe an incident of bullying, they can intervene by asking the bully to consider the consequences of his or her actions and think about how others feel. By talking calmly, yet firmly, to the bully, the teacher can make it clear that such behavior is unacceptable. Teachers can show the bully alternate ways to talk, interact, and negotiate; at the same time, they can encourage victims to assert themselves. By doing so, the teacher is showing the bully and the victim that action is being taken to stop the bullying. Acting promptly can prevent the bullying from escalating.

When interacting with children on a one-on-one basis, teachers should provide encouragement that acknowledges specific attributes, rather than dispensing general praise, approval, or admiration ("I am so glad that you have done a great job; it is wonderful; yours is one of the best projects") that may appear to be contrived. Expressions of specific encouragement ("You seem to be pleased and very interested in your project, and it appears you have worked on it for many days and used many resources to find answers to your questions"), as opposed to general praise, are descriptive, sincere, take place in private, focus on the process, and help children to develop an appreciation for their efforts and work. While developing children's self-esteem is a worthwhile goal, false praise may instead promote narcissism and unrealistic self-regard. Teachers should avoid encouraging children to think highly of themselves when they have not earned it (Baumeister, 2001; Hitz & Driscoll, 1988).

Additional long-term strategies may include encouraging children to resolve their own problems and using peers to mediate between bullies and their targets. Furthermore, teachers can spend time helping children to form ties with peers who can offer protection, support, security, and safety, thus helping to reduce children's exposure to bullying (Kochenderfer & Ladd, 1997; Ladd, Kochenderfer, & Coleman, 1996).

SUMMARY

Bullying and teasing are an unfortunate part of too many children's lives, leading to trouble for both bullies and their victims. Children who are bullied come to believe that school is unsafe and that children are mean. They may develop low self-esteem and experience loneliness. Children who continue to bully will have difficulty developing and maintaining positive relationships. A comprehensive intervention plan that addresses the needs of the school, the classroom, teachers, children, and families can be developed and implemented to ensure that all children learn in a supportive and safe environment.

References

Batsche, G. M., & Knoff, H. M. (1994). Bullies and their victims: Understanding a pervasive problem in the schools. *School Psychology Review, 23,* 165–174.

Baumeister, R. (2001). Violent pride: Do people turn violent because of self-hate, or self-love? *Scientific American, 284,* 96–101.

Bushman, B. J., & Baumeister, R. F. (1998). Threatened egotism, narcissism, self-esteem, and direct and displaced aggression: Does self-love or self-hate lead to violence? *Journal of Personality and Social Psychology, 75,* 219–229.

Frieman, M., & Frieman, B. B. (2000). *Reducing harassment in elementary school classrooms using high school mentors.* (ERIC Document Reproduction Service No. ED 439 797).

Froschl, M., & Sprung, B. (1999). On purpose: Addressing teasing and bullying in early childhood. *Young Children, 54,* 70–72.

Gropper, N., & Froschl, M. (1999). The role of gender in young children's teasing and bullying behavior. Montreal, Canada. (ERIC Document Reproduction Service No. ED 431 162).

Hitz, R., & Driscoll, A. (1988). Praise or encouragement? New insights into praise: Implications for early childhood teachers. *Young Children, 42,* 6–13.

Katz, L. G. (1993). *Distinctions between self-esteem and narcissism: Implications for practice.* Urbana, IL: ERIC Clearinghouse on Elementary and Early Childhood Education.

Katz, L., & Chard, S. (2000). *Engaging children's minds: The project approach* (2nd ed.). Stamford, CT: Ablex.

Kochenderfer, B. J., & Ladd, G. W. (1996). Peer victimization: Cause or consequence of school maladjustment? *Child Development, 67,* 1305–1317.

Kochenderfer, B. J., & Ladd, G. W. (1997). Victimized children's responses to peers' aggression: Behaviors associated with reduced versus continued victimization. *Development and Psychopathology, 9,* 59–73.

Ladd, G. W., Kochenderfer, B. J., & Coleman, C. (1996). Friendship quality as a predictor of young children's early school adjustment. *Child Development, 67,* 1103–1118.

Lambert, E. B. (1999). Do school playgrounds trigger playground bullying? *Canadian Children, 42,* 25–31.

Lickona, T. (2000). Sticks and stones may break my bones AND names WILL hurt me. Thirteen ways to prevent peer cruelty. *Our Children, 26,* 12–14.

Loeber, R., & Dishion, T. J. (1984). Boys who fight at home and school: Family conditions influencing cross-setting consistency. *Journal of Consulting and Clinical Psychology, 52,* 759–768.

Morris, V. G., Taylor, S. I., & Wilson, J. T. (2000). Using children's stories to promote peace in classrooms. *Early Childhood Education Journal, 28,* 41–50.

Noll, K., & Carter, J. (1997). *Taking the bully by the horns.* Reading, PA: Unicorn Press.

Olweus, D. (1991). Bully/victim problems among schoolchildren: Basic facts and effects of a school based intervention program. In D. J. Pepler & K. H. Rubin (Eds.), *The development and treatment of childhood aggression* (pp. 441–448). Hillsdale, NJ: Lawrence Erlbaum.

Olweus, D. (1993). Victimization by peers: Antecedents and long-term outcomes. In K. H. Rubin & J. B. Asendorf (Eds.), *Social withdrawal, inhibition, and shyness in childhood* (pp. 315–341). Hillsdale, NJ: Lawrence Erlbaum.

Olweus, D. (1997). Bully/victim problems in school: Facts and intervention. *European Journal of Psychology of Education, 12,* 495–510.

Roland, E. (1989). Bullying: The Scandinavian research tradition. In D. P. Tattum & D. A. Lane (Eds.), *Bullying in schools* (pp. 21–32). London: Trentham Books.

Saufler, C., & Gagne, C. (2000). *Maine project against bullying. Final report.* Augusta, ME: Maine State Department of Education. (ERIC Document Reproduction Service No. ED 447 911).

Schwartz, D., Dodge, K. A., & Coie, J. D. (1994). The emergence of chronic peer victimization in boys' play groups. *Child Development, 64,* 1755–1772.

Slee, P.T. (1995). Bullying in the playground: The impact of interpersonal violence on Australian children's perceptions of their play environment. *Children's Environments, 12,* 320–327.

Slee, P. T., & Rigby, K. (1994). Peer victimisation at school. *AECA Australian Journal of Early Education, 19,* 3–10.

Smith, P. K., & Sharp, S. (1994). The problem of school bullying. In P. K. Smith & S. Sharp (Eds.), *School bullying* (pp. 1–19). London: Routledge.

Vladimir, N., & Brubach, A. (2000). *Teasing among school-aged children.* (ERIC Document Reproduction Service No. 446 321).

Whitney, I., Rivers, I., Smith, P. K., & Sharp, S. (1994). The Sheffield project: Methodology and findings. In P. K. Smith & S. Sharp (Eds.), *School bullying* (pp. 20–56). London: Routledge.

Janis R. Bullock is Professor, Early Childhood Education, Department of Health and Human Development, Montana State University, Bozeman.

Classroom Problems That Don't Go Away

Laverne Warner and Sharon Lynch

Wade runs "combat-style" beneath the windows of his school as he makes his getaway from his 1st-grade classroom. It is still early in the school year, but this is the third time Wade has tried to escape. Previously, his teacher has managed to catch him before he left the building. Today, however, his escape is easier, because Mrs. Archie is participating with the children in a game of "Squirrel and Trees" and Wade is behind her when he leaves the playground area. She sees him round the corner of the school, and speedily gives chase. When she reaches the front parking lot of their building, however, she cannot find him. Wade is gone!

Experienced and inexperienced teachers alike, in all grade levels, express concern about difficult classroom problems—those problems that don't ever seem to go away, no matter what management techniques are used. Wade's story and similar ones are echoed time and again in classrooms around the world as adults struggle to find a balance between correcting children's behavior and instructing them about self-management strategies.

Educators emphasize an understanding of appropriate guidance strategies, and teachers learn about acceptable center and school district policies. An abundance of books, videotapes, and other teacher resources are available to classroom practitioners to enhance their understanding of appropriate guidance strategies. Professional organizations such as the Association for Childhood Education International define standards of good practice. Textbooks for childhood educators define well-managed classrooms and appropriate management techniques (e.g., Marion, 2003; Morrison, 2001; Reynolds, 2003; Seefeldt & Barbour, 1998; Wolfgang, 2001).

Despite this preparation, educators daily face problems with guiding or disciplining children in their classrooms. Understanding the developmental needs of children and meeting their physical needs are two ingredients to happy classroom management. It is also important to look at the larger problems involved

when children's misbehaviors are chronic to the point that youngsters are labeled as "difficult." Are these children receiving enough attention from the teacher? Are they developing social skills that will help them through interactions and negotiations with other children in the classroom?

Mrs. Archie's guidance philosophy is founded on principles that she believes are effective for young children. Taking time at the end of the day to reflect on Wade's disappearance, Mrs. Archie concluded that she had done what she could, as always, to develop a healthy classroom climate.

She strives to build a classroom community of learners and act with understanding in response to antisocial behavior in the classroom, and she knows that the vast majority of children will respond positively. Mrs. Archie's classroom layout promotes orderly activity throughout the day and is well-stocked with enough materials and supplies to keep children interested and actively engaged in their learning activities. Although the activities she provides are challenging, many simple experiences also are available to prevent children from being overwhelmed by classroom choices.

Furthermore, Mrs. Archie's attitude is positive about children, like Wade, who come from families that use punitive discipline techniques at home. Her discussions with Wade's mother prior to his escape had been instructive, and she thought that progress was being made with the family. Indeed, when Wade arrived at home the day he ran off, his mother returned him to school immediately.

So what is the teacher to do about children, like Wade, with chronic and intense behavioral difficulties? If serious behavior problems are not addressed before age 8, the child is likely to have long-lasting conduct problems throughout school, often leading to suspension, or dropping out (Katz & McClellan, 1997; Walker et al., 1996). Since the window of opportunity to intervene with behavior problems is narrow, childhood educators must understand the nature of the behavior problem and design an educative plan to teach the child alternative approaches.

The ABC's of the Problem

The first step in analyzing the behavior problem is to determine the "pay-off" for the child. Challenging behaviors usually fall into one of the following categories: 1) behavior that gets the child attention, either positive or negative; 2) behavior that removes the child from something unpleasant, like work or a task; 3) behavior that results in the child getting something she or he wants, like candy or a toy; and 4) behavior that provides some type of sensory stimulation, such as spinning around until the child feels dizzy and euphoric.

To understand the pay-off for the child, it is important to examine the ABC's of the behavior: the antecedents, behaviors, and consequences associated with the problem. The *antecedent* requires a record, which describes what was happening just prior to the incident. The actual *behavior* then can be described in observable, measurable terms: instead of saying that the misbehaving child had a tantrum, detail that he threw himself to the floor, screamed, and pounded his fists on the floor for four minutes. Finally, we examine the pay-off (*consequences*) for the behavior.

Did the behavior result in close physical contact as the child was carried into the adjoining room and the caregiver attempted to soothe him? Did the behavior result in his being given juice so that he could calm down? Did the behavior result in scolding by the teacher, providing the kind of intense individual attention that some youngsters crave because it is the only demonstration of love and caring they have experienced? When teachers and caregivers examine the ABC's of the behavior, they are better able to understand the child's motivation, establish preventive strategies, and teach alternative social skills the child can use to meet his or her needs.

Prevention Strategies

Mrs. Archie knows that she needs to learn specific strategies that will help her work with "difficult" behaviors, like those of Wade, because these problems certainly don't seem to go away on their own. The following intervention methods are designed to preempt anti-social behaviors and often are referred to as prevention strategies. It is always better to prevent the behavior as much as possible.

Accentuate the Positive For the child who demonstrates inappropriate behavior to gain attention, the teacher should find every opportunity to give the child positive attention when he or she is behaving appropriately. Often, these opportunities to "catch the child being good" occur relatively early in the day. When children receive plenty of positive attention early in the day and the teacher continues to find opportunities for praise and attention as the day goes on, the child is not as likely to misbehave for attention as his need is already being met (Hanley, Piazza, & Fisher, 1997). This intervention is based on the principle of deprivation states. If the child is deprived of attention and is "hungry" for adult interaction, he will do anything to gain the attention of others, even negative attention.

Player's Choice When educators see a negative pattern of behavior, they can anticipate that the child is likely to refuse adult requests. This is often referred to as "oppositional behavior." A teacher may remark, "It doesn't matter what I ask her to do, she is going to refuse to do it." One successful strategy for dealing with this type of oppositional behavior is to provide the child with choices (Knowlton, 1995). This approach not only gives the child power and control, but also affords the child valuable opportunities for decision making. Example of choices include, "Do you want to carry out the trash basket or erase the chalkboard?," "Do you want to sit in the red chair or the blue chair?," or "Do you want to pick up the yellow blocks or the green blocks?"

The teacher must be cautious about the number of choices provided, however. Many children have difficulty making up their minds if too many choices are presented—often, two choices are plenty. Also, adults need to monitor their own attitude as they present choices. If choices are presented using a drill sergeant tone of voice, the oppositional child is going to resist the suggestions.

On a Roll When adults anticipate that a child is going to refuse a request, teachers can embed this request within a series of other simple requests. This intervention is based on the research-based principles of high-probability request sequences (Ardoin, Martens, & Wolfe, 1999). The first step in this procedure is to observe the child to determine which requests she consistently performs. Before asking the child to perform the non-preferred request, ask her to do several other things that she does consistently. For example, 8-year-old Morgan consistently resists cleaning up the dollhouse area. While she is playing with the dollhouse, her teacher could ask her to "Give the dolls a kiss," "Show me the doll's furniture," and "Put the dolls in their bedrooms." After she has complied with these three requests, she is much more likely to comply with the request to "Put the dolls away now" or "Give them to me."

Grandma's Rule This strategy often is referred to as the Premack Principle (Premack, 1959). When asking a child to perform an action, specifying what he or she will receive after completing it more often ensures its completion. Examples here include: "When you have finished your math problems, then we will go outside," "When you have eaten your peas, you can have some pudding," and "After you have rested awhile, we will go to the library."

A Spoonful of Sugar Helps the Medicine Go Down This principle involves pairing preferred and non-preferred activities. One particular task that is difficult for preschoolers, and many adults, is waiting. Most of us do not wait well. When asking a child to complete a non-preferred activity such as waiting in line, pairing a preferred activity with the waiting will make it more tolerable.

Businesses and amusement parks use the principle of pairing when they provide music or exhibits for customers as they wait in line. Similarly, with young children, teachers can provide enjoyable activities as children wait. Suggested activities that can be used during waiting periods include singing, looking at books, reading a story, or holding something special such as a banner, sign, or toy.

Another difficult activity for many young children is remaining seated. If the child is given a small object to hold during the time she must remain seated, she may be willing to continue sitting for a longer period. The principle of pairing preferred and non-preferred activities also gives the child increasing responsibility for her own behavior, instead of relying on teacher discipline.

Just One More This particular intervention is most effective when a child behaves inappropriately in order to escape a low-preference task. The purpose of the intervention is to improve work habits and increase time on task. The first step is to identify how long a particular child will work at a specific task before exhibiting inappropriate behavior. Once the teacher has determined how long a child will work on a task, the teacher can give the child a delay cue to head off misbehavior. Examples of delay cues are "Just one more and then you're finished," "Just two minutes and then you're finished," or "Do this and then you're finished."

In this intervention, a teacher sets aside preconceived ideas about how long children *should* work on a task and instead focuses on improving the child's ability to complete tasks in reference to his current abilities. As the children's challenging behaviors decrease, the adult gradually can increase the time on task, and the amount of work completed, before giving them the delay cue and releasing them from the task.

The More We Get Together Another way to improve task completion is by making the job a collaborative effort. If a child finds it difficult to complete non-preferred activities, then the instructor can complete part of the task with the student. For example, when organizing the bookshelf, the adult completes a portion of the task, such as picking up the big books as the student picks up the little books. She prefaces that activity by stating, "I'll pick up the big books, and you pick up the little books." As the child becomes more willing to complete her part of the task, the caregiver gradually increases the work expectations for the child while decreasing the amount of assistance.

Communication Development

In addition to preventing inappropriate behavior, another tactic is replacing the problem behavior by teaching the child alternative behaviors. The key to this process is "functional equivalence." Teachers must determine the *function* or pay-off for the inappropriate behavior and then teach an alternative *equivalent* action that will service the same purpose as the negative behavior. This often is referred to as the "fair pair" rule (White & Haring, 1976). Rather than punishing the behavior, teaching children a better way to behave assists in meeting their needs.

Bids for Attention The first step in addressing attention-seeking negative behaviors is to reduce their occurrence by providing plenty of attention for the child's appropriate behaviors. The next step is to teach the child appropriate ways to gain attention from others. Most children learn appropriate social skills incidentally from their family and teachers; some children, however, have learned negative ways to gain social attention. Some of the social skills that may need to be taught include calling others by name, tapping friends on the shoulder for attention, knowing how to join others in play, and raising one's

hand to gain the teacher's attention. Numerous other social skills may require direct instruction. Any time a behavior is considered inappropriate, adults need to teach the child a better way to have his needs met.

When teaching social skills to chldren, break the skill into a maximum of three steps. Then model the steps and have the child demonstrate the skill. Provide positive and negative examples of the step and have the children label the demonstration as correct or incorrect. Use class discussion time to role-play and talk about when this particular social skill is appropriate. Throughout the day, set up situations that allow practice of the social skill and encourage the child to use the new skill. Finally, promote carry-over of the skill by communicating with the family about the social skills instruction in order for the child to practice the social skills outside of the classroom—on the playground, in the lunch room, and at home.

Ask for Something Else If we know that the child has disruptive behaviors when presented with tasks that are disliked, then the teacher can present the child with an alternative task or materials, something she likes, *before* the problem behavior occurs. Then the child can be taught to ask for the alternative activity or object. When the child requests the alternative, provide it and preempt the negative behavior. In this way, children can learn to communicate their needs and prevent the challenging behavior from occurring.

Ask for Help Many children behave disruptively because they are frustrated with a task. Teachers usually can determine when the child is becoming frustrated by observing and reading non-verbal communication signals. Possible signs of frustration might be sighing, fidgeting, reddening of the face, or negative facial expressions. Noticing these signs helps the teacher know that it is time to intervene. Rather than offering help when the child needs it, the teacher says, "It looks like you need some help. When you need help, you need to tell me. Now you say, 'I need help.'" After the child has responded by saying, "I need help," the teacher provides assistance. This strategy is much more effective if the group already has role-played "asking for help."

Ask for a Break This strategy is similar to the two listed above; in this case, educators teach the child to ask for a break during a difficult and frustrating task. Prior to presenting the task, the teacher can explain that she knows that the activity can be difficult, but that the child can have a break after spending some time working hard at it. Then, the child can be taught to request a break while other students are engaged in various tasks.

Although teachers would like to think that instruction and activities are always fun for children and that learning should be child-directed, certain important activities must be mastered if children are to become successful in school. Especially as children progress into the primary grades, teachers expect them to work independently on pencil-and-paper tasks. Teaching youngsters communication skills that will help them handle frustration and low-preference activities will improve their outcomes as learners in school and in life.

Reviewing Options

Mrs. Archie, in reviewing her options for working with Wade, is gaining confidence in her ability to work more carefully with the family and with Wade to ensure his successful re-entry to her classroom. Her resolve is to continue developing a "community of learners" (Bredekamp & Copple, 1997) by helping Wade become a functioning member of her group. She intends to teach him how to enter a play setting, negotiate for what he wants in the classroom, and learn how to make compromises, while nurturing him as she would any child. These are goals that she believes will help turn around Wade's negative behavior.

Mrs. Archie also knows that her administrator is a caring woman, and, if necessary, Wade could be placed in another classroom so that he could have a "fresh start" with his entry into school. Her hope is that this will be a last-resort strategy, because she understands how much Wade needs a caring adult who understands him and his needs. Her phone call to Wade's mother at the end of the day will be friendly and supportive, with many recommendations for how the school can assist the family.

A Long-Term Plan

Most children with chronic difficult behaviors did not learn them overnight. Many of these children experience serious on-going problems in their families. As teachers, we cannot change home dynamics or family problems. Sometimes a parent conference or parent education groups can be helpful, as the family learns to support a difficult child at home. With others, we do well to teach the child socially appropriate behavior in the classroom. As a child learns socially appropriate behavior in school, she learns that the behavior is useful in other settings. Often, the school is the only place where the child has the opportunity to learn prosocial behaviors. Children's negative behaviors may have, in a sense, "worked" for them in numerous situations for a substantial period of time. When we work to teach the child a better way to get his or her needs met, we must recognize that this process takes time and effort. When we as educators invest this time and effort with children during childhood, we are pro-

viding them with the tools that can make the difference in their school careers and in their lives.

References

Ardoin, S. P., Martens, B. K., & Wolfe, L. A. (1999). Using high-probability instruction sequences with fading to increase student compliance during transitions. *Journal of Applied Behavior Analysis, 32*(3), 339–351.

Bredekamp, S., & Copple, C. (Eds.). (1997). *Developmentally appropriate practice in early childhood programs* (Rev. ed.). Washington, DC: National Association for the Education of Young Children.

Hanley, G. P., Piazza, C. C., & Fisher, W. W. (1997). Noncontingent presentation of attention and alternative stimuli in the treatment of attention-maintained destructive behavior. *Journal of Applied Behavior Analysis, 30*(2), 229–237.

Katz, L., & McClellan, D. (1997). *Fostering children's social competence: The teacher's role.* Washington, DC: National Association for the Education of Young Children.

Knowlton, D. (1995). Managing children with oppositional defiant behavior. *Beyond Behavior, 6*(3), 5–10.

Marion, M. (2003). *Guidance of young children* (3rd ed.). Englewood Cliffs, NJ: Prentice Hall.

Morrison, G. (2001). *Early childhood education today* (8th ed.). Englewood Cliffs, NJ: Prentice Hall.

Premack, D. (1959). Toward empirical behavior laws: I. Positive reinforcement. *Psychological Review, 66,* 219–233.

Reynolds, E. (2003). *Guiding young children* (2nd ed.). Mountain View, CA: Mayfield.

Seefeldt, C., & Barbour, N. (1998). *Early childhood education: An introduction* (4th ed.). Columbus, OH: Merrill.

Walker, H. M., Horner, R. H., Sugai, G., Bullis, M., Sprague, J. R., Bricker, D., & Kaufman, M. J. (1996). Integrated approaches to preventing anti-social behavior among school-age children and youth. *Journal of Emotional and Behavioral Disorders, 4*(4), 194–209.

White, O. R., & Haring, N. G. (1976). *Exceptional teaching.* Upper Saddle River, NJ: Merrill/Prentice Hall.

Wolfgang, C. H. (2001). *Solving discipline and classroom management problems* (5th ed.). New York: John Wiley and Sons.

Laverne Warner is Professor, Early Childhood Education, and Sharon Lynch is Associate Professor of Special Education, Department of Language, Literacy, and Special Populations, Sam Houston State University, Huntsville, Texas.

From *Childhood Education*, Winter 2002/2003, pp. 97-100. © 2002 by the Association for Childhood Education International.

CHILDREN AND GRIEF: THE ROLE OF THE EARLY CHILDHOOD EDUCATOR

Andrea Ruth Hopkins

Early childhood educators cannot shield children from learning about death. Children witness death in many different forms, from a neglected houseplant to a favorite pet dying; from a cartoon show character flattened by a steamroller to TV images of exploding airliners and collapsing buildings during the September 11 terrorist attacks. As educators we have no choice about whether or not children receive death education; our only choice is how developmentally appropriate that education will be (Fox 2000).

Perceptions of death and developmental stages

A grieving child's perception of death relates directly to the child's level of cognition. Perceptions of death change as children progress through developmental stages. A clear understanding of these perceptions is essential for educators wishing to respond appropriately and helpfully to a grieving child's unique needs.

Infants and toddlers

Piaget theorized that children birth through age two are in the *sensorimotor stage* of development (Berk & Winsler 1995). During this period they develop a complex behavioral system, with strong attachments to parents and other intimate, dependable caregivers in their lives. Mutual attachment behavior protects the young and vulnerable child from danger. Instinctive behaviors such as smiling, babbling, and crying engage the caregiver in interactions, ensuring that the baby's emotional, physical, and social needs are met (Black 1998). Separation from the primary caregiver is likely to be met with vigorous protestations. The outcomes from a tragic loss are far-reaching, according to researcher Bette Glickfield. In her 1993 study she found the presence of a consistent and emotionally nurturing caregiver during the formative years to be the only reliable predictor of later attachment style in bereaved children (Glickfield 1993).

Preschoolers' Grasp of the Concept of Death

Four subconcepts of death—finality, inevitability, cessation, and causality—are related to the thinking of a child in the preoperational stage. *Finality* refers to the understanding that once a living thing dies, it will never be alive again. Preschool children are unable to comprehend death's permanence. A child may want to write or call the person who died in an effort to continue a physical relationship (Trozzi 1999). For example, after a tragic apartment fire left a young child dead, his classmates discussed the event. One child wasn't sure just who had died. "Carlos comes to breakfast," one of the other children assured him. "I'll show you who he is when he comes to breakfast tomorrow."

The concept of *inevitability* is knowledge that death will occur sometime to every living thing. Preschoolers usually deny the possibility of a personal death. They may see death as something avoidable or an event that happens only to others.

Cessation connotes the realization that there are neither biological nor psychological signs of life present in someone who is dead. The preoperational thinker believes death is a state of reduced functionality, that there are distinctions or degrees of death (Nagy 1948). The cessation of visible aspects of functioning, such as sight, hearing, and motion, is more easily grasped by two- to five-year-old children than is cessation of cognitive functions of feeling, thought, and consciousness.

Causality requires understanding that there are physical or biological reasons death occurs. The abstract thinking necessary to comprehend this makes it the most difficult concept for preschoolers to understand. They may cite external causes for the death rather than biological factors. Children's "magical thinking" may lead them to see unrelated events as a cause or explanation. False assumptions about the cause may include a feeling of responsibility or blame. A child who shouts, "I wish you were dead! I hate you!" to a sibling, friend, or parent will almost certainly feel completely responsible for any accident or tragedy that might befall that person.

Timmy, Who Loved Dinosaurs

Maria Trozzi, director of the Good Grief Program at Boston Medical Center, relates how one teacher dealt with children's need to understand death's permanence (1999). The teacher consulted Trozzi after a child in her first-grade class died from a brain tumor. She had told the children that Timmy died from an illness in his head that had stopped his brain and the rest of his body from working. However, each morning when attendance was taken, the children would say, "You forgot Timmy." Trozzi advised the teacher to ask, "Is Timmy here?" Despite their expectation that he might return, the children replied, "No, Timmy died."

The teacher had considered removing Timmy's desk, because it was a painful reminder to her. Trozzi advised her to leave the desk in place for a while so the class could use it to commemorate Timmy. The teacher asked the class what to do with Timmy's desk.

The children knew Timmy had loved dinosaurs, so they raised money to purchase books about dinosaurs. Inscribed in the front of each book was the message, *To our friend Timmy, who loved dinosaurs.* They placed his desk in a back corner of the classroom, decorated it with dinosaur stickers, and left the books on the desktop. Pillows and a rug finished off Timmy's Corner, a favorite spot for free reading time.

The children in this classroom sent a clear message: Timmy and his time in the classroom were important.

Talking to Families

Traumatic loss can overwhelm the adults in a family to the point where they may deny, ignore, or overlook their children's feelings (Naierman 1998). Teachers need to take time to talk to parents or other adult family members about problems or changes seen in a grieving child. They can remind them that even small deviations in a routine can be terrifying for children who have experienced loss, and that separation anxiety is a typical reaction for a child experiencing an unfamiliar situation (Farish 1995). Teachers can suggest that parents allow the grieving child to bring an item from home for comfort, or encourage parents to stay longer when bringing in or dropping off the child.

A baby or toddler who loses a parent or other attachment figure needs a stable environment, predictable schedules, and lots of comforting, touching, hugging, and holding by someone who loves her.

For babies younger than six months, the concept of death can be summed up in the phrases "all gone" and "out of sight, out of mind." From six months on a baby is somewhat aware of the absence of an attachment figure and may express limited grief (Papenbrock & Voss 1988) or react to the loss of attention, altered routines, and changes in the environment. Babies and toddlers are sensitive to the stress and emotions of those around them. They may experience temporary delays in motor development as their energy is invested in the process of grieving rather than in new physical or emotional growth (Grief Resource Foundation 1990).

A baby or toddler in the sensorimotor stage who loses a parent or other attachment figure needs a stable environment, predictable schedules, and lots of comforting, touching, hugging, and holding by someone who loves her (Papenbrock & Voss 1988) to help restore some of the security threatened by the loss. When the child is older, the primary caregiver can guide him through an understanding of the earlier loss (Furman 1990).

Older toddlers and preschoolers

Piaget's next cognitive stage, *preoperational,* encompasses children ages two to five. The preoperational child's thinking is characterized as magical, egocentric, and causal (Goldman 1998). Preschoolers believe strongly in the power of their wishes, which often leads them to conclude that death is temporary, reversible, or partial. (See "Preschoolers' Grasp of the Concept of Death.") In Maria Nagy's (1948) landmark study of children's conceptions of death, children ages three to five denied death as a natural and final process. They saw death as a departure—a further existence in changed circumstances for the person who died.

Preschoolers tend to respond to death with periods of anger, sadness, anxiety, and angry outbursts. They are also likely to show regressive behaviors and physical disturbances, as mentioned with toddlers (Farish 1995). Appropriate adult responses to a preschooler coping with death include clear communication about the death, reassurance that the child's needs will be met, acceptance of the child's reactions to the death, and plenty of hugging and loving reassurance.

Kindergartners and young schoolagers

Young school-age children from five through nine have reached the *concrete operational stage* of development. They are curious and realistic, and most have mastered some universal concepts, including irreversibility. While they are capable of expressing logical fears and thoughts about death, their understanding of finality can bring on deep emotional reactions (Goldman 1996). They may alternately deny feelings and experience deep anxiety. Fears of further abandonment and intense feelings of loss complicate the grieving process (Christian 1997).

Observable symptoms of and behaviors due to the stress of bereavement vary. Aggressive behaviors and temper tantrums are common in children who feel out of control. Sleep disorders may indicate fear or anxiety. Regression, also common, is an attempt by the grieving child to return to a more secure time in his or her life (Alderman 1989).

A Letter to Parents

Dear Families:

I am writing with sadness to tell you that Rosey, our class rabbit, died yesterday. He died at the Animal Medical Center in the examining room. I was able to be with him, as was the veterinarian from the emergency room. Here are some things we will tell the children.

Rosey died from rabbit pneumonia, which is an infection in the lungs. People cannot get this disease from animals. The veterinarian said it is almost impossible to notice any symptoms of this illness in time to treat it. Rosey suffered no pain or discomfort. When an animal dies at the animal hospital, the doctors and their helpers bury the body. It is sad when pets die—teachers and children feel sad and miss them. Rosey's death may remind them of deaths of loved ones or of pets.

We will tell the children [about Rosey's death] after assembly tomorrow and invite them to participate in a discussion. They will also be invited to help create a Rosey memory book in which they can contribute feelings about the loss of Rosey or happy memories they have of him.

During the upcoming days, some children may speak often of Rosey, while others will be more reticent. Please share your child's response with us. We, of course, will share any school discussions with you, as well as our Rosey memory book.

Warmly,

The Teachers

Source: Reprinted, by permission of the publisher, from E. Winter, "School Bereavement," *Educational Leadership,* vol. 57, no. 6 (2000).

Children need adult permission to act out, talk about, and interpret their thoughts and feelings about death, a topic adults tend to avoid with young children.

A delayed reaction months after the death is as legitimate as one occurring immediately after the loss (Farish 1995). Reprocessing takes place throughout the bereaved child's development. Years after the death the child will revisit the loss, trying to understand it from the vantage point of his or her current developmental perspective (Perry 1996).

Teachers' role

Three basic responsibilities regarding death education rest with the early childhood educator: to help children feel safe while acknowledging the reality of death, to promote an accepting classroom atmosphere where children's feelings are supported, and to provide developmentally appropriate learning opportunities that allow children to discuss death. Each of these functions plays an important role in developing young children's attitudes and understandings about death.

Helping children feel safe

Helping children feel safe while acknowledging the reality of death requires acceptance of children's views of death as one aspect of their normal curiosity about the everyday world. Teachers need to provide clear, simple facts that a child can comprehend, while avoiding confusing, abstract euphemisms, like equating death with sleep.

In one nursery school, teachers trying to deal effectively with the topic of death drew up some guidelines (Galen 1972). The primary guideline concerns the importance of teachers using the proper perspective. This means accepting preschoolers' views about death as part of their growing curiosity about and understanding of everyday phenomena. Children need adult permission to act out, talk about, and interpret their thoughts and feelings about death, a topic adults tend to avoid with young children.

Early childhood educators can ask themselves two questions before they react with ingrained discomfort to any child's question or comment regarding death:

- How would I treat this action/comment/question if it were not about death?
- What is the child really seeking by his or her action/comment/question? (Galen 1972)

If adults find children's repeated questions about death disconcerting, they should keep in mind that it is very common and completely normal for children to ask the same questions over and over again. This doesn't mean that the answers they give are inadequate, but rather that the children are seeking reassurance and trying to make the information fit their understandings (Cohn 1987). Children gain a sense of control by discussing their fears (Sandstrom 1999).

Creating a supportive classroom

The second function of the early childhood educator in death education is to promote a classroom atmosphere wherein the children's feelings are accepted and supported. The teacher should emphasize to the children through words and actions that there is nothing too sad or too terrible to talk about with a caring adult. Sensitive acknowledgment and support greatly assist children in sorting out their many difficult emotions (Cohn 1987). Teachers must never minimize children's feelings by distracting them or encouraging them to cheer up. The normal process of grieving is necessary if the child is to move on toward understanding a loss and resolving pain.

Educators must acknowledge grief with compassion and support. Providing extra comfort, reassurance, and security in the form of extra hugs, hand holding, and empathic

Teaching about Death through the Life Cycle of Plants

Grief educator Erna Furman strongly advocates providing emotionally neutral opportunities to learn about life and death in the preschool curriculum: "A basic concept of death is best grasped, not when a loved one dies, but in situations of minimal emotional significance, such as with dead insects or worms" (1990, 16). More involved than merely planting seeds in paper cups and watching them grow, her educational goal in using the life cycle of plants is to help young children begin to understand life, growth, death, and generational sequence.

Parent involvement is an integral component of Furman's life cycle curriculum. Parent participation stimulates children's interest and helps them understand—often for the first time—the growth cycle of flowers or vegetables. Parents can support and extend their children's learning at home. When enthusiasm for the life cycle is sparked, entire families may find enjoyment through shared gardening activities, outings to farms, shopping at farmers' markets, or visiting apple orchards.

The key element to the success of the life cycle curriculum, believes Furman, lies in the enthusiasm of the teacher. The teacher must wholeheartedly enjoy and respect the way nature works as well as the way children learn. Furman surmises that one reason her curriculum has been so well received may be that it provides an all-too-rare opportunity to really understand a common experience. It becomes a base of information from which further learning is motivated and, as she states, "engenders hope and trust that more things will, with effort, make sense and bring a feeling of mastery" (Furman 1990, 20).

For example, a teacher might provide props and materials children can use to establish a veterinarian's office. A doctors' kit, stuffed animals, blankets, scales, and pictures of animals create a setting in which children can interact and discuss illness and death in a safe manner. Grieving children can use these props to engage in play that helps them deal with some emotion-laden issues. Teachers observing the play can gain a better perspective of children's progress through their grief "journey" (Greenberg 1996). Clear communication with parents supporting a grieving child's need for these expressions is essential (see "Talking to Families").

Offering developmentally appropriate death education

The third function of the educator's role is to provide developmentally appropriate learning opportunities that discuss death (Crase & Crase 1995). There is great value in teaching young children about death before it enters their lives in an intimate way. Children exposed gradually to small doses of frightening or sad experiences may be able to work through them successfully (Ketchel 1986). Extending this understanding helps prepare children for other more personal losses.

Classroom activities and experiences that can help children understand death in developmentally appropriate ways include something as simple as having live plants in the classroom. Children can help care for the plants, experiencing firsthand that all living things share a need for food, water, and light. (See "Teaching about Death through the Life Cycle of Plants.")

The teacher should emphasize to the children through words and actions that there is nothing too sad or too terrible to talk about with a caring adult.

Live pets reinforce these concepts also. When a classroom pet dies, teachers sometimes respond by shielding children from the death. Rather, this should be used as an opportunity to answer children's questions and reinforce their understanding of the life cycle.

One first-grade classroom learned this lesson during a unit on hatching butterflies. (Hofschield 1991). The first of four butterflies to hatch was born with curled, malformed wings. The first-graders had many concerns and questions about the butterfly. The teacher channeled the children's interest into a focus on disability awareness. The students became very protective of the butterfly, which they named Popcorn. They checked on Popcorn often, verbally encouraging him and feeding him with an eyedropper.

Later that week the children noticed that Popcorn was not moving. The teacher gently lifted him onto a tissue and sat down with the children. She explained that the butterfly had died. Together they talked about the learning and

verbalizations is crucial. These efforts let a child know she is safe and that someone is there to care for her. The classroom structure and limits can bring a welcome feeling of normalcy to a grieving child. Emphasizing familiar routines, playing soothing music, using a calm voice—these strategies offer comfort as well as model coping skills a bereaved child can use (NAEYC 2001). They also show the other children appropriate ways to interact with their bereaved classmate.

Teachers can anticipate children's anger and plan activities that help them express and release anger in healthy ways. Many elements of early childhood classrooms can serve as tension releasers for children dealing with overwhelming emotions. Children can channel physical energy into sensory experiences such as sand and water play or manipulating clay and playdough. Opportunities and materials for emotional expression abound in the dramatic play center, block area, and puppet theater.

Play is an effective means for a child to work through grief. More than a game, acting out death, dying, funerals, and associated feelings can greatly assist children in reducing anxieties. Death play, while not necessarily initiated by the teacher, should be supported rather than discouraged if it occurs spontaneously.

growing they had all experienced because of Popcorn. Some children cried. Later that day, the children buried Popcorn in the school yard, each taking an opportunity to say something about the butterfly.

Reflecting later on the experience, the teacher realized that not only had the children learned scientific knowledge from the butterfly unit, but they also had matured through the group discussions and subsequent individual journal entries in which they wrote about their feelings. In the following weeks the teacher saw the children become more thoughtful toward and accepting of those around them (Hofschield 1991). Perhaps the loss created a shared bond among the children, as well as teaching empathy and tolerance for others.

There is great value in teaching young children about death before it enters their lives in an intimate way.

When the class rabbit died unexpectedly at one school, the teachers saw the opportunity to model mourning and assist children in processing an emotional loss (Winter 2000). The teachers sent a letter home (see "A Letter to Parents") to families in an effort to keep school and home discussions consistent.

Allowing children to watch the decay of something organic, such as a carved pumpkin or a piece of fruit, is another way to help them gain a better understanding of what happens to living organisms after death (Miller 1996). The item, enclosed in a heavy zipper bag or other transparent container, can be examined every few days by the class, and the changes noted. It is important for teachers to emphasize the process of nature, rather than revulsion, when discussing the changes (Miller 1996).

Conclusion

While early childhood educators may wish to protect children from negative or painful experiences, they are also aware that one of their primary tasks is to help children deal with strong emotions in healthy ways. Perhaps at no other time is this responsibility as difficult as when a young child experiences loss through death. An early childhood educator who creates a safe atmosphere for children's concerns, outlets for children's strong emotions, and appropriate life cycle experiences in the classroom can foster resiliency and coping skills that will assist children during an initial loss and help strengthen them for a lifetime.

Resources for helping children understand life and death

Fiction for children ages 3 and up

Anderson, J. 1994. *The key into winter.* New York: Albert Whitman. An allegorical story mixing fantasy and reality. The march of the seasons is the metaphor for the passages of life. Ages 4–8.

Brown, M. 1995. *The dead bird.* New York: Harper Trophy. A gentle story of a group of children who discover a dead bird and bury it with a simple ceremony. Ages 4–8.

Buscaglia, L. 1983, *The fall of Freddy the Leaf.* New York: Holt, Rinehart, & Winston. Freddy and the other leaves pass through the seasons. This parable helps explain the delicate balance between life and death. Ages 4–10.

Clifton, L. 1983. *Everett Anderson's goodbye.* New York: Henry Holt. Everett has a difficult time dealing with his father's death. Ages 3–8.

DePaola, T. 1973. *Nana Upstairs and Nana Downstairs.* New York: G. P. Putnam's Sons. Little Tomie loves his grandmother and shares many special times with her. Her death leaves him sad and in need of his family's understanding. Ages 3–8.

D'Esopo, K. 1995. Barklay and Eve Series. Westfield, CT: Pratt Resource Center. This series of three books helps children through times of family loss. It aids in cultural awareness in times of grief. The titles include *Together We'll Make It through This, Sitting Shiva,* and *Precious Gifts: Barklay and Eve Explain Organ and Tissue Donation.* Ages 3–8.

Good Cave, A. 1998. *Balloons for Trevor: Understanding death* (Comforting Little Hearts series). St. Louis, MO: Concordia. Interactive pages help parents and children work through issues together. Ages 4–8

Gregory, V. 1992. *Through the Mickle Woods.* Boston: Little, Brown. After his wife's death, a grieving king journeys to an old bear's cave in the middle of the Mickle Woods, where he hears three stories that help him go on living. All ages.

Joslin, M. 1999. *The goodbye boat.* Grand Rapids, MI: Eerdmans. This simple, beautiful story is told with only a handful of words. It represents visually the stages of grief. Baby–Pre-K.

Kirkpatrick, J. 1999. *Barn Kitty.* Santa Fe, NM: Arzo. *Barn Kitty* provides a gentle approach to the subject of death—touching and sure to generate discussion among young children. Ages 4–7.

O'Toole, D. 1998. *Aarvy Aardvark finds hope.* Burnsville, NJ: Mt. Rainbow. This story about animals presents grief, sadness, and eventual resolution after death. Ages 5–8.

Varley, S. 1984. *Badger's parting gifts.* New York: Morrow. After his death, Badger's friends recall their memories of him. All ages.

Nonfiction for children ages 5 to 12

Blackburn, L. 1991. *I know I made it happen: A book about children and guilt.* Omaha, NE: Centering. Sometimes children's magical thinking and guilt make them think they have caused the death of a loved one.

Carney, K. 1995. *Barklay and Eve series.* Westfield, CT: Pratt Resource Center. This series of three books was designed to help children through times of family loss and is written from the perspective of the Jewish religion.

Heegaard, M. 1992. *When someone very special dies.* Minneapolis, MN: Woodland. Young children can use this workbook to help them express their grief.

Mellonie, B., & R. Ingpen. 1987. *Lifetimes: The beautiful way to explain death to children.* New York: Bantam. Life cycles of plants, animals, and people are discussed. The book explains why some lifetimes are shorter.

Mundy, M. 1998. *Sad isn't bad: A good grief guidebook for kids dealing with loss*. St. Meinrad, IN: Abbey. This book affirms that even after loss, the world is still safe and grief eventually lessens.

Nystrom, C. 1992. *What happens when we die?* Chicago, IL: Moody. From a Christian perspective this book answers children's questions about death.

Palmer, P. 1994. *I wish I could hold your hand*. Manassas Park, VA: Impact. This gentle book helps children identify their feelings about loss and assures and comforts them.

Rogers, F. 1982. *When a pet dies*. New York: G. P. Putnam's Sons. This "first experiences" book addresses and affirms questions and feelings children have after the death of a pet. It discusses the importance of memories.

References

Alderman, L. 1989. *Why did daddy die? Helping children cope with the loss of a parent*. New York: Pocket Books.

Berk, L., & A. Winsler. 1995. *Scaffolding children's learning: Vygotsky and early childhood education*. Washington, DC: NAEYC.

Black, D. 1998. Bereavement in childhood. *British Medical Journal* 316 (7135): 93–133.

Christian, L. 1997. Children and death. *Young Children* 52 (4): 7680.

Cohn, J. 1987. The grieving student. *Instructor* (January): 76–78.

Crase, D. R., & D. Crase. 1995. Responding to a bereaved child in the school setting. ERIC ED 394 655.

Farish, J. 1995. *When disaster strikes: Helping young children cope*. Washington, DC: NAEYC.

Fox, S. S. 2000. *Good grief: Helping groups of children when a friend dies*. Boston, MA: New England Association for the Education of Young Children.

Furman, E. 1990. Plant a potato—Learn about life and death. *Young Children* 46 (1): 1520.

Galen, H. 1972. A matter of life and death. *Young Children* 27 (6): 351–56.

Glickfield, B. D. 1993. *Adult attachment and utilization of social provisions as a function of perceived mourning behavior and perceived parental bonding after early parental loss*. Detroit, MI: University of Detroit Mercy.

Goldman, L. 1996. *Breaking the silence: A guide to help children with complicated grief*. Bristol, PA: Taylor & Francis.

Goldman, L. 1998. Helping the grieving child in school. *Healing* 3 (1). Available online: www.kidspeace.org/healingmagazine/issue5/therapist.asp [access date: 7 November 2001].

Greenberg, J. 1996. Seeing children through tragedy: My mother died today—When is she coming back? *Young Children* 51 (6): 76–78.

Grief Resource Foundation. 1990. *Helping young children cope with loss*. Dallas: Author.

Hofschield, K. 1991. The gift of a butterfly. *Young Children* 46 (3): 36.

Ketchel, J. 1986. Helping the young child cope with death. *Day Care and Early Education* (Winter): 24–27.

Miller, K. 1996. *Crisis manual for early childhood teachers*. Beltsville, MD: Gryphon House.

NAEYC. 2001. Helping young children in frightening times. *Young Children* 56 (6): 6–7.

Nagy, M. 1948. The child's theories concerning death. *The Journal of Genetic Psychology* 73: 327.

Naierman, N. 1998. Grieving kids need guidance. *Early Childhood News* (March/April): 50–53.

Papenbrock, P., & R. Voss. 1988. *Children's grief: How to help the child whose parent has died*. Redmond, WA: Media.

Perry, B. 1996. Children and loss. Available online: http://teacher.scholastic.com/professional/bruceperry/childrenloss.htm [access date: 7 November 2001].

Sandstrom, S. 1999. Dear Simba is dead forever. *Young Children* 54 (6): 14–15.

Trozzi, M. 1999. *Talking with children about loss*. New York: Penguin.

Winter, E. 2000. School bereavement. *Educational Leadership* 57 (6).

Andrea Ruth Hopkins, M.Ed., is an early childhood educator with the St. Paul public schools. She teaches both in early childhood family education and in school readiness programs. Andrea is also a volunteer facilitator for the Minnesota Valley Children and Grief Youth Coalition.

From *Young Children,* January 2002, pp. 40-47. © 2002 by the National Association for the Education of Young Children. Reprinted by permission.

UNIT 5
Curricular Issues

Unit Selections

Key Points to Consider

- Describe the critical role teachers play in developing appropriate curricula for young children.

- What are some of the important components of education in Reggio Emilia classrooms?

- How can teachers provide an environment that is appropriate for all kindergarten age children to learn?

- What information should teachers be sending to parents about their children's early literacy experiences?

- What are some of the key essentials of early literacy instruction?

- How can physical activity be enhanced during the early childhood years?

 **Links: www.dushkin.com/online/**
These sites are annotated in the World Wide Web pages.

Association for Childhood Education International (ACEI)
http://www.udel.edu/bateman/acei/

Early Childhood Education Online
http://www.ume.maine.edu/ECEOL-L/

International Reading Association
http://www.reading.org

Teacher Quick Source
http://www.teacherquicksource.com

Teachers Helping Teachers
http://www.pacificnet.net/~mandel/

Awesome Library for Teachers
http://www.neat-schoolhouse.org/teacher.html

Future of Children
http://www.futureofchildren.org

National Institute on the Education of At-Risk Students
http://www.cfda.gov/public/viewprog.asp?progid=1062

In developing curriculum for young children, teachers and administrators are interested in various strategies and techniques that can further positive educational experiences. The lead article, "Understanding Curriculum: An Umbrella View", helps teachers evaluate the steps they take in planning challenging yet appropriate curriculum for preschool age children. Preschool teachers generally are not tied to state or district mandated curricula. Therefore, they have tremendous freedom as well as tremendous responsibility to plan learning experiences that will allow children to develop a lifelong love of learning along with the necessary skills they will need to be successful.

Programs that follow the philosophy of the Reggio Emilia schools of north central Italy are gaining more and more attention in their second decade of popularity with American Educators. In "Reggio Emilia: New Ways to think About Schooling," Rebecca New presents an excellent overview of Reggio classrooms for those not familiar with the approach. The total focus on the interests of the children help to guide Reggio teachers to provide an environment where investigation and exploration are central to the curriculum. The analogy of children in a Reggio Emilia preschool enjoying a leisurely learning journey vs. children in a typical U.S. preschool program participating in a race to see who can get to the end first works well when thinking about the two approaches.

Again this year the ongoing focus on kindergarten readiness is evident in "Emergent Curriculum and Kindergarten Readiness". Schools that offer a pre-kindergarten or developmental kindergarten class are missing the whole point of the kindergarten. Teachers in preschool and kindergarten, more than at any other level, are responsible for differentiating the curriculum and planning activities to meet the needs of all children. When the kindergarten is a place where all children who are age eligible to attend are welcomed into a classroom well equipped to meet their needs and interest we will have made great strides. Until then, we keep moving ahead at a slow pace.

In the article, "Learning Centers: Why and How," the reader who is unsure about how to develop appropriate learning centers in his or her classroom is encouraged to give it a try. The children, when given the opportunity, will provide additional suggestions of activities and will continue to contribute to the learning. Teachers can begin developing effective learning centers by collecting a variety of materials that will encourage the children to explore and manipulate as they develop skills for enhancing thinking, socializing, and creativity.

The poor physical condition of young people in America today is cause for great concern. Teachers of young children play a vital role in encouraging a lifelong enjoyment of physical activity. The authors of "Improving Public Health Through Early Childhood Movement Programs" provide suggestions for developing a preschool movement program. Ideas for specific activities are included.

One of the responsibilities of teachers that is often neglected is documenting and communicating the learning going on in the classroom. Teachers get so involved in the day-to-day teaching that they often forget to keep track of what the children are doing and to provide ways for families and administrators to become familiar with the learning opportunities in the classroom.

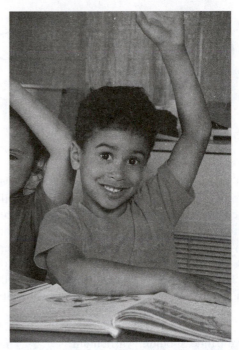

Young children are eager to delve into curriculum that is compelling. Activities that will allow them to investigate, dig deep, and roll up their sleeves and get involved are the types of learning experiences that send the message "learning is fun, and I can be successful." What is often presented is watered down, teacher directed, and lacking in true discovery. When we rob children of contributing to the learning process by providing all of the neatly cut papers for them to glue or worksheets for them to complete, we take away their desire to explore and investigate. When their learning is served to them on a platter, they never learn that they can gather information by themselves. Become a facilitator for learning instead of a dispenser of information.

Included are four articles addressing early literacy, the current hot topic in early childhood education. President George W. Bush has brought the battle over the best way for young children to learn how to read to the attention of parents and educators across the country with his request for $45 million for preschool reading research. What teachers do know about early literacy is the importance of a partnership between the home and school in introducing printed communication to young children. In addition to the article "The Essentials of Early Literacy Instruction" and "The Right Way to Read" are "Fostering Language and Literacy in Classrooms and Homes" and "Helping Preschool Children Become Readers: Tips for Parents." All four articles focus on the importance of families in the process.

A number of the articles in unit 5 provide opportunities for the reader to reflect on the authentic learning experiences available for children. How can they investigate, explore, and create while studying a particular area of interest? Make children work for their learning. This unit is full of articles addressing different curriculum areas. Active child involvement leads to enhanced learning. Suggestions for project-based activities in mathematics, science, and technology are also included. Again, the theme runs deep. Hands-on = Minds on!

Understanding Curriculum: An Umbrella View

By Judith Colbert, Ph.D.

What is curriculum? Chances are, the first response that comes to mind is that curriculum is a written document outlining topics to be covered or activities that will take place at a given time. Its format may range from a short-term plan, to a large book or e-document that sets out a step-by-step learning process that may take months to complete. But is there more to curriculum? If learning occurs all of the time, shouldn't curriculum have a wider meaning, something closer to "everything that happens"? Within that definition, wouldn't curriculum include both what is planned and what is unplanned?

A Double Perspective

Truth is, it is important to think of curriculum in both ways. Try to imagine curriculum as something that grows along a line that starts with a narrow, very specific view and extends to a wider, all-encompassing view. Another way of looking at curriculum is to picture it as a giant umbrella. This umbrella shelters a rich mixture of experiences that include not only the planned and unplanned events that occur in the child care setting, but also what occurs in the world beyond that may have an impact on what children learn. It is important to think of curriculum from this double perspective for two reasons.

1. **Having a specific plan matters.** The authors of *Eager to Learn* (2000), a report of the National Academy of Sciences, say that, although they cannot identify a "single curriculum or pedagogical approach," children who attend "well-planned, high quality early childhood programs in which curriculum aims are specified and integrated across domains" are "better prepared" for formal schooling (Bowman, Donovan, & Burns, 2000, p.6). In short, teachers in all settings need to have a plan for daily activities that meets specific goals.

2. **The big umbrella view also matters.** Everything that happens to each of us, teaches us something. What happens in the wider world influences what happens in the classroom. The character of curriculum is achieved from being embedded in "contexts of the larger society" that "interact with teachers, learners, other curriculum developers, and the culture of classroom life all at once—each interacting with and influencing the others" (Schubert, 1986, p. 9).

What Are the Responsibilities of Teachers?

Unlike children, adults have the ability to analyze their experiences, learn from what seems valuable, and reject what is inappropriate or appears to be of no benefit. Adults interacting with children have to recognize that children watch and learn from the adults in their midst, and are vulnerable to the effects of what is happening around them at all times, not just in formal teaching moments. If teachers do not wash their hands, the observant child is likely to ask, "Why should I?" As a result, teachers have additional responsibilities to 1) Model appropriate behavior; 2) Respond to unexpected events and integrate them into existing activity plans; 3) Filter external events; and 4) Provide a context for learning.

A Traditional Role

In carrying out these responsibilities, teachers fill a traditional role described by Joseph Schwab, an important researcher in the education field. Schwab (1973) described curriculum in relation to interactions among four elements: learner, teacher, subject matter, and environment, or milieu, as he called it. He saw curriculum as the product of a dynamic process, captured by a fifth element, a curriculum-developer who is sensitive to the nature of the individuals involved, the topics being considered, and the setting where learning is to occur.

All of this may sound familiar to teachers in early childhood settings who in most cases also fill a role, both formally and informally, that could best be described as a "curriculum developer." You focus on the learner when you try to "match" what happens to the "varying needs of the children" (Crosser, 1996) and to achieve what NAEYC calls "developmentally appropriate practice" (Bredekamp & Copple, 1997). You make decisions about how you interact with the children. For example, you decide whether you will be directive and instruct the children or whether you will permit what happens to emerge by standing aside and allowing the children to make choices. In either case, your decision is likely based on both what is appropriate to the child and situation, and your own preferred style. In addition, you search out and respond to subject matter and, finally, consider details of the setting as a member of a profession that has long understood that the arrangement and content of the environment influences what is learned (Colbert, 1997a).

Questions to Answer

In describing the process of curriculum development, Schwab was building on the work of an even earlier pioneer, Ralph Tyler. In 1980, Tyler's *Basic Principles of Curriculum and Instruction* (1949) was rated, with John Dewey's *Democracy and Education,* one of the two most influential books on curriculum thought and practice (Harold Shane, cited by Schubert, 1986, p. 171). In this influential work, Tyler proposed that curriculum-developers answer four basic questions related to:

- **Purpose** - What educational purposes should the school/child care program seek to attain?
- **Learning Experiences** - How can learning experiences be selected which are likely to be useful in attaining your learning objectives?
- **Organization** - How can learning experiences be organized for effective instruction?
- **Evaluation** - How can the effectiveness of learning experiences be evaluated? (See Schubert, p.171).

More than 50 years after they were formulated, Tyler's (1949) questions continue to be of value. They provide a framework for developing planned curriculum and helping teachers integrate unplanned events occurring both inside and outside the child care setting. As these questions are considered in more detail below, it is important to remember that each is related to the one that precedes it. In sequence, they create a cycle that moves from purpose to evaluation and generates yet another cycle, as the results of evaluation lead to the establishment of yet another purpose.

Purpose

The very first question teachers should ask is, "What is the purpose of what we are doing?" The purpose of any learning activity should be described clearly so that it is objective, measurable, and specific. For example, if you say that your purpose is to help children understand "bad weather," you are likely to have difficulty evaluating the results of your efforts. "Bad" is a subjective word. A rainstorm that spoils a picnic is "bad weather" but one that ends a drought is "good." "Weather" is also a very general word. It applies to a whole range of conditions. If you are not sure what "bad weather is" it is very difficult to evaluate whether your curriculum successfully helped children to understand the concept. On the other hand, if you say that your purpose is to help children understand a specific aspect of weather, such as rain, wind, or snow, you can find out from their drawings and discussions if they understand those specific conditions. It is also important to be clear at the very beginning about the purpose of what is happening in relation to both the "big picture" and the specific children who will experience the curriculum.

Linking Your Purpose to the Big Picture

Purposes that focus on the big picture illustrate how what happens relates to program philosophy. For example, consider how a sudden rainstorm might affect a planned program of activities in three early childhood settings, with different program philosophies, whose characteristics are revealed in distinctive responses to the question, "What is the purpose of what you are doing?" In each case, the teacher has an opportunity to integrate this unplanned event into existing curriculum plans:

- **Teacher #1:** We are providing a safe place for children. It is likely that this program is providing basic custodial care with minimum focus on curriculum. The teacher monitors the class to ensure that the children are safe, but pays little or no attention to what the children might learn. For example, if a rainstorm arises, they will bring the children indoors where they are warm and dry, but will make little attempt to discuss what is happening outside.
- **Teacher #2:** We are providing a safe place where children can develop emotionally, socially, cogni-

tively, and physically. The children in this program are likely to be exposed to a wide variety of experiences. In programs that focus on child development and where teachers are responsive to change, a rainstorm might lead to rapid revision of the planned curriculum. The teacher is likely to encourage spontaneous discussion topics such as what is rain, where does lightening come from, or what it means to be afraid of loud noises.
- **Teacher #3:** We are providing a safe place where children can develop emotionally, socially, cognitively, physically and gain respect for the world around them. In addition to focusing on child development, this program includes concern for the environment. In such a program, the teacher might respond as described in the second example, however, the discussion might also focus on the importance of rain as a source of water for all living things and a necessary ingredient in the production of food.

In every case, broad, "big picture" curriculum decisions are linked to ideas about the program's purpose or goals that are embedded in program philosophy. A clear understanding of the link between program philosophy and what happens in the child care setting helps determine answers to curriculum questions for the children in your care.

Learning Experiences

Answers to questions about your purpose provide a context for curriculum development, but do not give you enough information for creating learning experiences for specific children. For that information, it is helpful to consider what Schwab's four curriculum elements—the learner, the teacher, the subject matter and the environment—contribute to individual learning experiences.

The Learner

Decisions about what to put in a curriculum plan, or how to integrate spontaneous events into an existing plan must be made with knowledge of the specific children involved. That knowledge comes from at least two sources: what

Curriculum Development in Action

Purpose: To reduce conflict in the child care setting and help a specific child, Zack, participate more effectively in group activities.

Situation: Ellen has been a preschool teacher for several years. She knows that the character of the room changes from time to time and that the behavior of one child can make a difference. Recently she has noticed an increase in the amount of conflict among the children. Every time there is an outbreak, it seems that Zack is somehow involved.

Analysis of Behavior: Zack plays well when he is alone or in a small group and seems to prefer being in a quiet corner with a few playthings. However, he is always at the center of a dispute when he is with a large group of children. On the one hand, she thinks that Zack has difficulty socializing with others, but he functions well in small groups so simply relating to others may not be his problem. Given that the group size seems to be related to the problem, she is wondering about the level of stimulation. After all, he is usually fine when he has just a few playthings in a quiet corner.

Solution: Ellen decides to tailor the curriculum for Zack by including activities that would permit her to relate differently to him, depending on the situation. When he is alone or in small groups, she gives him freedom to choose his activities, but when he is involved in more complex situations, she takes a more directive approach and intervenes before trouble develops. Over time, she structures learning experiences that foster success in increasingly complex situations. She tries to ensure that he does not have to confront an overwhelming number of toys, and gradually increases the number over time. She creates a classroom environment with clear pathways and quiet areas where only a few children can gather, and provides ample "cool down" time by alternating periods of high activity throughout the day. As time passes, she records her observations of Zack's behavior and discusses her findings with his parents to determine whether her interventions are resulting in less conflict in the classroom and helping Zack to participate more effectively in group activities.

---

the teacher has learned about child development, and what the teacher has observed about the behavior of the specific children for whom the curriculum is being designed.

From the outset, curriculum developers consider the age and abilities of individual learners. Training and experience will give them a general idea of what is appropriate for children of a specific age. Only careful observation of individual children, however, will tell them what is important for a specific child to learn, and what is the best approach for helping that child to grow and develop. Teachers, therefore, need to make notes describing behaviors that are either positive or negative and take time later to reflect on how what they have observed might influence the activities they plan.

The Teacher

When planning curriculum, it is also important to think about the role the teacher will play in fulfilling its purpose. On the one hand, the teacher may be directive and require the children to be passive recipients of specific facts and skills. On the other, the teacher may be reactive, remaining in the background while the children largely determine what happens. In such cases, what results is often called an "emergent curriculum."

Allowing children to appear to take the lead in curriculum development does not mean teachers are idle. Teachers are busy observing, organizing, and responding. Wien, Stacy, Keating, Rowlings, and Cameron (2002) provide an excellent description of an emergent curriculum project that illustrates aspects of the teacher's role. Most of the teachers in the project were unfamiliar with emergent curriculum, however, the authors saw this lack of experience as an advantage: "It allowed them to take each step slowly and to observe children's responses carefully. Gradually, they created new possibilities for curriculum." In this project, each of the children received a handmade cloth doll with no features. After some discussion, the children set about to correct this deficiency in a variety of ways. As they did so, one teacher reports struggling "trying not to control" where the children put eyes on their dolls" (Wien et al., 2002, p. 34). Wien et al. acknowledges the difficulty of the process: "It wasn't easy. With planning that is responsive rather than programmed, teachers don't know what comes next until they collaborate on devising the best plan to suit the children's responses and interests" (pp. 36-37).

For some, the teacher's role in emergent curriculum is too passive. For example, researchers at Project Spectrum,

a 10-year research project established to test Howard Gardner's theory of multiple intelligences, regard learning as a complex interaction between the learner, the teacher, and the environment. In their view, the teacher is actively involved and provides support through what they call "scaffolding and bridging" (Chen, Krechevsky, Viens, & Isberg, 1998, p. 63). In contrast to the emergent curriculum study, Spectrum researchers believe that "teachers need to act as coaches and facilitators to guide and challenge students' learning and thinking. We encouraged the teachers to ask children thought-provoking questions and to pose problems, suggest different hypotheses, and urge children to test these hypotheses in a variety of ways." (Chen et al., 1998, p. 63; cited Colbert, 2000, p. 8-9).

From time to time, depending on circumstances, teachers are likely to adopt all three roles—directive, reactive, and interactive. As they do, it is important to recognize that the role they play helps shape what happens and, as a result, what the children learn.

Subject Matter

In planning curriculum, teachers can choose from a wide range of topics. As Tyler (1949) suggests, it is important that the subject matter supports the curriculum purpose. The purpose of the curriculum mentioned above is to teach children about weather. Clearly the subject matter for the learning experience should relate to weather. On the other hand, the curriculum may be designed to fulfill a much more fundamental purpose and weather-related topics may be only vehicles for encouraging the development of more basic skills and abilities. For example, on a rainy day, the children might exercise their mathematical skills by collecting and measuring how much rain has fallen. They might develop their artistic ability by drawing a variety of cloud formations or by using cotton balls to create a 3-D tactile version of the clouds in the sky. They might also write a poem about rain or learn some of the scientific thinking about the causes of thunder and lightening. They might talk about how they feel when there is a storm and whether it helps to be with friends.

Many readers will recognize these as activities that support Howard Gardner's multiple intelligences (Gardner, 1993; Colbert, 1997a). Whether they concentrate on Gardner's intelligences or some other learning theory, teachers who establish curriculum goals that focus on the individual child, rather than on a specific topic, have a foundation for flexibility. Although they might have planned to discuss bugs, body parts or some other topic, they can shift easily to rain if a sudden storm should arise and still accomplish their curriculum goals.

The Environment

Finally, the nature and organization of the environment contributes to the learning experience. As long as concerns about the safety of the children have been addressed, curriculum developers can shape the children's learning experience through the decisions they make about the physical environment. One obvious question to consider is whether an activity is more appropriate for indoors or outdoors. More complex questions relate to the organization of the space, which is closely related to both teacher roles and educational philosophy (Colbert, 1997a). For example, space that includes open pathways to activity areas promote children's independence and free teachers to work with individual children. In contrast, space encourages

wandering and conflict when it includes pathways that interrupt existing activities or that lead to dead ends or activities which do not hold the children's attention. Teachers in such settings spend much of their time sorting out conflicts and directing group behavior, at the expense of attention to individual children.

Organization

Having explored the learning experience from a number of perspectives, it is important to consider how those experiences are going to be organized to fulfill the purpose of the curriculum. When thinking about organizing a curriculum plan that will unfold over time, it is important to start with basic information or foundation skills and build toward more complex subject matter and abilities. When organizing a plan for daily activities, teachers must consider routines (diaper changing, washroom visits, lunch) and transitions (the times between activities such as line-ups) as well as learning activities. When organizing learning activities, it is important to consider a blend of quiet and strenuous activities, and ensure that major events are not planned for times when the children are tired or hungry. Teachers can solve many behavior management problems by scheduling events at times of the day when children are most able to participate. Once again, careful observation of the children's behavior provides clues to the ways in which the organization of activities can make positive contributions to the achievement of curriculum goals.

Evaluation

Finally, Tyler's fourth question requires that some means be in place to evaluate whether curriculum purposes are being fulfilled. Answering that question requires closing the circle, returning to the beginning of the cycle, and considering once again, "What is the purpose?" Evaluation will only be effective if the purpose has been clearly stated and if observations along the way provide evidence that either supports the achievement of a specific purpose or indicates that it has not been met. In either case, the results of the evaluation set the stage for the next curriculum cycle—findings from one cycle lead to the formulation of

new purposes in the next. If the evaluation suggests that learning has occurred, it is time to move on to new challenges. If it suggests that there is more to learn, the lesson can be repeated, with adjustments based on what has been observed.

Conclusion

Clearly, what happens in classrooms is based on observation and careful planning. No matter how careful the preparation, however, what happens is also beyond the control of any individual and cannot be fitted into any one theory of curriculum development. Children, like adults, learn from everything that happens. Curriculum is, in fact, a giant umbrella that shelters a myriad of events. A solid grounding in curriculum theory and a good idea of who participates and what questions to ask can help teachers and caregivers establish and achieve appropriate curriculum goals, and respond more effectively to everything that happens inside and outside the child care setting.

Judith Colbert, Ph.D., is a consultant who specializes in early care and education. She is the author of several articles on curriculum and a major study on the relationship between brain research and curriculum.

References

Bowman, B., Donovan, M.S. & Burns, M. S. (Eds.) (2000). *Eager to learn: Educating our preschoolers.* Executive Summary, Report of the Committee on Early Childhood Pedagogy established by the National Research Council. Washington, DC: National Academy Press. [Full report published 2001.]

Bredekamp, S. & Copple, C. (Eds.) (1997). *Developmentally appropriate practice in early childhood programs serving children from birth to age 8.* Revised Edition. Washington, DC: NAEYC.

Chen, J., Krechevsky, M., & Viens, J. with Isberg, E. (1998). *Building on children's strengths: The experience of Project Spectrum.* Project Zero Frameworks for Early Childhood Education, Vol. 1, Ed. Gardner, H., Feldman, D. & Krechevsky, M. NY: Teacher's College Press.

Colbert, J. (1997a, May-June). Classroom design and how it influences behavior. *Earlychildhood NEWS,* IX (3).

Colbert, J. (2000). *Brain research and curriculm: Perspectives on intelligence and learning.* Waterloo, Canada: author.

Crosser, S. (1996, September-October). The butterfly garden: Developmentally appropriate practice defined. *Early Childhood News,* VIII (5).

Gardner, H. (1993). *Frames of mind: The theory of multiple intelligences.* 10th Anniversary Edition. NY: Basic Books.

Shane, H. (1980). Significant writings that have influenced the curriculum: 1906-1981. *Phi Delta Kappan,* 62(5), 311-314 [cited by Schubert].

Schubert, W. (1986). *Curriculum: Perspective, paradigm, and possibility.* NY: Macmillan Publishing Company.

Schwab, J.J. (1973). The practical 3: Transition into curriculum. *School Review,* 508-509.

Tyler, R. (1949). *Basic principles of curriculum and instruction.* Chicago, IL: University of Chicago Press.

Wien, C., Stacey, S., Keating, B., Rowlings, J. & Cameron, H. (2002). Handmade dolls as a framework for emergent curriculum. *Young Children,* 57(1), 33-38.

Reggio Emilia:
New Ways to Think About Schooling

The Reggio Emilia approach offers educators a catalyst for change and for developing new kinds of collaboration in teaching and learning.

Rebecca S. New

How can parents ensure that young children are ready for school? How should teachers prepare for the children who arrive? Which assessment strategies can enhance students' learning, inform teacher practice, and engage parents in their children's education experiences?

These questions continue to plague educators despite dramatic new insights into children's early brain development and vastly improved theoretical understandings of how children learn (Bransford, Brown, & Cocking, 2000). Faced with expanding curriculum mandates amid draconian budget cuts, U.S. public schools have become the target of political rhetoric and tough-love reform initiatives. Opinion surveys convey little improvement in public satisfaction with U.S. schools; worse still, students often describe school as "boring, irrelevant, and mindless" (Carpenter, 2000, pp. 383-384). What's a teacher to do?

Go to Italy! Over the past decade, a small but growing number of elementary educators across the United States have joined their early childhood colleagues in finding new ideas and inspiration from the early care and education pro-

gram of the city of Reggio Emilia in northern Italy. Reggio Emilia is also increasingly a source of new ideas for educators in more than 40 countries, from Brazil to Tanzania to the Philippines.

How Did It Begin?

The town of Reggio Emilia lies in a prosperous area of northern Italy known for its civic engagement. Following World War II, a small group of parents began Reggio Emilia's municipal early childhood program, which thrived under the leadership of early childhood educator Loris Malaguzzi and the hard work of hundreds of parents and teachers. After decades of innovation and experimentation, city leaders sent traveling exhibitions throughout Europe and to the United States to share the Reggio Emilia approach. As news of Reggio Emilia spread, educators, parents, and policymakers began to take note.

What Is the Reggio Emilia Approach?

Embedded in the Reggio Emilia approach to education is an image of children, families, and teachers working together to make schools dynamic and democratic learning environments. Reggio Emilia has attracted educators interested in

- The role of the classroom environment in children's learning;

- Long-term curriculum projects that promote inquiry among teachers and children;

- Partnerships with parents that include collaboration in the learning process;

- Documentation for observation, research, and assessment; and

- "The hundred languages of children"—children's multiple means of expression and understanding (Edwards, Gandini, & Forman, 1993, 1998).

A visitor to a Reggio Emilia classroom finds an inviting environment, with adult- and child-sized furnishings, plants and natural light, large panels documenting the children's ideas, and very few commercially produced materials. The children are deeply immersed in their own dramatic or constructive play, or perhaps they are in small groups with a teacher, exploring how best to design the highways around a block city, construct a functioning water fountain for the birds, or draw a life-size dinosaur to scale. Later on, the teachers, armed with tape recorders and their own drawings, discuss the children's ideas as they plan for the next day.

A return visit in the evening might find groups of parents poring over the teachers' photos and notes and discussing how best to help their children express their mathematical ideas about distance and speed, or their quandaries about the meanings of love, or their fears of the dark, or, more recently, of pending war. On another evening, parents work in the kitchen with the cook, sharing recipes and making friends as they debate current events. Imbued in these activities are a deep respect for children's intelligence and a commitment to adult engagement.

Reggio Emilia's education philosophy resonates with key ideas in contemporary education, including Howard Gardner's theory of multiple intelligences, Lev Vygotsky's notions of the role of symbolic languages in cognition, James Comer's ideas about parental involvement, and Nel Nodding's challenge to create caring schools. Many educators note Reggio Emilia's similarities to John Dewey's education philosophy and to the play-based learning of British Infant Schools in the early 1970s. These key ideas run counter to a subject-centered, outcomes-based view of education and have challenged educators to rethink the purpose and scope of what they do.

Reggio Emilia and Early Childhood Educators

Historically, such challenges to the utilitarian approach to education have been more popular among early childhood educators than among elementary school educators. Partly because of the relatively autonomous status of early education outside mainstream public education in the United States, its educators have often felt freer to consider alternative approaches to learning (New, 2002). Nearly a century ago, the ideas of Germany's Friedrich Froebel influenced the establishment of the U.S. kindergarten as a place for children to learn in a nurturing and carefully planned environment. Italy's Maria Montessori furthered the development of environments and materials designed specifically for young children. British Infant Schools and the project approach are more recent international influences on early childhood education.

Reggio Emilia's ideas did not, however, always resonate with early childhood educators. When the approach first came to the attention of U.S. educators in the 1980s, early childhood educators had translated Piaget's interpretations of children's cognitive development into an emphasis on individual children learning in isolation from classmates. They viewed play as central to children's learning and teacher-directed activity as unnecessary or even counterproductive. Reggio Emilia served as a powerful catalyst in reexamining these beliefs and their associated theories (New, 1997) and revealed some of the biases embedded within the field's traditional views (Bredekamp, 2002). The guidelines for developmentally appropriate practice developed in 1987 by the National Association for the Education of Young Children (Bredekamp, 1987) had paid scant attention to these ideas, but the 1997 guidelines frequently cite examples from Reggio Emilia to illustrate principles of social cognition, scaffolding, and the role of symbolic languages in knowledge construction (Bredekamp & Copple, 1997).

Reggio Emilia's Appeal for Elementary Educators

The academic goals of elementary education have often been at odds with the developmental approach of early childhood education. Many parents and teachers continue to raise concerns about children arriving in structured and academically focused elementary classrooms for which their previous child-centered classrooms have failed to prepare them.

Elementary educators find that Reggio Emilia offers new perspectives on many current issues, including notions of readiness and transitions from home to school, ways of promoting family engagement in children's learning, the benefits of looping and multi-age grouping for using children's relationships to promote academic achievement, and the importance of staffing practices, such as teams of teachers, to promote professional development. The greatest attraction, however, is the way in which Reggio Emilia stimulates a rethinking of what schools do.

Embedded in the Reggio Emilia approach to education is an image of children, families, and teachers working together to make schools dynamic and democratic learning environments.

Reggio Emilia has helped bridge the divide between early and elementary educators in three ways: by revealing new ways for promoting children's academic learning in the realm of big ideas; by offering documentation as a tool for studying, sharing, and planning children's education experiences; and by provoking a new way to think about the role of the teacher.

New Possibilities for Children's Learning

Reggio Emilia's optimistic and respectful image of the child has influenced educators' views of what and how children learn. Conflicts between academic goals and child-initiated activities have lost their punch as teachers have experienced the benefits of hypothesis-generating projects rich and varied enough to provide authentic learning experiences for both adults and children. As children work together—for example, to create the rules for an athletic event—teachers notice how far they stretch their mathematical skills of measurement, estimation, and computation. Signs and invitations for such events serve as forms of authentic assessment when they reveal emerging skills and future learning goals. As teachers provide materials and purposeful questioning, they relish the ease with which children become deeply engaged in their projects.

Many of the values and practices associated with Reggio Emilia's interpretation of curriculum appeal to U.S. educators who have tired of standardized interpretations of effective teaching and children's learning. Thus, an elementary special education teacher in New Hampshire was inspired by Reggio Emilia to use collaborative projects to address individual education plan goals, taking her students with special needs into the community to explore their curiosities about plumbing and public transportation. An intern in a 1st grade class in a small Massachusetts fishing town drew on state-mandated curriculum goals while responding to children's anxieties about the impact of changing fishing regulations on their families' lives. The resulting community-based project included interviews with parents, tours of fishing plants, and the creation of a board game based on new federal regulations.

Documentation for Discussion and Discovery

When U.S. educators first began to adopt the Reggio Emilia approach, they often confused Reggio Emilia's concepts of documentation with traditional child-centered observations. As teachers began to share and discuss the meanings of their photos, tape recordings, and samples of children's work with other colleagues and children's families, however, they learned how to "make learning visible"—their own and that of the children they teach. Project Zero's uses of documentation strategies to capture children's individual learning within the context of group experiences has also helped U.S. educators to see the value of the pedagogical strategy of long-term projects (Project Zero & Reggio Children, 2001). In groups and as individuals, U.S. teachers are now sharing their ideas, experiences, frustrations, and inspirations through national and statewide conferences, an e-mail forum, and a Reggio Emilia Web site (http://ericeece.org/reggio.html).

The Role of the Teacher

What attracts educators most to Reggio Emilia's approach is how it changes their understandings of themselves—as teachers, as citizens, and as learners. U.S. teachers have reached the limits of their tolerance for the go-it-alone approach to teaching. More than half of the teachers responding to a 1990 Carnegie Foundation survey noted the limited time for meeting with colleagues, and less than 10 percent were satisfied with the opportunities available for them to establish collegial relationships (Darling-Hammond & Sclan, 1996).

The role of the teacher inherent in Reggio Emilia's approach offers new hope for lonely educators and corresponds with recent research on teacher collaboration (Cochran-Smith & Lytle, 1993; Fu, Stremmel, & Hill, 2002). Teams of teachers, such as those at the Crow Island School in Winnetka, Illinois, now travel together to workshops and conferences, bringing back new ideas to discuss with the whole faculty. School-based groups in Ohio participate in monthly statewide Reggio study groups. Massachusetts teachers meet regularly to share their documentation of children's learning in gatherings sponsored by Project Zero at Harvard University. Collaboration also involves parents: Two teachers in Ohio, frustrated by the problem of birthday parties in an economically and religiously diverse classroom, turned the issue over to the parents, setting the stage for more active partnerships with children's families throughout the year. All of these experiences have transformed the teacher's role from single expert to collaborative participant in an adult learning community (New, 2000).

Challenges and Possibilities

The reasons for Reggio Emilia *not* having much impact on U.S. elementary education are numerous. International education research has a poor track record for influencing changes in U.S. education practice in grades 1-12. Skeptics of Reggio Emilia's relevance to U.S. classrooms cite cultural challenges associated with Italy's philosophical roots, including the cultural support for close relationships between teachers and parents. Reggio Emilia's goals also stand in sharp contrast to a growing emphasis in the United States on high-stakes testing, a view of teachers as tools rather than decision makers, and a focus on individual learning in a competitive environment.

Others point to the practical challenges of building sustained relationships in an increasingly fragmented and hurried society; of planning curriculum that will be responsive to the diverse needs of children and families; and of finding the time, resources, and support necessary for what is surely more rewarding work—but also more work. Still others join me in cautioning against the idea that any one city, program, or set of guidelines can adequately determine what and how children are educated.

And yet there are many reasons to be optimistic about Reggio Emilia's usefulness in helping U.S. educators rethink their approach to public education. Of all of its features, Reggio Emilia's reconceptualization of the working environment of teachers may have the most to offer. The respect for children and parents is central, but the international success of Reggio Emilia's example is surely due to the respect given to teachers—as capable of asking good questions, willing to debate with one another, and committed to consultation with children's families. Even middle school teachers are beginning to think about how to adapt the Reggio Emilia approach to their instruction (Hill, 2002).

Of all its features, Reggio Emilia's reconceptualization of the working environment of teachers may have the most to offer U.S. educators.

Anderson (2000) notes that new ideas in education often weave in and out of public awareness for years, waiting for the right time and place for implementation. He argues that new common ground serves as a foundation for current reform initiatives, including the convergence of a shared understanding that

the rigid graded structure of schools must be overhauled; self-containment in any professional role is less than desirable.... classrooms must become busy, active, even noisy ... curriculum shouldn't be strictly compartmental-ized; high expectations are good; participation of all players is essential and workable. (p. 403)

Reggio Emilia has much to contribute to helping to make these changes more desirable and, therefore, more likely. Such changes would go a long way toward contributing to a more dynamic culture of education as envisioned by Bruner (1996) and living up to John Dewey's faith in schools as catalysts for societal change. There has never been a better time to give it a try.

References

Anderson, R. H. (2000). Rediscovering lost chords. *Phi Delta Kappan, 81*(5), 402-404.

Bransford, J., Brown, A., & Cocking, R. R. (Eds.) & Committee on Developments in the Science of Learning, National Research Council. (2000). *How people learn: Brain, mind, experience, and school* (Expanded ed.). Washington, DC: National Academies Press.

Bredekamp, S. (1987). *Developmentally appropriate practice in early childhood programs serving children from birth through age 8.* Washington, DC: National Association for the Education of Young Children.

Bredekamp, S. (2002). Developmentally appropriate practice meets Reggio Emilia: A story of collaboration in all its meanings. *Innovations, 9*(1), 11-15.

Bredekamp, S., & Copple, C. (Eds.). (1997). *Developmentally appropriate practice in early childhood programs* (Rev. ed.). Washington, DC: National Association for the Education of Young Children.

Bruner, J. (1996). *The culture of education.* Cambridge, MA: Harvard University Press.

Carpenter, W. A. (2000). Ten years of silver bullets: Dissenting thoughts on education reform. *Phi Delta Kappan, 81*(5), 383-389.

Cochran-Smith, M., & Lytle, S. L. (Eds.). (1993). *Inside/outside: Teacher research and knowledge.* New York: Teachers College Press.

Darling-Hammond, L., & Sclan, E. M. (1996). Who teaches and why. In J. Sikula (Ed.), *Handbook of research on teacher education* (2nd. ed., pp. 67-101). New York: Macmillan Library Reference.

Edwards, C. P., Gandini, L., & Forman, G. (1993). *The hundred languages of children: The Reggio Emilia approach to early childhood education.* Norwood, NJ: Ablex.

Edwards, C. P., Gandini, L., & Forman, G. (1998). *The hundred languages of children: The Reggio Emilia approach—advanced reflections* (2nd ed.). Greenwich, CT: Ablex.

Fu, V. R., Stremmel, A. J., & Hill, L. T. (Eds.). (2002). *Teaching and learning: Collaborative exploration of the Reggio Emilia approach.* Upper Saddle River, NJ: Merrill/Prentice-Hall.

Hill, L. T. (2002). A journey to recast the Reggio Emilia approach for a middle-school. In V. Fu, A. Stremmel, & L. Hill (Eds.), *Teaching and learning: A collaborative exploration of the Reggio Emilia approach* (pp. 83-108). Upper Saddle, NJ: Merrill/Prentice-Hall.

New, R. (1997). Reggio Emilia: An approach or an attitude? In J. Roopnarine & J. Johnson (Eds.), *Approaches to early childhood education* (Rev. 3rd ed.). Columbus, OH: Merrill.

New, R. (2000). *Reggio Emilia: Catalyst for change and conversation.* (EDO-PS-00-15). Champaign, IL: ERIC/EECE Clearinghouse on Elementary and Early Childhood Education.

New, R. (2002). Culture, child development, and early childhood education:Rethinking the Relationship. In R. Lerner, F. Jacobs, & D. Wertleib (Eds.), *Promoting positive child, adolescent, and family development.* Thousand Oaks, CA: Sage.

Project Zero & Reggio Children. (2001). *Making learning visible: Children as individual and group learners.* Reggio Emilia, Italy: Reggio Children.

Rebecca S. New is an associate professor in the Eliot-Pearson Department of Child Development, Tufts University, 105 College Ave., Medford, MA 02155, becky.new@tufts.edu.

From *Educational Leadership*, April 2003, pp. 34-38. Reprinted with permission of the Association for Supervision and Curriculum Development. © 2003 by ASCD. All rights reserved.

Emergent Curriculum and Kindergarten Readiness

Deborah J. Cassidy, Sharon Mims, Lia Rucker, and Sheresa Boone

Recently, the focus on "readiness" in early childhood education in the United States has increased dramatically in the face of growing concerns about the number of failing students and failing schools. The National Education Goals Panel (Shore, 1998) endorses an approach to school readiness that focuses on five domains of children's development and learning: physical health and motor development, social and emotional development, approaches toward learning, language development, and cognition and general knowledge. Both the National Education Goals Panel, Goal 1 Ready Schools Resource Group and the National Association of State Boards of Education emphasize the following important points about school readiness: 1) all children are to be ready to benefit from school, 2) readiness constitutes much more than knowing the ABC's and numbers, and 3) as the backgrounds of children vary, it is not appropriate to expect all children to have a common set of skills as they enter school (North Carolina School Improvement Goal Panel Ready for School Goal Team, 2000).

It is important to note, however, that the concept of "readiness" cannot be addressed by focusing only on the children. We must scrutinize the environment into which they are entering. The following four "Cornerstones of Ready Schools" are identified in *School Readiness in North Carolina* (2000) as the requisite components of school settings that allow children to be successful:

- Knowledge of growth and development of typically and atypically developing children

- Knowledge of the strengths, interests, and needs of each individual child

- Knowledge of the social and cultural contexts in which each child and family lives

- The ability to translate developmental knowledge into developmentally appropriate practices.

The concept of "ready schools" implies the need for flexibility to address individual differences in the physical environment, in the curriculum, and in the teaching strategies employed. The degree to which the professionals in our schools possess an in-depth knowledge of child development, and their ability to use this knowledge when making decisions about individual chil-dren, is a fundamental determinant of children's success, regardless of their individual "readiness."

In spite of the promising language regarding "ready schools" and developmental readiness of *individual* children in recent documents on school readiness, the pervasive sentiment still seems to be that many young children are inadequately prepared for the rigors of an often inflexible public school curriculum. The response of many preschools, child care programs, and public schools to the barrage of information indicating that young children arrive at kindergarten unprepared has been a rapid retreat "back to the basics." This usually means a more academic and highly structured approach to early childhood education.

> *The concept of "readiness" cannot be addressed by focusing only on the children. We must scrutinize the environment into which they are entering.*

The available research on child-centered, developmentally appropriate curriculum models indicates, however, that such a retreat is unwarranted. High-quality, developmentally appropriate curricula have been shown to result in positive cognitive and social outcomes for young children (Cost, Quality, & Child Outcomes Study Team, 1995; Marcon, 1999; Schweinhart & Weikart, 1998). It is essential, however, for programs that espouse more child-centered and developmentally appropriate curriculum approaches to articulate the many cognitive, social, emotional, and physical developmental accomplishments of their curricula. Only then can they answer those parents, kindergarten teachers, and public school administrators who question how a play-based approach to educating young children can serve as preparation for kindergarten.

This article describes the curriculum activities in one child-centered, developmentally appropriate child care facility preschool classroom. In particular, it explains how activities are selected according to children's needs, interests, and abilities, and how the activities address the core competencies mandated by the public school system in kindergarten. This emergent or "grassroots" curriculum (Cassidy & Lancaster, 1993; Cassidy & Myers, 1987) is based on specific observations made of individual and small groups of preschool children. Teachers in this classroom of 3- to 5-year-olds use daily planning to respond to observed behaviors, and then facilitate learning and development for each individual child. Since this child care facility is located in the state of North Carolina, the authors delineate which competencies from the North Carolina Standard Course of Study for Kindergarten (North Carolina State Department of Public Instruction) are addressed through the activities.

When planning an activity, the teachers first considered the child's (or group of children's) interest and how they could extend the interest to increase understanding and learning.

The various activities described here address competencies at or beyond the competency levels required in kindergarten. In the science area, for example, preschool children were involved in higher level skills of exploration and use of the scientific method—skills not included in the state Standard Course of Study until the 1st, 2nd, or even the 3rd grade. The Kindergarten Standard Course of Study for science requires competencies in areas such as identifying animal appearance and measuring growth and changes. The classroom pets provided an ongoing opportunity to learn such concepts, while also providing opportunities to learn about pet care. Another focus of the kindergarten science curriculum is to understand weather concepts. Each day, classroom conversations focused on daily and seasonal changes in weather and temperature. The lists of competencies in each activity description are not exhaustive. Indeed, they capture only a small number of the learning objectives met through the activities.

The Preschool Classroom

During the 6-month period of time described in the following curriculum strands, there were 15 children in this classroom, ranging in age from 3 to 5. Planning in this particular classroom is observation-based. When planning an activity, the teachers first considered the child's (or group of children's) interest and how they could extend the interest to increase understanding and learning. Then they shaped the activity to accommodate specific skills. If children demonstrated interest, or if similar play was observed in other areas, then the activities were further extended. Children also could request specific activities. The same activity could be repeated or altered to increase a child's experience/involvement and to target specific skills. Such

repetition was an important part of this classroom and allowed children to experience mastery and develop feelings of self-competence. Strands of interest (represented by child play) and planned activities extended from day to day, sometimes lasting for months.

Treasure Hunts

TREASURE HUNT

Social Studies Curriculum **Grade: Kindergarten**
Competency Goal 8:

8.2. Construct simple maps, models, and drawings of home, classroom, and school settings.

Science Curriculum **Grade: One**

Competency Goal 2: The learner will build an understanding of solid earth materials.

2.02. Classify rocks and other earth materials according to their properties: size, shape, color, and texture.

Competency Goal 3: The learner will build an understanding of the properties and relationships of objects.

3.01. Determine the many ways in which objects can be grouped or classified.

Treasure hunting was a tremendous source of interest and the basis for many classroom activities from September to March. This strand was completely child-initiated; original activities began as a result of child requests and ideas. Related play often continued outside of planned activities, and lasted the entire school year, despite gaps of several weeks between the planned activities. The children began in September by hiding classroom treasures and creating their own treasure chests. In planned extensions, the children made their own treasure, complete with foil, glitter, glue, and cellophane. The children also conducted treasure hunts, which involved marking the spot where the treasure was hidden with an "X." For subsequent hunts, the children asked teachers to draw maps of the classroom and playground, putting an "X" to mark the spot of the treasure. These activities ignited the children's imagination, and laid the groundwork for role-playing and developing their sense of visual representation through creating and using maps.

The teachers continued the activities with more maps and hidden eggs. At snack time one day, the children used graham crackers, peanut butter, and raisins to create edible treasure maps. Several children began to design their own more traditional maps. The purchase of a related computer game further reinforced and enhanced the interest in this topic.

One of the teachers visited a gem mine in the mountains of North Carolina and brought back buckets of dirt and sand in which the children could search for treasure. As they found the gems/"treasure," the children discovered the properties of the stones, and determined how they were alike and different, and why. The children then classified the gems, expanding their knowledge about solid materials in the earth. The children eventually put the gems to use again as hidden treasure.

The children used their literacy skills daily to plan and create increasingly detailed treasure maps. One day a parent brought in a box of household materials for the classroom. One of the items was a jewelry box that reminded the children of a treasure chest. They began to build forts for the treasure chest and the treasure hunts became more of a large-group activity.

Bookmaking

BOOKMAKING

English Language Arts Curriculum **Grade: Kindergarten**

Competency Goal 1: The learner will develop and apply enabling strategies and skills to read and write.

1.03. Demonstrate decoding and word recognition strategies and skills.
- Recognize and name upper case and lowercase letters of the alphabet.
- Recognize some words by sight, including a few common words, one's own name, and environmental print such as signs, labels, and trademarks.
- Recognize most beginning consonant letter-sound associations in one-syllable words.

Competency Goal 4: The learner will apply strategies and skills to create oral, written, and visual texts.

4.02. Use words that name and words that tell action in a variety of simple texts.

4.03. Use words that describe color, size, and location in a variety of texts (e.g., oral retelling, written stories, lists, and journal entries of personal experiences).

Competency Goal 5: The learner will apply grammar and language conventions to communicate effectively.

5.01. Develop spelling strategies and skills by:
- Representing spoken language with temporary and/or conventional spelling.
- Writing most letters of the alphabet.
- Analyzing sounds in a word and writing dominant consonant letters.

Science Curriculum **Grade: Kindergarten**

Competency Goal 4: The learner will increase his/her understanding of how the world works by using tools.

4.02. Determine the usefulness of tools to help people: scissors, pencils, crayons, etc.

In December, many of the children began to make their own books by stapling, taping, and gluing paper together. Some children cut pictures from magazines and glued them into their books, while others drew their own pictures. Teachers capitalized on this interest and enhanced literacy skills by planning bookmaking activities related to other activity strands, such as creating a book about feelings.

The children remained primarily interested in creating their own books, and so the teachers followed their lead. Many of the children were becoming interested in learning letters and writing words/stories in their books. The children began asking the teachers to write the words in the books as they dictated the story. They also asked teachers to write words for them on separate paper, and then they copied the letters into their books. Some children who were familiar with letters asked teachers to spell the words orally while they wrote the letters. Others were ready for the teachers to help them sound out words phonetically, so that they could try to write the words on their own. Some of the children could spell many common words, and used a rich vocabulary to tell their stories.

The children used different tools to assist them in the bookmaking process. Some children cut and glued pictures from magazines, while others drew their own pictures. Some asked teachers to write dictated stories, others copied letters and words teachers wrote for them, while still others only needed the word to be spelled orally or sounded out for them. Scissors, pencils, and crayons were used by most of the children. These tools were useful in helping the children create individual products.

As the children continued to extend their own ideas, repeat similar stories, and observe others' books, they developed more advanced skills. This strand allowed the teachers to observe and naturally extend literacy skills, such as letter recognition, writing development, and top-to-bottom and left-to-right orientation. The activity also boosted children's phonetic awareness and their understanding of story development. Many of the stories were drawn from the children's personal experiences and generated a sharing of ideas and interest in the work of others.

Classroom Garden

In December the children continued to talk about a garden they had grown on the playground the previous year. They were extremely interested in using the spray bottles to water the new plants that one of the teachers had donated to the classroom. The children began to compare the different types of plants found in the classroom—how they grew, or the similarities and differences in their appearance. They also observed that certain plants produce food, and others do not.

The teachers wanted to build on the children's skills of observation and their appreciation of nature. As it was not possible to grow an outdoor garden during that time of year, they assisted the children in sprouting beans in the classroom. In January the children and teachers planted bulbs and began to chart their growth. The children's discussion of different types of seeds and uses for them led to art activities in which they used seeds to make necklaces, collages, media table experiences, etc. The class also made plans to grow a vegetable garden the next month, and they began to plant some of the plants in the classroom. The children discussed when they needed to plant indoors and why, as well as when plants could be planted outdoors.

GROWING THINGS

Science Curriculum   **Grade: Kindergarten**

Competency Goal 1: The learner will build an understanding of similarities and differences in plants and animals.

1.01. Identify the similarities and differences in plants: appearance, growth, change, and uses.

1.02. Identify the similarities and differences in animals: appearance, growth, change, and purpose.

1.03 Observe the different ways that animals move from place to place, and how plants move in different ways.

1.04. Observe similarities of humans to other animals, such as basic needs. Observe how humans grow and change.

Competency Goal 2: The learner will build an understanding of weather concepts.

2.03. Observe the seasonal and daily changes in weather (e.g., temperature changes).

Competency Goal 3: The learner will build an understanding of the properties/movement of common objects and organisms.

3.03. Describe motion when an object, a person, an animal, or other living creature moves from one place to another.

Grade: One

Competency Goal 1: The learner will build an understanding of the needs of living organisms.

1.01. Learn why plants need air, water, nutrients, and light.

Competency Goal 2: The learner will build an understanding of solid earth materials.

2.03. Determine the properties of soil (e.g., its capacity to retain water and ability to support life).

Grade: Two

Competency Goal 1: The learner will build an understanding of plant and animal life cycles.

1.01. Analyze the life cycle of plants, including reproduction, maturation, and death.

Grade: Three

Competency Goal 1: The learner will build an understanding of plant growth and adaptations.

1.03. Analyze plant structures for specific functions: growth, survival, and reproduction.

1.04. Determine that new plants can be generated from such things as seeds and bulbs.

As a result of these activities, the children gained an understanding that without water, light, and nutrients, the plants and sprouts would not thrive. They also began to understand the properties of soil (e.g., how the soil absorbed or retained water, and how soil supports plant life). By taking care of the plants, the children could observe how the plants grew from day to day and week to week. They could observe whether the plant survived, and when or if it reproduced. As they cared for the plants, the children observed the life cycle of a plant: how a plant grew more leaves as it reproduced, how it matured, and how some eventually died.

Discussions about growing things eventually extended to people and animals. One of the student teachers provided a butterfly habitat, through which children were able to observe the development of butterflies from larvae. The children compared one state of growth to another as the larvae became caterpillars, then butterflies. Caterpillars grown from larvae and chrysalises developed into butterflies. By watching these processes, the children could identify similarities and differences (appearance, growth, change, and purpose) in animals. Comparisons were suggested for consideration, such as human babies and caterpillars need kinds of food that older humans and butterflies may not need to eat. Every living thing, however, needs a source of food or nutrients to sustain life. Also, those needs change at different times or stages in life. The children were able to observe these stages and the requirements of each stage. The butterfly habitat allowed the children to observe not only the development of a butterfly, but also its movement in different states. The butterfly habitat also allowed the children to observe and chart how butterflies and caterpillars move differently to get from one place to another. The class eventually released the butterflies.

Discussing Feelings

In November the teachers initiated several group meeting discussions regarding feelings, with the purpose of helping the children develop a set of classroom rules. They believed that helping the children understand and recognize their own feelings would provide a base on which the children could develop relevant, functional guidelines for classroom behavior. Group-time discussions about feelings and their causes led to the creation of classroom books about feelings in which children used literacy skills and creativity. The children either drew or cut out magazine pictures and dictated the text of their stories to the teachers. During group time, the students made lists and charts, so they could compare and contrast their opinions.

Discussions about different feelings and personal reactions led to comparisons of physical characteristics. The children worked on life-sized "Me" pictures for several days in December. In February, they were still talking about their similarities and differences, so the teachers planned an activity in which the children mixed paints to develop colors that would most closely resemble their skin colors, and then again worked on self-portraits.

The children had enjoyed earlier activities that involved tape recording their voices and then identifying each voice. The teachers

FEELINGS/AWARENESS OF SELF AND OTHERS

Healthful Living Curriculum   *Grade: Kindergarten*

Competency Goal 2: Stress management.

2.1. Naming feelings.

2.2. Verbalizing feelings.

2.3. Accepting the normalcy of feelings.

Social Studies Curriculum   *Grade: Kindergarten*

Competency Goal 2: The learner will infer that individuals and families are alike and different.

2.1. Describe aspects of families.

2.2. Distinguish likenesses and differences among individuals and families (particularly with reference to cultural differences and skin color).

Competency Goal 6: The learner will characterize change in different settings.

6.1. Describe changes in oneself.

Science Curriculum   *Grade: Kindergarten*

Competency Goal 1: The learner will build an understanding of the similarities and differences in plants and animals.

1.04. Observe how humans grow and change.

planned another activity in which each child read a book into a tape recorder. As a group, over several days, the children listened to the tapes and discussed the voices, as well as the story. By February, the children were able to recognize that they were not static; they began to view themselves as growing and changing beings. A growth chart that was updated over the course of the year recorded changes in height, so that the children would have further concrete evidence of change over time.

Conclusions

It is clear that play in this classroom addressed many of the goals for children's learning in kindergarten, as well as those for 1st and 2nd grade. The children were enthusiastic about the activities because the teachers built and planned them around the children's interests. The curriculum in this classroom was not only developmentally appropriate and child-centered, it also served to prepare children for kindergarten. With experience in a high-quality, developmentally appropriate classroom such as this one, children will more likely be adequately prepared for the ever-increasing rigor of kindergarten competencies.

Regardless of the curriculum adopted in the pre-kindergarten or child care classroom, however, exposure to appropriate and stimulating curriculum does not ensure that all children will master concepts. It is critical that a developmentally appropriate curriculum be coupled with a developmentally appropriate assessment system that documents the progress of each child in the classroom. Many children will fail in a kindergarten or preschool environment that favors a rigid pass/fail system, attempts to measure only "facts," and in which assessment is conducted in artificial and unnatural settings. Indeed, the only way for children to be successful under such circumstances is for teachers to teach to the test under typical test-taking conditions. Under such conditions, however, it will be difficult to determine what children really know, especially if they are unaccustomed to such environments, as is often the case for children who come from developmentally appropriate classrooms. Only through developmentally appropriate curriculum and assessment, such as portfolio documentation, can we be assured that each child is adequately prepared for kindergarten.

Furthermore, three other essential components must be in place to effectively meet the needs of preschoolers:

• Teachers must be knowledgeable and able to facilitate learning for each child. They must possess a keen understanding of children's development and how the young child learns. An ability to determine the children's abilities, individual personalities, family cultures, and priorities also is critical. Teachers' role in observing the children's interests and ongoing play was the catalyst for creating this educationally stimulating environment. Their ability to capture crucial information that was relevant to this group of children, and to utilize it as the basis of their curriculum, transformed "ordinary" preschool activities into an extremely rich and stimulating learning environment.

• Communication with parents is essential in helping them understand how a play-based curriculum prepares children for kindergarten. Because play is such an enjoyable and engaging experience for children, it is sometimes difficult for parents to see how children learn through a play-based curriculum, particularly when many adults view play as fun but superfluous, and "work" as valuable but not usually enjoyable.

• Communicating with kindergarten teachers and administrators about best practices in preschool education, and its relationship to kindergarten entry, also is critical. Many public school personnel are unfamiliar with best practices in preschool education and need articulate preschool teachers to explain the relationship between play and the competencies and expectations of kindergarten.

With the guidance of knowledgeable teachers, these children were truly prepared for kindergarten and enjoyed learning during their preschool years. Teachers can educate parents and administrators about how a child-centered curriculum is also a readiness curriculum.

Summary

Much has been written, discussed, and opined about kindergarten readiness. Unfortunately, a recurrent underlying assumption places the burden of becoming ready solely on young children and their families. All too often, children are forced to be "ready" for an inappropriate environment that contains few of the components that would make it "ready" for them. Children *can* be "ready" for kindergarten, given an early education environment that 1) is engaging, age-appropriate, and child-centered; 2) includes a curriculum and assessments system that provides for individual differences; and 3) provides knowledgeable teachers who are responsive and capable of facilitating learning.

References

Cassidy, D. J., & Lancaster, C. (1993). The grassroots curriculum: A dialogue between children and teachers. *Young Children, 48*(6), 47-51.

Cassidy, D. J., & Myers, B. K. (1987). Early childhood planning: A developmental perspective. *Childhood Education, 64,* 2-8.

Cost, Quality, & Child Outcomes Study Team. (1995). *Cost, quality, and child outcomes in child care centers. Public report* (2nd ed.). Denver, CO: Economics Department, University of Colorado at Denver.

Marcon, R. A. (1999). Differential impact of preschool models on development and early learning of inner-city children: A three cohort study. *Developmental Psychology, 2,* 358-375.

National Research Council. (2000). *Eager to learn.* Washington, DC: National Academy Press.

North Carolina State Department of Public Instruction. *North Carolina Standard Course of Study.* Retrieved December 15, 2002, from www.dpi.state.nc.us/Curriculum

North Carolina School Improvement Goal Panel Ready for School Goal Team. (2000). *School readiness in North Carolina: Strategies for defining, measuring, and promoting success for all children.* Raleigh, NC: North Carolina State Board of Education.

Schweinhart, L., & Weikart, D. (1998). Why curriculum matters in early childhood education. *Educational Leadership, 55,* 57-60.

Shore, R. (1998) *Ready schools.* Washington, DC: Goal 1 Ready Schools Resource Group, National Education Goals Panel.

Deborah J. Cassidy is Associate Professor, Department of Human Development and Family Studies, and Sharon Mims is Director, Child Care Education Program, University of North Carolina at Greensboro. Lia Rucker is Training Coordinator and Sheresa Boone is Outreach Training Coordinator, North Carolina Rated License Assessment Project.

LEARNING CENTERS: WHY AND HOW

One of the most accepted practices in early childhood education is that classrooms are organized into interest areas or learning centers. Children paint in the art center, work puzzles in the manipulatives center, and look at books in the library center, for example.

Why organize space in this way?

Meeting children's needs

A well-organized and creative classroom reflects children's interests, needs, developmental levels, and learning styles. It invites children to explore and discover. It offers security and safety. And it allows children to develop meaningful relationships with other children and adults.

The key to creating effective environments for young children is to know how they develop. Children grow and develop at unique rates, but almost all follow a predictable sequence of development. For example, an infant is likely to sit unassisted before pulling up to stand. Teachers who understand developmental sequences and can mark developmental milestones—particular skills we expect most children to acquire by a certain age—are likely to prepare the best environments for learning and socializing. We know, for example, that most 10- to 12-month-olds are afraid of strangers, that 18- to 26-month-old toddlers are wobbly walking, and that 5-year-olds are eager to help with chores. This kind of knowledge helps teachers respond to children and can help direct the curriculum and room arrangement.

Goals for every child

Many early childhood educators describe a set of life-long learning skills or universal goals that help prepare children to become cooperative and competent members of society. These include:

- **Self-regulation**—understanding and accepting rules for yourself and the sake of the community.
- **Problem-solving skills**—working to negotiate and resolve conflicts.
- **Initiative**—evaluating a situation and being willing to try to improve it.
- **Trust**—developing honesty and steadfastness in relationships.
- **Independence**—taking responsibility for your own successes and failures.
- **Creativity**—approaching ideas and tasks with initiative, playfulness, and inventive thinking.

Curriculum planning and room arrangement for all ages of children supports these goals. You build trust in infants when you respond promptly to crying and cuddle often. You help toddlers develop self-regulation and independence when you have a low shelf for book storage. And similarly, you support creativity and initiative when you let 4-year-olds plan and dig a corner of the playground for a vegetable garden.

Infants and toddlers

Infants and toddlers learn about their world through their senses—by

Toys and materials for babies

Make sure toys and materials are in good condition, have no sharp or broken parts, and are non-toxic. Check sizes with a choke tube to make sure infants can't swallow or choke on toys. Wash and sanitize all toys after each use.
- mirrors
- musical toys
- chew toys
- busy boards
- balls
- shape sorters
- blocks
- dolls
- books
- mobiles
- wheel toys
- squeeze toys
- rings and chain links that snap or hook together
- household pots, wooden spoons, plastic cups, and cardboard boxes
- nesting blocks, barrels, and bowls

seeing, touching, tasting, hearing, and smelling. Infants and toddlers need to touch, manipulate, and interact with things to know them. To learn, babies need environments that allow—and encourage—the exploration of real materials. Babies build skills when adults respond to them consistently and support their curiosity and developing skills in a safe, supportive way.

The primary activities for infants—diapering, eating, and sleeping—require specific equipment and carefully arranged space. Discovery or exploration zones are additional secure spaces where the youngest children can explore their surroundings. For the youngest infants this might mean a floor blanket with a mirror propped nearby, a mobile to watch, and a hanging cloth ball to kick.

As infants become more mobile, this exploration zone expands. It could include a corner for crawling over pillows and a different area for play with dolls and soft toys. Expand and equip classroom discovery areas to respond to the developmental needs and interests of growing toddlers.

Most toddlers and 2-year-olds depend upon someone else to satisfy their needs, offer support, and entertain. This means they typically play alone or in the presence of another child but with little interaction—unless there is an attractive toy in someone else's hands. Language is limited, so communication is often physical. Toddlers are not yet able to understand the feelings of someone else (empathy) and instead tend to be self-focused.

For a toddler environment to be effective it must be safe and spacious. Because toddlers aren't able to share toys, be sure to provide duplicates of favorite playthings. Use low dividers to help children focus their activities—trains in that corner and housekeeping here. Encourage self-help skills by providing shelves and baskets for toy storage—and encouraging the children to help at cleanup time.

Preschoolers

Three- to 5-year-old children are often described as preschoolers. Preschoolers are active, eager learners. They are constantly exploring, manipulating, and experimenting with the environment to learn more about it. They still rely heavily on their senses but are beginning to think abstractly, to use symbols, and to reason. They learn best when they can use real materials, reflect on what happens, and draw conclusions—what we call "cause and effect."

Preschoolers gradually become less self-centered and begin to understand the viewpoints of others. This allows play to become more cooperative—a key to increased language experiences, problem solving, and experimentation. Increasing physical coordination and strength allows preschoolers to handle new materials, build creatively, and initiate new activities.

Standard materials for the block center

- unit blocks—at least 100
- hollow blocks
- cardboard blocks
- human figures
- animal figures—domestic, farm, and jungle
- vehicles
- measuring tools
- labeled storage shelf

Learning centers

The developmental skills of preschoolers require less space for sleeping, eating, and toileting and more space for play and discovery. Arranging that space in learning centers allows children to play cooperatively and investigate language, roles, materials, and relationships. Learning centers encourage children to work and learn at their own pace, with materials that meet individual needs and levels of development.

Common learning centers include places for art, block play, dramatic play or housekeeping, science and discovery, music, math and manipulatives, a library and listening equipment, and an outdoor play area. In each learning center the aim is to encourage children to work independently in a safe, teacher-monitored atmosphere, on activities that are clear, stimulating, and meaningful.

Space learning centers according to their use. The art center is best placed near a sink, and the library away from water and paint, for example. Consider electricity needs, natural light, floor surfaces (absorbent rug or easy-to-clean vinyl), and storage. Make sure all furniture is child-sized and that materials for the

center are arranged attractively and within children's reach. Try to include math- and literacy-building materials into the activity of each center. For example, post maps and building plans near the block center, encourage children to sign their art work, and supply nature guides and measuring tools in the discovery center. Label learning materials and all areas of the classroom so children will learn to associate written words with information and direction.

Block center

Blocks offer children an opportunity to build representations of structures in their world. There are many kinds of blocks: unit blocks, large hollow blocks, and cardboard blocks made from recycled cardboard boxes. Each kind helps children understand size, spatial relationships, balance, and organization.

For successful construction, unit blocks should relate to each other mathematically—each block is twice as long or wide as the one preceding it in size. A properly built set of unit blocks is not inexpensive, but with proper care will be the most enduring purchase a program can make.

Locate the block center in a corner of the classroom, out of the traffic path, and preferably on a low-pile rug (to absorb sound). Placing the center near the dramatic play center encourages children in the two areas to interact. Place a low, sturdy shelf next to one wall for block storage. Outline each size of block on the shelf with paint or tape to help children evaluate the available materials—and to help with cleanup time. A cardboard box with a jumble of blocks thrown in is not inviting to children and doesn't encourage the proper care of classroom materials.

Encourage increasingly complex constructions by providing an adequate number of blocks, by scheduling long periods of play, and allowing children to leave their structures in place overnight. You may want to help them post a "Building under construction" sign. Tape a building zone on the floor to discourage accidental building collapse.

Set guidelines for safe block play. "Tear down with hands not feet." Kicking down a building is disrespectful of the materials. Limit building height to one a child can see over—"Build to your nose." Encourage children to work together to carry heavy hollow blocks.

Art center materials

- crayons
- markers
- chalk
- colored pencils
- variety of papers
- scissors
- paste
- glue
- collage materials
- brushes
- watercolor paints
- clay
- smocks
- printing stamps
- containers for materials
- display areas
- drying space for finished products
- tempera paints—liquid and dry
- play dough and sculpting tools
- woodworking bench, hammer, nails, and goggles

Art center

The art center supports children's creativity and artistic expression. Typically it contains a standing easel, a tabletop work surface, and non-toxic materials for painting, cutting, drawing, stamping, pasting, and sculpting. A box of beautiful junk—shells, ribbon, cloth scraps, colored wire, textured paper, and wallpaper samples—encourages experimentation and creative expression. Successful, child-centered art centers focus on the process of making art, not on its product. Therefore, it does not contain teacher-made patterns, models, coloring books or sheets, or materials that demand adult direction. Provide containers for different kinds of materials. Make sure children can choose materials from the art shelf, use them, and return the materials to their proper storage space.

Encourage children to investigate, but not destroy, art materials. To be a successful artist, you need to know your materials and how they work. To use scissors, for example, you need to develop small finger muscles and coordination. Help children build these skills by providing numerous opportunities for children to practice with scissors. Similarly, children need to experiment to discover how much water makes watercolor paint runny and pale and how much permits vivid color and paint control. It's this experimentation that teaches children how to be artists.

Help children develop independence and self-reliance by having art smocks available. Buy or make smocks that children can put on and take off without adult assistance. Keep a pile of old newspaper handy for protecting the floor or table during messy art activities. Show how to use a sponge or paper towel to wipe up spills rather than to smear and dribble. Less experienced artists may be confused by too many paint colors and large jugs of glue. Help them out by providing small cups or squeeze bottles for glue and limiting the colors of paint to three. As children master materials they will be able to regulate their choices of materials and methods.

Encourage children to talk about their art by asking questions like, "Tell me about your picture" rather than by making observations that may or may not be accurate. What you see as a yellow car may, in fact, be the artist's interpretation of a submarine. Remember it's the process of art, not the product, that develops skills and confidence. Avoid rushing the art process; give children time to make as many and as elaborate pieces as they want.

To save money in the art center, consider mixing powered tempera yourself rather than buying it already mixed. Make your own modeling and sculpting mixtures as well. Ask parents to donate collage materials, interesting paper, and storage containers.

Dramatic play

The dramatic play center is sometimes called the home center, the

Common dramatic play themes

- florist shop
- restaurant
- post office
- train station
- veterinarian and doctor offices
- barber shop
- astronauts and space exploration
- camping
- farming and ranching
- fire fighting
- business office
- grocery store

housekeeping center, or the home life center. Whatever the name, it is the place where children explore the activities and relationships of the real world. In it children can investigate roles—being a mommy, a doctor, or a construction worker. They build language and communication skills, practice negotiation and problem-solving, and develop literacy skills using menus, lists, messages, cookbooks, or order forms.

Dramatic play centers usually contain child-sized kitchen equipment—stove, refrigerator, and sink (either manufactured from wood or modified from large cardboard boxes), dishes, pot and pans, cooking utensils, mops, brooms, and telephone. Additionally the center usually contains dress-up clothes, dolls, a rocking chair, and standing mirror.

Prop boxes make it easy to expand the home center so that children have opportunities to explore occupations and activities. As you gather materials, remember math and literacy-building props—tickets and pretend money for the train ride or a clipboard, paper, and pencil for bird watchers, for example. Ask parents to help you gather dress-up clothes, tools, and supplies for the prop boxes.

Science center

The science center, sometimes called the discovery center, is a place where children can explore, discover, evaluate, and draw conclusions about materials. Children use their senses to explore both physical and biological science. Science is always hands-on and is never magic.

Choose a classroom location that offers natural light. If possible, place the center near an electrical outlet. Some teachers position the science center near the manipulative center so that many materials can be shared. Storage is important because you will rotate some materials and equipment. You do, however, need space for classroom pets, plants, and specifically planned activities.

The sand and water table is an important addition to the science center, though it has uses in almost every area of the classroom. Help keep children healthy by draining and sanitizing the table at the end of every day.

Music

The music center invites children to investigate sound, rhythm, movement, and song. Music appreciation begins early for children—some say before birth. Build on this natural interest with daily activities that include singing, dancing, and playing music. Typical music centers contain rhythm instruments, a record or cassette player, and a box of scarves or ribbon batons for movement activities. A piano, autoharp, or guitar will enrich the center.

The music and movement center is likely to be noisy and active. Place it where the noise and children's movement won't disturb those working in the library and discovery centers, for example. A nearby electrical outlet is important if you want to use recorded music. Store rhythm instruments on a low shelf so children are free to play music throughout the day.

Movement activities can range from singing a finger play or swaying to a recorded tune to dancing and jumping activities that involve the whole body. As you plan movement activities, consider the ways children can use their bodies to make and respond to music.

- **Arm and body movement**—swinging, clapping, reaching, stretching, waving, carrying, patting, bouncing, pounding, punching air, shaking, tugging, twirling, swimming, drooping, and swaying
- **Finger movements**—pinching, tickling, grasping, squeezing, tying, tapping, snapping, rolling, clapping, scratching, and pointing
- **Leg and foot movements**—creeping, kicking, stomping, tip-toeing, tapping heels, spinning, tapping toes, hopping, jumping, leaping, sliding, rolling ankles, bending, and standing on one foot

Movement activities help children learn directions—up, down, back, forward, above, in a circle, to the side of, in back of, between, and across. They also help reinforce vocabulary as you suggest that children move quietly, loudly, joyfully, heavily, slowly, sadly, or quickly, for example.

Singing in the classroom—whether a cleanup song before lunch or a finger play during a large group time—is an extension of the music center. In general, songs for children have the following characteristics:

- limited vocal range
- simple, meaningful, easy-to-remember words
- clear, steady rhythm
- short length
- subjects that children are familiar with

Teach new songs with your own voice—with or without an instrument—or with a recording. Your singing voice is not important—the song is what children respond to.

Manipulative center

In the manipulative center children discover mathematical concepts by working with shape, size, classifica-

Supplies for the manipulative center

- flannel board and figures
- counting pegs and boards
- geo board and rubber bands
- parquetry tiles
- plastic locking blocks
- number strips
- abacus
- egg cartons and muffin tins
- puzzles
- pretend money
- colored beads
- storage containers
- counting collections
- spinners
- dice
- stacking and nesting containers
- balance scale
- lengths of cord

tion, counting, sequence, and order. These math activities are not limited to a particular center. Instead, math experiences enrich all areas of the classroom: dividing clay, comparing the size of hamsters, setting the table for snack, and weighing the pecans found on the playground. Often, however, teachers do focus on math in the manipulative center. Here children can move, sort, combine, and compare small objects—and see mathematical relationships.

The manipulative center is easy to position in the classroom. It requires only a table and comfortable chairs for the children, and a nearby storage area. Some teachers find that providing carpet squares for manipulatives helps children confine their work, especially when they are working with materials that easily roll off the table. Check school-supply catalogs for ideas of which material to include in the center. Then develop a plan to collect or construct your own materials.

Always introduce activities in the manipulative center. Match the activity with the developmental level of the child, and then expand it as the child develops new skills. For example, stringing beads can be a simple exercise in coordination and preci-

sion—get the bead on the string. Make it a more complex activity by providing a pattern card—red-blue-yellow-red-blue-yellow—and challenge the child to match the color pattern of beads on the string to that on the card.

Managing puzzles for the manipulative center is sometimes a headache. Make organization easier by buying only the sturdiest puzzles. Wooden inlay puzzles are the most durable, but heavy cardboard and plastic inlay puzzles can also last several years with careful use. Invest in a puzzle rack that helps children take puzzles off of the shelf without a spill. Code the backs of puzzle pieces so you can easily identify which piece belongs where. An easy way to do this is to write a symbol or numeral on the back of all the puzzle pieces—all 11 pieces of the balloon puzzle have a star on the back, for example.

Library

The purpose of the library center is to help children become book lovers —eager readers who know where to turn for information and entertainment. The library center frequently includes equipment for listening to books as well as looking at them.

Place the library in a quiet corner of the classroom with good lighting. Make the space inviting by displaying books neatly and providing comfortable chairs or fluffy floor pillows for readers. Some teachers include a table for writing activities in the library center.

Teach children how to care for books. Books are for reading and don't belong scattered on the floor. Show children how to turn pages carefully, and to help you make repairs.

Practice reading books aloud to children. If you're reading to a large group, face the group and hold the book to one side of your face. Make sure all the children can see the pictures. Introduce the book by telling the children the book's title and author: "We're going to read *When Will It Be Spring* by Catherine Walters." Give a one-sentence summary of the book: "It tells about a baby bear who learns how seasons change." Read the book, pausing to answer ques-

tions or to repeat a passage. Allow time to discuss the book after you've finished reading. Ask open-ended questions about a character or action: "Why did Alfie ask his mother about the coming of spring?" Offer other activities to a child who loses interest.

Enlist the aid of parents in helping to maintain the library. Make a list of books you'd like for the classroom and post it for parents to see. Ask families to give books to the class in honor of birthdays and other celebrations. If you want children to be able to listen to a book on tape, ask parents to do the recording. Store the tape with the book—children can listen to the words and "read" along.

Materials for the outdoor classroom

- balls
- hoops
- balance beam
- ropes
- tunnels
- sand and sand toys
- dramatic play props
- ladders
- tires
- art supplies
- blocks
- puzzles
- wheel toys
  - —wagons
  - —tricycles
  - —scooters
- water
  - —hose
  - —water table or similar tub
  - —measuring containers
- garden tools
  - —child-sized shovels, rakes, trowels
  - —watering cans or hose

Outdoors

The outdoors expands the space for any learning center—yes, it's great to do art or build with blocks on the playground. But the outdoors also Loffers a unique environment for experimentation and discovery—for growing a garden, observing weather, riding wheel toys, and watching cloud movement, for example.

Give children safe opportunities for outdoor play every day. Regularly check to make sure equipment is suitably anchored, that fall zones are well cushioned, and that riding toys are in good repair. Consider dividing the playground into zones or areas designated for swinging and climbing, for wheel toys, for quiet, restful activities, and for gardening. The best playgrounds include shady areas, grass, hard tracks (for riding toys), and provision for water play, digging, rolling, running, and climbing.

Plan outdoor activities and equip playground areas as carefully as you do indoor interest centers.

Resources

Art center

Cherry, Clare. *Creative Art for the Developing Child.* Morristown, N.J.: Fearon Teaching Aids, 1972.

Schirrmacher, Robert. *Art and Creative Development for Young Children.* Albany: Delmar Publishers, 1988.

Block center

Hirsch, Elizabeth. *The Block Book.* Washington, D.C.: National Association for the Education of Young Children, 1974.

MacDonald, Sharon. *Block Play.* Beltsville, Md.: Gryphon House, 2001.

Walker, Lester. *Block Building for Children.* Woodstock, N.Y.: Overlook Press, 1995.

Science and discovery center

Holt, Bess-Gene. *Science with Young Children.* Washington, D.C.: National Association for the Education of Young Children, 1977.

Levenson, Elaine. *Teaching Children About Science.* New York: Prentice Hall, 1985.

Petrash, Carol. *Earthways.* Beltsville, Md.: Gryphon House, 1992.

Williams, Robert A., Elizabeth Sherwood and Robert Rockwell. *More Mudpies to Magnets.* Beltsville, Md.: Gryphon House, 1990.

Rockwell, Robert, Robert Williams, and Elizabeth Sherwood. *Everybody Has a Body.* Beltsville, Md.: Gryphon House, 1992.

Music

Blood-Patterson, Peter, Ed. *Rise Up Singing: 1200 Songs, Words, Chords and Sources.* Bethlehem, Pa.: Sing Out Publications, 1988.

Cherry, Claire. *Creative Movement for the Developing Child.* Morristown, N.J.: Fearon Teaching Aids, 1971.

Math and manipulatives

Copley, Juanita V. *The Young Child and Mathematics.* Washington, D.C.: National Association for the Education of Young Children, 2000.

Baratta-Lorton, Mary. *Workjobs.* Menlo Park, Calif.: Addison Wesley, 1972.

Gilbert, La Britta. *I Can Do It! I Can Do It!* Beltsville, Md.: Gryphon House, 1984.

Moomaw, Sally and Brenda Hieronymus. *More Than Counting.* St. Paul, Minn.: Redleaf Press, 1995.

Library and listening

Armington, David. *The Living Classroom: Writing, Reading, and Beyond.* Washington, D.C.: National Association for the Education of Young Children, 1997.

Jalongo, Mary Renck. *Young Children and Picture Books.* Washington, D.C.: National Association for the Education of Young Children, 1988.

Neuman, Susan, Carol Copple, and Sue Bredekamp. *Learning to Read and Write.* Washington, D.C.: National Association for the Education of Young Children, 2000.

Outdoors

Rivkin, Mary S. *The Great Outdoors.* Washington, D.C.: National Association for the Education of Young Children, 1995.

Rockwell, Robert, Elizabeth Sherwood and Robert Williams. *Hug a Tree.* Beltsville, Md.: Gryphon House, 1983.

Tilgner, Linda. *Let's Grow.* Pownal, Vt.: Storey Communications, 1988.

General environment

Houle, Georgia Bradley. *Learning Centers for Young Children.* West Greenwich, R.I.: Consortium Publishing, 1987.

Isbell, Rebecca and Betty Exelby. *Early Learning Environments that Work.* Beltsville, Md.: Gryphon House, 2001.

From *Texas Child Care*, Spring 2002, pp. 30-42. © 2002 by Texas Workforce Commission.

Improving Public Health Through Early Childhood Movement Programs

Clersida Garcia, Luis Garcia, Jerald Floyd, and John Lawson

Early childhood is a unique period of life, a time when children are developing physically, emotionally, intellectually, and socially. Providing a movement development program at this early age enables children to acquire fundamental motor skills and the feeling of competence in movement. Once in place, these skills serve as the foundation for building more complex motor skills later in life. Early development of competence in movement has the potential to create a healthy habit of physical activity participation.

While learning motor skills is rewarding in itself, it also has significant health benefits. Research has demonstrated that virtually all individuals will benefit from regular physical activity. The Surgeon General's report on physical activity and health concluded that moderate physical activity can substantially reduce the risk of developing or dying from heart disease, diabetes, colon cancer, and high blood pressure (U.S. Dept. of Health and Human Services, 1996). If more Americans were physically active, our health care expenses would be reduced and the quality of our lives would improve.

Common sense suggests that happy and successful experiences early in life predispose people to enjoy physical activity. If that is true, school administrators, early childhood educators, motor development specialists, and physical educators have a tremendous opportunity to influence the health of the next generation by providing movement program opportunities to young children.

This article discusses how movement programs can help young children develop fundamental movement patterns and healthy, active lifestyles while learning cognitive and psychosocial concepts. In addition, it describes specific techniques and approaches that educators can use to promote physical activity.

These techniques can give children positive, developmentally appropriate experiences with the ABCs of movement skills, thereby inspiring continued participation in and enjoyment of physical activity.

Public Health Goals for Physical Activity

In January 2000, the U.S. Department of Health and Human Services (USDHHS) launched Healthy People 2010, a comprehensive, nationwide health promotion and disease prevention agenda, which calls for Americans to increase their daily physical activity (USDHHS, 2000). Looking at the current level of physical activity, there is reason for great concern.

A significant portion of the United States population is sedentary. Forty percent of the adult population reported that they engaged in no leisure-time physical activity, while children and adolescents reported that they ride a bicycle on 2.4 percent of all trips two miles or less (USDHHS, 2000). As a result of our lack of exercise, too many of us are at risk for cardiovascular disease and other diseases. The problem is made worse by our being overweight and eating unhealthy diets. According to the National Center for Chronic Disease Prevention and Health Promotion (NCCDPHP, 2000), the percentage of overweight and obese children has more than doubled between 1980 and 1994, with 10 percent to 15 percent of children and adolescents being overweight. Sixty percent of five-to-ten-year-old obese children already have at least one risk factor for cardiovascular disease, and 25 percent of obese children have two or more risk factors (NCCDPHP, 2000). Young people are at particular risk for becoming sedentary as they grow older (President's Council on

Figure 1. Developmentally Appropriate Activity

In this self-paced activity, a child throws different kinds, sizes, and weights of balls while learning to place the throwing arm and stepping leg in position.

Figure 2. Integrating Other Domains

While playing "Pretending to Be Grownup People," these "firefighters" will earn play money for completing their job (negotiating obstacles) and then use the money to buy healthy food.

Figure 3. Meaningful Activity

Activities need to have a purpose that children understand. "Feeding the Animals" was a favorite.

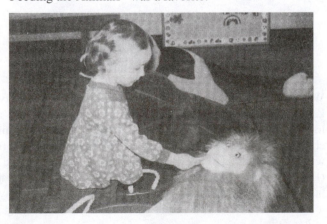

Figure 4. Hand-Eye Coordination

In another purposeful activity, "Going to Fish," children practice hand-eye coordination to connect their magnetic hook to the fish in the lake.

Figure 5. Agenda-Setting Activity

Children explore different means of transporting blood (blue bean bags represent deoxygenated blood; red bean bags represent oxygenated blood) to various body parts.

Figure 6. Creative Spontaneity

Children throw objects across a "river." Soon after, they spontaneously began to jump over the river. Activities that allow such creative spontaneity will engage children's interest longer.

Physical Fitness and Sports, 2001). Even among children aged three to four years, those who are less active tend to remain less active after the age of three than most of their peers (Pate, Baranowski, Dowda, & Trost, 1996). Viewed together, these statistics are quite alarming. Therefore, encouraging moderate and vigorous physical activity among youths seems essential.

Why are people inactive? No one knows the answers for sure. However, Barnett and Merriman (1991) have identified three misconceptions about early physical activity and motor skill development that may be partly responsible for the pattern of physical inactivity and the health problems our youth and adult populations are experiencing today.

Misconception #1: Children are "naturally" predisposed to vigorous activity. Various studies suggest that this is a false assumption and support early intervention. Cardiovascular disease has been detected among young children (NCCDPHP, 2000; Newman, Freedman, & Berenson, 1986). Furthermore, cardiovascular disease risk factors in children are increasing and have been tracked from childhood into adulthood (Nicklas, Webber, Johnson, Srinivasan, & Berenson, 1995). Today's youths are more sedentary than any previous generation. Nader, et al. (1995) found that young girls and boys between the ages of four and seven years showed similar deficiencies in physical activity at home. Not surprisingly, more children than ever have risk factors for cardiovascular and other diseases. High-tech toys and technological recreation often worsen these trends, encouraging children to sit for hours in front of the television or the computer screen rather than using their bodies. To counteract these influences, children need to be encouraged, instructed, and exposed to physical activity in order to develop the habits and dispositions to be physically active for life.

Misconception #2: Children "naturally" develop the fundamental motor skills they need through undirected play. Systematic observation of children demonstrates that they do not naturally develop fundamental motor skills. Many children never develop certain mature patterns of fundamental motor skills; as a result, they perform poorly as they get older. Furthermore, these early failures can damage the child's self-esteem, leading to statements like "I can't dance," or "I can't throw." A vicious circle may start, in which young people feel embarrassed. They know that they can't move efficiently; they feel awkward, uncoordinated, and inhibited, and therefore learn to avoid movement. Movement is no longer associated with joyful self-expression, but with failure and humiliation.

Longitudinal studies on the development of throwing (Garcia & Garcia, in press) found that this fundamental skill does not automatically mature. Most young children in this study began to perform at a mature stage of throwing after a year and a half of instruction and more than 400 trials. In other words, children need instruction, encouragement, and a lot of practice to achieve mature stages of this skill.

Misconception #3: Movement programs take away time and resources from other, more important educational activities. In fact, children's domains do not develop in isolation from one another. Cognitive, affective, social, and motor skills are interdependent. They should also be integrated in our movement curriculum designs and teaching practices. Movement pro-

Figure 7. Designing Equipment for Success

This child uses a suitable paddle: wide, light, and with a small grip. The balloon is set on a ring so it will stay in place before being hit.

All photos courtesy of the authors

grams can be more effective if they include activities that enhance cognitive, affective, and social development. At the same time, activities that develop those other domains have greater impact when they include movement and movement-related concepts (e.g., see Block, 2001; Block & Campbell, 2001). As we will suggest below, a developmental curriculum of movement activities includes all domains of development.

In conclusion, the misconceptions about physical activity and motor skill development in early childhood have had serious adverse effects on our youth and adult populations. The unique developmental opportunity offered by early childhood movement experiences is crucial to the overall health status of our youth and adult populations. We need to pay greater attention to the development of movement skills and to patterns of activity during the early childhood years. Once children develop sedentary habits, they are not likely to become more physically active as they grow to adulthood.

Designing and Developing the Preschool Movement Program

We know from common observation that there are at least two keys to developing successful movement programs: (1) allowing children to have fun with the activity, and (2) teaching children the fundamental motor skills. When children have fun with movement, they develop favorable attitudes toward it (Henderson, Glancy, & Little, 1999). An educational approach built on enjoyment helps to ensure that children will view physical activity positively, and thus will be predisposed to engage in it.

Figure 8. The Effect of Actions

Children kick plastic bottles toward targets. They said they liked the sounds the bottles made when kicked and the sounds of the bottles hitting the targets or the wall.

But having fun isn't enough. Many children have fun on the playground but never develop the basic skills they need. Thus, another key to a successful program is to teach children those basic motor skills using a developmentally and instructionally appropriate approach.

How do we design a successful early-childhood movement program? Garcia (1994) demonstrated that such programs are based on three principles:

1. Activities must be developmentally appropriate. Children's activities should accommodate a variety of individual characteristics and needs, including overall developmental status, previous movement experiences, fitness and skill level, body size, interests, and motivations. Children must be interested in the activities and have a choice—there is a great risk of destroying a positive attitude by forcing or pressuring children into performing activities they are not ready to try, or in contexts that make them uncomfortable.

Development programs provide the opportunity for active learning—learning through motion, through play, and through guided discovery. An example of this approach appears in figure 1, which shows children throwing objects of different kinds, sizes, and weights at a variety of targets. The children are allowed to make choices of distance, targets, and equipment. They pace their own activity while the teacher focuses on the opposition of the throwing arm to the stepping leg.

2. Activities should integrate and reinforce other developmental domains besides the physical domain. Physical, emotional, social and cognitive development are interrelated. Learning in one domain affects the others, and children are always striving to make connections between domains (National Association for Sport and Physical Education, 1994). Physical activities can be planned to engage children's imagination, their capacity for thinking and planning, and their ability to empathize and cooperate.

In figure 2, children are using different locomotor skills in a gamelike situation called "Pretending to be Grownup People," in which an obstacle course challenge becomes their 'job.' After they are paid for finishing their job, they go to the grocery store to buy food. In the store they use the food pyramid to make healthy choices to place in a table setting. Afterwards, the instructor talks with the children about their choices and helps them to identify the foods found in the pyramid. This is an exciting game with a lot of pretending and physical activity, and its similarity to life events enables children to transfer and relate the information to their real life.

3. Activities should have contextual reinforcement. A well-planned movement curriculum can fill children with enthusiasm for physical activity, but those children must receive encouragement to use their physical skills elsewhere—in the home, in other classes, and among their peers. Teachers and program administrators can help to make sure their students receive that kind of encouragement by communicating with other teachers, parents, and the community at large. They can also include incentives for children to use their skills outside of class as a part of their curriculum.

Activities should occur in environments similar to those that children experience daily. By building associations between those environments and pleasurable physical activities, teachers increase the likelihood that children will continue to engage in movement on their own.

Research has shown that children continue to participate in physical activity when movement activities are meaningful to the children themselves (Garcia, 1994). The movements must have a purpose that children can understand. For instance, when asked which of several activities they liked best, children typically responded that they liked "feeding the animals" (figure 3). This was an activity in which they moved back and forth using different locomotor skills to get food and feed stuffed animals. They also liked it "when the activity kept going," as it did in the grocery store activity, in which they bought one food item and set the table each time. Both of these are activities in which the children repeatedly go around obstacle courses.

Obstacle courses are a favorite of children, especially when the course provides personal excitement, such as crawling through a "tunnel." Other examples of "purposeful" activities include "delivering mail," "visiting the zoo," and "going to fish" (figure 4). Children perform locomotor activities and utilize arm and leg strength to get into the lake before "going to fish." During the fishing action (connecting the end of the fish pole to the magnet on the fish), children practice hand-eye coordination skills. These activities include locomotor activities that relate to things the children can do in the course of their daily life outside school. All these activities have strong associations across the developmental spectrum, from physical to cognitive.

In addition, Garcia (1994) has shown that children continue to participate when activities include prompts or situations that allow them to develop their own agenda. Such situations typically lead to discoveries or exercise of the imagination. One agenda-setting activity (figure 5) allowed children to explore different ways of transporting blood (beanbags) to different body parts and organs.

Several pictures of the body parts were posted for guidance and motivation. All children were willing to move around to bring blood to all the body parts. Another activity provided children with pieces of small equipment (ropes, ribbons, hoops) and encouraged them to use those items in creative forms of activity.

Teachers facilitated and guided the children, posing questions and appropriate challenges. Children responded with a variety of movements. After the activity, children's typical comments included: "I played with the rope, and pretended it was a snake," "I used the rope as my choo-choo train," and "I like to turn it over my head." Another agenda-setting activity asked children to imagine that they were throwing things over a "river." Soon, children were jumping into the imaginary river, just as they might if they really were playing on a riverbank. When movement activities allow for creative spontaneity and adaptation of this kind, children remain engaged in them longer (figure 6).

Garcia (1994) found that children continue activities when they experience success in the task at hand. Success is more likely if physical activities are designed and equipment is adjusted to correspond with children's individual skill levels. In figure 7, the size and weight of the ball and racquet conform with the child's individual skill level and success rate.

When success rates are high, children try their best virtually every time. When asked why they repeated certain actions many times, children's responses included: "I like when I hit the clown and he goes down and goes up again—it's funny;" "I like kicking the shaker bottles," and "I like the sound they make" (figure 8). They like to see the impact of their actions. This reinforces the notion that children like to exert control over the situation. When they are able to influence the situation, children tend to balance their challenges and successes in ways that keep them engaged and ensure a positive experience.

By applying the principles illustrated in this section, movement education programs can help children master fundamental motor skills. Equally important, they can help children develop positive associations with activity that will predispose them favorably toward physical activity in other areas of their lives. These are prerequisites of a lifetime of healthful and joyful physical activity.

References

Barnett, B. & Merriman, W. (1991). Misconceptions in motor developments. *Strategies, 5*(3), 5–7.

Block, B. A. (2001). Literacy through movement: An organizational approach. *Journal of Physical Education, Recreation & Dance, 72*(1), 39–48.

Block, B. A., & Campbell, E. F. (2001). Reinforcing literacy through movement for children with hearing disabilities. *Journal of Physical Education, Recreation & Dance, 72*(7), 30–36.

Garcia, C. (1994). Motivating fundamental motor skills learning in preschool children. *Journal of Sport and Exercise Psychology, 16*(Suppl. 94), S55.

Garcia, C., & Garcia, L. (in press). Examining developmental changes in throwing: A close up look. *Motor Development Research & Reviews*.

Henderson, K., Glancy, M., & Little, S. (1999). Putting the fun into physical activity. *Journal of Physical Education, Recreation & Dance, 70*(8), 43–45, 49.

Nader, P. R., Sallis, J. F., Broyles, S. L., McKenzie, T. L., Berry, C. C., Davis, T. B., Zive, M. M., Elder, J. P., & FrankSpohrer, C. C. (1995). Ethnic and gender trends for cardiovascular risk behaviors in Anglo and Mexican-American children, ages four to seven. *Journal of Health Education, 26*(2, Suppl.), S27–35.

National Association for Sport and Physical Education. (1994). Developmentally appropriate practices in movement programs for young children. Reston, VA: Author.

National Center for Chronic Disease Prevention and Health Promotion. (2000). Preventing obesity among children. *Chronic disease notes and reports, 13*(1), 1–4.

Newman, W. O., Freedman, D. S., & Berenson, G. (1986). Regulation of serum lipoprotein levels and systolic blood pressure to early atherosclerosis. The Bogalusa Heart Study. *New England Journal of Medicine, 314,* 138–144.

Nicklas, T. A., Webber, L. S., Johnson, C. C., Srinivasan, S. R., & Berenson, G. S., (1995). Foundations for health promotion with youth: A review of observations from the Bogalusa Heart Study. *Journal of Health Education, 26*(2, Suppl.), S18–26.

Pate, R. R., Baranowski, T., Dowda, M., & Trost, S. G., (1996). Tracking of physical activity in young children. *Medicine and Science in Sports and Exercise, 28*(1), 92–96.

President's Council on Physical Fitness and Sports. (2001). Healthy people 2010: Physical activity and fitness. *Research Digest*, Series 3, No. 13.

U.S. Department of Health and Human Services. (2000). *Healthy People 2010.* Washington, DC: Author.

U.S. Department of Health and Human Services. (1996). *Physical activity and health: A report of the Surgeon General.* Atlanta, GA: Centers for Disease Control and Prevention.

Clersida Garcia is an associate professor, Luis Garcia is an assistant professor, and Jerald Floyd is a professor emeritus of the Department of Kinesiology & Physical Education at Northern Illinois University, DeKalb, IL, 60115. John Lawson is an assistant professor of communications at Robert Morris College, Pittsburgh, PA, 15108.

Reprinted with permission from the January 2002 issue of *Journal of Physical Education, Recreation & Dance*, pp. 27-31, 53, a publication of the American Alliance for Health, Physical Education, Recreation and Dance, 1900 Association Dr., Reston, VA 20191, www.aapherd.org.

THE ESSENTIALS OF EARLY LITERACY INSTRUCTION

Kathleen A. Roskos, James F. Christie, and Donald J. Richgels

The cumulative and growing research on literacy development in young children is rapidly becoming a body of knowledge that can serve as the basis for the everyday practice of early literacy education (IRA & NAEYC 1998; National Research Council 1998; Yaden, Rowe, & MacGillivary 2000; Neuman & Dickinson 2001; NAEYC & NAECS/SDE 2002). Although preliminary, the knowledge base outlines children's developmental patterns in critical areas, such as phonological and print awareness. It serves as a resource for designing early literacy programs and specific instructional practices. In addition, it offers reliable and valid observational data for grounding approaches to early reading assessment.

That we know more about literacy development and acquisition, however, does not let us escape a central issue of all early education: What *should* young children be learning and doing before they go to kindergarten? What early literacy instruction should children receive? What should it emphasize—head (cognition) or heart (motivation) or both?

Real-life answers to these questions rarely point directly to this or that, but rather they are somewhere in the middle, including both empirical evidence and professional wisdom. While we will continue to wrestle with these complicated questions, we must take practical action so that our growing understanding in early literacy supports the young child as a wholesome, developing person.

What then are the essentials of early literacy instruction? What content should be included, and how should it be taught in early education settings? Our first response to these complex questions is described below in a skeletal framework for action. We briefly define early literacy, so as to identify what young children need to know and be able to do if they are to enjoy the fruits of literacy, including valuable dispositions that strengthen their literacy interactions. Then we describe two examples of instruction that support children's reading and writing learning before they enter the primary grades.

With the imagery of Pip's remark from *Great Expectations* in mind, we hope to show that well-considered early literacy instruction is certainly not a bramble-bush for our very young children, but rather a welcoming environment in which to learn to read and write.

THE LEARNING DOMAIN

Today a variety of terms are used to refer to the preschool phase of literacy development—emerging literacy, emergent reading, emergent writing, early reading, symbolic tools, and so on. We have adopted the term *early literacy* as the most comprehensive yet concise description of the knowledge, skills, and dispositions that precede learning to read and write in the primary grades (K–3). We chose this term because, in the earliest phases of literacy development, forming reading and writing concepts and skills is a dynamic process (National Research Council 1998, 2000).

Young children's grasp of print as a tool for making meaning and as a way to communicate combines both oral and written language. Children draw and scribble and "read" their marks by attributing meaning to them through their talk and action. They listen to stories read aloud and learn how to orient their bodies and minds to the technicalities of books and print.

When adults say, "Here, help me hold the book and turn the pages," they teach children basic conventions of book handling and the left-to-right, top-to-bottom orientation of English. When they guide children's small hands and eyes to printed words on the page, they show them that this is the source of the reading and that the marks have meaning. When they explain, "This says 'goldfish'. Do you remember our goldfish? We named it Baby Flipper. We put its name on the fishbowl," they help children understand the connection between printed words, speech, and real experience.

Children's early reading and writing learning, in other words, is embedded in a larger developing system of oral communication. Early literacy is an emerging set of relationships between reading and writing. These relationships are situated in a broader communication network of speaking and listening, whose components work together to help the learner negotiate the world and make sense of experience (Thelen & Smith 1995; Lewis 2000; Siegler 2000). Young children need

Essential Early Literacy Teaching Strategies

Effective early literacy instruction provides preschool children with developmentally appropriate settings, materials, experiences, and social support that encourage early forms of reading and writing to flourish and develop into conventional literacy. These basics can be broken down into eight specific strategies with strong research links to early literacy skills and, in some cases, with later elementary-grade reading achievement. Note that play has a prominent role in strategies 5, 6, and 8. Linking literacy and play is one of the most effective ways to make literacy activities meaningful and enjoyable for children.

1. Rich teacher talk

Engage children in rich conversations in large group, small group, and one-to-one settings. When talking with children,

- use rare words—words that children are unlikely to encounter in everyday conversations;
- extend children's comments into more descriptive, grammatically mature statements;
- discuss cognitively challenging content—topics that are not immediately present, that involve knowledge about the world, or that encourage children to reflect on language as an object;
- listen and respond to what children have to say.

2. Storybook reading

Read aloud to your class once or twice a day, exposing children to numerous enjoyable stories, poems, and information books. Provide supportive conversations and activities before, during, and after reading. Repeated reading of favorite books builds familiarity, increasing the likelihood that children will attempt to read those books on their own.

3. Phonological awareness activities

Provide activities that increase children's awareness of the sounds of language. These activities include playing games and listening to stories, poems, and songs that involve
rhyme—identifying words that end with the same sound (e.g., Jack and Jill went up the hill);
alliteration—recognizing when several words begin with the same sound (e.g., Peter Piper picked a peck of pickled peppers);
sound matching—deciding which of several words begins with a specific sound (e.g., show a child pictures of a bird, a dog, and a cat and ask which one starts with the /d/ sound).
Try to make these activities fun and enjoyable.

4. Alphabet activities

Engage children with materials that promote identification of the letters of the alphabet, including

- ABC books
- magnetic letters
- alphabet blocks and puzzles
- alphabet charts

Use direct instruction to teach letter names that have personal meaning to children ("Look, Jennifer's and Joey's names both start with the same letter. What is the letter's name? That's right, they both start with j").

5. Support for emergent reading

Encourage children to attempt to read books and other types of print by providing

- a well-designed library center, stocked with lots of good books;
- repeated readings of favorite books (to familiarize children with books and encourage independent reading);
- functional print linked to class activities (e.g., daily schedules, helper charts, toy shelf labels);
- play-related print (e.g., signs, menus, employee name tags in a restaurant play center).

6. Support for emergent writing

Encourage children to use emergent forms of writing, such as scribble writing, random letter strings, and invented spelling, by providing

- a writing center stocked with pens, pencils, markers, paper, and book-making materials;
- shared writing demonstrations in which the teacher writes down text dictated by children;
- functional writing opportunities that are connected to class activities (e.g., sign-up sheets for popular centers, library book check-out slips, Do not touch! signs);
- play-related writing materials (e.g., pencils and notepads for taking orders in a restaurant play center).

7. Shared book experience

Read Big Books and other enlarged texts to children, and point to the print as it is read. While introducing and reading the text, draw children's attention to basic concepts of print such as

- the distinction between pictures and print;
- left-to-right, top-to-bottom sequence;
- book concepts (cover, title, page).

Read favorite stories repeatedly, and encourage children to read along on the parts of the story they remember.

8. Integrated, content-focused activities

Provide opportunities for children to investigate topics that are of interest to them. The objective is for children to use oral language, reading, and writing to learn about the world. Once a topic has been identified, children can

- listen to the teacher read topic-related information books and look at the books on their own;
- gather data using observation, experiments, interviews, and such;
- use emergent writing to record observations and information; and
- engage in dramatic play to consolidate and express what they have learned.

As a result of such projects, children's language and literacy skills are advanced, and they gain valuable background knowledge.

writing to help them learn about reading, they need reading to help them learn about writing; and they need oral language to help them learn about both.

What early literacy instruction should children receive? What should it emphasize—head (cognition) or heart (motivation) or both?

Young children need writing to help them learn about reading, they need reading to help them learn about writing; and they need oral language to help them learn about both.

NECESSARY CONTENT AND DISPOSITIONS IN EARLY LITERACY

Early literacy holds much that young children might learn. Yet we cannot teach everything and must make choices about what content to teach and which dispositions to encourage. High-quality research provides our best evidence for setting priorities for what to address and how.

Recent reviews of research indicate at least three critical content categories in early literacy: oral language comprehension, phonological awareness, and print knowledge. They also identify at least one important disposition, print motivation—the frequency of requests for shared reading and engagement in print-related activities, such as pretend writing (Senechal et al. 2001; Layzer 2002; Neuman 2002; Lonigan & Whitehurst in press).

Children need to learn mainstay concepts and skills of written language from which more complex and elaborated understandings and motivations arise, such as grasp of the alphabetic principle, recognition of basic text structures, sense of genre, and a strong desire to know. They need to learn phonological awareness, alphabet letter knowledge, the functions of written language, a sense of meaning making from texts, vocabulary, rudimentary print knowledge (e.g., developmental spelling), and the sheer persistence to investigate print as a meaning-making tool.

Content of Early Literacy Instruction

Teaching preschool children

- what reading and writing can do
- to name and write alphabet letters
- to hear rhymes and sounds in words
- to spell simple words
- to recognize and write their own names
- new words from stories, work, and play
- to listen to stories for meaning

Valuable Dispositions of Early Literacy Instruction

Cultivating preschool children's

- willingness to listen to stories
- desire to be read to
- curiosity about words and letters
- exploration of print forms
- playfulness with words
- enjoyment of songs, poems, rhymes, jingles, books, and dramatic play

---

WRITTEN LANGUAGE IS HARDER TO LEARN THAN ORAL

Learning an alphabetic writing system requires extra work. Both spoken and written language are symbol systems for representing and retrieving meanings. In spoken language, meaning making depends on phonemes or sounds. As children gain experience with the language of their community, they learn which words (or sequences of phonemes) stand for which concepts in that language. For example, children learn that the spoken word *table* in English or *mesa* in Spanish names a four-legged, flat-topped piece of furniture.

Writing and reading with an alphabetic system involve an extra layer of symbols, where the phonemes are represented by letters. This means that beginners must both learn the extra symbols—the letters of the alphabet—and raise their consciousness of the phonemes (because, while speaking and understanding speech, we unconsciously sequence and contrast phonemes).

Speakers, for example, understand the two very different concepts named by the words *nail* and *lane* without consciously noticing that those words are constructed from the same three phonemes (/n/, /A/, and /l/), but in different sequences. When children learn to read, however, they must pay attention to those three phonemes, how they are sequenced, and what letters represent them.

Invented spelling is a phonemic awareness activity that has the added advantage of being meaningful and functional (Richgels 2001). Children nonconventionally but systematically match sounds in words that they want to write with letters that they know. For example, they may use letter names and sounds in letter names (/ch/ in H, /A/ as the name of the letter A, and /r/ in R) when spelling *chair* as HAR. Invented spelling begins before children's phonemic awareness is completely developed and before they know all the names of the letters of the alphabet. With encouragement from adults, it develops through stages that culminate in conventional spelling.

The meanings of both spoken and written language serve real purposes in our daily lives (Halliday

1975). We usually do not speak without wanting to accomplish something useful. For example, we might want to influence others' behavior ("Would you turn that down, please?"), express our feelings ("I hate loud music"), or convey information ("Habitual listening to loud music is a danger to one's hearing"). Similarly, with written messages we can influence behavior (NO SMOKING), express feelings (I ❤ NY), and inform (Boston 24 mi) while serving such added purposes as communicating across distances or preserving a message as a record or a reminder.

These added purposes require that written messages be able to stand on their own (Olson 1977). Written language is decontextualized; that is, the sender and receiver of a written communication usually do not share the same time and space. The writer is not present to clarify and extend his or her message for the reader. This means that young readers' and writers' extra work includes, in addition to dealing with phonemes and letters, dealing with decontextualization.

WHY DO THE EXTRA WORK?

Historically, societies have found the extra work of writing and reading to be worthwhile. The extra functions of written language, especially preserving messages and communicating across distances, have enabled a tremendous growth of knowledge. Individual children can experience similar benefits if teachers help them to acquire the knowledge and skill involved in the extra work of reading and writing while always making real to them the extra purposes that written language serves. We must cultivate their dispositions (curiosity, desire, play) to actively seek, explore, and use books and print. As they learn what letters look like and how they match up with phonemes, which strings of letters represent which words, and how to represent their meanings in print and retrieve others' meanings from print, they

must see also how the fruits of those labors empower them by multiplying the functionality of language.

With speech, children can influence the behavior of others, express their feelings, and convey information. A big part of motivating them to take on the extra work of reading and writing must be letting them see how the permanence and portability of writing can widen the scope of that influencing, expressing, and informing. Young children who can say "No! Don't!" experience the power of spoken words to influence what others do or don't do—but only when the speakers are present. Being able to write *No* extends the exercise of that power to situations in which they are not present, as morning kindergartners Eric, Jeff, Zack, and Ben realized when they wrote NOStPN (No stepping) to keep afternoon kindergartners from disturbing a large dinosaur puzzle they had assembled on the classroom floor (McGee & Richgels 2000, 233–34).

W ritten language is decontextualized; that is, the sender and receiver of a written communication usually do not share the same time and space.

THE PRACTICE OF EARLY LITERACY INSTRUCTION: TWO EXAMPLES

Unlike the very real and immediate sounds and meanings of talk, print is silent; it is obscure; it is not of the here and now. Consequently, early literacy instruction must often be explicit and direct, which is not to say that it must be scriptlike, prescriptive, and rigid (Schickedanz 2003). Rather it should be embedded in the basic activities of early learning long embraced by early education practice and research. These include reading aloud, circle time, small

group activities, adult-child conversations, and play.

Teachers can embed reading and writing instruction in familiar activities, to help children learn both the conventions of print and how print supports their immediate goals and needs. The two examples below show how what's new about early literacy instruction fits within tried-and-true early education practice.

INTERACTIVE STORYBOOK READING

Reading aloud has maximum learning potential when children have opportunities to actively participate and respond (Morrow & Gambrell 2001). This requires teachers to use three types of scaffolding or support: (a) before-reading activities that arouse children's interest and curiosity in the book about to be read; (b) during-reading prompts and questions that keep children actively engaged with the text being read; and (c) after-reading questions and activities that give children an opportunity to discuss and respond to the books that have been read.

Instruction can be easily integrated into any of these three phases of story reading. This highly contextualized instruction should be guided by children's literacy learning needs and by the nature of the book being read:

- information books, such as Byron Barton's *Airport*, can teach children new vocabulary and concepts;
- books, songs, and poems with strong rhymes, such as Raffi's *Down by the Bay*, promote phonological awareness; and
- stories with strong narrative plots, such as *There's an Alligator under My Bed*, by Mercer Mayer, are ideal for generating predictions and acquainting children with narrative structure, both of which lay a foundation for reading comprehension.

In addition, most books can be used to teach print recognition, book

Shared Reading to Learn about Story Plot

Here is how one teacher reads *There's an Alligator under My Bed*, by Mercer Mayer, to a group of four-year-olds.

Before reading. The teacher begins by saying, "Let's look at the picture on the cover of the book. [Shows a boy in bed with an alligator sticking out from beneath] The boy in this story has a *big* problem. Can anyone guess what that problem is?"

After the children make their guesses, the teacher points to the title and says, "The title of this book is *There's an Alligator under My Bed*. So Suzy and Joey were correct in guessing what the boy's problem is. How do you think the boy will get rid of the alligator?"

After several children share their predictions, the teacher begins reading the book aloud.

During reading. After reading the first section of the book, which introduces the boy's problem, the teacher pauses and asks, "Do you have any other ideas about how the boy might get rid of the alligator?"

The teacher reads the next two pages, which detail the boy's plan to leave a trail of bait to the garage, and then pauses to ask the children what the word bait means.

After reading the next section, in which the boy lays out a trail of food, the teacher asks, "What do you think the alligator is going to do?"

Finally, after reading the rest of the story, in which the alligator gets trapped in the garage, the teacher points to the note the boy left on the door to the garage and asks, "What do you think the boy wrote in his note?"

After reading. The teacher sparks a discussion of the book by asking several open-ended questions, such as "What did you like best about the story?" and "How would *you* have gotten rid of that alligator?"

Later, the teacher does a follow-up small group activity—to reinforce a sense of story plot, she helps children sequence a few pictures of the main story events.

---

concepts (e.g., cover, page), and concepts of print (e.g., print vs. pictures). Of course, instruction should be limited to several brief teaching points per reading so children can enjoy the read-aloud experience. Enjoyment and building positive dispositions should always be given high priority when reading aloud. For an example of how a teacher might do an interactive story reading session with *There's an Alligator under My Bed*, see "Shared Reading to Learn about Story Plot."

LITERACY IN PLAY

The general benefits of play for children's literacy development are well documented, showing that a literacy-enriched play environment exposes children to valuable print experiences and lets them practice narrative skills (Christie & Roskos 2003). In the following example, two preschoolers are playing in a restaurant activity center equipped with wall signs (Springville Restaurant), menus, pencils, and a notepad:

Food server: Can I take your order?

Customer: [Looks over the menu] Let's see, I'd like some cereal. And how about some orange juice. And how about the coffee with that too.

Food server: We don't have coffee. We're all runned out.

Customer: Okay, well . . . I'll just take orange juice.

Food server: [Writes down order, using scribble writing] Okay. I'll be right back with your order. (Roskos et al. 1995)

Here, the customer is using the literacy routine of looking at a menu and then placing an order. If the menu is familiar and contains picture cues, some emergent reading might also be taking place. The food server is using another routine—writing down customer orders—and is practicing emergent writing. In addition, the children have constructed a simple narrative story, complete with a problem (an item is not available) and a resolution (drop that item from the order).

A Vygotskian approach to developing mature dramatic play also illustrates the value of tangible play plans for helping children to self-regulate their behaviors, to remember on purpose, and to deliberately focus their attention on play activity—foundational cognitive skills of reading and writing (Bodrova & Leong 1998). We have found that preschoolers often spend more time preparing for their dramatizations than they spend acting out the stories. For example, one group of four-

year-olds spent more than 30 minutes preparing for a pizza parlor story (organizing felt pizza ingredients, arranging furniture for the pizza kitchen, making play money, and deciding on roles) and less than 10 minutes acting out the cooking, serving, and eating of the pizza meal. One would be hard pressed to find another type of activity that can keep young children focused and "on task" for this length of time.

Specific to early literacy, descriptive research shows that a literacy-in-play strategy is effective in increasing the range and amount of literacy behaviors during play, thus allowing children to practice their emerging skills and show what they have learned (Neuman & Roskos 1992). Evidence is also accumulating that this strategy helps children learn important literacy concepts and skills, such as knowledge about the functions of writing (Vukelich 1993), the ability to recognize play-related print (Neuman & Roskos 1993), and comprehension strategies such as self-checking and self-correction (Neuman & Roskos 1997). Like storybook reading, the literacy learning potential of play can be increased when it includes before, during, and after types of scaffolding as illustrated in "Guided Play to Explore New Words and Their Sounds."

Guided Play to Explore New Words and Their Sounds

With the teacher's help, the children are creating a gas station/garage play center as part of an ongoing unit on transportation.

Before play. The teacher provides background knowledge by reading *Sylvia's Garage*, by Debra Lee, an information book about a woman mechanic. She discusses new words, such as *mechanic, engine, dipstick, oil*.

Next, the teacher helps the children plan the play center. She asks children about the roles they can play (e.g., gas station attendant, mechanic, customer) and records their ideas on a piece of chart paper. She then asks the children to brainstorm some props that they could use in their center (e.g., signs, cardboard gas pump, oil can, tire pressure gauge) and jots these down on another piece of chart paper. The children then decide which props they will make in class and which will be brought from home, and the teacher or a child places an *m* after each make-in-class item and an *h* after each from home item.

During the next several days, the teacher helps the children construct some of the make-in-class props, such as a sign for the gas station ("Let's see…*gas* starts with a *g*. Gary, your name also starts with a *g*. Can you show us how to write a *g*?").

The list of props from home is included in the classroom newsletter and sent to families.

During play. The teacher first observes the children at play to learn about their current play interests and activities. Then she provides scaffolding that extends and enriches children's play and at the same time teaches important literacy skills. She notices, for example, that the mechanics are not writing out service orders or bills for the customers, so she takes on a role as an assistant mechanic and models how to write out a bill for fixing a customer's car. She monitors her involvement to ensure close alignment with children's ongoing activity.

After play. During small group activity time, the teacher helps children with a picture-sort that includes pictures of people and objects from their garage play. They sort the pictures into labeled columns according to beginning sounds—/m/ *(mechanic, man, map, motor)*; /t/ *(tire, tank, top, taillight)*; and /g/ *(gas, gallon, garden, goat)*. They explore the different feel of these sounds in the different parts of their mouths. They think of other words they know that feel the same way.

After modeling, the teacher gives the children a small deck of picture cards to sort, providing direct supervision and feedback.

CLOSING

We are gaining empirical ground in understanding early literacy learning well enough to identify essential content that belongs in an early childhood curriculum. Increasingly, the field can articulate key concepts and skills that are significant and foundational, necessary for literacy development and growth, research-based, and motivational to arouse and engage children's minds. The need to broadly distribute this knowledge is great—but the need to act on it consistently and carefully in instructional practice is even greater, especially if we are to steer children clear of the bramble-bushes and on to be successful readers and writers.

REFERENCES

Bodrova, E., & D. Leong. 1998. Development of dramatic play in young children and its effects on self-regulation: The Vygotskian approach. *Journal of Early Childhood Teacher Education* 19 (2): 115–24.

Christie, J., & K. Roskos. 2003. Literacy in play. In *Literacy in America: An encyclopedia of history, theory and practice*, ed. B. Guzzetti, 318–23. Denver, CO: ABC-CLIO.

Halliday, M.A.K. 1975. *Learning how to mean*. New York: Elsevier.

IRA & NAEYC. 1998. Joint Position Statement. Learning to read and write: Developmentally appropriate practices for young children. *Young Children* 53 (4): 30–46. Online (overview): www.naeyc.org/resources/position_statements/psread0.htm

Layzer, C. 2002. Adding ABCs to apple juice, blocks and circle time. Paper presented at the conference, Assessing Instructional Practices in Early Literacy and Numeracy, September, in Cambridge, Massachusetts.

Lewis, M. 2000. The promise of dynamic systems approaches for an integrated account of human development. *Child Development* 71: 36–43.

Lonigan, C., & G. Whitehurst. In press. Getting ready to read: Emergent literacy and family literacy. In "Family literacy programs: Current status and future directions," ed. B. Wasik. New York: Guilford.

McGee, L.M., & D.J. Richgels. 2000. *Literacy's beginnings: Supporting young readers and writers*. 3d ed. Needham, MA: Allyn & Bacon.

Morrow, L., & L. Gambrell. 2001. Literature-based instruction in the early years. In *Handbook of early literacy research*, eds. S. Neuman & D. Dickinson, 348–60. New York: Guilford.

NAEYC & NAECS/SDE (National Association of Early Childhood Specialists in State Departments of Education). 2002. Joint Position Statement. Early learning standards: Creating the conditions for success. Online: naeyc.org/resources/position_statements/earlylearn.pdf

National Research Council. 1998. *Preventing reading difficulties in young children*. Washington, DC: National Academy Press.

National Research Council. 2000. *From neurons to neighborhoods: The science of early childhood development*. Washington, DC: National Academy Press.

Neuman, S.B. 2002. What research reveals: Foundations for reading instruction in preschool and primary education. Handout of the U.S. Department of Education's Early Educator Academy, 14–15 November, in Los Angeles.

Neuman, S.B., & D. Dickinson, eds. 2001. *The handbook of early literacy research*. New York: Guilford.

Neuman, S.B., & K. Roskos. 1992. Literacy objects as cultural tools: Effects on children's literacy behaviors in play. *Reading Research Quarterly* 27 (3): 202–35.

Neuman, S.B., & K. Roskos. 1993. Access to print for children of poverty: Differential effects of adult mediation and literacy-enriched play settings on environmental and functional print tasks, *American Educational Research Journal* 30 (91): 95–122.

Neuman, S.B., & K. Roskos. 1997. Literacy knowledge in practice: Contexts of participation for young writers and readers. *Reading Research Quarterly* 32 (1): 10–33.

Olson, D.R. 1977. From utterance to text: The bias of language in speech and writing. *Harvard Educational Review* (47): 257–81.

Richgels, D.J. 2001. Invented spelling, phonemic awareness, and reading and writing instruction. In *Handbook of early literacy research*, eds. S.B. Neuman & D. Dickinson, 142–55. New York: Guilford.

Roskos, K., C. Vukelich, J. Christie, B. Enz, & S. Neuman. 1995. Linking literacy and play. Videotape (12 min.) and facilitator's guide. International Reading Association.

Schickedanz. J. 2003. Engaging preschoolers in code learning. *In Literacy and young children*, eds. D. Barone & L.

Morrow, 121–39. Newark, DE: International Reading Association.

Senechal. M., J. LeFevre, K.V. Colton, & B.L. Smith. 2000. On refining theoretical models of emergent literacy. *Journal of School Psychology* 39 (5): 439–60.

Siegler, R. 2000. The rebirth of children's learning. *Child Development* 71 (1): 26–35.

Thelen, E., & L.B. Smith. 1995. *A dynamic systems approach to the development of cognition and action.* Cambridge, MA: The MIT Press.

Vukelich, C. 1993. Play: A context for exploring the functions, features, and meaning of writing with peers. *Language Arts* 70: 386–92.

Yaden, D., D. Rowe, & L. MacGillivary. 2000. Emergent literacy: A matter (polophony) of perspectives. In *The handbook of reading research*, vol. 3, eds. M. Kamil, P.B. Mosenthal, P.D. Pearson, & R. Barr, 425–54. Mahwah, NJ: Erlbaum.

Kathleen A. Roskos, Ph.D., is the director of the Ohio Literacy Initiative at the Ohio Department of Education and is a professor at John Carroll University in Cleveland. She coordinated Bridges and Links, one of the first public preschools in Ohio, and is instrumental in the development of content guidelines in early literacy. Kathleen studies early literacy development, teacher cognition, and the design of professional education for teachers.

James F. Christie, Ph.D., is a professor of curriculum and instruction at Arizona State University in Tempe, where he teaches courses in language, literacy, and early childhood education. His research interests include children's play and early literacy development. James is the president of the Association for the Study of Play.

Donald J. Richgels, Ph.D., is a professor in the literacy education department at Northern Illinois University in DeKalb, where he teaches graduate and undergraduate courses in language development, reading, and language arts.

Beyond the Journal. This article also appears on NAEYC's Website: www.naeyc.org.

Illustrations © Diane Greenseid.

The Right Way to Read

In the old days, preschoolers had no more pressing business than to learn how to play. New research shows that they benefit from instruction in words and sounds.

BY BARBARA KANTROWITZ AND PAT WINGERT

WHEN YOU WALK THROUGH THE brightly colored door of the Roseville Cooperative Preschool in northern California, you're entering a magical, pint-size world where 3- and 4-year-olds are masters of the universe. At the science table, they use magnifying glasses to explore piles of flowers, cacti and shells. In the smock-optional art area, budding da Vincis often smear blotches of red, blue and yellow directly on the table. (It's wiped off with a damp cloth when the next artist steps up.) There are ropes for climbing and two loft areas: one carpeted and filled with books and a dollhouse, and the other with a clear Plexiglas floor, perfect for keeping an eye on the activities below. There are no letters or numbers on the walls to distract from this focused play. The only rule, says director and founder Bev Bos, is that the kids

are in control. "I tell other teachers, 'Forget about kindergarten, first grade, second grade'," she says. "We should be focusing on where children are right now."

THE NEW THINKING: Without early, explicit instruction in the relationship between letters and sounds, a significant number of young children may be at risk for serious reading problems throughout their lives

Sounds like an idyllic preschool learning environment, right? Wrong, according to a growing number of early-education researchers. Until quite recently, Bev Bos's

philosophy was the standard at preschools around the country, and there are still lots of teachers who passionately defend the idea that they should be helping kids feel secure and learn to play well with others, not learn the three Rs. But researchers now say the old approach ignores mounting evidence that many preschoolers need explicit instruction in the basics of literacy—the stuff most of us started to learn in first grade, how words fall on a page and the specific sounds and letters that make up words. New brain research shows that reading is part of a complex continuum that begins with baby talk and scribbles, and culminates in a child with a rich vocabulary and knowledge of the world. While some children acquire the literacy skills they need by osmosis, through their everyday experiences, many don't. Most at risk are children of poverty, who are twice as likely to have serious trouble reading. But studies have also shown that at least 20 percent of middle-class children have reading disabilities and that early intervention could save many of them from a lifetime of playing catch-up.

Earlier this month the increasingly fractious schoolyard brawl—between old-style educators who fear kids will be pushed to read and the new guard who fear they won't be pushed enough—became even more heated when President George W. Bush rolled out his early-childhood-education plan. Bush put himself squarely in the early-reading camp when he proposed retraining all 50,000 Head Start teachers in the most effective ways to provide explicit instruction in the alphabet, letter sounds and writing—whether through responsive reading to kids, early writing experiences or carefully designed group projects. He also wants Head Start to use a detailed literacy-screening test and asked for an unprecedented $45 million for preschool-reading research. Bush's domestic-policy adviser, Margaret Spellings, says preschool teachers shouldn't be afraid of these changes. "This is not about putting little kids in desks at age 3," Spellings says. "This is about doing things right from the beginning of life. It's the social-emotional *plus* the cognitive."

HEAD START'S WAY:
Youngsters growing up in low-income neighborhoods are the most likely to have reading problems, but they may also need extra help with social-emotional development and health care

That hasn't reassured many preschool teachers, nor the National Head Start Association, which has vigorously attacked the Bush plan. "There's far more to children's development than just reading," says Cynthia Cummings, executive director of Community Parents Inc., a Head Start program in the Bedford-Stuyvesant section of Brooklyn. "We have children who come in who are not potty trained, who don't know how to sit down in a chair, who have difficulty following a routine, who may have some other types of delays that will affect their language. You have to address those." This holistic approach could get a boost this week, when

Sen. Ted Kennedy, a longtime supporter of Head Start, is expected to introduce legislation that would create a comprehensive early child-care system, with reading readiness—the main focus of the Bush plan—as just one component.

Both sides in this debate agree that young children learn best when their five senses are engaged, when teachers and parents provide hands-on ways to master important language skills. But teachers like Bev Bos worry that making the ABCs a top priority will mean "drill and kill" instead of rich language experiences. "I'm afraid kids won't have any childhood," Bos says. Preliteracy advocates admit there's a danger that the new ideas will be incorrectly implemented. They say teacher training will help, and they stress that in the most effective preliteracy programs, there is no "reading hour" or all-group instruction, no teacher with a pointer at the head of the class. The goal isn't to get all kids actually decoding words at 4 or 5—though some may be ready to do that—but rather to expose them to the basics. The kids think they're just having fun when they play word games with blocks, although their teachers know better.

At the Children's Village Child Care Center in Philadelphia, nearly 200 children, many from non-English-speaking homes, spend much of their day engaged in activities specifically designed to develop pre-reading skills. There are lots of alphabet puzzles and games, as well as reading and writing areas full of books, crayons, pencils and paper. The school's library includes bilingual Chinese-English children's books because many of the parents are Chinese immigrants. "We want to encourage parents to read to the children, no matter what the language," says director Mary Graham.

One morning last week, Miranda Tan, who just turned 5, worked with her teacher, Norma Bell, on her "phonics writing book." In it, she practices what is often called invented spelling—writing down words as they sound rather than as they are actually spelled. Early-reading proponents say it would be more accurate to describe this practice as "phonics writing," to get across the message that it's an exercise in phonemics (the way letters represent sounds) rather than true spelling. Miranda's book is titled "My Big Sister," and the first page offers a drawing of a girl with a blue face, pink hair and a brown dress. Underneath, written in shaky print, is "c e s my sistr kli." Bell reads it back to her and then writes, "This is my sister Kelly" underneath Miranda's sentence.

Early-literacy advocates say this kind of detailed instruction is especially important for the kids in the poorest neighborhoods who have the least exposure to books and sophisticated use of language. In one study, researchers found that children of poverty start school with a vocabulary of only about 10,000 words, compared with 40,000 for kids from middle-class homes. Bush has said that statistics like these prompted him to target poor kids, especially Head Start participants. As the governor and First Lady of Texas, Bush and his wife, Laura, were impressed by the success of the preliteracy curriculum at the Margaret Cone Head Start Center in Dallas. Until a few years ago, more than a quarter of the children coming into the program at the age of 4 scored in the bottom 1 percent of a national preschool test. Even more troubling, the same group had even lower scores after a year at the Cone Center, despite special funding from Texas Instruments that gave them access to high-quality health care, often cited as a factor in school success.

THE OLD THINKING: Many
preschool teachers were taught that they should concentrate on helping kids feel confident and learn to get along with other children. More academic work could wait until first grade.

All that changed when the Cone Center adopted a curriculum developed at Southern Methodist University. Every child now wears a name tag, a visual and personal reminder of their link to the world of print around them. Teachers spend time with kids in small groups talking about word sounds and letter names. Children are encouraged to talk in sentences, use new words and stick to proper English. When the new curriculum was introduced, some Cone teachers were dubious. "I didn't think it would go over," says Vina Dawson, a Head Start teacher for more than 13 years. The emphasis on literacy was the exact opposite of all the child-development training she has received. But, Dawson says, "the test scores prove it works." By the end of third grade, 55 percent of the children who attended both Cone and a local elementary with a strong literacy emphasis were reading at grade level, compared with 5 percent in the control group.

Getting a Jump on Literacy

Reading doesn't just happen automatically for every youngster. And while the jury's still out on how young is too young to get started, here are 10 things parents can do to get the ball rolling:

1 Talk with your kids: Children pick up quickly on the sounds and rhythms of language. Keep the banter going. It will help them grasp the rudiments of conversation. • Provide a running commentary on both your activities and your child's. • Follow up on what your child says. • Recite rhymes, repeating your child's favorites.

2 Read with them every day: Reading to kids boosts their knowledge and vocabulary. It introduces them to the mechanics of literacy—like turning pages and reading from left to right. • Pick a regular reading time when stories can be enjoyed at a relaxed, unhurried pace. • Take books along on errands. • Make sure Mom's not doing all the work. Boys who associate reading with women might dismiss it as a "girl thing."

3 Choose your books wisely: Find books on subjects that interest them—they'll enjoy reading more. • Get them involved in choosing their books. • Find books related to current events in their lives, such as on starting school or about a recent vacation destination.

4 Surround your child with books: Children love having familiar stories nearby that they can go back to again and again.

• You can find cheap, used books at yard sales, thrift stores and library sales. • Consider subscribing to a children's magazine. This way your child has something to look forward to in the mail every month. • Make sure they see you reading.

5 Slow down and enjoy reading aloud: Don't just drone along. Kids pick up on boredom and lose interest quickly. Add some drama to your voice, act out different characters and put yourself into the story. • Pose questions about the story, and follow up on theirs. • Pause here and there so kids have time to take things in.

6 Read stories over and over: It takes a long time for kids to take it all in, and they love familiar stories where they know what's coming next. • Tape yourself reading your child's favorite stories so kids can hear them when they want.

7 Foster their awareness of letters and print: Point out familiar letters in their everyday lives, such as the "S" in "Sesame Street." • Buy them plastic letters to play with or make some. • Write their names on possessions like lunchboxes. • Give them writing supplies when they play games like house or hospital.

8 Surround them with writing tools: All kids like having a varied supply at their disposal. • Provide them with different kinds of papers, as well as markers, crayons and pens. • Encourage kids to tell you stories, write them down, then read them back to them.

9 Don't pressure them: Nagging your kids about what they read may turn them off to reading in general. • Comic books and sports magazines are better than no reading material at all. • Agree to take turns in choosing their bedtime stories. • Ask your librarian for books that are both entertaining and educational.

10 Show your appreciation: Nothing encourages good reading habits like positive reinforcement. • Display your child's writing in prominent places, such as the refrigerator door. • Don't jump on every mistake a child makes while reading aloud, especially if it doesn't change the gist of the story. • Talk with your kids about what they are reading and writing in school.

SOURCES: NATIONAL ASSOCIATION FOR THE EDUCATION OF YOUNG CHILDREN, INTERNATIONAL READING ASSOCIATION. TEXT BY JOSH ULICK.

Results like that are dramatic, but early-reading advocates say that literacy training can work just as well on kids who aren't poor. Many researchers believe that significant numbers of middle-class children could avoid being labeled learning-disabled if they got early help with language and letters. Teachers are already being encouraged to seek consultations with speech therapists for kids who are slow to talk, since language problems can be a precursor to reading difficulties. Following the example of Texas, a number of states are also considering screening preschoolers and kindergartners for early signs of dyslexia so problems can be treated early. That could save districts money and give more resources to kids with severe learning problems that aren't so easily remedied.

The new literacy-rich curriculum could use projects to teach kids multiple skills. That's the central concept at the Early Childhood Education Center in Oglesby,

Ill., two hours southwest of downtown Chicago. A typical project gives 3- to 5-year-olds the task of researching pizza. They begin by asking questions posted on the classroom walls. What is the crust made of? What is the shovel for putting the pizza in the oven? Are there other ways to get pizza besides from a pizza place? They get answers by visiting local pizza parlors and making and decorating their own pies. In the process, they measure ingredients, chart their progress and write about their experiences. "We aren't 'teaching reading'," says Sallee Beneke, the director, "but we are teaching the precursors to reading by encouraging children to understand that things we draw and write about can be useful for communication."

The fight over what's best for the pizza makers and the finger painters won't be resolved quickly. But some major change seems inevitable. Even Bos is always looking for creative ways to use language. One morning last week she played the autoharp in the indoor play area as youngsters hopped around and made up their own lyrics. Then she read them a book one mother had brought in, "Piggie Pie," with no clear ending. Bos encouraged the kids to pick their own conclusion. Would the witch eat the wolf for lunch or just make him a burger? As usual, there were no easy answers.

With NADINE JOSEPH *and* KAREN SPRINGEN

Fostering Language and Literacy in Classrooms and Homes

David K. Dickinson and Patton O. Tabors

We based our study on the theoretical assumption that rich language experiences during the preschool years play an important role in ensuring that children are able to read with comprehension when they reach middle school.

Early childhood educators should be delighted. Bolstered by the accumulating research on the importance of early literacy, policymakers are beginning to craft policies with the potential to benefit young children. Researchers with long-standing interest in early literacy now hold major posts in the U.S. Department of Education, and new funding initiatives are being launched to fuel research and expanded services. The Head Start Bureau, which has begun to require programs to track the growth of individual children, has greatly expanded efforts to support children's intellectual growth, giving literacy special attention. States also are focusing new attention on early literacy.

However, we must be aware that heightened visibility brings risks. The new emphasis on accountability will put added pressure on teachers to raise children's scores on assessments. To meet this challenge and take advantage of the current climate, now is the time for early childhood educators to ensure that programs are of the highest quality. Staff at all levels must have a basic understanding of what early literacy is and an awareness of the experiences that support its development. Without such understanding there is a danger that programs will be mandated to address literacy skills in ways that neglect what we know about how children construct literacy. And well-meaning teachers may be tempted to return to heavy-handed didactic instructional methods that have been discouraged for years. Of particular concern is the possibility that early literacy efforts will take a single-minded focus on print-related dimensions and fail to recognize that *oral language* is the foundation of early literacy.

This article discusses how early childhood programs can make a different through classroom-based experiences and by efforts of preschool staff to help parents communicate with their children in ways that build the language skills critical to early literacy. We do not discuss developing phonemic awareness or knowledge of the alphabet and other print-based activities in the classroom, not because they are of less importance, but because we wish to highlight the importance of oral language. In the rush to embrace literacy in early childhood settings, we fear that oral language may be overlooked.

Thinking about early literacy

In 1987 we (that is, the authors, Catherine Snow, and many others) began the Home-School Study of Language and Literacy Development, an intensive examination of how parents and teachers support the development of language skills in young children from families with low incomes. Children living in poverty are less likely to become successful readers and writers—yet many *are* successful. What makes the difference? We wanted to identify the strengths in homes and in preschool programs that can build strong language and literacy foundations, so that we can ultimately make these strengths part of all children's lives. To accomplish this goal, we followed children from preschool through seventh grade (and, more recently, into high school).

Here we briefly summarize some of the key findings of the language and literacy development of 74 of the children during the preschool time period (Dickinson & Tabors 2001). Their families were eligible for Head Start, but about half used state vouchers to attend private programs. They lived in eastern Massachusetts, and all families reported that they used English in the home. We based our study on the theoretical assumption that rich language experiences during the preschool years play an important role in ensuring that children are able to read with comprehension when they reach middle school (Snow & Dickinson 1991). This hypothesis is supported by the findings of other researchers that children's language and literacy skills in kindergarten are strongly related to later academic success (Snow et al. 1991; Cunningham & Stanovich 1997; Whitehurst & Lonigan 1998).

Face-to-face talk relies on gestures such as pointing to objects, intonation, and the speakers' shared experience.

To capture the rich details of home and classroom life, we audiotaped conversations in both classrooms and homes and interviewed mothers and teachers about their experiences with the children (see Dickinson & Tabors 2001 for details). From this information we sought to identify the kinds of interactions and experiences that made a difference in children's later literacy skills. To see what effect these preschool interactions and experiences had on literacy development, we administered a battery of language and early literacy tasks to the children on a yearly basis, beginning in kindergarten. We assessed the children's ability to understand words, their ability to produce narratives, and their emergent literacy skills, including letter knowledge, early reading and writing, and phonemic awareness.

The language skills needed to build the foundation of reading and writing fall into different clusters (Snow & Dickinson 1991). Some skills are required to carry on informal conversations with friends and relatives. What's typical of these interactions is that people understand the meaning of the interaction largely because the ongoing activity makes clear what they are talking about. For example, you probably would be baffled if you were simply to read a transcript of talk that occurred during peekaboo or the feeding of a baby. Face-to-face talk relies on gestures such as pointing to objects, intonation, and the speakers' shared experience.

Another cluster of language skills is needed when people must make sense of words without all these immediate supports. They need to understand language apart from the face-to-face contexts where it is produced. For such occasions people need skill in constructing extended discourse that conveys new information that is not available from what one can see and hear. Later academic work, including comprehension of most texts, requires these abilities. We expected that certain experiences would build the specialized kinds of language skills that children need to become literate. Indeed, our analyses of homes and classrooms revealed three dimensions of children's experiences during the preschool and kindergarten years that are related to later literacy success:

- **Exposure to *varied vocabulary*.** Knowing the "right word" is vital if one is to communicate information clearly. Large vocabularies have long been known to be linked to reading success

(e.g., Anderson & Freebody 1981); they also are a signal that children are building the content knowledge about the world that is so critical to later reading (Neuman 2001).

- **Opportunities to be part of conversations that use *extended discourse*.** Extended discourse is talk that requires participants to develop understandings beyond the here and now and that requires the use of several sentences to build a linguistic structure, such as in explanations, narratives, or pretend talk.

- *Home and classroom environments* **that are cognitively and linguistically stimulating.** Children are most likely to experience conversation that include comprehensible and interesting extended discourse and are rich with vocabulary when their parents are able to obtain and read good books and when their teachers provide classrooms with a curriculum that is varied and stimulating.

The adults used techniques like definitions and synonyms, inference and comparison, the child's prior experience, or the semantic, social, or physical context to help the children understand what the new words meant.

We now will discuss each of these dimensions, describing what we found in the homes and the preschool classrooms that the 74 children attended. We spotlight one child in the study, a boy named Casey, who had both a very supportive family and a very supportive classroom environment.

Varied vocabulary

Opportunities to hear and use a variety of new and interesting words in conversations with adults were especially important to children in our study. These conversations happened at home and in preschool classrooms.

At home

For the Home-School Study we recorded the children in conversation with their mothers during book readings and toy play sessions and with their mothers and other members of their families during mealtimes. In all three conversational contexts we found the adults using new and interesting words with the children. Even more important, we found that the adults used techniques like definitions and synonyms, inference and comparison, the child's prior experience, or the semantic, social, or physical context to help the children understand what the new words meant (Tabors, Beals, & Weizman 2001).

Some families used these techniques more than others—Casey's family, for example, used more new and interesting words than the average for the whole group. How often new words were used also made a difference. On average, children whose families used more new words understood more words and had better emergent literacy skills later in kindergarten.

Teachers who use interesting and varied words may help to create a vocabulary-rich environment—a classroom in which children are exposed to and encouraged to use varied words.

In the classroom

We taped child and teacher conversations in the classrooms during free play, group times (Dickinson 2001b), book reading (Dickinson 2001a), and mealtime (Cote 2001). Across all these settings, children benefited from conversations that included more varied vocabulary. Interestingly, what mattered was not just the variety of words that the teachers used, but also the variety of words that the children used as they spoke with the teachers. We studied only one or two children in each classroom, so this finding suggests that their language growth was bolstered by input from teachers as well as from other children. We speculate that teachers who use interesting and varied words may help to create a vocabulary-rich environment—a classroom in which children are exposed to and encouraged to use varied words.

Extended discourse

Extended discourse is an important contributor to children's language and literacy development. Adults can extend or draw out their talk with children, enriching the conversation and helping children go beyond the here and now. Again, both home and preschool may be settings for this discourse.

At home

In looking at the transcripts of the conversations we recorded with parents and children reading books together, playing with toys, and during mealtimes, we found that each of these settings provided opportunities for extended talk that helped the children recognize and use these types of talk later in school. To see what we mean by extended discourse, let's listen as Casey's mother reads a book about elephants. This mother doesn't just read the book with her child; she also discusses it at length with him, helping him understand the information and tying it to his personal experience.

Mother: [reading] "African elephants have a dip in their backs. They also have ridges on their trunks, which end

in two points. Asian elephants have smoother trunks that end in just one point." See the dip in his back?
Casey: I know why he's different. He has them [pointing to tusks], and he doesn't.
Mother: He has tusks. Well, this is a female. [reading] "Asian elephants often live in forests and swamps. This Asian cow elephant lives in Nepal, a small country north of India."
Casey: Ma! In India?
Mother: Yeah, do you know somebody from there? Deepack? Your friend? Yeah. [reading] "African elephants live in the plains as well as forests. This African elephant lives in the open grassland. It flaps its huge ears to help keep cool in the hot African sunshine." Because it's very hot in Africa. (Dickinson & Tabors 2001, 39)

Casey's mother is using what we call *non-immediate talk*—that is, she gives Casey information beyond what is immediately available from the book. This type of conversation is an important preparation for talk about books at school (De Temple 2001).

Other types of extended discourse we found in the transcripts were fantasy talk during toy play (Katz 2001) and explanations and narratives during mealtimes (Beals 2001). The important thing about all of these forms of extended discourse is that they occurred during normal conversations in everyday activities. Some families used these types of talk more often than others, and their children were better at telling a narrative in kindergarten than were children who had less exposure to extended conversations.

Free play, or choice time, is the ideal opportunity for children to engage in pretend talk, a type of extended discourse that predicts stronger language and literacy development.

In the classroom

Free play, or choice time, is the ideal opportunity for children to engage in pretend talk, a type of extended discourse that predicts stronger language and literacy development. Ann Greenbaum's skilled conversations demonstrate some of the features of teachers' extended discourse that are especially powerful supports for children's oral language. In her exchange about sharks, she built on and extended the children's comments and used varied words ("You must be very brave and daring men to go down there").

Another important but more subtle feature of Ann's knack for conversation is her ability to fine-tune the balance between talking and listening to the children. In looking at the ratio of teacher-to-child talk, we found that children did better on our language and literacy assessments when preschool teachers talked less during free play. This finding may reflect the fact that teachers are better attuned to children when they listen more. It also might point to the benefit of allowing children to put their ideas into words.

We also examined teacher-child talk during group meetings and large-group book reading. During group meeting times we found that the percentage of all talk that provided children with information or engaged them in thoughtful discussions was predictive of later development. Similarly, during book reading sessions, conversations encouraging children to think about the story were beneficial. The following is a conversation that occurred as the teacher read a book in which a child finds a dinosaur and brings it home. The poor dinosaur is overwhelmed by loud noises. Here we see the teacher using extended discourse to encourage the children to analyze the dinosaur's reaction and to recognize the emotion of fear.

Teacher: How do you think Dandy feels, Susan?
Susan: Bad.
Teacher: Why?
Susan: Everybody take a look at the picture.
Teacher: I think he not only feels sad, he feels very—
Children: Happy.
Teacher: I don't think so. What did Dandy do when the truck came?
Todd: Shook.
Teacher: He was scared—he shook. And what did he do when the airplanes zoomed overhead? And when the train roared by? Did Dandy like loud noises?
Children: No!
Teacher: How is Dandy going to feel with all this?
Children: Bad. Sad.
Teacher: Not only sad. What else?
Children: Mad!
James: Scared!
Teacher: You got it, James! He's going to be very scared! (Dickinson & Tabors 2001, 190–91)

There was an interesting difference between the kind of discourse that was most beneficial in the two settings. During free play, relaxed back-and-forth exchanges with limited amounts of teacher talk proved helpful, but teacher efforts during group times to keep individual children talking detracted from the group experience. This result may show that when teachers engage in excessively long interactions with one child, the other children "tune out."

Environments that support oral language

Visits to the children's homes and classroom occurred only once a year during the study because of the large amount of language data that we collected each visit. Although we were able to collect a great deal of information about the types of talk used in these contexts on those particular days, we realized that we couldn't

know how often such conversations occurred in normal home life or during the typical preschool day. For these reasons, we interviewed mothers and teachers to help us understand how supportive the overall environment was for the children's language and literacy development.

In the home

We used the mothers' answers to a cluster of questions to see how the home environment supported children's language and literacy development. Questions included:

- How often do you read to your child?
- Does anyone else read to your child and how often?
- How many children's books do you own?
- Do you get books from the library or bookstore?
- Do you read anything else with your child?

We found a lot of variation on this measure of home support for literacy. Not surprisingly, Casey's mother scored the highest in the entire sample on the answers to these questions. Casey was hearing many books and other materials read to him by a lot of different people. His family was buying books in addition to getting them from the library. How did this low-income family, and others with high support for literacy, manage to buy books? Many of the mothers mentioned that they always asked relatives to give their children books on special occasions and that they were always on the lookout for books at tag sales.

Of course, having the books is only the first step in the process. It is also necessary to have willing readers who use the books for enjoyment and to expand the children's knowledge of the world. In this study the children whose mothers reported high support for literacy at home scored well in kindergarten on all three measures of early literacy (receptive vocabulary, narrative production, and emergent literacy).

In the classroom

We interviewed the preschool teachers to discover how they typically organize their classroom day and to learn what they saw as their primary educational goals. We also observed the classroom environments to learn about the curriculum.

We found differences in the pedagogical emphasis of teachers. Some valued social and emotional development highly, others stressed academic growth, and some placed high values on both (Smith 2001). Our conversations revealed how the teachers allocated their classroom time. One of the striking things we found was the large variation in the amount of time teachers reported setting aside for book reading. When the children in our study were four years old, somewhat more than 25% of the teachers reported planning for more than 51 minutes of book reading a week, whereas about 17% reported planning for reading 15 minutes or less per week.

When we looked at what teachers told us about their pedagogical beliefs and their ways of organizing time, we did not find much consistency between belief and practice. We also did not find much evidence that teachers' beliefs were related to children's growth. This set of findings suggests that many preschool teachers may lack well-articulated systems of belief that link understanding of the nature of language and literacy development with notions of effective classroom practices.

Other dimensions of the classroom environment did relate to children's later language and literacy development. One such dimension, the quality of the curriculum, was exemplified in Casey's classroom. For example, after the firefighters demonstrated their equipment to the class and introduced new words and concepts, the teacher extended that experience. We also found that children's later development was more positive if the classroom had a writing center and the teacher planned times for small-group activities.

Our data strongly indicate that it is the nature of the teacher-child relationship that makes the biggest difference in early literacy.

Our measures of the classroom environment were far less potent predictors of later language and literacy than our measures of teacher-child interaction. Our data strongly indicate that it is the nature of the teacher-child relationship and the kinds of conversations that they have that makes the biggest difference to early language and literacy development.

Oral language/literacy support at home and school: The long-term benefits

We were interested in what effects different home and preschool environments, and various combinations of home and preschool environments, had on these children's kindergarten skills and on their more long-term academic achievements. To chart children's growth we individually assessed our children in kindergarten, using tasks that tapped language skills (receptive vocabulary, story understanding and production) and early literacy knowledge (letter knowledge, environmental print "reading," writing, phonemic awareness). Each year we continued to test children, and when they were in elementary school we began to use standardized reading tests.

How important was the home environment in comparison to the school environment—and vice versa? And how much could we predict about these children's later accomplishments based on what we knew about their abilities in kindergarten?

Apparently, the level of language and literacy skill that the children had acquired by the end of their kindergarten year provided a strong basis for the acquisition of literacy and vocabulary skills in the later elementary years.

Let's start with the last question. What we found was that the scores that the kindergartners achieved on the measures (receptive vocabulary, narrative production, and emergent literacy) were *highly predictive* of their scores on reading comprehension and receptive vocabulary in fourth and in seventh grade. Apparently the level of language and literacy skills that the children had acquired by the end of their kindergarten year provided a strong basis for the acquisition of literacy and vocabulary skills in the later elementary years. Although this is perhaps not entirely surprising, it does confirm that for this group of children early learning set the stage for later literacy acquisition in school.

If kindergarten skills are so important, we need to know the relative contributions of home and preschool to children's kindergarten skills. When we looked at each of the three kindergarten measures one at a time, we found that the significant predictors of narrative production were home environmental variables, while home and preschool environment variables were both significant in explaining children's scores in receptive vocabulary and emergent literacy. For these reasons, it was extremely important that we had collected data on interactions and experiences from both the home and the classroom.

For Casey, who came from a supportive home and attended a preschool where language development was a main goal, the combined interactions and experiences provided him with strong scores in both understanding words and emergent literacy in kindergarten, in comparison with the other children in the study.

But not all of the children in the study came from environments as supportive as Casey's. What about them? What if a child from a home with lots of rich talk and exposure to books attends a preschool that does not support emergent literacy? Or what about the child who gets little support for language and literacy development at home, but attends a high-quality preschool with a wonderful language- and literacy-rich environment? Can either of these environments compensate for the other?

Using the data from the Home-School Study, we developed analyses to look at these hypothetical situations—the high-home/low-preschool language and literacy environment combination and the low-home/high preschool language and literacy environment combination. What we found is that, while a child with a high-home/low-preschool combination would score *below* the mean for the sample on all three measures of kindergarten abilities, a child with a low-home/high-preschool mix would score *above* the mean. The implication is that excellent preschools can compensate for homes that have well-below-average language and literacy support—at least as reflected in the children's kindergarten skills (Dickinson & Tabors 2001, 326).

Based on our results, we strongly believe that the early childhood period is key to getting children off to a strong start in language and literacy. Our research suggests that policymakers' attention to literacy skills must include attention to building early foundations in rich oral language, both at home and in preschool. Everyday activities can develop varied vocabulary, engage children in complex uses of language that go beyond the here and now, and surround children with environments that support language and literacy development. For this to happen, we must help all preschool teachers understand the major role they play in supporting children's long-term development. These teachers must deepen the knowhow required to constantly extend children's oral language while they also encourage phonemic awareness and writing skills. Rather than adding an extra burden, this attention to language development is likely to create livelier, more enjoyable experiences for both teachers and children. Finally, teachers also must actively reach out to families, building on their strengths while guiding them toward the kinds of home language and literacy activities that will help their children achieve the educational success that families desire for their children. With these early language experiences, children will be far more likely to acquire the specific reading and writing skills needed for school success.

References

Anderson, R. C., & P. Freebody. 1981. Vocabulary knowledge. In *Comprehension and teaching: Research reviews*, ed. J. T. Guthrie, 77–116. Newark: DE: International Reading Association.

Beals, D. E. 2001. Eating and reading: Links between family conversations with preschoolers and later language and literacy. In *Beginning literacy with language: Young children learning at home and school*, eds. D. K. Dickinson & P. O. Tabors, 75–92. Baltimore: Paul H. Brookes.

Cote, L. R. 2001. Language opportunities during mealtimes in preschool classrooms. In *Beginning literacy with language: Young children learning at home and school*, eds. D. K. Dickinson & P. O. Tabors, 205–21. Baltimore: Paul H. Brookes.

Cunningham, A. E., & K. E. Stanovich. 1997. Early reading acquisition and its relation to reading experience and ability 10 years later. *Developmental Psychology* 33 (6): 934–45.

De Temple, J. M. 2001. Parents and children reading books together. In *Beginning literacy with language: Young children learning at home and school*, eds. D. K. Dickinson & P. O. Tabors, 31–51. Baltimore: Paul H. Brookes.

Dickinson, D. K. 2001a. Book reading in preschool classrooms: Is recommended practice common? In *Beginning literacy with language: Young*

children learning at home and school, eds. D. K. Dickinson & P. O. Tabors, 175–203. Baltimore: Paul H. Brookes.

Dickinson, D. K. 2001b. Large-group and free-play times: Conversational settings supporting language and literacy development. In *Beginning literacy with language: Young children learning at home and school*, eds. D. K. Dickinson & P. O. Tabors, 223–55. Baltimore: Paul H. Brookes.

Dickinson, D. K., & P. O. Tabors, eds. 2001. *Beginning literacy with language: Young children learning at home and school*. Baltimore: Paul H. Brookes.

Katz, J. R. 2001. Playing at home: The talk of pretend play. In *Beginning literacy with language: Young children learning at home and school*, eds. D. K. Dickinson & P. O. Tabors, 53–73. Baltimore: Paul H. Brookes.

Neuman, S. B. 2001. Essay Book Review: The role of knowledge in early literacy. *Reading Research Quarterly* 36 (4): 468–75.

Roach, K. A., & C. E. Snow. 2000. *What predicts fourth grade reading comprehension?* Paper presented at the annual conference of the American Education Research Association, New Orleans, April.

Smith, M. W. 2001. Children's experiences in preschool. In *Beginning literacy with language: Young children learning at home and school*, eds. D. K. Dickinson & P. O. Tabors, 149–74. Baltimore: Paul H. Brookes.

Snow, C. E., & D. K. Dickinson. 1991. Skills that aren't basic in a new conception of literacy. In *Literate systems and individual lives: Perspectives on literacy and schooling*, eds. A. Purves & E. Jennings. Albany: State University of New York (SUNY) Press.

Snow, C. E., W. S. Barnes, J. Chandler, I. F. Goodman, & L. Hemphill. 1991. *Unfulfilled expectations: Home and school influences on literacy*. Cambridge, MA: Harvard University Press.

Tabors, P. O., D. E. Beals, & Z. O. Weizman 2001. "You know what oxygen is?" Learning new words at home. In *Beginning literacy with language: Young children learning at home and school*, eds. D. K. Dickinson & P. O. Tabors, 93–110. Baltimore: Paul H. Brookes.

Whitehurst, G. J., & C. J. Lonigan. 1998. Child development and emergent literacy. *Child Development* 68: 848–72.

David K. Dickinson, Ed.D., is a senior research scientist in the Center for Children and Families at the Education Development Center, Inc., in Newton, Massachusetts, and an affiliate with CIERA (Center for the Improvement of Early Reading Achievement), based at the University of Michigan. David directed the aspects of the Home-School Study that dealt with classrooms and is now developing and studying professional development efforts that build on language and literacy in the classroom.

Patton O. Tabors, Ed.D., a research associate at the Harvard Graduate School of Education since 1987, has been involved in research related to language and literacy acquisition of both young English-speaking and second-language-learning children. She is author of *One Child, Two Languages: A guide for Preschool Educators of Children Learning English as a Second Language* and coeditor of *Beginning Literacy with Language: Young Children Learning at Home and School.*

Portions of this article were excerpted from D. K. Dickinson and P. O. Tabors, eds., *Beginning Literacy with Language: Young Children Learning at Home and School* (Baltimore: Paul H. Brookes, 2001).

Helping Preschool Children Become Readers: Tips for Parents

by Dr. Ann S. Epstein, Director, Early Childhood Division

Parents and other family members lay the foundation for reading and writing long before children enter school. To help preschoolers begin to develop these skills at home, parents need to provide two things:

- **Experiences with language**—having conversations, playing games with language and sounds
- **Experiences with print**—reading to children, giving children tools for reading and writing.

Learning to read and write should be pleasurable; it does not require tedious drills or forced memorization. When learning is fun, children develop good attitudes toward schooling as they master valuable skills. Below are 12 things parents can do to make learning enjoyable and meaningful. These ideas build on children's natural desire to communicate and can easily be included in family routines.

1. Have daily conversations with children.

Listening and speaking are the foundation of reading and writing. When parents converse with children, they should listen patiently, even if it means waiting for children to form their thoughts and words. Adult patience creates a climate in which children feel free to talk.

Children like to talk about themselves, their interests, and their feelings. If parents talk about the things children care about, children will be eager and natural speakers. There are many things parents can do with their children to encourage conversation, for example:

- Looking at pictures in the family photo album and talking about the people and celebrations
- Joining children's pretend play, letting the child be the leader
- Providing materials and sharing the child's favorite activities, such as drawing, building with blocks, racing toy cars, or baking cookies
- Attending sporting events, going for walks, digging in the yard, marking a snow fort, or collecting bugs

To help the conversation along, parents can make encouraging comments ("I see you made a red circle") and repeat the child's remarks ("You're happy because Kyla invited you to her party"). An occasional open-ended question is fine, especially to seek information ("What are you going to serve at your 'tea party'?"). However, too many questions tend to stifle conversation.

Conversation sets the stage for having fun with language. Singing songs, telling stories, reciting rhymes, and moving to rhythmic chants all help children develop *phonological awareness—the ability to perceive the sounds of language.* For example, the repeated words in "Row, Row, Row Your Boat" help make children aware of the sounds that make up these words. Nursery rhymes like "Eensy, Weensy Spider" call attention to words with the same ending sound, as does encouraging children to make up new endings to familiar rhymes: "Jack be nimble, Jack be red, Jack jump over the _____."

> **12 things you can do to help your preschooler become a reader**
>
> 1. Have daily conversations with your child.
> 2. Keep lots of print and writing materials in your home.
> 3. Set up a reading and writing space for your child.
> 4. Let your child see you read and write.
> 5. Read with your child every day.
> 6. Point out reading and writing in everyday activities.
> 7. Make a message board.
> 8. Encourage your child to "read."
> 9. Display your child's writing.
> 10. Make a bank or file of words your child likes to write.
> 11. Go to the library with your child.
> 12. Use television and technology wisely.

When parents point out the individual sounds in words, they promote *phonemic awareness. A phoneme is the smallest unit of sound in the lan-*

guage. It can be the sound made by a single letter, such as /s/, or a letter combination, such as /sh/. *Phonemic awareness is knowing that words are made up of sequences of these individual sounds. Phonics, the next step in learning to read, is knowing sound-letter relationships.* For example, a parent might say *"Mommy and muffin… those both start with the /m/ sound, that's the letter m."* If a child asks how to spell *dog,* a parent can say, "It starts with the sound /d/, and the letter *d* looks like this." Parents and children can also play games with alliteration, that is, with words that start with the same sound. For example, a parent can put three objects that start with the /b/ sound in a bag (such as a ball, block, and barrette) and the child can find something else that begins with *b* to put in the bag. Guessing games are also fun: "I'm thinking of something in the refrigerator that starts with the /g/ sound—gggg. What do you think it is?"

2. Keep lots of printed materials and writing materials in the home.

Homes should be filled with interesting things to read, including illustrated storybooks, nonfiction books, homemade books, magazines, photo albums, newspapers, catalogs, seed packets, greeting cards, flyers, take-out menus, manuals, junk mail, maps, and so on. Children, like adults, need variety.

Parents should also keep on hand many different types of writing materials, including crayons, markers, chalk, pens and pencils, paper in different sizes and colors, stationery, stamps and ink pads, wooden and plastic letters for tracing and copying. Tools for making books, such as tape, scissors, staplers, a hole punch, and string, will also encourage writing.

Reading and writing supplies do not need to be expensive. Parents can reuse and recycle materials or buy children's books at yard sales, resale shops, and used-book sales at the library. They can also add their own printing around the house, such as labels for things the child uses every day ("toy box" or "dishes"). Reading and writing materials should be placed where children can easily see

and reach them, for examples, on low shelves or in baskets and crates.

3. Set up a reading and writing space for children.

To convey the importance of reading and writing, parents can set up a special space for these activities. It may be a quiet place or somewhere close to the center of action, whatever is most inviting for the child and will keep his or her attention. This space should include materials that belong to the child alone and do not have to be shared with adults or other children in the household. This will encourage the child to think of the area as his or her own play or work space. Parents can offer the child a choice of spending quiet time in this special area instead of taking a nap. Or, they can set aside another regular time each day when the child can choose to go to this area.

4. Let children observe parents reading and writing.

Young children imitate their parents, so modeling reading and writing at home is very important. When parents pick up a newspaper or book instead of turning on the television, they send a powerful message about the pleasure as well as the usefulness of reading. At the dinner table, parents can briefly describe something interesting they have read, or mention some reading and writing they did at work that day. Children should see their parents writing, whether they are paying bills or writing an e-mail message to a friend. If a child wants to know something, a parent might say, "Let's look that up in the dictionary [or in the encyclopedia or on the Internet]." This shows children that written sources provide information and that answering questions can be an adventure.

5. Read with children every day.

Parents should set aside a regular time each day to read with their children. This might be at bedtime, after school, early in the morning—whatever works in the family schedule. They should read in a comfortable place, without a lot of distractions, where they can snuggle or sit side by side with their child. Children should

be able to see and touch the book while parents read to them.

Reading with children will be most beneficial if parents follow these simple techniques:

- **Be familiar with the book.** If the book is new, parents should try to read it themselves beforehand.
- **Read slowly but naturally.** Pronouncing the words carefully helps to build children's vocabulary.
- **Read with interest.** An expressive voice shows interest and engages the child.
- **Use different voices.** This helps children differentiate the characters and their qualities.
- **Use a finger to follow the words.** This shows the connection between spoken and written words. Children will learn to associate sounds with specific letters and letter combinations.
- **Stop reading to talk about the book.** Children want to talk about the pictures, story, and characters. If a book is familiar, they might predict what will happen next or imagine different events and endings.
- **Extend the reading.** Reading is enriched when children represent the events or characters through drawing and play-acting. Other ideas include visiting places and doing things that appear in the book or making up stories and games that build on the book's ideas.

There should be a variety of books to choose from and the child should make the choice, even if it is often the same book. Repetition helps children understand the forms of written language and begin to recognize familiar words and letters. Here are some guidelines to help parents choose storybooks for their young child's library:

- **Illustrations.** Are the drawings, paintings, or photographs visually pleasing? Do the people represent a variety of races, ages, and abilities?
- **Story line.** Is it written in the language the child speaks? Will the activities and messages make sense to the child? Will it encourage discussion?

- **Child interest.** Will the child be curious about the characters and what happens to them? Will the child look at the book alone, even when an adult is not available for reading?
- **Adult interest.** Is it a book the parent wants to read and talk about with the child? Is the parent prepared to answer whatever questions the child may have about the book?

6. Call children's attention to reading and writing in everyday activities.

Children are curious about the daily activities adults view as commonplace. Their natural interest provides many opportunities for parents to call attention to reading and writing. These opportunities include making grocery lists and finding matching coupons; pointing out letters and words on signs and buildings while riding in the car or taking a walk; looking up addresses and phone numbers before going places or making calls; reading maps; reading team names and scores aloud at sporting events; looking at the weather report in the newspaper; reading menus at restaurants or making up menus at home; writing and illustrating children's favorite recipes; labeling pictures in the family photo album; writing thank-you notes; reading the television guide and making a list of the shows the family will watch; writing and mailing fan letters to children's favorite performers and athletes.

7. Make a message board.

A message board lets children know the family's plans for the day. This can be especially important on weekends, when routines may vary. The message board can be a dry-erase board, a chalkboard, or just a pad of paper. The board should be hung at the child's eye level for easy visibility and so the child can add his or her own messages. Each day, the parent and child can draw a few simple pictures and label them with easy words. For example, a picture of a swing on one line and a grocery cart with the word *store* on the next line would indicate they were going to the playground and then the supermarket. Parents should encourage children to predict what will happen based on the picture and word messages. At the same time they are learning to read, children are learning about sequences, an important concept in math.

8. Encourage children to "read."

Young children "read" in many ways. Before they read actual words, children pretend to read. They follow the pictures in a familiar book, tell the story from memory, or make up their own narrative. With lots of exposure to books, they come to understand basic print concepts, such as turning pages from front to back, reading from top to bottom, and following lines from left to right. Parents can promote children's early reading in several ways. They can encourage young children to read to them, to other family members, even to dolls and stuffed animals. As children begin to write, parents can ask them to read their words. If a child asks the parent to take dictation, either the parent or child can read back the words. It is important for parents to write down the child's exact words. This establishes the direct connection between spoken and written language.

9. Display children's writing.

Parents should display all the different forms of children's writing, including scribble letters and words based on word sounds (for example, *bg* for *big.*). They can also take photos of and display temporary writing (for example, made with sticks in the mud or sand on a tray). Writing should be mounted at the child's eye level so it can be easily seen. It can be attached with tape, pins, clips, or any other household fasteners. Display surfaces include the refrigerator, a wall, a bulletin board, a bookcase, the side of a dresser, the front of a kitchen cabinet; sticky notes can be stuck to the computer, papers hung from a mobile, and so on. If other family members comment on the writing, children will have a sense of its importance and of their accomplishment.

10. Make a word bank or word file.

A word bank is an illustrated dictionary or file of words a child uses in talking, reading, and writing. It organizes the words that are important to the child. A word bank can be created with an old recipe box and index cards, or with a loose-leaf notebook. Each word is put on a separate card or page, written in large and clear letters. Next to the word, the parent or child draws a picture that illustrates it. The cards or pages are then placed in alphabetical order. A word bank should be kept in a place where the child can easily reach it and look up words on his or her own. Whenever the child asks for help writing or spelling a word, the parent can refer the child to the existing list or help the child add a new entry to the word bank.

11. Take children to the library.

Libraries offer books and other reading materials, usually at no cost. Parents should find out where the nearest public library is located or if it sends a bookmobile to their neighborhood. Their child's preschool or day care center may also have a lending library. Library visits should occur frequently, preferably on a regular schedule (for example, every Saturday after soccer practice). A child should have his or her own library card and a tote bag to carry and store books.

Children can check out books, magazines, cassette tapes, and CDs with stories, information, poems and songs. They should pick the items that interest them. Parents can point out something they think is interesting, but in the end the child should make the choice. Children should also be the judge of whether a book is too easy or too hard. Reading or re-reading easy books can build a child's confidence. On the other hand, if a difficult book is interesting enough, the child may be up to the challenge of reading it. If a book is boring or *too* difficult, a child will simply set it aside and pick up something of greater interest.

Many libraries also have regular story hours and other events for young children. Sometimes they have exhibits, for example, an art show by a local artist. Looking at the exhibit together and talking about it is another good way for parents to help develop their child's language skills.

12. Use television and technology wisely.

Young children learn best by doing, not by watching. Television and computers can play a part in early learning but should not replace active exploration and social interaction. Viewing should be limited to one or two programs a day. Parents should look for shows that help develop the intellectual and social skills children need when they enter school, and they should watch and talk about these programs with their child. If the family has a computer, parents should buy software designed for young children. Drawing and writing programs that allow children to create and read their own pictures, words, and stories are more interesting and promote a wider range of skills than programs limited to memorization and practice.

Finally, parents should remember that they are not alone in helping their child along the path to literacy. They can talk to their child's teacher, the librarian, and other parents. They can share the books and activities their family enjoys and get others' ideas on how to support children's learning at home. With a parent's encouragement, a child will enter school ready to learn how to read and write. With a parent's example, a child will become an adult who reads for information and pleasure.

From *High/Scope ReSource*, Summer 2002, pp. 4-6. © 2002 by High/Scope Press.

Index

Test Your Knowledge Form

We encourage you to photocopy and use this page as a tool to assess how the articles in *Annual Editions* expand on the information in your textbook. By reflecting on the articles you will gain enhanced text information. You can also access this useful form on a product's book support Web site at *http://www.dushkin.com/online/*.

NAME: DATE:
_____

TITLE AND NUMBER OF ARTICLE:
_____

BRIEFLY STATE THE MAIN IDEA OF THIS ARTICLE:

_____

LIST THREE IMPORTANT FACTS THAT THE AUTHOR USES TO SUPPORT THE MAIN IDEA:

_____

WHAT INFORMATION OR IDEAS DISCUSSED IN THIS ARTICLE ARE ALSO DISCUSSED IN YOUR TEXTBOOK OR OTHER READINGS THAT YOU HAVE DONE? LIST THE TEXTBOOK CHAPTERS AND PAGE NUMBERS:

_____

LIST ANY EXAMPLES OF BIAS OR FAULTY REASONING THAT YOU FOUND IN THE ARTICLE:

_____

LIST ANY NEW TERMS/CONCEPTS THAT WERE DISCUSSED IN THE ARTICLE, AND WRITE A SHORT DEFINITION: